12/18/1997

To Margaret &

How I wish I could have given this book to you and Ronald. He would have enjoyed this so much. May you gain an enhanced appreciation for the great leadership and profound sacrifice of our pioneer fathers.

I appreciate your wonderful friendship and all you have done for me and for my family over the years and especially for your love and devotion to my exceptional brother.

Love,

Ronnie

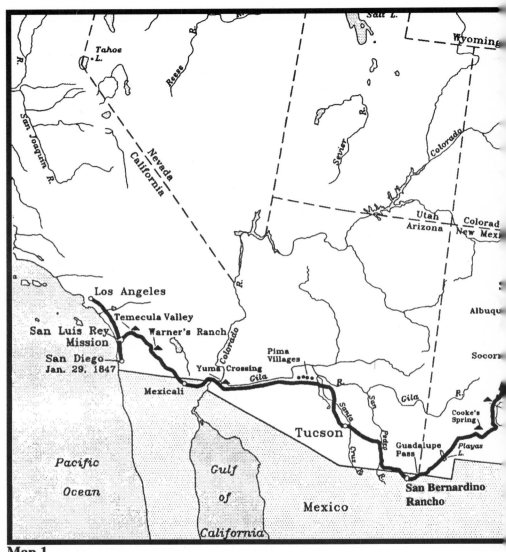

Map 1

1846-1847
Mormon Battalion Route
Council Bluffs, Iowa to San Diego, California

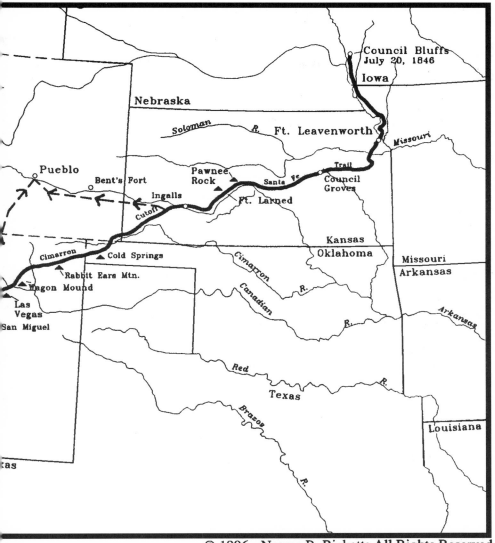

Council Bluffs
July 20, 1846

Iowa

Nebraska

Soloman R.   Ft. Leavenworth

Missouri

Pawnee
Rock   Santa Fe   Trail   Council
Groves

Pueblo

Bent's Fort   Ingalls

Cutoff   Ft. Larned

Kansas
Oklahoma

Missouri
Arkansas

Cimarron   Cold Springs

Rabbit Ears Mtn.   Cimarron   R.

Wagon Mound   Canadian

Las
Vegas

San Miguel   Arkansas

Red   R.

Texas

Brazos   R.

Louisiana

...as

R.

—————— Mormon Battalion

▬ ▬ ▬ ▬ Sick Detachments

– – – – States not in existence

▲ Camp Site

The Mormon Battalion

U.S. ARMY OF THE WEST
1846–1848

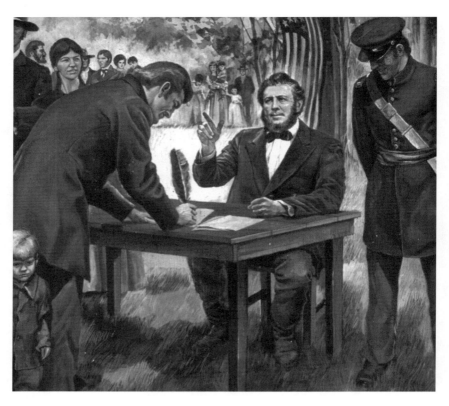

Brigham Young enrolling volunteers in the Mormon Battalion as Colonel James Allen watches, Council Bluffs, Iowa. Painting by Dale Kilbourn, © Church of Jesus Christ of Latter-day Saints, Salt Lake City, Utah; used by permission.

The Mormon Battalion

U.S. ARMY OF THE WEST
1846–1848

Norma Baldwin Ricketts

Foreword by
David L. Bigler

UTAH STATE UNIVERSITY PRESS
LOGAN, UTAH
1996

Utah State University Press
Logan, Utah 84322–7800

Typography by WolfPack
Cover design by Michelle Sellers

Cover illustration:

The Mormon Battalion by George M. Ottinger, © Church of Jesus Christ of
Latter-day Saints, courtesy of the Museum of Church History and Art, Salt
Lake City, Utah; used by permission.

Library of Congress Cataloging-in-Publication Data

Ricketts, Norma B. (Norma Baldwin)
    The Mormon Battalion : U.S. Army of the West, 1846-1848 / Norma
Baldwin Ricketts ; foreword by David L. Bigler.
        p. cm.
    Includes bibliographical references and index.
    ISBN 0-87421-216-2 (cloth). — ISBN 0-87421-215-4 (paper)
    1. Mexican War, 1846-1848—Campaigns—Southwest, New. 2. Mexican
War, 1846-1848—Campaigns—California. 3. United States. Army.
Mormon Battalion—History. 4. Mexican War, 1846-1848—Regimental
histories. 5. Mexican War, 1846-1848—Participation, Mormon.
6. Mormons—Southwest, New—History. 7. United States. Army.
Mormon Battalion—Registers. 8. Southwest, New—History, Military.
9. California—History, Military. I. Title.
E405.2.R53 1996
973.6'24—dc20   96-35706
                                                        CIP

Contents

Maps

Illustrations

Foreword

David L. Bigler

When Philip St. George Cooke of the First Dragoons took command of the Mormon Battalion at Santa Fe in October, 1846, he was deeply disappointed at the "extraordinary assignment" he had been given. The thirty-seven-year-old professional soldier had hoped to win glory and advancement at the seat of conflict in the war with Mexico. Instead he had been handed the most remarkable body of volunteers ever to report at Fort Leavenworth for duty in the U.S. Army.

It hardly took eighteen years of service on the American frontier for the six-foot-four officer to see that some of the men assigned to his command were "too old," others "too young," and that the whole outfit was "embarrassed by many women." Cooke also thought his untrained soldiers often showed "great heedlessness and ignorance, and some obstinacy." It was certainly true that these men usually marched to a different drummer than the one to which he was accustomed.

The newly promoted lieutenant colonel would change his mind by the time his Mormon footmen, trimmed to an efficient body of 335, had reached California, completing one of the longest marches in the annals of military history. Of all the apocryphal stories about the battalion, the one that rings most true is that Cooke bared his head in tribute to his former comrades when in 1858 he rode into Great Salt Lake City at the head of the Second Dragoons, a unit in Albert Sidney Johnston's Utah Expedition.

By then, it would have been difficult to find many noteworthy events in western history during the important period of 1846 to 1848 in which members of this company, so unique in the annals of American military history, did not somehow take part. They made possible the 1847 Mormon move to Utah, occupied California for the United States, took part in the 1848 discovery of gold at Sutter's Mill, opened the Mormon-Carson Emigrant Trail over the Sierra Nevada, and drove the first wagons over the Spanish Trail and Hensley's Salt Lake Cutoff of the California Trail.

These and other exploits have been more or less recognized over the years. Not so well known or understood, however, has been the larger role the Mormon Battalion performed in American and western history. Too often historians have seemed to adopt the limited outlook of Daniel Tyler as reflected in his highly partisan and outdated account, *A Concise History of the Mormon Battalion in the Mexican War, 1846–47*, first published in 1881.

From that perspective, the march of the volunteers appears to go forward as a kind of heroic, self-contained epic possessing little relation to the world around it. For Latter-day Saints, the story is without question inspirational and faith promoting. But the failure to step back and see it in relation to the larger picture of American history has resulted in the undervaluing or forgetting altogether of some of the command's most notable contributions.

To focus, for example, on the battalion's Battle of the Bulls as a significant event in itself overlooks the important relationship that exists between this bovine encounter on southern Arizona's San Pedro River and President James Polk's plan to take over the region that now forms most of the American Southwest. The connection between the bull fight and Manifest Destiny lies in the answer to an obvious question: Where did the wild bulls come from in the first place?

All those belligerent bulls came from an abandoned ranch established in 1822 by one Ignacio Perez under a grant from the Mexican government to create a buffer against Apache incursions from the east. By 1846, however, the invading warriors had overrun the region and turned Perez's 73,240-acre spread and its animals into their own game preserve, where they hunted the cattle left behind as they did any other game. Easiest to bring down safely were the cows and calves, which left the bulls to grow older, wilder, and more aggressive.

As this episode illustrates, except for a little island of soldiers and their suffering families at Tucson, the northern Sonoran region had reverted to Indian control by 1846, and the Hispanic frontier had effectively retreated south of the present international border between Arizona and Mexico. The Mormon Battalion's march across the Southwest demonstrated that Mexico's claim on the region was hollow and that an expansionist president's bid for sovereignty was as good as that of anyone else except native Indians, including the Pima and Papago but not including the Apaches, who were themselves not original inhabitants.

Nor was the brief, but exciting, fight with these dangerous animals the only evidence that the land could belong to whoever had the will to occupy, govern, and defend it. The most effective means of conquest, employed by both Cooke and General Stephen W. Kearny, was not muskets or money but the promise to protect the inhabitants from hostile Indians. Easily given, such pledges took forty years to fulfill.

More immediate dividends came from the battalion's work to open a wagon road from New Mexico to southern California, but in another often overlooked respect. The new road would demonstrate that a route west, well to the south of the Gila River's upper reaches, was not only feasible but the way of the future.

Cooke's decision to march due west from the old Spanish road that ran between the abandoned Santa Rita copper mines and Janos, Mexico, was not taken in answer to the prayers raised by spiritual leader Levi Hancock. Cooke's purpose was to find a shortcut to San Bernardino Spring, a historic site on today's Mexican border in Arizona and the destination he had in mind all along. The alternative was to go the long way around by known roads to the south, via Janos and Fronteras, where the battalion might be exposed to military garrisons at both places.

Portions of the new route, known as Cooke's Wagon Road, would become thoroughfares for emigrants on the southern trail to California, for the San Antonio-San Diego Mail Line, and for the Butterfield Overland Stage. By demonstrating the importance of the Gila River's southern tributaries as corridors of commerce and travel, the battalion influenced the decision to acquire in 1854 a block of land of almost incomparable worth. This was the some 30,000 square-mile section that now encompasses southern Arizona, including Tucson, and known as the Gadsden Purchase.

On completing its epic march, the battalion finally gave General Kearny the force he needed to back up his mandate from President Polk to occupy and govern California for the United States. Prior to the Gold Rush, the non-Indian inhabitants of California numbered fewer than 15,000. Some 335 Mormon muskets under a capable officer, like Cooke, were more than enough for Kearny to uphold his authority against rebellious Californians, hostile natives, or his reckless countrymen, Commodore Robert Stockton and John C. Frémont.

These and other contributions make gratifying indeed the growing interest in recent years in the Mormon Battalion story and the large and significant role it played. For as time goes on, it becomes increasingly clear that the occupation of New Mexico and California during the Mexican War was among the most decisive chapters in all of American history.

Yet the role of the Mormon volunteers in these events has not only been understated, but many questions about this singular company have for too long gone unanswered. Considering that Mormon annals usually number cows and chickens, it is puzzling that more has not been done simply to identify the exact number and correct names of those who enlisted in Iowa, much less tell what finally became of them.

In this landmark work, historian Norma Baldwin Ricketts has now given the story of the Mormon Battalion the comprehensive treatment it deserves. To this subject she brings a heartfelt interest sustained over many years and exceptional gifts as a researcher and writer, which make her uniquely qualified to write this book.

Not only has the author placed the battalion in the larger context it merits, she has also provided a valuable source of new information about the company and its members. For the first time, her work presents an accurate roster, lists dependents, and identifies who went where by name and number over the three-year period 1846 to 1848 and beyond.

Especially noteworthy are the author's treatment of a subject too long ignored, the women of the Mormon Battalion, and her success in throwing new light on the role of battalion members or veterans in the early history of California. In the process, she has demonstrated that she is a foremost authority on this important subject and has made a significant contribution to Mormon, western, and American history.

Preface

For many years the historic journey of the Mormon Battalion has been, for me, a story waiting to be told. My interest began in the early 1960s while living in California. The gold rush era was fascinating. I became aware of Mormons in California very early, some as long as two years before Brigham Young and the pioneer company arrived in Salt Lake Valley in July 1847. As I studied the books written on the battalion up to that time, I found accounts incomplete, leaving many questions unanswered. The battalion was five hundred straight-backed soldiers marching in unison with muskets on their shoulders from Fort Leavenworth to San Diego, a group of nameless faces serving a year in the United States Army of the West.

Who were these soldiers, how did they endure months of constant hunger and thirst, inadequate clothing and no shoes? Why did nearly one third never reach California? Seventy-nine men reenlisted for an additional six months, another untold story. Mormon folklore contains numerous stories about the pioneers walking across the plains, the handcart companies that were pushed and pulled along the trail, and the trials of the early settlers in Salt Lake Valley. Yet, few stories could be found that told of the courage, hardships, faith, and perseverance of the battalion soldiers.

This dearth has been corrected recently to a great extent by several excellent publications of individual journals, whose editors have provided readers not only with an understanding of a particular journal, but with invaluable footnotes as well. Two examples are David L. Bigler's *The Gold Discovery Journal of Azariah Smith* and Will Bagley's *Frontiersman: Abner Blackburn's Narrative.* However, areas of the battalion experience still remained unknown. As an example, the movement of the men after discharge was lacking. For me, the cycle was incomplete ending the story in California. The men must return to their families and church. Only then would the saga of the Mormon Battalion be finished. The existing overview beginning with enlistment and ending with discharge simply was not enough.

My original intention was to extract individual stories and weave them together to bring the Mormon Battalion into the twentieth century, to read, to enjoy, and to learn of their challenges and accomplishments. I wanted to show these men as real people with real problems day after day, who somehow managed to fulfill their commitment under very difficult circumstances. The resulting battalion stories could then take their place among Mormon folklore and be told over and over.

One of the unique characteristics of the battalion is the large number of daily journals. A careful study of these pioneer writings reveals much more than a recitation of miles traveled, weather conditions, and campsites. Tucked into each journal is a story here and there and then another, stories that run the gamut of emotions, stories telling too much and yet not enough. These unforgettable stories provide glimpses into the soldiers' lives and connect us to the men who wrote them.

Unexpectedly, early research provided two additional avenues to be considered. First, the battalion became a giant jigsaw puzzle. A sentence in one journal provided a better, more complete understanding of facts in other journals. Comparing several journals on a specific day revealed an incredible amount of information. Because of the men's honest, realistic style of recording events, pieces of information from journal to journal fit perfectly. Once these pieces were put together, as the face of the puzzle grew, it seemed the resulting information should not be lost again. I began an elaborate system of cross filing names and events in order to preserve the data. The corroboration the diaries gave each other was fascinating and consistent. One only has to compare the same date in available diaries to confirm a fact and to obtain a more complete picture of what was happening.

For example, when Company B was stationed in San Diego, four men recorded the same incident, all incomplete. The first said a sailor named Beckworth was baptized in the ocean. The second told the name of the sailor's ship. The third diarist wrote only the name and company of the man performing the baptism, while a fourth thought this was the first Mormon convert in California.

This is the resulting entry for April 18, 1847, using these four diaries. The words are theirs, only the arrangement is mine: "A sailor named Beckworth from the ship *Congress* was baptized in the ocean, probably the first Mormon convert in California. He was baptized by William Garner of Company B."

For years it has been puzzling how Samuel Lewis went to Salt Lake Valley. He was discharged in Los Angeles in July 1847, worked at Sutter's Fort for a short time. Several records indicate he reached Salt Lake in December 1847. Yet there was no known group of discharged veterans who went to Utah at that time, so the puzzle remained. Recently, I was rereading Abner Blackburn's journal. Blackburn spent the winter of 1846–47 in Pueblo with the sick detachments and did not travel to California with the original battalion. He went to California in the summer of 1847 with James Brown to collect the mustering-out pay of the Pueblo soldiers and stayed in California only a short time. While writing about the return trip from California to Salt Lake Valley, Blackburn mentioned they were joined by Samuel Lewis for the return trip. This Brown group arrived in Utah in December 1847. The question of how Lewis reached Salt Lake Valley in midwinter was solved. This is an example of how information fits together from one journal to another even though at first thought one would not be inclined to make this pairing because Lewis was in California and Blackburn was in Pueblo.

Another fact that became evident during early research was the participation of battalion members in major historical events in early California history. It seemed once these men were identified as participating in these historic moments, their names should be preserved. There was no desire or attempt to turn them into superheroes using impressive-sounding adjectives. It was enough just to identify them as being in a particular place at a certain time.

There were six men known as *The California Star* Express riders. For many years, only the names of three were known. After several years of research, the names of two more were located. Finally, in 1992 the name of the sixth rider was found. Since these six men participated in a major event in California history, it is gratifying to know they are all identified.

Another benefit of this cross-filing, all done before I became familiar with computers, was unexpected. The actual number of men serving in the battalion has fluctuated in heretofore published accounts. To my knowledge, there never has been an official roster established. The total enlistees have varied from 500 (five companies at 100 each) to as high as 540 men. During the course of this work each name was studied from the mustering-in roster, the mustering-out roster, the pension records, and individual journals and histories. When duplicates were removed, and other problems were cleaned out, the reconstructed roster matches that which Lieutenant Colonel James Allen and William Coray recorded just prior to arriving at Fort Leavenworth. Both Allen's record and Coray's journal state there were 474 enlisted men and 22 officers, totaling 496. A month later, during the second roster count, again recorded by Coray, the figure is the same: 496. The analysis and description of how the final enrollment in the battalion reached 496 is presented in Appendices A–G. This may be the most significant contribution of this work.

How to connect so many facts together in a cohesive manner while retaining historical accuracy was the next decision. I decided to tell their stories by combining many journals to form a composite picture of a day-by-day account of this epic march. Actual words, thoughts, phrases, and, sometimes, entire sentences from various journals were selected. These were then arranged to tell what happened on the trail each day of their year in the army, from July 1846 to July 1847. No adjectives were added, no conversation was built, and no emotion supplemented that of the pioneer diarists. Spelling was not changed in quotations and only light punctuation was added. A tight journalistic style of writing was utilized to match the frugal style of most pioneer diarists. I hope this method will animate the human aspect of this historic journey.

The battalion diarists wrote on small pages under difficult circumstances; it is a wonder they wrote at all, but they did. Their personalities frequently peak out as the pages flip by. Azariah Smith, a sweet-spirited young man, saw rainbows after a storm while others wrote about the mud. Some recorded brief half sentences using no subject; others wrote in greater detail. One very methodical journalist recorded events so repetitiously it was as if he filled out a blank form each evening. Abner Blackburn made me laugh out loud—and more than once. William Coray's journal is quoted extensively because he wrote in greater detail than most of his comrades, providing new insight into several events on the trail. Also, his entries previously have not been quoted frequently because a typed copy of his journal was not located until 1994. Prior to that his writings were available only in the Journal History of the Church of Jesus Christ of Latter-day Saints, a compilation of the daily events in early Mormon history as extracted from individual journals.

In most journals the date, campsite, and miles traveled are difficult to locate because they are scattered through the body of the journal. To facilitate following the journey, these facts have been highlighted in italics at the beginning of the entry for each day.

The date in a diary occasionally may be off by a day or two from another. Perhaps one chronicler wrote at night and another wrote the next morning. Frequently, an entry will read, "Two days ago . . . " and this makes a date vary briefly in some instances. In most cases, however, the diaries coincide again in a day or two. I have shown the location of each day's travel as a prominent place or area they departed, passed, traveled through, or reached that day. Occasionally, these place names are those battalion members used, but these generally are identified with more common names.

Mileage traveled each day varies from soldier to soldier. One man records ten miles while another writes twelve miles for the same day. Perhaps one overestimated while the next understated the distance. By using the same source throughout, the mileage is consistent.

Segment maps, showing all routes used by the battalion, are included. These maps do not have the detail trail historians need to track and preserve trails. Rather they are provided to assist the reader gain a visual concept of this long and arduous journey and of how many steps, day after day, it takes to fill six months.

When the spelling of a last name varied, I used the spelling on the headstone if known. If not, the name on the mustering-out list was used. There are hundreds of names in the pages ahead and, for the most part, both first and last names are used. There simply were too many Williams, Georges, and Henries to do otherwise. Only Azariah could be used singly since no one else had his name. Using both names, although slightly repetitious at times, provides proper identification and saves countless hours of future research. The reader is invited to enjoy the face and story of the moment without trying to remember all the names.

History constantly unfolds—lost journals will be found in dusty trunks, additional documents will come from unexpected sources, and new research will be released, all before the ink on this work can dry. Hopefully, these efforts will allow readers to become acquainted with and to enjoy the battalion's story 150 years after its incredible journey. Perhaps historians will find this work a starting point to which they can add new pieces of the battalion puzzle as they are found.

Constructing this manuscript over the past six years has been a rewarding and, at times, a surprising experience. Journals and needed information have been received unexpectedly from unusual sources. At times it seemed as if pieces were guiding themselves to the puzzle and my job was merely to put them in place.

With keen observations and usually strict adherence to the truth, these men were chroniclers of history. Without meaning to do so, they also became master storytellers with unforgettable voices. Each individual story, when lifted from its journal, provides a unique view of the writer's world and becomes part of a complex, big picture. Suddenly there are no more blank faces; each has a name and each shines in the spotlight when his story is being told.

The time has come to write *finis* to this manuscript. It is hard, very hard, to put it down. Tomorrow's mail may bring another piece of the puzzle.

Acknowledgments

During the past thirty-five years descendants of the Mormon Battalion have been most generous in sharing journals, family histories, and anecdotal information. Therefore, it is necessary to reach across the years and express appreciation to all those who shared their valuable items with me. Since there literally are dozens of you, too many to name, I hope you will recognize excerpts from your ancestor's journal and enjoy reading his name and story. Without your collective material, this story could not have been written in its present form.

I gratefully acknowledge the assistance of many individuals over nearly four decades of research and writing as well as individuals who have responded to this specific project.

Robert E. Coates, director, Mormon Battalion Memorial Visitors Center, Church of Jesus Christ of Latter-day Saints, San Diego, was most helpful. Sincere appreciation goes to Matthew Heiss, Mary S. Kiessling, and Grant Allen Anderson, all of the Historical Department, Church of Jesus Christ of Latter-day Saints, Salt Lake City, for research assistance. Archivist Michael Landon, also with the LDS Church Historical Department, and historians Will Bagley and Lorin K. Hansen have been kind to advise and encourage my efforts; Diane Parkinson, librarian, Brigham Young University, Provo, Utah, helped with several problem areas; Joseph Rinker provided Catholic research; Tom Mahack and Ben E. Lofgren walked the trail from Pleasant Valley over Carson Pass, logging nightly stops and mileage. Sincere appreciation to them for making map 7 possible.

Staff of the following libraries have been particularly helpful during the past four decades: San Diego Public Library, San Diego; Los Angeles Public Library, Los Angeles; Salt Lake City Public Library, Salt Lake City; the Bancroft Library, University of California, Berkeley; California Room, California State Library, Sacramento; and Oakland Public Library, Oakland. Special mention must be made of the late James de T. Abajian, librarian, California Historical Society, San Francisco, who guided and directed my initial research during the early 1960s and taught me the importance of meticulous research. The five series of pioneer history published by the Daughters of Utah Pioneers have been used to locate leads for journals, histories, and biographical information.

To my daughter, Susan Green; Frank Lombard; and Crystal Baldwin, acknowledgment not only for many constructive suggestions and hours of editing, but, most of all, thanks for believing in the concept and encouraging me over the years. To my sons, Robert A. Ricketts and John L. Ricketts, whose loving support and belief that I could do it were greatly appreciated, and to Jean and Nagatoshi Kami, who introduced me to the computer and guided me through the early days at the keyboard, thereby speeding this endeavor to conclusion by at least two years, my heartfelt gratitude; to Paul Jennings and Gordon Jennings, who answered urgent calls when the computer stopped me cold, sincere appreciation and thanks. Finally, I want to recognize John R. Alley, executive editor, Utah State University Press, Logan, whose suggestions, editing, and quest for excellence have brought this manuscript to its present form.

In every undertaking there are those who keep one on course and moving forward with wise counsel, constructive criticism, and kind encouragement. Sincere appreciation to Ben E. Lofgren and David L. Bigler for so doing.

Written, retrospectively, in 1887:

I often wonder why no writer . . . ever dares to list the services of that Battalion to our country in the Mexican War.

—John J. Riser
Private, Company C,
Mormon Battalion

Brigham Young's address prior to the departure of the Mormon Battalion, Council Bluffs, Iowa. Painting by C. C. Christensen, © Church of Jesus Christ of Latter-day Saints, Salt Lake City, Utah; used by permission.

Introduction

Mobbings, murders, expulsions, and religious bigotry often were the lot of members of the Church of Jesus Christ of Latter-day Saints from its beginning in New York state in 1830. Church members were forced to flee from New York to Ohio and Missouri in the mid-1830s. The Ohio Saints arrived in Missouri just in time to witness the final expulsion during the winter of 1838–39. From 1839 to 1844, Illinois seemed to be a haven for the peaceful way of life these outcasts sought, but the cycle repeated itself. After the murder of their leader, Joseph Smith, and his brother Hyrum in 1844, the Latter-day Saints experienced increased persecution. Under Brigham Young, the Mormon Church began its exodus west from Nauvoo across the frozen Mississippi River in January 1846 to escape the armed mobs and continued persecution.

From the Mississippi River to Council Bluffs, Iowa, there were approximately 20,000 Mormons scattered on the prairies in a thin line that stretched more than four hundred miles. They had only what they could load into wagons or carts, along with cattle, pigs, chickens, sheep, and a few horses. Although several temporary settlements were built along the four hundred–mile route, thousands were camped by the roadside in wagons, tents, and dugouts. The winter just past had been severe, one of exposure, illness, and hunger.

Under such conditions it is easy to understand the disbelief with which the Mormons greeted the army recruiting officers who arrived at Mount Pisgah, Iowa, June 26, 1846. Captain James Allen brought an order from Colonel Stephen W. Kearny, First Dragoons, U.S. Army of the West, Fort Leavenworth, Kansas, authorizing him to enlist five hundred Mormon volunteers to help secure California in the war with Mexico.[1]

The Mormons had many reasons to be reluctant to enlist: They had received no protection from persecution and mob action in Missouri and Illinois; their families were destitute and spread over a wide area; and they had hundreds of miles of hostile Indian territory to cross. They were worried how their families would survive another bitter plains winter, and they were concerned about protection for their families in this unfamiliar

1

western frontier. The call to arms had come at a time when the fleeing emigrants were the least prepared to provide men: "Surprised as we were at the government's demand, we were still more so to think our leaders would entertain for a moment the idea of compliance therewith" (James S. Brown).[2]

Hosea Stout's infant son died in his arms while fleeing from Nauvoo. His response to the request for a battalion was strong and immediate: "I was glad to hear of war against the United States and was in hopes it might never end until they were entirely destroyed for they had driven us into the wilderness."[3] Henry Bigler wrote:

> This body . . . [was] made up from the camp of Latter-day Saints just after the expulsion from their homes . . . then to cap the climax the government would call for five hundred of our best men to go and help fight their battles. . . . Here were the Saints with their wives and children in an Indian country, surrounded by savages, without a house, and a scanty supply of provisions . . . to leave them thus to go at the call of our country, to say the least, was rather trying.[4]

What the Mormons didn't know was that Brigham Young had solicited help from the United States Government. He sent Jesse C. Little To Washington, D.C., to see what aid, if any, could be secured. His people were in such dire straits Young wanted to get some type of government assistance in the forced exodus. He offered to haul supplies for the army, to establish posts, or to render any service needed to earn enough to buy supplies, wagons, and teams for the western migration. None of these proposals was accepted, but the timing of Little's visit may have played a major role in the enlistment of the Mormon Battalion.

President James K. Polk and members of Congress had adopted the policy of Manifest Destiny, the idea of extending national boundaries from the Atlantic to the Pacific. Only the Mexican provinces of California and New Mexico prevented Manifest Destiny from becoming a reality. President Polk also did not want the area to fall under British or French rule. Neither did he want a large body of Mormons joining forces with Britain or France.

Trouble had existed for some time between Mexico and the United States over the western boundary of Texas. When Texas was annexed to the United States on December 29, 1845, it reawakened the anger of the Mexican government, which bitterly disputed the borders of Texas set up by the United States. On January 13, 1846, President Polk ordered General Zachary Taylor to march to the eastern bank of the Rio Grande River, claiming it to be the western boundary of the nation. Mexico insisted that the Nueces River one hundred miles to the east was the true western boundary of Texas and that General Taylor's advance was an act of agression.[5]

The first blood was shed on April 25, 1846, when a band of Mexican troops crossed to the eastern side of the Rio Grande and attacked Taylor's company of American soldiers. General Taylor won battles at Palo Alto and Reseca de la Palma and forced the Mexicans back across the Rio Grande. The news of this action was communicated to President Polk, who sent a message to Congress asserting that war existed by an act of agression by Mexico on American soil. The date was May 13, 1846. President Polk met again with Jesse Little on June 5 and informed Little that the Mormons would be protected in California and that five hundred to one thousand men would be taken there to participate in the war with Mexico. Little accepted the offer on behalf of the Mormon Church and left Washington to notify Brigham Young. It did not fall upon Little, however, to deliver the news. Someone else reached the Mormons first. On the president's authority, General Kearny sent Captain James Allen to recruit the Mormon volunteers. Since there were enough volunteers from other areas, Kearny only requested five hundred men from the Mormons.

Kearny, who was in Fort Leavenworth, began building the Army of the West. He sent for two captains and their commands, Captain E. V. Sumner and Captain Philip St. George Cooke, to rejoin the regiment, the First Dragoons, at Fort Leavenworth. Kearny next sent Captain James Allen, First Dragoons, to enlist the Mormons. When Kearny left Fort Leavenworth, the Army of the West consisted of the First Dragoons and a regiment of Missouri Mounted Volunteers under Colonel Sterling Price. Later Company F, Third Artillery, and a regiment of New York Infantry Volunteers joined him in California as did the Mormon Battalion.

Polk's next step was to order General Taylor to conquer Mexico City. General John Wool formed a column at San Antonio, Texas, for the invasion of Chihuahua, and Colonel Stephen W. Kearny was to organize a force to conquer New Mexico and California. On June 24, 1846, President Polk sent Commodore John D. Sloat of the Pacific Squadron the following confidential order: "If you ascertain with certainty that Mexico has declared war against the United States, you will at once possess yourself of the port of San Francisco, and blockade and occupy such other ports as your forces may permit."[6]

In obedience to these instructions, Sloat occupied Monterey July 7 and issued a proclamation announcing that "henceforth California will be a portion of the United States." Mexico's General José Castro and his army fled south from Monterey with Sloat's arrival. Under Sloat's orders Captain John B. Montgomery, of the USS *Portsmouth*, and his crew raised the American flag over Yerba Buena (San Francisco) on July 9, 1846.

At this time another problem was developing in northern California. A group of ranchers heard rumors that Mexican authorities were going to drive all Americans out of California. Banding together under William B.

Ide, this small rebel group stormed the military post at Sonoma on June 14, 1846, and captured, among others, Mariano G. Vallejo, one of California's wealthiest citizens. These rebels declared California to be an independent republic with Ide as president. They raised a home-made flag, showing a field with a crudely drawn bear and a star, which gave the incident its name—the Bear Flag Revolt.[7] California was a republic for fourteen days until John C. Frémont arrived and raised the American flag.

Frémont and his group of topographical engineers joined with the Bear Flaggers into what was known as the California Volunteers. When Frémont and his California Volunteers arrived in Monterey July 19, he wanted to join Commodore Sloat's command to legitimize his rebel forces. Sloat would not muster Frémont's band into United States service and opposed Frémont's proposal to march against Santa Barbara and Los Angeles. Commodore Robert F. Stockton arrived and took command from Sloat July 25. Stockton commissioned Frémont's troops as the Navy Battalion of Mounted Riflemen and sent Frémont and the California Volunteers by sea to San Diego to cut off the remnants of Castro's fleeing army. Stockton sailed down the coast to San Pedro.

General Castro continued his flight into Mexico and Governor Don Pio Pico fled to lower California. Without opposition, Frémont and Stockton occupied Los Angeles August 14, 1846, and the conquest of California was complete. Four days later, Stockton formally annexed California to the United States and appointed John C. Frémont as its military governor or commandant. Stockton also divided California into three military districts placing Archibald Gillespie in command in Los Angeles, Frémont in Monterey, and himself in San Diego. He sent Kit Carson overland with dispatches announcing the conquest of California. Carson left Los Angeles September 5, 1846, with the news the Mexican generals were in flight, all ports and towns were occupied, the people were reconciled to American rule, and Frémont was the military governor, stationed in Monterey.

The natives in Los Angeles rebelled against Lieutenant Gillespie's arrogant control and arbitrary regulations. Led by General José Maria Flores and other Californians, the rebels gave Gillespie the choice of fighting or evacuating Los Angeles. Taking the latter course, Gillespie fled to San Pedro and embarked on a merchant ship. The Californians increased the scope of their rebellion and Americans fled from Santa Barbara and San Diego. Commodore Stockton began the reconquest of southern California when he returned to San Pedro October 27, 1846. Without horses, he was unable to lead his soldiers to Los Angeles. Stockton was content to reoccupy San Diego. Frémont left northern California November 30, 1846, with the California Volunteers, traveling south through California's central valleys.

During this same period General Kearny and Captain Cooke and their troops continued on their way to California. They had nearly reached Albuquerque when Kearny received an express message from Colonel Price telling of the death of Lieutenant Colonel Allen, commander of the Mormon Battalion, at Fort Leavenworth. He decided to send Cooke back to Santa Fe to assume command of the Mormon Battalion when it arrived. He instructed Cooke to bring the battalion and to make a wagon road to the Pacific. Kearny continued on to California. Cooke left Kearny at La Joya, New Mexico, October 3 for Santa Fe. He was assigned three men, two of whom he left to guard his baggage until he returned. The third, a bugler, traveled with him to Santa Fe. When Cooke assumed command of the battalion, his rank became lieutenant colonel.

Kearny entered San Diego December 12, 1846, and met with Commodore Stockton. He told Stockton President Polk wanted Kearny to be the governor of California, but Stockton was not convinced. In spite of their differences, the two commanders combined their forces and, under joint attack, defeated a force of Californians at the San Gabiel River in the Battle of the Mesa January 9. They entered Los Angeles January 10 unopposed.

The Californians, defeated in the battle with Stockton and Kearny, fled northward where they met Frémont on his southward trip and surrendered to him. Together with Frémont, they signed the Cahuenga Capitulation January 13, 1847. Under the agreement, the Californians agreed to deliver their arms to Frémont and to refrain from participation for the duration of the Mexican War. Frémont did not require an oath of allegiance to the United States and extended amnesty to the Californians who had violated their paroles. John C. Frémont signed the Cahuenga Capitulation as the "Military Commandant of California." Two weeks later the Mormon Battalion arrived. With strict discipline and long, hard days of marching, Cooke and the battalion arrived in San Diego January 29, 1847, without firing a single shot. California was under American rule, but it took another year with several main encounters, all in Mexico, before the war was over officially.[8]

After the initial opposition, Brigham Young and the governing council of the Mormon Church met little resistance as they urged the men to enlist and to prove their loyalty to America. The clothing allowance of $3.50 a month, plus their monthly pay, would produce much-needed cash. Forming the battalion also provided for five hundred men to reach California at government expense. By this time Brigham Young and the other leaders realized it would not be possible to move the displaced emigrants west immediately. They made receiving permission to remain on Indian lands through the approaching winter season a condition for forming the battalion. Allen met with leaders of the Potawatomi and arranged a treaty for the Mormons to remain temporarily on Indian lands.

At first recruits were slow to sign up. After the men understood the feelings of their leaders, the murmuring stopped. Upon learning that Mormon Church officials approved of enlisting, one eighteen-year-old boy wrote:

> This was quite a hard pill to swallow—to leave wives and children on the wild praries, destitute and almost helpless, having nothing to rely on only the kindness of neighbors, and go to fight the battles of a government that had allowed some of its citizens to drive us from our homes, but the word comes from the right source and seemed to bring the spirit of conviction of its truth with it and there was quite a number of our company volunteered, myself and brother among them. (Zadock K. Judd)[9]

After Brigham Young delivered an eloquent appeal for volunteers, the quota was reached in less than two weeks. Brigham Young promised the men:

> You are now going into an enemy's land at your country's call. If you live your religion, obey and respect your officers, and hold sacred the property of the people among whom you travel, and never take anything but what you pay for, I promise you in the name of Israel's God that not one of you shall fall by the hand of the enemy. Though there will be battles fought in your front and in your rear, on your right hand and on your left, you will not have any fighting to do except with wild beasts.[10]

This battalion was unique in several ways. First, all of its members belonged to the Mormon Church except six soldiers, the commanding officer (Captain Allen), and a handful of regular army officers. A religious group had been asked to form a military unit solely from its own members. The church was only sixteen years old; the men had joined the church because of sincere, personal conviction. They were not just members. Many held offices in the church's lay priesthood, being either elders, seventies, or high priests. All of their officers, except three, had been to the Mormon temple in Nauvoo, Illinois. This meant the officers had received certain sacred ordinances reserved for members endeavoring to live up to all the teachings of the Mormon Church.[11]

The volunteers voted unanimously to have Brigham Young and the Council of Twelve Apostles, the governing body of the Mormon Church, nominate the officers, both commissioned and non-commissioned. The soldiers, therefore, were committed to obedience to their officers ecclesiastically as well as by military jurisdiction.

On Saturday, July 18, President Brigham Young and Apostles Heber C. Kimball, Parley P. Pratt, Willards Richards, John Taylor, and Wilford Woodruff met in private council with the commissioned and non-commissioned officers on the banks of the Missouri River. The church officials gave the men "their last charge and blessings, with a firm promise that on condition of faithfulness their lives should be held in honorable remembrance to all generations."[12] They instructed the officers to be "as fathers to the privates, to remember their prayers, to see that the name of Deity was strictly observed and revered, and that virtue and cleanliness were strictly observed." Young also told them "a private soldier is as honorable as an officer if he behaves as well." No one was distinguished as being better flesh and blood than another. Brigham Young continued: "Honor the calling of every man in his place. . . . keep neat and clean, teach chastity, gentility, and civility. Swearing must not be admitted, insult no man. Let no man be without his undergarment. . . . keep neat and clean."[13]

The men were sworn in and what a group it was. Recruited from a church that had suffered from war and bloodshed, the volunteers had no knowledge of army regulations, no marching experience, and no desire to be soldiers. These men enlisted as a "mission" for their church, paying first allegiance to their religious leaders and second to the army officers. They believed their enlistment to be divinely ordered and thought they were doing more than just marching to California. They believed they were working to "build up the Kingdom of God." This loyalty to the Mormon Church at times caused conflict with military authority.

The battalion was made up of men representing various occupations and backgrounds, ranging in age from fourteen years (Alfred Higgins) to sixty-eight years old (Samuel Gould). Although the requested age was from eighteen to forty-five years, several youths who had not yet reached eighteen were able to join. A few older men also enlisted. Many volunteers were foreign born, representing Sweden, Norway, Wales, Ireland, Germany, and England, which provided the largest number. All of the existing states were represented except Florida, Louisiana, and Texas.

When the five companies were complete, there were 496 men listed on the company rosters. Three other Mormons were on the command roster and one man joined up at Fort Leavenworth, making a total of five hundred volunteers in the battalion. Four others, including Captain Allen, completed the command staff. Thirty-one wives of battalion members accompanied their husbands. Although twenty signed up as laundresses, only the names of eighteen laundresses have been identified. To date, only two women are known to have been mentioned in journals as doing laundry for a soldier. In both cases, the soldier paid them for doing his washing. There is no record located that confirms the women were ever paid by the army. Forty-four children accompanied the thirty-one

couples. Three of them, and nine other boys, for a total of twelve, served
as aides to the officers in the battalion. Jefferson Hunt and his wife, Celia,
took seven children along. Other large families included James P. Brown,
four children; Montgomery Button, four; Nelson Higgins, six; and Sebert
Shelton, seven. Only four of the wives and one child who wasn't an aide
reached California.

Of historical note is the fact that the first children of American citizens born in two western states—California and Utah—were from this
group: Diego Hunter, son of Jessie and Lydia Hunter, in California and
Elizabeth Steele, daughter of John and Catherine Steele, in Utah.

In addition to the thirty-one battalion couples, there were two other
couples (Jane and John Bosco and Rebecca and Elijah Smith) who started
the journey. The men were teamsters and did not belong to the battalion.
Only Rebecca Smith, who went to Pueblo with the Brown sick detachment,
survived. The other three died en route. One soldier took his mother
along with his wife and two children.

The men were aware that their actions reflected on the Mormon
Church. When the commanding officer made an unpopular decision,
William Coray wrote: "We durst not rebel for fear of after claps coming on
the church."[14]

The first four companies of the battalion left Council Bluffs and
began their trek Monday morning, July 20, 1846. The fifth company started the next day. Arriving at Fort Leavenworth, Kansas, August 1, 1846, the
men were issued supplies and equipment. They decided to travel in their
own clothes and send most of the clothing allowance of $42 to their fami-
lies and their church. This, they thought, was part of their duty and the
call of their mission.

The group left Fort Leavenworth August 12, 1846, and began one of
the longest infantry marches in United States history. When the battalion
left Fort Leavenworth to start its journey west, it was without uniforms,
without military discipline or training, and handicapped by the presence
of wives and families and by a leadership divided between military and religious authority. What they did have was a promise that none of them
would be lost fighting the enemy. Brigham Young later said: "The brethren
who went into the battalion went with as good hearts and spirits, according
to the extent of their understanding, as ever men went upon missions in
the world, and they manifested a readiness to do anything required of
them. . . . perhaps no other set of men under the same circumstances
would have done better . . . the character that you bear . . . is good."[15]

They were real people with complex every-day problems. There was
conflict between military and church authority. Yet they maintained the
belief that they were engaged in a calling their church leaders had given
them. Throughout all their trials and hardships, the journals used in this

work did not reveal a single instance of questioning their service in the U.S. Army or their loyalty to the Mormon Church. William Wood, Company C, wrote to his non-Mormon parents in England, telling them about enlisting in the battalion and his trip to California. He was in Los Angeles, with a few months remaining before being discharged, when he wrote: "I have crossed the continent of America from the Atlantic to the shores of the Pacific. Yet my mind is not changed at all in regards to the religion I profess to believe. I know that it is true and that all men, sooner or later, will know it."[16] After one particularly difficult period with human endurance almost spent, a soldier stood up and drew from his pocket a small American flag, saying, "This flag, brethren, was made for me by my wife before we left the States. It is for this, comrades, that we toil, and for a home for the Church."[17]

When the battalion arrived in Santa Fe on October 9, Lieutenant Colonel Philip St. George Cooke, U.S. Army, became its commander. Colonel Cooke was a strict disciplinarian, pointing his speech with invectives. One diarist recorded he had "a rare combination of swear words." The soldiers often were upset by his use of swearing when giving orders, yet they came to respect and trust him. He, in turn, developed a great admiration for the pluck, stamina, and loyalty of these men. Colonel Cooke's insistence upon order, discipline, and systematic procedure contributed heavily to the success of the expedition. After arriving in California, Cooke read an official communication congratulating the soldiers upon completing the journey under adverse conditions and blazing a road to the Pacific Ocean. This communiqué softened the attitude of the Mormons toward their commander and they began to appreciate Cooke's strengths.[18]

The lack of food, water, and clothing caused unbelievable hardship and suffering as they traveled. The men sold buttons off their coats to Indians for food. At one point James S. Brown traded his belt for a hatful of ground acorn mush and, holding up his pants with one hand and his hat full of mush in the other, joined his messmates like a conquering hero. Again and again, they boiled bones and scraped hides to survive. They sucked nourishment from the soft edges of hooves and horns and roasted intestines: "I eat guts for the first time today though many have eat them before" (Henry Standage).[19]

During the march the men suffered most for lack of water while crossing the deserts. Mirages mocked their thirst and they filled their mouths with buckshot and small stones to stimulate the flow of saliva. With faces blackened by the sun, and with sunken eyes, they often fell by the way exhausted. Stronger companions carried water back to them at night after camp was made. Three sick detachments, totaling 156 men, were sent back to winter in Pueblo.

With ranks depleted by the three groups on detached service, 335 men reached San Diego January 29, 1847. With them were the four women and one child who had made the entire trip to California. Upon reaching California, there was little resemblance to an army. They were a group of men in ragged clothing, most without shoes, so emaciated that all military drill and discipline had been suspended. It was enough merely to finish the journey. They had started with twenty-five government wagons and twelve private wagons and had reached their destination with five government wagons and three private wagons. They also brought several cannon and other ordnance of war. Colonel Cooke succeeded in blazing a wagon road to California as directed.

In California they fought no battles. The war with Mexico was almost at an end by the time they arrived except for a few skirmishes with Indians. Company B was assigned to peacetime garrison duty in San Diego. The other four companies were sent to Los Angeles, also for peacetime duty. The battalion was discharged at Fort Moore in Los Angeles July 16, 1847. At that time they did not know how far west Brigham Young and the Mormon immigrants had traveled or where the church would settle. Nor did they know that before they reached their families and the church they would participate in several important historical events in the early days of California's golden era.

On April 5, 1848, Brigham Young wrote: "The enlistment of the Mormon Battalion in the service of the United States, though looked upon by many with astonishment and some with fear, has proved a great blessing to this community. It was indeed the temporal salvation of our camp."[20]

CHAPTER ONE

The Enlistment

1846

Fri., June 26, Mt. Pisgah, Iowa. Five men, in army uniforms and with a baggage wagon, rode into camp. They talked with William Huntington, who was in charge, and Apostle Wilford Woodruff.[1] There was instant alarm when the Saints saw the uniforms. Women rounded up their children and hid them while men reached for their rifles. They thought the soldiers might be spies trying to find out how many Mormons were here and what their plans were. It was only two years since Joseph Smith, the Mormon prophet, was murdered and the sight of the soldiers and the uniforms brought it all back.

Sat., June 27, Mt. Pisgah. The leader of the men who had arrived the day before was Captain James Allen, First Dragoons, U.S. Army of the West. He brought four dragoons with him. With Huntington's permission, the men gathered in the bowery and Allen told them he had a request from the president of the United States to enlist five hundred Mormons in the army for twelve months during the war with Mexico.[2] The volunteers would go to Fort Leavenworth for supplies and then to California, where they would be discharged in a year.

The captain asked for healthy men, eighteen to forty-five years old, to make five companies of about one hundred soldiers each. The enlisted men were to choose their own officers consisting of a captain and a first and second lieutenant for each company. The volunteers would be allowed to keep their guns and accoutrements at the end of their service. Twenty women, four for each company, were to serve as laundresses and to receive rations and other allowances. Taking the men would cause serious hardships on families left behind. Many thought it was a plan to destroy the Mormons. Since the government hadn't offered any protection from the mobs in Missouri and Illinois, there was doubt about sending men to

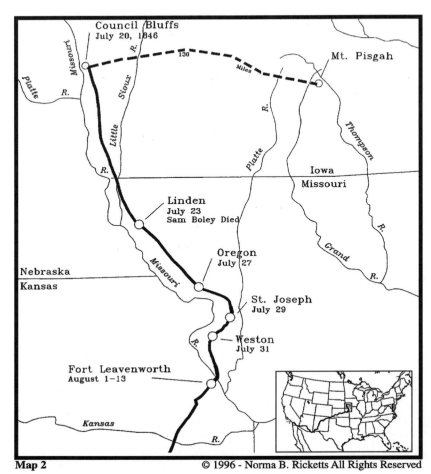

1846-1847
Mormon Battalion Route
Council Bluffs, Iowa to Ft. Leavenworth, Kansas

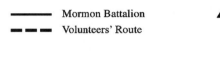

—————— Mormon Battalion
━ ━ ━ ━ Volunteers' Route

fight for the United States at this time. Huntington sent a letter by messenger to Brigham Young at Council Bluffs to tell him about the captain's proposition.[3]

Sun., June 28, Mt. Pisgah. Everyone talked about the war and the government's request. Hosea Stout thought it was a plot to bring trouble to the Mormons. William Hyde said it would be very hard to leave his wife, children, and aged parents "in the midst of wild Indian country with only a wagon box for a home."[4] Captain Allen left for Council Bluffs to see Brigham Young.

Mon., June 29, Mt. Pisgah. Talk about the war continued. Most denounced the idea of Mormons enlisting. Abraham Day said, "Here is one man who will not go."[5] The women felt the request was unfair, that the Saints had given enough and owed the government nothing. The men were anxious to hear what Brigham Young thought about Allen's proposal.

Wed., July 1, Mt. Pisgah. There was a lot of talk in camp. Melissa Coray wanted to go with her husband and said she didn't see why women must always stay behind and worry about their husbands when they could just as well march beside them.[6]

Sat., July 4, Mt. Pisgah. More talk and agitation. Dimick Huntington's wife was distraught at the thought of his leaving. George Taggart talked with William Huntington and Ezra T. Benson and told them he "wished to do that which would be productive of the most good in building up the Kingdom of God." Their counsel to him was "the importance of the case requires every man should go."[7]

> I felt indignant toward the Government that had suffered me to be raided and driven from my home. I made the uncouth remark that "I would see them all damned and in Hell." I would not enlist. On the way to the Bluffs we met President Brigham Young, Heber C. Kimball and W. Richards returning, calling for recruits. They said the salvation of Israel depended upon the raising of the army. When I heard this my mind changed. I felt that it was my duty to go. (Daniel B. Rawson)[8]

> As soon as the authority of the church made known their desires for us to enlist, I wished to go. Brother Miller tried to influence me to stay, but Brother Brigham had said he wanted all young men to go that could, so I was determined to go. (Henry G. Boyle)[9]

Mon., July 6, Mt. Pisgah. Brigham Young, Heber C. Kimball, and Willard Richards arrived from Council Bluffs with Allen and his men. Allen stood in an empty wagon while announcing his message to the gathered exiles. Allen explained that thousands of volunteers were ready to enlist in the United States Army in the Mexican War. Through the benevolence of President James K. Polk, five hundred Mormons could enlist. Brigham Young said it was no hoax, that it was the first time the government had "stretched its arm to our assistance."[10] Young stated enlisting would prove loyalty to the country. Further, the wages would help their families and the Mormon Church. Everyone listened attentively to the call of the church leaders. After the meeting the band commenced playing and marching. Parley P. Pratt called to the brethren to fall in line. It was a stirring scene. Charles Hancock was the first to step up and Brigham Young signed young Charles's name with a flourish as the first volunteer. Sixty men signed up.

Wed., July 8, Mt. Pisgah. Sixty-six men volunteered. Others were thinking about signing up. There was a feeling of sadness and worry among the wives and families. The volunteers left for Council Bluffs after receiving military advice from Charles C. Rich, who had been a general in the Nauvoo Legion, the Mormon militia.

Thurs., July 9, Mt. Pisgah. Brigham Young and other Mormon Church authorities left for Council Bluffs in the late afternoon to enlist volunteers there.

Fri., July 10, Mt. Pisgah. More men enlisted. Several women also signed with their husbands. The mood in camp was one of worry and grave concern. Captain Allen and Indian Agent R. B. Mitchell issued a proclamation at Council Bluffs granting permission to the Mormons for a portion of them to reside on Potawatomi land. Captain Allen did this in the name of the president of the United States.

Sun., July 12, Mt. Pisgah. Although it was hard to see families separated and the sadness in everyone's eyes, the murmurings stopped after President Young said, "This thing is from above for our good."[11]

Mon., July 13, Council Bluffs, Iowa. The volunteers and families from Mt. Pisgah arrived. Twenty-two-year-old John J. Riser was traveling with his brother in the Mormon exodus from Nauvoo when they heard about the government's request for a battalion. John Riser probably was the only man eager to enter the military service:

This news aroused in me such a desire to reach the place of enlistment that I could hardly await the time until we should reach the place as I feared that I would be too late to offer my services to my country, and so I left the slow-going company behind and went ahead on foot to reach the camp where the enlisting took place, but I found there was plenty room for more. I had a great love for adventure and I had no doubt I inherited this military ardor from my forefathers who had seen much service in the wars of Germany. I had myself enrolled in Company C . . . to serve one year, but with this enlistment commenced a series of hardships which I however cheerfully encountered and without complaint and became a true soldier.[12]

Tues., July 14, Council Bluffs. Brigham Young announced that even though the battalion was part of the regular army, under Captain Allen, the battalion could appoint its own company leaders. The men voted to have President Young and the council choose the officers and non-commissioned officers of the five companies. Brigham Young next appointed the officers of each company. Some officers decided to take their wives and children along. More men signed up. Israel Evans and Isaac Carter, both eighteen and quite short, were turned down by the recruiting officer as "under size." Then they stood on a stump behind someone and were accepted. Lot Smith was afraid he might not measure up to the required height, so he raised up on his toes. Jacob Butterfield, 6'2", thought he was the tallest man to volunteer. Alonzo Raymond had an affliction for a considerable time, which the doctors told him was incurable. Heber C. Kimball saw him resting by the side of the road and asked him what was troubling him. Alonzo told of his illness. Kimball told him to enlist in the battalion and promised him he would recover and be able to complete the march. Alonzo enlisted in Company D.

Thurs., July 16, Council Bluffs. About 450 men gathered in the square in the morning. An American flag was "brought out from the store house of things rescued" when they fled from Nauvoo and "was hoisted to a tree mast and under it the enrollment took place."[13] Samuel Rogers and William Johnstun had cut the liberty pole for the flag a few days before.

Colonel Thomas Kane, a longtime friend of the Mormons, was in camp and assured them enlisting was the right thing to do. Captain Allen assumed command after mustering the men into the army for one year. He had spent twenty-one days recruiting the battalion. Some of the delay was due to the scattered condition of the emigrants. After being among the Mormons for three weeks, Captain Allen said they "came into the service very readily and will . . . make an active and efficient force."[14]

Plans were made to leave as soon as more men signed up for the fifth company. Captain Allen announced the group was to be known as the Mormon Battalion, U.S. Army of the West. The men went eight miles to Sarpy's, a French trading post on the Missouri River, where each man was issued a blanket, coffee, and sugar.[15] Most then returned to Council Bluffs for a final farewell to wives and families.

Fri., July 17, Council Bluffs. Sidney Willes was baptized this afternoon. He and his brother, Ira, were the only ones in their family to join the Mormon Church. Both were in Company B. Dimick Huntington signed up for Company D. His wife believed she would never see him again and was distraught. He laid his hands on her head and blessed her in the name of the Lord that they would see each other again and spend many happy years together. William Casper left his wife and baby in care of her sixteen-year-old brother. He told his wife, "Sarah Ann, you are in the hands of the same God as I am. May He bring us together again."[16]

When the companies paraded and were inspected by Colonel Allen, one man was rejected in Company B. The battalion was under pay from this date.

Sat., July 18, Council Bluffs. A drum tattoo brought the men to attention for roll call by company. Then Brigham Young and Apostles Heber C. Kimball, John Taylor, Orson Pratt, and Wilford Woodruff met with both officers and non-commissioned officers in a poplar grove near the river. After exhorting the officers to be "fathers to their companies and manage their men by the power vested in the priesthood," Brigham Young concluded by explaining the plan of emigration to go to the Great Basin, where they would have protection against mobs and where they could build temples. He also told them they would be "dismissed about 800 miles from us."[17]

The enlisted men cleared an eight-rod square while the meeting was going on. They stomped the grass down until it was smooth enough to dance. After the meeting with the officers, the church leaders, together with their wives, began the dancing with a double cotillion. It was a signal for the festivities to begin.

Captain Pitt's Brass Band played until the sun went behind the hills. All church authorities and officers and soldiers of the battalion joined in. There was "perfect order . . . all was still and quiet . . . nothing was heard but the music"—violins, horns, sleigh bells, and tambourines. What a merry dance it was. A sister with light hair, dark eyes, and a soprano voice, sang a touching song, accompanied by a quartet:

> By the rivers of Babylon we sat down and wept.
> We wept when we remembered Zion.

Many listening had tears in their eyes. "An elder asked the blessing of heaven on all who, with a purity of heart and brotherhood of spirit, had mingled in that society, and then all dispersed."[18] Thomas Kane was in attendance.

Sun., July 19, Council Bluffs. In his Sunday sermon Brigham Young and the apostles said again it was right to serve in the battalion. All took courage from their words. Company E was filling up. Abraham Day, who said he wouldn't sign up, was in Company E. Dimick Huntington arranged for his wife and three children to go with him. William Kelley, assigned to Company A, married his sweetheart, Anna Farragher, in the evening. She did not go on the march.[19]

A Sabbath meeting was held at Redemption Hill at Council Bluffs. Three apostles spoke—John Taylor, Parley P. Pratt, and Wilford Woodruff. After the meeting another thirty or forty volunteers signed up.

Mon., July 20, along the Missouri River, 10 miles. Allen and the first four companies started for Fort Leavenworth. Wives, mothers, and children cried as the men marched away. It was difficult for the men as well. They didn't take food with them, only a little flour and parched corn, since they didn't want to take food away from families left behind. They each had one blanket to use both as a bottom and top as they slept. Captain Allen led out along the east bank of the Missouri River for the two-hundred-mile journey to Fort Leavenworth. Zacheus Cheney wrote, "I tell you, on that day the tears fell like rain drops."[20] But loyalty to their church leaders was paramount to men such as David Pettegrew: "I then left my family in the care of my son-in-law . . . because I was counselled by President Young to go with the Mormon Battalion, it being a particular request."[21]

Tues., July 21, Glenwood, Iowa, 4 miles. Dough was mixed by opening up a bag of flour and pouring a little water into a hollowed-out place in the flour. When the water and flour were mixed, each man got a branch like a walking stick, went to the sack and took a lump of dough. He pulled the dough out into a long string and wrapped it around and around the stick. Then it was held close to the fire until it was considered baked. Hard rain during the day made conditions muddy and miserable for walking. It was a trial for Thomas Dunn to leave his wife and baby. He left in the afternoon to go back and tell her good-bye one more time. When the group stopped for the night, the men made brush shelters. Jesse C. Little came into camp during early evening. The rain continued all night and the men discovered their brush shanties did not provide much shelter. The fifth company left Council Bluffs.

Wed., July 22, Thurman, Iowa, 18 miles. Thomas Dunn returned this morning. He continued to grieve for his wife and was very worried about his elderly parents, who were living in a wagon box, and had no means of sustenance while he was gone. Captain Allen became Lieutenant Colonel Allen when the fifth company was filled. Jesse Little made encouraging remarks and bestowed his blessings upon the group. He talked about Samuel Boley, who was very ill. Colonel Allen was very kind to the men. As the companies started out in the morning, the musicians played "The Girl I Left Behind." The men in Company B purchased a baggage wagon and three yoke of oxen to pull it. The wagon and oxen cost each man $1.62 and each one was allowed to place 20 lb. of goods in the wagon. The fifth company caught up at Mosquito Creek.

Thurs., July 23, Linden, Missouri, 26 miles. Samuel Boley died during the night. This was the first death in the battalion. Wrapped in his blanket, he was buried in a rough lumber coffin on Mosquito Creek. He was a man of integrity and energy. During his illness he was nursed by the assistant surgeon, Dr. William McIntire. Jesse Little spoke kindly of Boley.

Fri., July 24, Rocky Port, Missouri, 5 miles. The weather was excessively hot. It was hard to walk in the boiling sun. Many began to fail and this was just the beginning. Colonel Allen wanted moderate marches, but Adjutant George Dykes, who had a horse, urged long marches. The men who were sick were annointed with oil and blessed by the laying on of hands. There was a great deal of drinking in Company E. Alonzo Raymond took his place on the march as he had recovered from his illness. He believed Heber C. Kimball's promise was fulfilled. John Steele drank freely from a cold spring during the day and suffered from it: "My bowels being empty not eating much today, it took hold and cramped my bowels and stomach and I was in exceeding pain; then the Elders laid hands on me and I got a little better so as to go along. The brethren stand this journey pretty well, some of them walked 25 miles without tasting a mouthful of anything and a scanty supper at that."[22]

Sat., July 25, 15 miles. No flour. Many went to bed fasting while others ate parched corn. Quite a few had sore feet as they were not used to long hours of marching. Thomas Dutcher was very ill.

Sun., July 26, Mound City, Missouri, 21 miles. Passed fields of potatoes, oats, and corn. Some items were appropriated as everyone was hungry:

> The farmers along the rout thought we were a rough sett. Chickens, ducks, pigs, and all kind of vegetables suffered without price. Some of those fellows would steal anything. One set of thieves carried [away] several beehives while the oners were at dinner. One soldier drove off a cow and milked her to the fort and then sold her for whiskey. (Abner Blackburn)[23]

> I was at one time traveling alone some little distance from the road and the company was ahead of me. I came across a man in his garden digging potatoes. I asked him civilly if he would give me two or three. He told me no and raised his hoe on me and told me to get out of his lot. I stood a few moments in a daring attitude and then stooped and picked up two or three potatoes, went a few steps to an onion bed, pulled up two or three of them and went on my way leaving a very mad man using very bad language while I was saying nothing. . . . Vegetables were a treat to persons living principaly on bread and bacon and were appropriated by some on the route as also chickens, honey, pigs, and roasting ears of corn and Col. Allen, being an old Soldier, seemed to think that it was a natural consequence. I remember at one time we made our camp close to a large corn field. The proprietor came to the Col. as soon as he seen that

camp was going to be made and requested the Col. to keep the boys out of the corn and he circulated that such request had been made and soon after fires had been kindled I happened to be to the Cols. and roasting ears were plentiful around it and much corn was consumed that night. (Henry W. Sanderson)[24]

My feet became very sore. My payne was savere, the sore had been of long duration. [I] opened it with my knive. Brother Gully and A Lytle & Pace ware very kind to me and done all they promised to do to see that no hardship was placed on me as I told them my health was poor. Marched 20 miles and camped. (Levi Hancock)[25]

Mon., July 27, Oregon, Missouri, 20 miles. The weary travelers had been without flour two days. Colonel Sterling Price came into camp with the load of flour from Fort Leavenworth, but would not deliver it to Quartermaster Sebert because Sebert was a Mormon. Insulted, Colonel Allen ordered the flour turned over immediately or Price would be placed under arrest. Upon hearing Allen's words, Price hurriedly followed the order and delivered the flour. The men cheered Colonel Allen's action.

Tues., July 28, Nodaway, Missouri, 18 miles. Passed through several small towns where former enemies from Missouri lived. They said they were misled and would like the Mormons back as neighbors. Philander Colton was surprised today when his young son, Charles, came into camp. He ran away to be with his father. He was only nine years old. Young Charles sang as the men sat around the campfire. His soprano voice, which was sweet with a plaintive quality, touched the men. Allen gave permission for him to continue with the battalion.

Wed., July 29, Mt. Pleasant, Missouri, 6 miles. The men marched in good order through St. Joseph, Missouri, with the fifes and drums setting a brisk pace. The Missourians thought the Mormons would turn down the request of the government for soldiers. They were surprised at the spirited march.

Thurs., July 30, near Bloomington, Missouri, 15 miles. Everyone was very hungry. Some men didn't set examples as Brigham Young asked. There were chickens, ducks, pigs, and vegetables taken from farmers along the way without permission.

Fri., July 31, near Watson, Missouri, 10 miles. A very strong wind came up during the night, which revived smouldering campfires. All tents were blown down around the men. Uprooted trees were scattered in all directions at the edge of camp, but not one fell into the camp. The streaks of lightning made a scene of terror. The men felt they were saved by God, since only one ox was killed by falling timber. Today they passed through Weston in time to music. The whole town was looking out their doors, astonished. They said only Mormons would have enlisted under such forbidding circumstances. The musicians really outdid themselves and kept the soldiers at a good pace playing such tunes as "Jefferson's Liberty" and "Over the River to Charley." With the left foot down at the beginning of a bar, five companies of Mormons marched through and turned three corners in the heart of town while onlookers were silent.

John Tippets saw John Eagle, one of the mob that murdered Joseph Smith, standing in the door of the stable. They camped a mile beyond town. The men washed and cleaned up as they expected to reach Fort Leavenworth the next day. Melissa Coray started washing for Samuel Rogers. The water was only three inches deep and had a very muddy bottom. John Tippets tried to wash his clothes, but the mud got on them and he couldn't wash it out. The companies had only a small amount of soap.

At night Colonel Allen and the orderlies prepared the first official roster—22 officers and 474 enlisted men for a total of 496 names on the company rosters.[26] Captain Allen had appointed three Mormons in Council Bluffs to command positions: First Lieutenant George P. Dykes as adjutant to assist Allen in handling correspondence, distributing orders, and as chief assistant to the commander and chief intermediary between the commander and the Mormon soldiers. Private James H. Glines became a sergeant major whose main duty was to assist Dykes. Private Sebert C. Shelton was appointed quartermaster sergeant in charge of distributing clothing, equipment, and other military goods. These three men, while serving on the command staff, were not counted on the company rosters. They and John Allen, who joined the unit at Fort Leavenworth, brought the total number of volunteers to five hundred.

William McIntire was named assistant surgeon of the battalion and served without military rank. His name, therefore, was not on the company rosters.[27]

Roster
Mormon Battalion, U.S. Army of the West

Command Staff

James Allen, Captain, promoted to Lieutenant Colonel
George W. Sanderson, Assistant Surgeon
William L. McIntire, Assistant Surgeon
Jeremiah Cloud, Major, Paymaster
George P. Dykes, 1st Lieutenant, Adjutant (Co. D)
James H. Glines, Sergeant Major, assistant to Dykes (Co. A)
Sebert C. Shelton, Quartermaster Sergeant (Co. D)

Company A

Officers, etc.:

Jefferson Hunt, Captain
George W. Oman, 1st
  Lieutenant
Lorenzo Clark, 2nd Lieutenant
William W. Willis, 3rd
  Lieutenant
Phineas R. Wright, 1st
  Sergeant (Until March 9,
  1847)
Ebenezer Brown, 2nd
  Sergeant
Reddick N. Allred, 3rd Sergeant
  (Quartermaster Sergeant on
  Feb. 11, 1847, when trans-
  ferred to command staff)

Alexander McCord, 4th
  Sergeant
Gilbert Hunt, 1st Corporal
Lafayette N. Frost, 2nd Corpo-
  ral (Died in San Diego)
Thomas Weir, 3rd Corporal
  (Reduced to Private, March
  9, 1847)
William S. Muir, 4th Corporal
  (1st Sergeant at mustering
  out)
Elisha Averett, Musician
Joseph W. Richards, Musician
  (Died in Pueblo)

Privates:

Allen, Albern
Allen, Rufus C.
Allred, James R.
Allred, James T. S.
Allred, Reuben W.
Bailey, James
Beckstead, Gordon S.
Beckstead, Orin M.
Bevan, James
Bickmore, Gilbert
Blanchard, Mervin S. (Died in
  Pueblo)
Brass, Benjamin
Bronson, Clinton D.
Brown, John
Brown, William W.
Bryant, John S.
Butterfield, Jacob K.
Calkins, Alva C.
Calkins, Edwin R.
Calkins, James W.
Calkins, Sylvanus

Casper, William W.
Chase, Hiram B. (4th Sergeant
  at mustering out)
Clark, Joseph L.
Clark, Riley G.
Coleman, George (Died en
  route to Pueblo)
Cox, Henderson (Murdered,
  Tragedy Spring)
Curtis, Josiah
Decker, Zachariah B.
Dobson, Joseph
Dodson, Eli
Earl, James C.
Egbert, Robert C.
Ewell, William F.
Fairbanks, Henry
Ferguson, James (Sergeant
  Major when transferred to
  command staff, October 15,
  1846)
Frederick, David I.

Garner, David
Glines, James H. (Sergeant Major when transferred to command staff)
Goodwin, Andrew
Gordon, Gilman
Hampton, James (Died en route to California)
Hawkins, Benjamin
Hewitt, Eli B.
Hickenlooper, William E.
Holden, Elijah E.
Hoyt, Henry P. (Died in Sierra Nevada)
Hoyt, Timothy S.
Hudson, Wilford H.
Hulet, Schuyler
Hunt, Marshall
Ivie, Richard A.
Jackson, Charles A.
Johnson, Henry M.
Kelley, Nicholas
Kelley, William
Kibby, James
Lake, Barnabas
Lemmon, James W.
Maxwell, Maxie
Mayfield, Benjamin F.
Moss, David
Naegle, John C.
Oyler, Melcher (Died in Pueblo)

Packard, Henry (Corporal at mustering out)
Perrin, Charles
Pierson, Ebenezer
Ritter, John
Rowe, Caratat C.
Sessions, John
Sessions, Richard
Sessions, William B.
Sexton, George S.
Shepherd, Marcus L. (Corporal at mustering out)
Steele, George E.
Steele, Isaiah C.
Swarthout, Hamilton
Taylor, Joseph A.
Thompson, John C.
Vradenburg, Adna
Weaver, Franklin
Weaver, Miles
Webb, Charles Y.
Wheeler, Merrill W.
White, Joseph
White, Samuel S.
Willey, Jeremiah
Wilson, Alfred G.
Winn, Dennis W.
Woodworth, Lysander
Wriston, Isaac N.
Wriston, John P.

Company B

Officers, etc.:

Jesse D. Hunter, Captain
Elam Luddington, 1st Lieutenant
Ruel Barrus, 2nd Lieutenant
Philemon C. Merrill, 3rd Lieutenant (Adjutant from Santa Fe to California)

William Coray, 1st Sergeant
William Hyde, 2nd Sergeant
Albert Smith, 3rd Sergeant
David P. Rainey, 1st Corporal
Thomas J. Dunn, 2nd Corporal
John D. Chase, 3rd Corporal
Edward Wilcox, 4th Corporal

William Hunter, Musician
(Drummer)

George W. Taggart, Musician
(Fifer)

Privates:

Alexander, Horace M. (Corporal on March 6, 1847)
Allen, Elijah
Allen, Franklin
Allen, George A.
Bigler, Henry W.
Bingham, Erastus, Jr.
Bingham, Thomas, Sr.
Bird, William
Bliss, Robert S.
Boley, Samuel (Died en route to Ft. Leavenworth)
Borrowman, John
Brackenbury, Benjamin
Brown, Francis
Bush, Richard
Bybee, John McCann
Callahan, Thomas W.
Camp, James G.
Carter, Isaac P.
Carter, Richard (Died en route)
Cheney, Zacheus
Church, Haden W.
Clark, George S.
Colton, Philander
Curtis, Dorr P.
Dalton, Henry S.
Dayton, Willard T.
Dunham, Albert (Died in San Diego)
Dutcher, Thomas P.
Eastman, Marcus N.
Evans, Israel
Evans, William
Follett, William A.
Freeman, Elijah N. (Died en route to Pueblo)
Garner, Philip

Garner, William A.
Green, Ephraim
Hanks, Ephraim K.
Harris, Silas
Haskell, George N.
Hawk, Nathan
Hawk, William
Hinckley, Arza E.
Hoffeins, Jacob
Hunter, Edward
Huntsman, Isaiah
Jones, David H.
Keysor, Guy M.
King, John M.
Kirk, Thomas
Lawson, John V.
Martin, Jesse B.
McCarty, Nelson
Miles, Samuel, Jr.
Morris, Thomas
Mount, Hiram B.
Murdock, John R.
Murdock, Orrice C.
Myers, Samuel
Noler, Christian
Owen, Robert
Park, James P. (1)
Park, James P. (2)
Pearson, Ephraim, Jr.
Pierson, Harmon D.
Prows, William C.
Richards, Peter F.
Rogers, Samuel H.
Simmons, William A.
Sly, James C.
Smith, Azariah
Steers, Andrew J.
Stevens, Lyman
Stillman, Dexter

Stoddard, John R.
Study, David
Walker, William H.
Watts, John S.
Wheeler, John L.
Whitney, Francis T.
Wilcox, Henry

Willes, Ira J.
Willes, W. Sidney
Winters, Jacob
Workman, Andrew J.
Workman, Oliver G.
Wright, Charles
Zabriskie, Jerome

Company C

Officers, etc.:

James Brown, Captain
George W. Rosecrans, 1st Lieu-
    tenant
Samuel Thompson, 2nd Lieu-
    tenant
Robert Clift, 3rd Lieutenant
Orson B. Adams, 1st Sergeant
Elijah Elmer, 2nd Sergeant
    (1st Sergeant at mustering
    out)

Joel J. Terrell, 3rd Sergeant
    (Private at mustering out)
David Wilkin, 4th Sergeant
Jabez Nowlin, 1st Corporal
Alexander Brown, 2nd Corporal
Edward Martin, 3rd Corporal
Daniel Tyler, 4th Corporal
Richard D. Sprague, Musician
Ezra H. Allen, Musician (Mur-
    dered, Tragedy Spring)

Privates:

Adair, G. Wesley
Babcock, Lorenzo
Bailey, Addison
Bailey, Jefferson
Barney, Walter, Sr.
Beckstead, William Ezra
Blackburn, Abner
Boyle, Henry Green
Brimhall, John
Brown, Jesse Sowell
Brownell, Russell G. (1st Cor-
    poral at mustering out)
Burt, William
Bush, William H.
Calvert, John H.
Carpenter, Isaac
Carpenter, William H.
Catlin, George W.
Clift, James
Condit, Jeptha S.

Covil, John Q. A.
Dalton, Edward
Dalton, Harry
Dodge, Augustus E.
Donald, Neal (Died in San
    Diego)
Dunn, James
Durphee, Francillo
Fellows, Hiram W.
Fife, John
Fifield, Levi J.
Forbush, Lorin E.
Gibson, Thomas
Gould, John C.
Gould, Samuel J.
Green, John W. (Died en
    route to Pueblo)
Hancock, Charles B.
Hancock, George W.
Harmon, Ebenezer

Harmon, Lorenzo F.
Hatch, Meltiar
Hatch, Orin
Hendrickson, James
Holdaway, Shadrack
Holt, William
Ivie, Thomas C.
Johnson, Jarvis
Johnstun, Jesse W.
Johnstun, William J.
Landers, Ebenezer
Larson, Thurston
Layton, Christopher
Lewis, Samuel
Maggard, Benjamin
McCullough, Levi H.
Mead, Orlando F.
Moore, Calvin W.
Mowrey, Harley W.
Mowrey, John T.
Myler, James
Olmstead, Hiram
Peck, Isaac
Peck, Thorit (Corporal as of
    June 2, 1847)
Perkins, David M.
Perkins, John (Died in
    Pueblo)
Pickup, George

Pierson, Judson A.
Pulsipher, David
Reynolds, William F.
Richie, Benjamin W.
Richmond, Benjamin B.
Riser, John J.
Rust, William W.
Shipley, Joseph
Shumway, Aurora
Shupe, Andrew J.
Shupe, James W.
Smith, Milton (Died en route
    to Pueblo)
Smith, Richard D.
Squires, William (Corporal at
    mustering out)
Thomas, Elijah
Thomas, Nathan T.
Thompson, James L.
Tindell, Solomon
Truman, Jacob M.
Tuttle, Elanson
Wade, Edward E.
Wade, Moses
Welch, Madison J.
Wheeler, Henry
White, John S.
Wilcox, Matthew
Wood, William

Company D

Officers, etc.:

Nelson Higgins, Captain
George P. Dykes, 1st Lieu-
    tenant (To command staff)
Sylvester Hulet, 2nd Lieutenant
    (Resigned April 10, 1847)
Cyrus C. Canfield, 3rd Lieu-
    tenant
Nathaniel V. Jones, 1st
    Sergeant (Private at muster-
    ing out)

Thomas S. Williams, 2nd
    Sergeant
Luther T. Tuttle, 3rd Sergeant
    (1st Sergeant at mustering
    out)
Alpheus Haws, 4th Sergeant
Arnold Stephens, 1st Corporal
    (Died in Pueblo)
John Buchannan, 2nd Corporal
William Coons, 3rd Corporal

Lewis Lane, 4th Corporal (Private at mustering out)

Privates:

Abbott, Joshua
Averett, Jeduthan
Badham, Samuel
Barger, William H. (Corporal as of March 18, 1847)
Boyd, George W.
Boyd, William W.
Brizzee, Henry W.
Brown, James P.
Brown, James S.
Button, Montgomery
Casto, James B,
Casto, William W.
Chase, Abner (Died en route to Pueblo)
Clawson, John R.
Cole, James B.
Collins, Robert H.
Compton, Allen
Cox, Amos
Curtis, Foster
Davis, Eleazer
Davis, James
Davis, Sterling
Douglas, James
Douglas, Ralph
Fatoute, Ezra
Finlay, Thomas B.
Fletcher, Philander
Forsgreen, John E.
Frazier, Thomas L.
Gifford, William W.
Gilbert, John R.
Gilbert, Thomas (Deserted August 23, 1846)
Gribble, William
Hendricks, William D.
Henrie, Daniel
Higgins, Alfred

Henry W. Jackson, Musician
Willard G. Smith, Musician

Hirons, James P.
Hoagland, Lucas
Holmes, Jonathan H.
Hunsaker, Abraham (Sergeant as of March 18, 1847)
Huntington, Dimick B.
Jacobs, Sanford (Corporal as of March 18, 1847)
Kenney, Loren E.
Lamb, Lisbon
Laughlin, David S.
Maxwell, William B.
McArthur, Henry M.
Mecham, Erastus D.
Merrill, Ferdinand
Mesick, Peter I.
Oakley, James E.
Owen, James C.
Peck, Edwin M.
Pettegrew, James P.
Rawson, Daniel B.
Raymond, Alonzo P.
Richmond, William
Roberts, Benjamin M.
Robinson, William J.
Rowe, William
Roylance, John
Runyan, Levi
Sanderson, Henry W.
Sargent, Abel M.
Savage, Levi
Sharp, Albert
Sharp, Norman (Died en route to Pueblo)
Shelton, Sebert (Quartermaster Sergeant on command staff; transferred back to company November 8, 1846)
Smith, John G.

Spencer, William W.
Steele, John
Stephens, Alexander
Stewart, Benjamin F.
Stewart, James
Stewart, Robert B.
Stillman, Clark
Swarthout, Nathan
Tanner, Myron
Thomas, Hayward J.

Thompson, Miles J.
Tippets, John H.
Treat, Thomas W.
Tubbs, William
Twitchell, Anciel
Walker, Edwin
Whiting, Almon
Whiting, Edmond
Woodward, Francis S.

Company E

Officers, etc.:

Daniel C. Davis, Captain
James Pace, 1st Lieutenant
Andrew Lytle, 2nd Lieutenant
Samuel L. Gully, 3rd Lieu-
   tenant (Resigned October
   19, 1846)
Edmund L. Brown, 1st
   Sergeant
Richard Brazier, 2nd Sergeant
Ebenezer Hanks, 3rd Sergeant
Daniel Browett, 4th Sergeant
   (Murdered, Tragedy Spring)

Stephen M. St. John, 2nd
   Corporal
John V. Binley, 3rd Corporal
   (Private at mustering out)
Roswell Stephens, 4th
   Corporal
James A. Scott, Corporal (Died
   in Pueblo)
Levi W. Hancock, Musician
   (Fifer)
Justice Earl, Musician
   (Drummer)

Privates:

Allen, John (Drummed out in
   Los Angeles, July 1847)
Bates, Joseph W.
Beddome, William
Beers, William
Brown, Daniel
Bulkley, Newman
Bunker, Edward
Burns, Thomas R. (Corporal
   at mustering out)
Caldwell, Matthew
Campbell, Jonathan, Jr.
Campbell, Samuel
Cazier, James
Cazier, John

Chapin, Samuel G.
Clark, Albert
Clark, Joseph
Clark, Samuel G.
Cox, John
Cummings, George W.
Davis, Walter L.
Day, Abraham
Dennett, Daniel Q.
Dyke, Simon
Earl, Jacob S.
Ewell, John M.
Fauney, Fredrick
Follett, William T.
Glazier, Luther W.

Harmon, Oliver N.
Harris, Robert, Jr.
Harrison, Isaac
Hart, James S.
Hess, John W.
Hickmott, John
Hopkins, Charles A.
Hoskins, Henry
Howell, Thomas C. D.
Jacobs, Henry B.
Jameson, Charles
Judd, Hyram
Judd, Zadock K.
Karren, Thomas, III
Kelley, George
Kelley, Milton (Died in Pueblo)
Knapp, Albert
Lance, William
McBride, Harlem
McClelland, William C.
Miller, Daniel M.
Miller, Miles
Park, William A.

Pettegrew, David
Phelps, Alva (Died en route to California)
Pixton, Robert
Porter, Sanford
Pugmire, Jonathan, Jr.
Richardson, Thomas L.
Roberts, Levi
Sanders, Richard T.
Scott, Leonard M.
Skeen, Joseph
Slater, Richard
Smith, David (Died in San Luis Rey)
Smith, Lot
Spidle, John
Standage, Henry
Strong, William
Tanner, Albert M.
West, Benjamin
Whitworth, Robert W.
Williams, James V.
Wilson, George D.
Woolsey, Thomas

Company	Officers	Non-Com.	Privates	Company
Company A	4	10	92	106
Company B	4	9	87	100
Company C	4	10	91	105
Company D	4	10	88	102
Company E	4	10	73	87
Total Volunteers in Mormon Battalion				500

There is little written about the women and children who went with the Mormon Battalion. Thirty-one wives of battalion members and three other women, with forty-four children, started the journey. Each company was allowed four laundresses, but to date only eighteen of the possible twenty have been identified.

Melissa Coray washed for Samuel Rogers and was paid 18½ cents. Rogers later hired Mary Luddington to do his washing for 50 cents a month. These are the only known references to women actually washing for any of the soldiers. In later years several women told their children that they cooked for the messes to which they and their husbands were assigned.

The men simply did not mention their wives, although when Colonel Cooke decided to send the wives to Pueblo with the sick soldiers in the Brown detachment, the husbands objected strenuously. John Steele and John Hess made a gallant plea which persuaded General Doniphan to allow them to go with their wives to Pueblo. Hess, who drove a supply wagon, told of packing his wagon in such a manner as to provide as much comfort as possible for the wives who rode in it. On December 5, when a bull was killed and cooked for the soldiers, Captain Hunter told his wife it was a heifer, hoping to make it more palatable for her.

Nathaniel Jones was married to Rebecca Burton, sister to Melissa Coray. Jones left his young wife and an infant to join the battalion. While the command was in San Luis Rey early in 1847, he wrote in his journal that Melissa had not been well for several days. This may have been the beginning of her pregnancy, since she delivered a son in Monterey the following October. Existing accounts have Melissa pregnant the entire trip, which would make her pregnant for fifteen months.

William Coray wrote about his wife on several occasions. On the march to California, Melissa Coray noticed the men were so hungry they ate their rations almost immediately upon receiving them. Melissa went to each mess in Company B and talked to the men about rationing their food over the entire allotment period instead of eating it during the first couple of days. Lydia Hunter and Melissa Coray, both in Company B, enjoyed riding together in the Hunter wagon, visiting and singing. When the team became weak and worn out as the trip progressed, Captain Hunter stopped their rides as he didn't want Melissa's extra weight in his wagon for the team to pull.

For some, the march was a honeymoon journey. James Brown married a widow, Mary McCree Black, on July 16, 1846. John and Mary Emeline Sessions were married in July prior to the departure of the battalion. William and Melissa Coray were married three weeks before the march began. In 1879 Melissa Coray Kimball (she had remarried after William's death) completed the necessary paperwork and applied to the United States government for the pension of William Coray. She received a reply from the Department of Interior, Pension Office, dated March 19, 1884: "The claimant having contracted a polygamous marriage prior to filing her claim, the case was found to be inadmissable, and was rejected in accordance with the provision of the Act of August 7, 1882."[28]

One journalist recorded that Stephen St. John and his daughter walked to the top of a nearby hill one evening while camped. His daughter was Harriet St. John Brown, wife of Daniel Brown, Company D. In Pueblo it was noted that Mary Brown, wife of Captain James Brown, went among the men "as a ministering angel." Celia Mounts Hunt took care of young Joseph Richards in Pueblo and gave him nourishment a few hours before he died. The women also prepared the bodies of the men who died in Pueblo for burial.

Eliza and James T. S. Allred were ill when they traveled with the Brown company to Pueblo. She gave birth to a baby en route, and, without proper assistance and medicine, the infant son died. Although records indicate the baby was born "on the plains" in Colorado, the exact date and location of the birth are not known. The Allreds left the battalion October 18 and reached Pueblo November 17, 1846, so the baby was born sometime between. James Allred stayed behind to dig a shallow grave for the child. After completing the heart-breaking task, he was so weak he couldn't travel quickly. He reached camp late at night and tried to console his distraught wife.

When John Hess and his wife Emeline arrived in Salt Lake Valley in July, 1847, after spending the winter in Pueblo, he wrote:

> I was now in a country that was untried, and one thousand miles from where any supplies could be obtained, with only the outfit of a discharged soldier, which consisted of a small tent, a sheer-iron camp kettle, a mess pan, two tin plates, two spoons, two knives and forks, a pair of blankets badly worn, two old quilts, ten pounds of flour, and my dear precious wife Emeline, who had been with me through all of the trials and hardships and had endured them all without a murmur. God bless her . . . had it not been for her noble spirit to comfort me, I think many times I should have almost despaired.[29]

The four women who reached California were divided—two in San Diego and two in Los Angeles. When word was received in Los Angeles about Lydia Hunter's death in San Diego, Phebe Palmer Brown went around to the tents and told the men about Lydia's passing. The three remaining women all reached Utah eventually, Melissa Coray first. The husbands of Susan Davis and Phebe Brown (Daniel Davis and Ebenezer Brown) reenlisted in the Mormon Volunteers, so the two women were in San Diego eight additional months after the battalion was discharged.

Jefferson Hunt's wife Celia and their seven children were with him. A few weeks before joining the battalion, Hunt became a polygamist by marrying Matilda Nease. Her brother and sister, later adopted by Jefferson Hunt, went along. Celia went to Pueblo in the Higgins detachment and Matilda went with the Brown group. Having two wives traveling with the battalion is interesting because polygamy had not been announced publicly at the time, although it had been practiced in Nauvoo secretly. Polygamy was announced in Salt Lake City in 1852.

Jesse D. Hunter also was a polygamist. He left his first wife, Kesiah, and five children behind. Their son William, who was fifteen years old, went with him as a drummer in Company B. His second wife, Lydia, whom he had married in Nauvoo, Illinois, February 2, 1846, accompanied him and served as a laundress for his company. Lydia died shortly after arriving in California. By 1849 Kesiah and the five children—Asa, Mary, Jesse, Samuel, and Martha—joined Hunter in California. The family, including William, went to the gold fields for a while, but all were listed back in San Diego on February 20, when the 1850 census was taken.

Women and Children Accompanying the Mormon Battalion

		Husband	Company
1.	Ruth Markham Abbott*	Joshua Abbott	D
2.	Susan Smith Adams*	Orson B. Adams	C
3.	Eliza Manwaring Allred	James T. S. Allred	A
4.	Elzadie E. Ford Allred*	Reuben W. Allred	A
5.	Agnes Brown*	Edmund L. Brown	E
6.	Eunice Reasor Brown	James Polly Brown	D
	Children: Neuman, Robert, Sarah, Mary Ann		
7.	Harriet St. John Brown	Daniel Brown	D
8.	Mary McCree Black Brown*	James Brown	C
	Children: George David Black, Mary's son by first husband, and an unnamed child by James's first wife, Martha Stephens		
9.	Phebe Draper Palmer Brown*	Ebenezer Brown	A
10.	Mary Bittels Button	Montgomery Button	D
	Children: James, Jutson, Louisa, Samuel		
11.	Melissa Burton Coray*	William Coray	B
12.	Susan Moses Davis	Daniel Coon Davis	E
	Children: Daniel C. Davis Jr., son of Daniel's first wife, Sophronia Fuller		

* Women known to be laundresses. There were twenty assigned, four to a company. Sarah Kelley was probably the fourth laundress for Company A. Sarah Ann Arterbury Church (wife of Haden Church, Company B) may have been the fourth laundress for Company B, but her participation in the march cannot be documented at this time.

13. Jane Wells Cooper Hanks*	Ebenezer Hanks	E
14. Emeline Bigler Hess*	John Hess	E
15. Sarah Blackman Higgins	Nelson Higgins	D
Children: Almira, Alfred,		
Driscilla, Nelson, Heber, Carlos		
16. Mary Ann Jameson Hirons	James P. Hirons	D
17. Celia Mounts Hunt (first wife)	Jefferson Hunt	A
Children: John, Jane, Harriet,		
Joseph, Hyrum, and twins Parley		
and Mary		
18. Matilda Nease Hunt (second wife)	Jefferson Hunt	A
Children: Peter Nease and Ellen		
Nease, brother and sister of		
Matilda, adopted by Hunt		
19. Lydia Edmonds Hunter*	Jesse D. Hunter	B
20. Fanny Allen Huntington	Dimick Huntington	D
Children: Lot Elisha, Martha Zina,		
Clark Allen		
21. Malinda Allison Kelley*	Milton Kelley	E
22. Sarah Kelley	Nicholas Kelley	A
Child: Parley		
23. Mary Eliza Clark Luddington*	Elam Luddington	B
Children: Angeline Adeline and		
one more		
24. Mary Emeline Sessions*	John Sessions	A
25. Martha Jane Sargent Sharp	Norman Sharp	D
Children: Martha's 10-year-old sis-		
ter, Caroline Sargent		
26. Elizabeth Trains Mayfield Shelton*	Sebert C. Shelton	D
Children: Caroline, Cooper,		
Thomas, Maria, and children		
from Elizabeth's first husband:		
Jackson Mayfield, John Mayfield,		
Sarah Mayfield		
27. Sarah Prunty Shupe	James W. Shupe	C
28. Catherine Campbell Steele*	John Steele	D
Child: Mary		
29. Sophia Tubbs*	William Tubbs	D
30. Isabella McNair Hunter Wilkin	David Wilkin	C
31. Albina Merrill Williams	Thomas S. Williams	D
Children: Caroline, Ephraim, and		
Albina's sister, Phoebe Lodema		
Merrill		

32.	Jane Bosco	John Bosco was a teamster for Jefferson Hunt. Jane and her husband died en route within a short time of each other and were buried side by side.
33.	Rebecca Smith	Elisha Smith was a teamster for Daniel Davis. He died en route and she went to Pueblo.
34.	Lena Monger Luddington, mother of Elam Luddington, traveled with Elam, his wife and two children.	

There were at least nine other young males, besides Neuman Brown, Robert Brown, and Nelson Higgins shown here, who accompanied the battalion as officers' aides (see appendix A).

Fort Leavenworth, 1846. Frontier Army Museum, Fort Leavenworth, Kansas; used by permission.

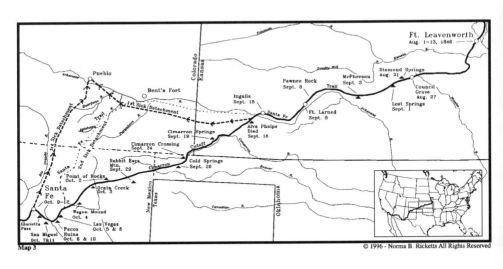

Map 3

1846-1847
Mormon Battalion Route
Ft. Leavenworth, Kansas to Santa Fe, New Mexico

——— Mormon Battalion
– – – Sick Detachments
· · · · · Santa Fe Trail
– — – States not in Existence
▲ Camp Site

N

CHAPTER TWO

Fort Leavenworth:
Knapsacks and Muskets

Sat., Aug. 1, Fort Leavenworth, Kansas. It took five hours to ferry across the river and reach Fort Leavenworth.[1] There were four hundred Missouri Volunteers and seventy regular soldiers at the garrison when the Mormons arrived. Other troops had gone to Santa Fe with Stephen W. Kearny. When the battalion stopped in the public square, several were shaking with chills and fever. Three heavy rainstorms en route had caused these malaria-like symptoms. Tents were issued, one for every mess of six men, but the tents were very hot when the sun was on them. The heat made more men ill. Each mess was to cook, eat, and sleep together. Some were homesick for their families. Ice cream was tasted by many for the first time at a cost of five cents.

Sun., Aug. 2, Fort Leavenworth. Services were held. George Dykes preached and mixed military talk in with his sermon. William Coray bought a quill pen and ink and paper at the fort and planned to carry them in a box in the baggage wagon. He noted, "The orderly sergeants of each company were required to make out a provision return for five days rations."[2] Harmony prevailed in the Mormon tents.

Mon., Aug. 3, Fort Leavenworth. The men were so anxious to get their muskets they lined up early in the morning. Colonel Allen said they'd want to throw them away before they got to California. The gun, a flint-lock musket, weighed twelve to fifteen pounds and carried an ounce ball one mile. The cartridge box was carried in a leather belt, two and one-quarter inches wide, over the left shoulder. The bayonet and scabbard were attached to a belt over the right shoulder. Each man had a knapsack for clothes and other necessities, which was carried in front. Their bedding was carried on their backs. When everything was in place, they were covered from neck to waist, plus carrying the musket in their hands.

They also had small cotton haversacks to carry dinner and sometimes a day or two of rations. Their canteens held three pints of water. Every man received a wide, heavy, white leather waist belt, with orders to keep it clean. This white belt was the only common article of a uniform the men had. The battalion was never a uniformed group.

> After the usual ceremonies of this war department or military post, the Battalion of Mormon officers and soldiers were ordered to stay on the grounds . . . that they might receive their arms and equipage. The brethren were very cheerful and happy, all but those sick brethren. . . . The adjutant ordered a shade to be erected in front of our tents, which order was strictly obeyed. Companies A and B received their arms and accoutrements in the P.M. and Captains Jefferson Hunt and Jesse D. Hunter gave their receipts for the same. (William Coray)

Tues., Aug. 4, Fort Leavenworth. The men drilled to learn how to form into ranks, and practiced using their guns. The officers allowed each company to buy a baggage wagon and a four-mule team to haul knapsacks and bedding.[3] Every mess received a camp kettle, frying pan, and coffee pot. The clothing money for the year, forty-two dollars, was issued. Most men sent this money to their families, except one dollar for the Twelve Apostles. All soldiers were required to sign receipts for their money. The paymaster was surprised that every man could sign his own name. Mary Luddington, one of the laundresses with Company B, agreed to do Samuel Rogers's washing for fifty cents a month. (It is not known why Rogers asked both Mary Luddington and Melissa Coray to wash his clothes.)

> After roll call the officers were busily engaged in giving receipts to the Quartermaster Sergeant for camp equipment received at Council Bluffs, also making requisition for stationery and other things. In the evening at the usual hour drums were beat . . . and all was silent, good order is observed here. The guard is strict. (William Coray)

Wed., Aug. 5, Fort Leavenworth. There was quarrelling and fighting among the soldiers from upper Missouri, who were in the fort when the battalion arrived. The day before, one of the Platte City Volunteers struck another with a hatchet, wounding him severely. The musicians from the battalion were examined by the fort musicians. All passed. Everyone was impressed with Justice Earl, an eighteen-year-old drummer with Company E. There was a lot of "humming and singing by the soldiers in their tents at night." William Hyde said it made him think of a Methodist camp meeting. At dark Orson Hyde, Parley P. Pratt, John Taylor, and Jesse Little rode into camp. The men rejoiced at their arrival. Colonel Allen seemed pleased to see the visitors too. The trio came to take the clothing pay back to the church and families. The monthly pay schedule was as follows:

Captain	$50 plus 20 cents per day rations
1st Lieutenant	$30 plus 20 cents per day rations
2nd Lieutenant	$25 plus 20 cents per day rations
1st Sergeant	$16
2nd Sergeant	$13
Corporal	$ 9
Musician	$ 8
Privates	$ 7

Cos. D & E received their arms this morning. A & B were making out their pay rolls in the Bachelors Block at which place the paymaster made his quarters. In the P.M. Co. B was called upon to appear at the door of the Block. They marched up after they had elected their 3d lieut, 4th sgt. and 4th corporal. (William Coray)

Thurs., Aug. 6, Fort Leavenworth. The troops purchased goods from the fort trader and local sutlers. Many crossed the river and bought needed items in Weston. Colonel Allen said Mormons, although not acquainted with military drills and regulations, obeyed commands better than most soldiers, that he "had not been under the necessity of giving the words of command the second time."[4] The men were pleased to hear his comments.

John Murdock tried to train a six-mule team and was run over by the wagon. The back wheels were locked and he was hurt seriously. The men, still thinking about their families, wrote letters to their wives and children. The weather continued very hot. One soldier said it was 135 degrees in the sun. William Hyde and Thomas Dutcher were both ill with fever. Samuel Rogers paid Melissa Coray 18½ cents for the washing she did for him. Sebert Shelton was relieved of his duties and Samuel Gully was promoted to assistant quartermaster.

Capt. Brown's company, Co. C, were called to receive their money. . . . the companies that had received their money were found liberally donating for the benefit of the poor and for the England missionaries, viz. Parley P. Pratt, Orson Hyde, and John Taylor who were then on their way to that place. . . . Elections were held in each company as in the first . . . the orderly sergeant[s] of each company [were] notified to form their companies on the right of companies . . . retreat about six o'clock P.M. (William Coray)

Fri., Aug. 7, Fort Leavenworth. The latecomers arrived today. Nicholas Kelley brought his wife and son. Others were William Park, Albert Sharp,

A Tarnscript of duplicaite invoice of Ordinance
Received in fort Levensworth

Invoice of Ordinance and Ordinance Store isued this 3ᵗʰᵈᵃʸ
of Augᵗ 1846. Agreable to Order For isue by Maj C Wharton
Commanding Fort Leavinsworth. to Capt. Jefferson Hunt
Commanding A Company of Mormon Volentiers
Mustered into the service of the United States

93	Muskets Complete
5	Cavelry Sabers brass mounted
93	Infantry Cart Boxes
93	Cart Boxe plates
93	Cart Box Belts
93	Bayonet scabords
93	Bayonet scabord Belts
93	Bayonet scabord Belt Plates
93	Waist Belts
93	Waist Belts Plates
93	Musket Gun Slings
93	Brushes & Piks
93	Musket screw Drivers
93	Musket Wipers
10	Musket Ball Screws
10	Musket spring Vices
93	Extra Flint Caps
4	Rifles Half Stᵗ. Harpers Ferry
	I certify that the above invoice is Corect.

P Flemming
Ord. Sergᵗ. U.S.A.

(Duplicates)

Accoutrements issued to Company A.

Rations issued to Company A.

Lieutenant Samuel Gully's receipt for equipment and animals issued to Company A. Documents on pages 38 and 39 from Archives, Historical Department, Church of Jesus Christ of Latter-day Saints, Salt Lake City, Utah; used by permission.

Thomas Gilbert, William Beddome and Robert Whitworth.[5] Jefferson Hunt and his two families also arrived.[6]

> Preparations . . . for marching, breaking mules, buying wagons, drawing knapsacks and haversacks, etc., were the principal business of the Battalion this day. About 2 o'clock P.M. Parley P. Pratt, Orson Hyde, John Taylor, Robert Pierce and Col. Little left camp, Parley Pratt taking the money sent back to the families and poor. They were accompanied by a guard of two of the old police, namely Andrew Lytle and Alonzo Clark. . . . this was kept very quiet all the time for fear evil designed persons might follow and rob them. (William Coray)

The uniform allowance Pratt took back totaled $5,860.

Sat., Aug. 8, Fort Leavenworth. A few men got drunk and one was put in the guardhouse. Levi Hancock, Company E, asked David Pettegrew to visit the tents and counsel against drinking, gambling, and swearing. During the trip from Council Bluffs, there were three hard rainstorms, all at night. With no tents and with everyone sleeping on the ground, the men were soaked thoroughly all three times. Blankets did not dry out between rainstorms and were used wet from night to night. During the daytime, the men traveled in wet clothing. Many continued to suffer with chills and high fever. The extreme heat caused additional discomfort. Jonathan Pugmire was detailed to do blacksmithing. He worked out in the open under the sun, which reflected off the limestone around him. He was working on a wheel and had given it the last stroke of his hammer when he fell to the ground in a raging fever.

Sun., Aug. 9, Fort Leavenworth. David Pettegrew visited each tent "and gave them certain instructions and the consequences that would follow if not obeyed."[7] Thomas Dunn said he had "kept himself from the drunkards this far and prayed to God he will ever be counted worthy to receive honor, glory, immortality and eternal life."[8] George Dykes said because Mormons were in the army they were not "at liberty to participate in evil practices common to such circumstances."[9]

Mon., Aug. 10, Fort Leavenworth. John Allen, a man at the fort, was baptized and joined Company E of the battalion. The weather continued to be unbearable. Many were ill from working in the sun. Azariah Smith said it was "hot enough to melt cheese." The companies were getting ready to leave. Goods were high priced in the fort store. Colonel Allen was very sick. Unless he improved greatly, he would not be able to continue the journey with the battalion.

Tues., Aug. 11, Fort Leavenworth. John Spidle was bit on the hand by a rattlesnake, which caused quite a commotion. The battalion learned the reason they were going to California was to reinforce General Kearny's

Army of the West in the war with Mexico. Extra supplies were sent to Bent's Fort so that when the battalion reached the fort they could replenish their supplies for the rest of the journey to Santa Fe.

Thurs., Aug. 13, Fort Leavenworth, 5 miles. Companies A, B, and E marched out, stepping lively as the musicians of the three companies played in unison. The plan was to start without Colonel Allen. Jefferson Hunt would be in charge until Colonel Allen recovered. The men liked Allen as he was kind to all. The soldiers discovered what it was like to carry the heavy musket and accoutrements of a foot soldier on a hot day with the dust flying in clouds. The provision wagon of Company B broke down and company members went without supper. It was seven hundred miles to Santa Fe.

> The other companies [C and D] remained behind to rig themselves out a little better for the journey. The three companies did not travel together as I had expected, but each one traveled to suit their own convenience. Company B continued in the rear of A and E, camped 5 miles from the Fort after the first day's travel. The other companies struck tents some 5 or 6 miles ahead. One of our teams remained behind having broken a wagon. The company missed supper. The Col. and his staff remained behind, giving the command to Capt. Hunt, ordering him to march on to Council Grove with ease. (William Coray)

Fri., Aug. 14, 6 miles. Companies A and E went ahead, followed by Company B. John Allen was confirmed a member of the Mormon Church. "All was peaceful" (William Coray).

> On this day the sick list was enlarged to nearly 15 in the morning in Company B alone, other companies in proportion. We missed breakfast. This day we . . . were hindered in consequence of the broken wagon until the Col. could forward another. H. W. Church having been on furlough returned to camp and Bro. Matthews arrived . . . they brought letters which had been sent from the Bluff to different parties in the battalion, bearing date of the 10th inst. Bro. Matthews had been sent on an express for a dr. from Ft. Leavenworth to wait upon Col. Kane, who was very sick at the camp of the Saints at Cutler's Park, to witness that he was not poisoned.[10]

Sat., Aug. 15, Wall Creek, 15 miles. Colonel Allen remained too ill to leave the fort. William Hyde, who had remained behind due to illness, caught up with the travelers.

> Started very early this morning. Our march was slow, the heat intense, the suffering of the sick intolerable, being huddled up

together in the baggage-wagon with camp kettles, mess-cans, etc., over the worst of roads. The cause of sickness I attributed mostly to the plums and green corn which we used so freely at the Fort. . . . The command of the Battalion rested upon Capt. Hunt, he being the first captain in the battalion. We marched . . . in a southwest course taking the old Santa Fe trail.[11] (William Coray)

Sun., Aug. 16, Mill Creek, 14 miles. Robert Bliss found a bee tree and about 20 lb. of honey. It made an excellent repast. Delaware and Shawnee Indians ferried the soldiers over the Kansas River in flat boats. "We traveled up one branch [of the river] called by the Indians Wakaroosa . . . where Captains Hunt and Davis and their companies were camped. We struck tents a little before sundown. There were 17 sick in our company [Co. B] at this time, five in Co. E. Co. A had left their sick back at the Ft. to be brought on in hospital wagons" (William Coray).

Mon., Aug. 17, Wakaroosa Creek, Kansas. Heavy rains spattered right through the tents and ran under them. All were thoroughly drenched. Colonel Allen sent another wagon of supplies from Fort Leavenworth. Each company had tasks assigned. "Burned a wood pit, set our black-smiths in the three companies at work in setting wagon tires" (William Coray).

Tues., Aug. 18, Wakaroosa Creek, Kansas. Forty to fifty beef cattle were missing. Later Indians brought them in for bounty. The men were bothered by lice and mosquitoes. They were on the Kansas River. The sutlers with their ten wagons came into camp. Known as the "scavengers of the trails," the sutlers sold clothing, some foodstuffs, and water, all at very high prices. Levi Hancock baptized Leonard Scott, Company E, into the Mormon Church and gave health blessings to others.

Wed., Aug. 19, Wakaroosa Creek, 4 miles. Companies C and D caught up with the three advance companies. There was joy at being united again. A furious storm hit just after camp was set up. Driving rain, hail, lightning, and peals of thunder roared from the West. A dark cloud engulfed the camp leaving only five of one hundred tents standing. It took six men to hold each tent from blowing away. Two heavy government baggage wagons were upset. It was a very frightening experience for the women and children, since many suffered from chills and fever. The twin babies of Captain Hunt had been ill before the storm. The Hunts' tent blew away and the babies were drenched.

The storm came with such violence that nothing could withstand its power—one blast—and then the tents with one accord lay a total wreck upon the field, covering their inmates with surprise and drenching them to the skin. I was in a tent with my family and grasped the tent and stood up and the rain ran down until it filled my boots and the hail stones came so hard that I was . . . ready to give up. It lasted half an hour. (John Steele)[12]

Since no one was injured or killed, there was rejoicing and singing when the storm was over as everyone gathered up the wreckage. Hancock thought it was a warning of the unholy actions of some of the soldiers.

Company B to which I belong had just arrived when it [storm] commenced and were in the act of pitching their tents and staking out their teams. The other companies had been on the ground long enough to have their tents up when the fury of the storm came upon us. Nearly every tent (and there were over a hundred) was blown flat to the ground. Several wagons were upset. The wind blew my small wagon about ten rods. I attempted to hold it as it started but finding that my attempt was in vain I reached for my wife, seized her by the arms and brought her to the ground on her hands and knees. As we recovered I took as I supposed the last look of my old wagon, whole and sound. We scampered to a wagon that stood near and clung to the wheels till it commenced hailing tremendously. My wife sprang into the wagon after she had been thumped by the hail awhile. It was with great difficulty that we kept the cover on the wagon. We were both as wet as we could be. Hats, caps, handkerchiefs, fragments of tents, and wagon covers could be seen flying in every direction, while the horses and mules in their fright had broken loose and scampered over the prairies. . . . my wagon . . . was found right side up. . . . It continued cloudy with occasional slight showers during the night. The guard had considerable difficulty in guarding the cattle this night. (William Coray)

Thurs., Aug. 20. The day was spent drying out and gathering up supplies that had been scattered in the storm. Clothes and knapsacks were hung up to dry. Cleaned guns. Lieutenant James Pace and Samuel Gully left for Fort Leavenworth to find out what Colonel Allen's condition was. Levi Hancock met with Captain Hunt and proposed that religious meetings be held. William Hyde, Daniel Tyler, and David Pettegrew talked in the meeting, followed by Captain Hunt, who gave a vigorous and passionate speech. Pettegrew noted, "Elder [Levi] Hancock with myself are called on by the officers in command to take charge of the spiritual affairs of the camp."[13] The soldiers sustained Levi Hancock as spiritual leader.[14] Robert Bliss said "the spirit of God was manifested and attended the word with power." After the meeting the men prayed in their messes for the sick, the battalion, and the families left behind, while the officers met to settle a serious difficulty between Captain James Brown and two of his lieutenants, George Rosecrans and Robert Clift:[15]

The Capt. overheard Clift, breathing out some threatenings and forming rash conclusions concerning him and was exasperated to such a degree that he seized his pistol (a six shooter) and declared he would shoot Clift, but fortunately he could not be found until the Capt.'s anger was appeased. Clift immediately preferred a charge against the Capt. who, finding himself about to be court martialed, was willing to make restitution and sought an opportunity to do so, but Clift was very indifferent and exclaimed with an air of importance, "My character as an officer in the army of the U.S. has been disgraced and this company must be satisfied before I will settle." But finally the Adjt. prevailed upon him to drop it if the Capt. would make acknowledgement to him and the company. He proceeded to do so and spoke a little too long to suit the two officious Lieuts. and they put him [Brown] under guard and Clift renewed his charges against him [Brown]. The secret of the matter appeared to be this: [They thought] Brown had done wrong and Rosecranse and Clift wanted to supplant him, which was evident from a toast meeting held in the evening of the 19th instant in Company C, Rosecranse and Clift being at the head enjoined it upon everyone to drink and give a toast expressive of their sentiments in regard to Capt. Brown and Higgins, the latter being the Captain of D Co. Cyrus Canfield, the 3rd lieu. of the 4th co. also craved the place of his capt. The toasts ran like this: Here is to Capt. Brown that he may be discharged and sent back to the Bluffs, he having disgraced himself as an officer and that his place may be filled by Lieut Rosecranse, who raised the co.

Here is to Capt. Higgins that he may be discharged and the one to take his place, meaning Canfield, who it rightfully belongs to. This meeting was held so that the aspirants might know whether their project would take or not. This, however, was not known to the council who met this day to deliberate over the matter. Capt. Hunt said this matter had grown completely out of hand. He and others gave the Capt and his subordinates a complete dressing out. Both parties made every acknowledgement asked for and the Capt. retained his standing.

So much for so much. It was agreed upon by the council to have meeting in the afternoon and a lecture by Elders Tyler and Hyde. Accordingly, at the appointed hour, the brethren convened. Meeting opened by Levi W. Hancock, who was the highest [ecclesiastical] authority in the battalion at this time. Elder Tyler spoke, followed by Hancock, Hyde, and Capt. Hunt; the latter told his feelings at considerable length and with great animation. He fairly laid the ax at the root of the tree and discountenanced vice in the strongest terms, which imparted a good spirit to the Battalion and checked insubordination materially. Capt Hunt advised the captains of cos. to get their men together often and pray for them, and teach them the principles of virtue and to be united with each other. After sundown Sgt. Maj. Glines arrived in camp with a small drove of cattle. He informed me that the Adjt. [Dykes] was 4 miles back with the sick who were left at the fort. (William Coray)

Fri., Aug. 21, Elm Grove, Kansas, 15 miles. Adjutant Dykes came in with the hospital wagon. He was upset that the battalion was not closer to Council Grove and talked to the captains about the sick, lack of order, and insufficient progress. Dykes said Colonel Allen was very ill. Prayers were said in the individual messes for Allen's recovery. Bigler said they prayed "lest a more tyrannical man take command." There was a meeting at night for the officers, but Captain Hunter refused to go because of high feelings. A few men in C and D didn't like their captains and were causing problems. Three men were blessed for their health and one was baptized for the remission of his sins. Azariah Smith and several comrades amused themselves by pitching dollars.

Adjt Dykes arrived . . . and inquired for the provisions of the battalion. Capt. Hunt could give him no information, having forgotten the orders of the Col, which were to continue a rapid march to Council Grove where they would all meet again. Here we were in a bad fix; our provisions 30 miles ahead and we almost out. (William Coray)

Sat., Aug. 22, Stone Coal Creek, Kansas, 12 miles. Elam Luddington's horses were lost in the morning and he was left behind to find them. After traveling a short time, they reached Coal Creek, which was difficult to cross. Long ropes were fastened on each side of the wagons, and ten to twelve men on each rope helped the teams cross the stream. Camped by a green, stagnant pond filled with tadpoles. The cool evening seemed to revive the sick. Their route followed the Santa Fe Trail to the Southwest.

I arrived at the fort . . . and learned the Colonel was not expected to live many hours . . . I remained through the day watching over the Colonel. At evening he was removed to his old quarters. Lieutenant Gully and myself followed in the procession, we remained with him through the night. His niece, a fine young lady . . . gave her special attention to him during the night. She was the only relative I heard of. (James Pace)[16]

Sun., Aug. 23, Allen's Grove, Kansas, 5 miles. Passed ruins of an ancient city. Some believed it was a Nephite city from the Book of Mormon.[17] Sanford Porter became ill while traveling today and fell behind. Camped at 110 Creek. Water was very scarce. Thomas Gilbert decided to leave the battalion and return to Fort Leavenworth.[18]

> the weather had been dry so long there was a scum over most of the water, which made it almost unfit for use. The face of the country is beautiful, all prairie for hundreds of miles. This morning Elam Luddington came up. William Hyde lost his pony. Our guide was taken very ill. (William Coray)

> The Colonel died at six o'clock A.M. August 23, 1846, at Fort Leavenworth, Kansas. . . . At his passing Major Horton, commander of the post, requested Lieutenant Gully and myself to his quarters. He suggested one of us should return to Council Bluffs and inform our president of our situation and return to the command as soon as possible. It was decided I should go, as Lieutenant Gully, as quartermaster had charge of our entire outfit. . . . I took my leave about noon August 23, being well fitted out with a good horse and other things necessary by order of Major Horton. . . . arrived at the camp of the Saints at Cutler's Creek, west side of the Missouri, 18 miles above Sarpee's Point, August 26, 10 A.M. I then sat in council answering questions, and receiving special counsel for the battalion. Howard Egan and John D. Lee accompanied me on my return. (James Pace)[19]

Mon., Aug. 24, Bluff Creek, Kansas, 15 miles. Weather was better. They nooned at Schwitzer's Creek. Towards evening they passed traders returning to the United States. Letters were written hastily to send to families in Council Bluffs with the traders. Sanford Jacobs caught up after suffering intensely and falling behind. While he was alone, he called upon the Lord in fervent prayer, asking that his life might be spared if he had further work to do. At that instant, he said, his pain left him and he was able to continue and catch up with his company. Robert Bliss, night guard, kept vigil with a loaded gun for the first time. Evening prayers were said in the messes.

> The health of the Battalion was very poor; there were from 70 to 80 on the list [sick] and convalescent. It was suggested to the cos. to have prayer together for the sick. This evening some traders passed us who were only 22 days from Santa Fe. They also informed us that Col. Kearny and co. left Bent's Fort for Santa Fe the same day they left Santa Fe. No prospect for fighting in Mexico. It was supposed, also that he [Kearny] would arrive at the place of destination on the 23rd inst. One of the traders was killed a few days ago while looking for his horse about 60 yards from their camp by an Indian. The traders in turn killed an Indian for revenge 2 nights after. (William Coray)

Tues., Aug. 25, Beaver Creek, Kansas, 14 miles. Struck tents early and traveled over prairie and small creeks. Caw Indians came into camp during the noontime stop. The creeks they passed abounded with grapes and plums.

Wed., Aug. 26, Bluff Creek, Kansas, 18 Miles. As they crossed Bluff Creek, Company C's wagon, carrying sick persons and flour, fell from the banks into the water. Two women and six men nearly drowned as they couldn't get out from under the wagon for a few minutes. They weren't hurt, only frightened and wet. Samuel Gully and Sebert Shelton arrived from Fort Leavenworth with a letter from Mormon officials and the sad news that Colonel Allen had died. William Hyde wrote it "struck a damper to our feelings. We considered him a worthy man and looked upon him as a friend."[20] Jefferson Hunt was especially affected by the loss of Colonel Allen:

> the death . . . shocked him [Hunt] very much, knowing the responsibility that would rest upon him, that he would have to take command, inexperienced as he was. Suffice it to say that it [Allen's death] caused more lamentation from us than the loss of a Gentile ever did before. Col. Allen was a good man. He stood up for our rights better than many of our brethren; he obtained for us a good fit out with plenty of provisions, was kind to the families journeying with us, fed private teams at public expense, was never abusive or tyrannical, which is the case with nearly all the regulars. In short he was an exception among officers of the U.S. Army. (William Coray)

Thurs., Aug. 27, Council Grove, Kansas, 7 miles. The companies marched to music into Council Grove. Captain Hunt was in charge as senior officer. Jane Bosco, whose husband was a teamster for Captain Hunt, died and was buried near camp. Council Grove was a government post used by soldiers and traders preparing to travel on the Santa Fe Trail. Wagons were repaired and supplies were replenished. The command acquired two cannon drawn by six horses each, a portable blacksmith shop and forty provision wagons. There were twelve family wagons and five private baggage wagons. Religious services were held. "The minds of the brethren were much engaged meditating upon our condition after the death of Col. Allen. To this end the council met and decided that Capt Hunt should lead the battalion. There were, however, two contrary minds as usual, viz. Lt Dykes and Shelton" (William Coray).

Fri., Aug. 28, Council Grove, Kansas. Traders from Santa Fe arrived and brought Sergeant Hyde's pony. He was not well and was very glad to get it back so he didn't have to walk. One of the letters from church officials instructed the men not to take medicine but to pray and bless the sick. Many were sick and were healed by laying on of hands. Merchants in thirteen baggage wagons joined the battalion to go to Santa Fe. They sold clothing, water, and other goods, all at very high prices.

Sat., Aug. 29, Council Grove, Kansas. During the morning the soldiers paid final respects to Colonel Allen.[21] Drums called all soldiers to order in a square with the officers in the center. After a song, Adjutant Dykes talked about the resurrection. Dykes' remarks "melted" Philip Thompson, a guide, to tears. Levi Hancock sang a solo. Captain Hunt exhorted the young men particularly to improve their conduct and to watch their profanity, pleading with them to act in a manner to secure the favor of heaven and the approbation of the community of Saints. David Pettegrew closed the meeting with prayer. Twenty-eight members of Captain Brown's "quarrelsome" company were baptized in the Neosho River for the remission of their sins. Two others were baptized into the Mormon Church for the first time.[22]

In the afternoon Lieutenant Andrew J. Smith, U.S. Army, and Dr. George Sanderson and staff arrived in camp. Smith came to take charge. Most of the men felt Captain Hunt should lead the battalion. Adjutant Dykes urged the men to accept Smith, saying he was a West Point graduate and knew army rules and regulations. Captain Hunt questioned Smith about carrying out Colonel Allen's plans and promises. Hunt was particularly concerned about the families traveling along. Smith said he would faithfully carry out Colonel Allen's promises. Upon a motion by Captain Higgins and seconded by Captain Davis, the officers voted to give the command to Smith. Only Captain Hunter and Lieutenants Lorenzo Clark, Samuel Gully, and William W. Willis voted to have Captain Hunt lead the battalion. The enlisted soldiers resented not getting to vote on the matter.[23]

Sun., Aug. 30, Council Grove, Kansas. Lieutenant Smith took command. Dr. Sanderson set up the hospital wagon and began seeing men who were sick. When the men learned Sanderson was from Missouri, they were apprehensive and thought he didn't like Mormons. John Bosco died and was buried beside his wife. He did not belong to the battalion. He and his wife were traveling with the Hunts. Orders were given at dark to be on the march early in the morning, so a small group of men under Elisha Averett went to a nearby hill by the light of the moon and carried large stones to build a cairn around the two graves, 10 ft. long, 7 ft. wide, and 2 ft. high. The center was filled with rock and the whole overlaid with uniform flat rocks. This was done to keep the wolves away. The names of the deceased were carved crudely on two rough stones placed at the top of the grave as headstones. The men enjoyed wild grapes found near this campsite.

Mon., Aug. 31, Diamond Springs, Kansas, 22 miles. The privates still didn't understand why Lieutenant Smith took command, but accepted it and thought time would tell if it was the right decision, leaving it in the hands of those who knew concerning the mission. Lieutenant Smith mustered the men, inspected their guns, and completed paperwork as regulations required. Smith ordered each man to take turn at guard duty and be on duty for twenty-four hours.[24]

There were 475 enlisted men and 21 officers on the battalion roster when the roster was reviewed on this date by Lieutenant A. J. Smith. The total number of 496 agreed with the first "official" roster made the night before entering Fort Leavenworth. One new member, John Allen, had been added at Fort Leavenworth, and Thomas Gilbert had deserted, so the total remained at 496. They had camped at Diamond Springs, where they found the best water so far on the journey. Fur traders, who traveled this route to the Rocky Mountains, named these springs because of their sparkle in dry surroundings. Several messes baked bread in the evening.

Tues., Sept. 1, Lost Springs, Kansas, 15 miles. Traveled over a flat, treeless prairie with large grasshoppers and wild sunflowers, three inches across. Dust clouds puffed small, hard objects into their eyes. There was no wood, so they dug narrow trenches in the ground and burned weeds to boil water for coffee and tea. Camped at Cottonwood Creek.

Wed., Sept. 2, Cottonwood Creek, Kansas, 26 miles. They entered Comanche territory where the Indians supposedly were very hostile. Many were sick. Dr. Sanderson forced everyone he saw to take calomel. It was a trying time. Some were too sick to report. Lieutenant Smith pulled several of the sick out of the wagons because they didn't report to the doctor. Nathaniel Jones, Company B, went to Smith and tried to explain the men weren't being disrespectful, that they were loyal, but had religious scruples against mineral medicine. Adjutant Dykes told Lieutenant Smith this wasn't so, and his statement made it harder on the men. If they didn't obey the colonel's orders, it would be mutiny. "Oh Lord! Deliver us from the hands of Doctor Sanderson" (David Pettegrew).[25]

David Pettegrew ordained William F. Ewell an elder in the Mormon Church. Sergeant Thomas S. Williams had purchased a team and wagon in Fort Leavenworth to haul a portion of Company D's knapsacks. He also allowed men who were sick to ride in his wagon. When Lieutenant Smith approached the wagon to pull the sick out, Williams ordered him to stop. Smith became angry and drew his sword and threatened to harm Williams if he allowed any more sick to ride. Williams grabbed the small end of his whip and told Smith he would strike him to the ground if he took a step forward. He also told Smith the wagon and team were his private property and he would haul whom he pleased. He said the sick men were his brothers and he would never leave one lying on the ground as long as his team could pull them. Smith left without taking any further action except to ask the name of the soldier.

The sickness increased. The diseases were principally ague and fever and billious and congestion. I was taken with the ague and fever this day but fortunately better provided for than many others having a wagon to ride in and a man to drive it. The Col. turned the sick all out of the wagons this day because they were not under the doctor's care. He said they might stay on the prairie if they would not submit to the order. Such indeed was the straits we were in and a narrower place no people was ever placed in. The Council [counsel] of the Church one way and the breaking of the commder's orders would be mutiny on the other hand, the church saying if you want to live, don't take medicine and if they didn't take medicine they could not ride. (William Coray)

Thurs., Sept. 3, near McPherson, Kansas, 25 miles. Dr. William L. McIntire, a member of the Mormon Church, was appointed assistant surgeon by Colonel Allen at the time of enlistment in Council Bluffs. He was not supposed to administer to his afflicted comrades unless ordered to do so by Sanderson. Once in a while he was able to help without Sanderson's knowledge. During the previous three days of walking, many were sick with ague and congestive fever. Sergeant Thomas Williams was driving his baggage wagon, with several men riding inside when Smith ordered them out. He asked Albert Dunham, one of the sick men, if he had taken any medicine. When Albert said "yes," the lieutenant asked him who ordered it. Upon learning he had taken medicine administered by Dr. McIntire without orders from the surgeon, the lieutenant said if any man in the battalion did the like again, he would cut his throat. Then he turned to Albert and said if he took medicine in the like manner again, he would tie a rope to his neck and drag him one day behind a wagon. In the evening the orderly sergeants were called together by the lieutenant and were told all sick were to report in person to Dr. Sanderson or they would be left on the prairie. The surgeon, while talking to the lieutenant, poured harsh curses on the men and said he would send as many to hell as he could. The men were not used to such language and concluded that the lieutenant was beginning to look very unlike Colonel James Allen. The men were in a quandary. Church leaders said not to take the medicine while military leaders ordered it to be done or Dr. Sanderson said he would send as many to hell as he could. They camped without food or water. William Hyde expressed the feelings of many men toward the doctor when he stated Sanderson was a "corrupt sample of the people we had just left in Missouri . . . who had stained their hands in the blood of the saints."[26]

Fri., Sept. 4, Little Arkansas River, Kansas, 18 miles. A miserable night with all blankets and clothes wet. The sick reported to Dr. Sanderson. He gave them calomel and arsenic. To those recovering he gave bitters of bayberry bark and camomile flowers. Some thought he wanted to kill them. He continued to curse all the time he was giving the medicine from an old, rusty spoon.

> If anything was ailing any of the men, if they had taken cold or had blistered feet through walking in poor shoes, or anything else, they would have to report at the sick call and the orderly sergeant would go with them to the doctor's quarters. After a light examination the doctor would give each one a nice little paper containing a dose of calomel. All were treated alike. They were told to take it with water before eating breakfast. The men fearing to be salivated would often bury it before getting back to camp . . . the doctor found out the men did not take calomel. After that they had to take it in his presence. During the time the men are on the sick list they are excused from guard duty, but had to carry their gun and knapsack. (Zadock K. Judd)[27]

Lieutenant Smith was checking on the sentinels to see if they were doing their duty when he was halted by Thomas Howell, one of the sentinels on guard. Smith mistakenly gave him the wrong signal and Howell held him a prisoner until the relief guard arrived. Smith was very upset but could fault no one but himself, since he had given the password for the previous night. Smith later remarked to another officer that the man who took him prisoner "would just as leave kill a man as look at him."[28] Howell's comrades found this amusing as he was known to be a very peaceful character.

The sun finally appeared in the afternoon and brightened the soldiers' outlook. They saw prickly pear cactus and other desert plants for the first time.

Sat., Sept. 5, Cow Creek, Kansas, 20 miles. All sick went to Dr. Sanderson to the tune "Jim Along Joe." The fifers played this tune each morning as the men walked to the "death" wagon. They found parsley plants along the trail and boiled them. With vinegar for seasoning, the men thought the parsley was first rate. Many were so tired they couldn't keep up and were scattered along the trail. Clusters of grapes were picked along Cow Creek. The troops caught up with the provision wagons. "Here we saw buffalo for the first time. The Missourians killed one and I got a piece" (William Coray).

Sun., Sept. 6, Plum Buttes, Kansas, 24 miles. Started without breakfast. Saw plum bushes, but no fruit. There were prickly pear cactus all along, but no water or wood. Burned buffalo chips as wood for first time and found the resulting smell to be very strong. They thought buffalo meat was good but tough. A thunderstorm came up suddenly. Lightning killed Dimick Huntington's cow. Luther Tuttle was very sick. The doctor thought it might be typhoid fever. When camp was breaking up, getting ready for the day's travel, Luther said: "Take me along with you as far as you can, then if I die, dig a hole and leave me by the way." He was afraid of the doctor's medicine. His companions put him and his blanket in an empty pork barrel. Several times during the day they gave him a drink of water. "We saw many buffalos. Lt. Merrill killed a young cow and I must say it was the tenderest meat I ever ate. We met a family here from Santa Fe, reported Kearny in peaceful possession of it. The citizens had sworn allegiance to the govt. and all this done without the first fire" (William Coray).

Mon., Sept. 7, Walnut Creek, Kansas. Left camp before sunrise. No breakfast. In the evening Lieutenant Smith paraded the soldiers for the first reading of army regulations. Once again Luther Tuttle traveled during the day in the barrel. At night he was lifted from the barrel and placed in his tent to sleep. One of his companions answered roll call for him.

> Camped on the Pawnee Fork. Passed the best tract of country to look at I had seen since I left the fort. Numerous herds of buffalo made the plains look quite black, as the caravan passed many of our boys gave them chase and succeeded in killing a number. They were principally bulls. The Indians had selected the cows . . . because of their being better meat. These animals had grazed the grass off short to the ground. Before we camped, it commenced raining and continued 4 or 5 hours very severe. The creek so high we could not cross. (William Coray)

Tues., Sept. 8, Ft. Larned, Kansas, 6 miles. Azariah Smith drove the Coray team. He liked doing it as there was a downpour and it was better than walking in the mud all day. Thousands of buffalo were passed and a few were killed for food. Traveled up the Arkansas River. Passed Pawnee Rock.[29] Robert Bliss and others carved their names on it. It was about forty feet high in the midst of the prairie with no other trees or rocks around it.[30] Several Indian attacks had occurred in the area, so the guard was doubled. The men were uncomfortable traveling all day in wet clothing. There was plenty of wood, useless because it was all wet, like the men. "This day . . . continued lowsy. I had succeeded [in breaking] the ague by this time by means of quinine and held myself present for duty" (William Coray). In the evening Lieutenant Smith called the captains and orderlies to his tent to go over muster lists.

Wed., Sept. 9, Pawnee Fork, Kansas, 12 miles. Azariah joined the Coray mess and helped Melissa wash. Levi Hancock found a piece of paper inside a cloth tied to a limb. The paper read, "Look out for Indians. We had a man killed here last night by Comanches May 31, 1846, signed BRAMFORD."[31] The river was very high and provided good water to drink. The banks were so steep wagons were eased down the banks with ropes. Men on the opposite bank used ropes to help teams pull the wagons up that bank. The water was cold and caused further discomfort for the men. In the evening Lieutenant Smith again called the captains and orderlies to his tent to go over muster lists.

> Camped on open prairie. Cooked our supper with buffalo dung. This morning I went to the surgeon to report the sick who were unable to walk. He said, "By G—, you bring them here. I know my duty." I went direct to the Col. to see if he upheld him in such conduct to which he replied he may send the asst. surgeon to see them. But frequently we carried the sick away to his quarters which was generally some ways for he was afraid to camp near us for fear of his life. (William Coray)

Thurs., Sept. 10, 20 miles. During the night a heavy wind blew all tents down. This morning the sick went to the "black wagon" of Dr. Sanderson. They didn't want to take his medicine, but he said they couldn't ride in the wagons unless they did.

Fri., Sept. 11, Coon Creek, Kansas, 12 miles. After sick call at sunrise, the companies crossed the prairie and reached the Arkansas River about noon. They followed the river and found it to be a curiosity. It appeared to be a river of sand with water breaking out here and there and then disappearing again. Plenty of fish for supper, but no timber. Using buffalo chips for fires caused the men to hold their noses when the chips started burning. Water was plentiful. Many washed clothes.

Sat., Sept. 12, Arkansas River, Kansas, 20 miles. Continuing along the river, they passed hundreds of white sand hills, many of them higher than the tree tops that drifted like snowdrifts. The plains were covered with buffalo bones. They met three men from Mississippi, all members of the Mormon Church. The leader was John Brown, whom they knew in Nauvoo while working on the temple and who told them there were fourteen Mormon families from Mississippi in Pueblo for the winter. Brigham Young had instructed him to take the Mississippi families west to Fort Laramie, where they were to meet Young and the body of the church going west. When the plans changed and the Mormons stayed in Council Bluffs until spring, the Mississippi company went back to Pueblo for the winter. Brown said they had a branch of the Mormon Church there. William Crosby and Daniel M. Thomas were with him. The trio was going back to Mississippi to get their own families and bring them west. The soldiers speared fish with their swords and bayonets for supper. Many were sick.

Sun., Sept. 13, Arkansas River, Kansas, 20 miles. Continued along the Arkansas River and passed large herds of antelope, buffalo, elk, wolves, and badgers. They had to dig holes in the sand to reach water. The scenery all day was sandy and dry, one eternal plain with no hills.

Mon., Sept. 14, Arkansas River, Kansas, 18 miles. Passed large piles of lime that was white like chalk but looked like plaster. The army animals were weak. Feed for the animals was very scarce, since the buffalo and other wild animals had eaten the grass. Azariah's eyes were sore again. Alva Phelps was very sick.

Tues., Sept. 15, Cimarron Cutoff, Kansas, 15 miles. The morning was cloudy. They crossed the Arkansas River at the point where the Cimarron Cutoff intersects the main road to Bent's Fort. They took the cutoff, which went south and west to Santa Fe. Before his death, Colonel Allen had sent their supplies to Bent's Fort. Plans had been changed when Kearny decided to continue to Santa Fe without waiting for them at Bent's Fort. The battalion had been redirected to Santa Fe using the Cimarron Cutoff instead of going to the fort, a change which caused their rations to be short. They now had no place to replenish supplies until Santa Fe. As they took the Cimarron Cutoff, they crossed the river. One wagon was upset and Francis Whitney, who was sick and riding in the wagon, was injured. They overtook five Missouri companies under Colonel Sterling Price and delivered the ammunition they had been hauling for Price's outfit. Lieutenant Smith notified Captain Higgins he would have command of a guard of ten men to take women and children to Pueblo. This was known as the family detachment. Levi Hancock was against this plan. He said Brigham Young and other church officials gave instructions to hold together, not to divide. Alva Phelps continued to be very ill. Azariah Smith took a mule to go get wood. The mule threw him off and returned to camp. Azariah's back was hurt in the fall. When he was walking back to camp, he saw a rattlesnake. They camped on the south side of the Arkansas River.[32]

> The stream glistened at the bottom, and along its banks were pitched a multitude of tents, while hundreds of cattle were feeding over the meadows. Bodies of troops, both horse and foot, and long trains of wagons, with men, women, and children, were moving over the opposite ridge and descending the broad declivity before us. These were the Mormon Battalion in the service of government, together with a considerable number of Missouri volunteers. The Mormons were to be paid off in California, and they were allowed to bring with them their families and property. There was something very striking in the half-military, half-patriarchal appearance of these armed fanatics, thus on their way with their wives and children, to found, it might be, a Mormon empire in California. We were much more astonished than pleased at the sight before us. In order to find an unoccupied camping-ground, we were obliged to pass a quarter of a mile up the stream, and here we were soon beset by a swarm of Mormons and Missourians. The United States officer

in command of the whole [Colonel Sterling Price] came also to visit us, and remained some time in our camp.

In the morning the country was covered with mist. We were always early risers, but before we were ready, the voices of men driving in the cattle sounded all around us. As we passed above their camp, we saw through the obscurity that the tents were falling, and the ranks rapidly forming; and, mingled with the cries of women and children, the rolling of the Mormon drums and the clear blast of their trumpets sounded through the mist. (Francis Parkman)[33]

Wed., Sept. 16, Cimarron Cutoff, Kansas. Alva Phelps died during the evening. His grave was dug by torch light on the south bank of the Arkansas River and was only four feet deep because of water seepage. Earlier in the afternoon he begged the doctor not to give him medicine. Dr. Sanderson, using horrible oaths, forced it down in his rusty spoon. A few hours later Alva died. The general feeling was that the doctor killed him. His body was placed in Henry Standage's tent for the night. Azariah's back was so sore from his fall he couldn't stand guard.

Captain Nelson Higgins left for Pueblo with a detachment of women and children and ten men. After it was learned a few days ago that a small group of Mormon Church members was wintering in Pueblo, Lieutenant Smith decided to send the Higgins detachment to Pueblo to lessen the number of women and children traveling with the battalion. There was sadness in camp about parting. Lieutenant Smith gave them thirty days' rations but through a mix-up the rations were not put into the one wagon they took. After the Higgins contingent left, planning began for the rest of the battalion to cross the desert ahead. The day was spent obtaining enough provisions for a couple of days and resting. Because their supplies went to Bent's Fort, Lieutenant Smith sent a messenger to Colonel Sterling Price requesting supplies. Price and the Missouri Volunteer Cavalry were ahead of the battalion. Colonel Price replied he "wasn't hauling provisions for Mormons." Lieutenant Smith sent back word that if provisions weren't sent "he would let loose the Mormons and come down upon them with his artillery."[34] Price sent the supplies. At night the men watched a meteor in the East that moved north and south and up and down. Levi Hancock thought it was a sign something soon would follow.

Thurs., Sept. 17, Cimarron Desert, Kansas, 25 miles. Alva Phelps was buried in the morning with a few remarks by Samuel Gully. He said, "We have death with us and hell immediately following in the way of our first surgeon."[35] Started across the Cimarron Desert. James Pace caught up with the battalion. Lieutenant Pace had left August 21 to see how Colonel Allen was. He then journeyed to Council Bluffs to tell Brigham Young about Allen's death. On his return to Fort Leavenworth he was given a fresh horse and grain and left the fort September 6. Howard Egan and John D. Lee accompanied him from Fort Leavenworth to here.

Lee and Egan had come to collect the pay to take back to Brigham Young and their families. Lee was dismayed at the condition and treatment of the battalion by Lieutenant Smith. He asked Smith and Captain Hunt to ride in Hunt's wagon. Lee charged Smith "with tyranny and oppression" and told him the men were ready to mutiny because of being forced to take Sanderson's medicine and cursings. He also spoke of the long, forced marches. The men riding in the wagon thought Lieutenant Smith might challenge Lee to a duel, but instead, when the wagon stopped to water the animals, Smith just walked away. "He [Lee] told Smith, 'In two minutes the battalion would have rebelled and taken your sweet life. When I came into camp this morning the people felt that they would not bear such things.' We marched 25 miles and camped without water, wood, or grass for the teams. The mules gave out and did not come up in one of our trains" (William Coray). The day was intensely hot, and they had no water.

Fri., Sept. 18, Sand Creek, Kansas, 26 miles. They saw a lake with mist rising from the water; it was far away. Next it looked like a lake of clear water, but it went on ahead of them. When they moved, it moved, and when they stopped, it stopped. It was a mirage, truly an aggravation when the men were so thirsty. Finally, they came to a stagnant pond, but had to drive buffalo out of it. The water was thick with buffalo urine, bugs, and rain water. The soldiers rushed to it, layed down, and sucked and strained the water through their teeth to keep from swallowing the bugs. Then they filled their canteens. Camped with no wood. Lee read three letters from Brigham Young. One told them to live by faith and leave the surgeon's medicine alone. The second stated Captain Hunt should lead after Colonel Allen died. Since Lieutenant Smith already was in command, nothing was done about this letter. The last letter told the men to turn their pay over to Lee to take back to Council Bluffs. Lee talked about these letters and got the men all stirred up. When they arrived at their camp site, the men had been without water for forty-eight hours. Later that night others became sick from drinking the tainted water earlier in the day.

Sat., Sept. 19, Cimarron Springs, Kansas, 10 miles. Started at 4 A.M. to get ahead of Price's Missouri troops. Stopped at 9 A.M. at Cimarron Springs. Found water by digging in a dry creek bed, but it tasted like epsom salts. Plenty of grass for animals and buffalo chips for fire. Many hurried and wrote letters to send with Lee and Egan when they took the money to Council Bluffs. Captain Hunt requested the soldiers' pay from the paymaster, who didn't have cash, so promised to pay them in Santa Fe. Lee and Egan decided to continue on until the battalion was paid.

Lieutenant Smith called the first sergeants of all companies together to find out why the men who were not on sick reports sometimes missed their assigned duties with other men standing in for them. William Coray told him the men didn't like the medicine and cursings of Dr. Sanderson so messmates often stood guard for the sick. Lieutenant Smith became angry and said if the sergeants wrote false reports, they would be put in irons. Later the captains held a meeting in Captain Hunt's tent and discussed the authority dividing the battalion. William Coray wrote, "So many a man has stood guard when he was scarcely able to stand alone determined, if possible, to adhere to the council of the Twelve and not take medicine."

Sun., Sept. 20, Cimarron River, Kansas, 10 miles. For about two hundred miles there had been little food and water for the men and a shortage of feed for the animals. Lieutenant Smith appeared to be using up men and beasts. Both teams and men failed frequently. Azariah Smith fixed the Coray wagon. As they traveled over a sandy riverbed, they saw many buffalo, antelope, deer, wolves, prairie foxes, prairie dogs, and jack rabbits. In the evening the officers met with John Lee and discussed the authority problem dividing the battalion. The captains had talked about it in their meeting the night before. Captain Hunter spoke about how Lee came and dictated to the battalion and criticized Lieutenant Smith. He said that Lee was out of place. Levi Hancock and David Pettegrew supported Lee, but Captain Hunt stood up and said he alone had the right to counsel. Lee said Hunt should stand up for his men more. The meeting adjourned with lots of opinions and nothing settled.

Mon., Sept. 21, Cimarron River, Kansas, 18 miles. Started this morning at 7 A.M. and traveled up the river until early afternoon. Azariah continued to drive the Coray team. The men dug about four feet in sand to reach water. When Samuel Rogers was on horse guard during the night, he heard Lieutenant Smith discussing the soldiers with the adjutant and the doctor. It appeared to Samuel they deliberately planned forced marches to make the men ill and force them to take the calomel or walk and do duty. Samuel Rogers said they seem determined to kill the soldiers. Azariah's eyes were sore again.

I threw all medicine sent me thereafter away and after a time the Dr seemed to surmise that there was something not exactly right and had me taken morning and evening to his tent and administered medicine with his own hand but not a bit of it got into my stomach as I would hold it in my mouth until I was taken out of the tent and then spit it out and through it all recovered to such an extent that I thought I could make a day's journey on foot. (Henry W. Sanderson)[36]

As they passed an extensive ancient water system, they thought about the Book of Mormon and its people, thinking that this land was once well populated and irrigated and now stood barren.

Tues., Sept. 22, Cimarron River, Colorado, 16 miles. Reveille at 4 A.M., roll call, and in motion by 6 A.M. Continued along the river, with rain in the evening. Men and teams gave out all along the way from exhaustion and sickness. The men went to sick call as the musicians played "Jim Along Joe." Lieutenant Smith tried to train the men to be marching soldiers. This idea was not practical. It was impossible to keep a marching cadence in long columns strung out over rough terrain and without proper shoes, food, or water. "The wind blew very hard. To keep my wagon from blowing off I tied it between the Captains and the baggage wagon. Reported all the sick for the first time to the Dr. this morning" (William Coray).

Wed., Sept. 23, Cimarron River, Wagon Body Spring, Oklahoma, 15 miles. During the night an ox fell into the hole dug for water and broke its neck. Continued traveling along the river. Brackish, salty water had "physicking" effect on everyone. When the men were digging for water, they found fish. At night the sergeants told Lieutenant Smith they opposed requiring the sick to report to the doctor. They told him Dr. Sanderson gave calomel for every disease whether it was boils, rheumatism, fever, or lame backs. Lieutenant Smith told the sergeants they were mistaken and nothing was resolved. Several mules were left to perish. During the night the wolves were noisy and bold.

> Orders were that no teams or men should leave without orders. We marched nearly 15 miles . . . very sandy all the way . . . teams gave out. A storm this evening with every appearance of the equinox. Sickness raged high—10 in our co. and from 35 to 40 in the battalion—some of them are very sick. William Hyde refused to parade the company. (William Coray)

Thurs., Sept. 24, Cimarron Crossing, Oklahoma, 18 miles. An early morning departure left behind several mules, horses, and oxen too weak to continue. Traveled over high ridges and barren desert. Lots of lizards, rattlesnakes, toads, tarantulas, and buffalo. The sand was deep and difficult to pass through. They reached the Cimarron crossing about four in the afternoon and camped with a group of traders in sight of two large mountains known as Rabbit Ears, a landmark for travelers. "Lt. Smith was heard to say he had not five friends in the battalion" (William Coray).

Fri., Sept. 25, Oklahoma, 18 miles. Passed through hills that looked like volcanoes had exploded long ago and camped about three o'clock. Some of the younger men climbed a rocky ridge and found a cave. Several Spaniards rode into camp.

Amongst them was a Spanish Hidalgo and his daughter with their rich caprisoned horses and their jingeling uniform. The Sinuretta lit off her horse like a nightengale. The whole camp was there in a minute. Their gaudy dress and drapery attracted all eyes. The dress of the Sinuretta is hard to describe, all the colors of the rainbow with ribbons and jewelry to match. She was the Rodope [?] of the great American plains. We gave them presents and made them welcome to our camp and also to martial music as a greeting. The damsel was struck with our drummer boy, Jessie [Justice C.] Earl, and his violin. He played "The Girl I Left Behind Me." She could not contain herself and with her companaros started a dance and made the dance fit the tune. (Abner Blackburn)[37]

The name of this river is Cimarron because it means "lost river" in Spanish. The reason of the Spaniards calling it so is because of its having no rise nor outlet, it frequently rises 18 inches within a few minutes and without any prospects of rain, but the water sinks away in the sand. As we ascended the bluffs, we came in sight of high craggy peaks, rugged rocks and high precipices. We met traders bound for the states. I had the pleasure of seeing a Spaniard in his native dress and cavalry mounting with his long spurs. As usual we cooked our supper with buffalo dung. (William Coray)

Sat., Sept. 26, Cold Springs on Santa Fe Trail, Oklahoma, 23 miles. Traveled on a trail over hills and rocks and camped on a ridge overlooking Cedar Springs. Azariah and others went about a mile away to get water and wood. Lieutenant Smith sent an express to General Kearny to ask him to wait in Santa Fe until the battalion could get there. They found cedar, spruce, and cottonwood for fires. Water was scarce. Lieutenant Luddington lost one of his ponies and had difficulty moving his wagon. He received permission from Lieutenant Smith to use a yoke of oxen.

Nothing new. Just go ahead seems to be the only word, no rest. March, march is the daily task. Day break brings reveilee, sick or well must go either to roll call or it's the doctor. Next, boys, get your breakfast, and strike your tents with all possible speed, then left, left, all day over the road through dust, over hills, and across valleys, some twelve, thirteen and eighteen miles. Halt, stack arms, pitch tents, run over all creation gathering buffalo chips, or a little brush and getting water, draw rations, cook supper, etc. While this is going on, roll call comes on again. By the time the evening chores are finished dark is at hand, attend to evening duties, go to bed and sleep on the rough cold ground with only one blanket and a thin tent to shelter from the cold. (James Scott)[38]

Sun., Sept. 27, New Mexico, 13 miles. Many antelope were shot and eaten at night for quite a treat. There was no wood, so they hunted buffalo chips to cook the antelope. The nightly battalion encampments generally covered from four to six acres with individual companies camped together. Elijah Allen was very ill and rode in the wagon all day. As he was lying in the wagon during the evening, he overheard Jesse Hunter, captain of Company B, remark that his illness was holding the company back. During the night he thought he was too sick to continue and did not want to hold up his company. He crawled out of the wagon into nearby bushes and thought he was going to die. The next morning, as he lay suffering, he heard the wagons pulling out. When the wagons were out of sight, he crawled back to the campfire and fell asleep.

John D. Lee, assisted by James Pace, Levi Hancock, Andrew Lytle, and William Hyde, devised a plan to replace Captain Jefferson Hunt with Quartermaster Samuel Gully. They couldn't get enough support, so the plan failed.

Mon., Sept. 28, McNees Creek, New Mexico, 18 miles. Azariah killed an antelope and he and two others brought it into camp. They also saw bears and wild turkeys. Azariah returned to his father's mess. He had been traveling with the Corays for a few days. When the boys checked to see how Elijah Allen was, he was not in the wagon, so they went back to find him. He was asleep by the fire of the previous campsite. They brought him into camp and he rode in the wagon again all day. By nightfall he felt better.

> This evening I was informed that a secret influence was used against Capt. Hunt at the same time holding up S. E. Gully as the only fit man to lead this Battalion and that Lee was at the head, assisted by Pace, Hancock, Lytle and William Hyde . . . and I must say that I could not suppress thoughts running through my mind, but I can keep from writing them. (William Coray)

Tues., Sept. 29, Rabbit Ears, New Mexico, 15 miles. After they passed Rabbit Ears, many teams and men failed for lack of food, water, and judgment of Lieutenant Smith.[39] Traveled until nine at night, hunting food for animals. While John Steele and Thomas Treat hunted antelope, they discovered stones placed in a large ring with a pile of stones in the center. Levi Hancock thought it was an old Nephite work.[40]

Wed., Sept. 30, Extra Valley, New Mexico, 25 miles. Traveled over sandy plain. Lots of rocks and high mounds. The men's coats were worn through on the shoulders by the constant rubbing of the muskets. Many shoulders were blistered. Plenty of antelope meat to eat. Lieutenant Smith had been in charge one month. The company orderly sergeants worked on the rosters in the evening. Lieutenant Smith accused the sergeants of neglecting their duties and not obeying orders of Quartermaster Gully. "The Col.

threatened to reduce me in the ranks for not communicating his orders to the captain" (William Coray).

Thurs., Oct. 1, New Mexico, 15 miles. They broke camp at daylight and traveled three miles, where they rested for four hours. About noon they passed a structure running north and south, which looked like an old fort. Nearby were channels that had carried water. It probably was the work of Pueblo Indians.

Fri., Oct. 2, Valley of Tears, New Mexico, 23 miles. Started early and marched several hours. When they finally stopped for breakfast, Levi Hancock, John King, and Lyman Stephens climbed a peak. Hancock built an altar and prayed. In the afternoon they met a number of Kearny's dragoons coming from Santa Fe. They said the battalion was to be in Santa Fe by October 10. Lieutenant Smith ordered an accelerated pace in order to reach Santa Fe by the tenth. William Follett called the lieutenant a "negro driver," so William Coray reported him. Follett was put under guard. William Walker and Jacob Butterfield couldn't keep up with the faster pace, so they, too, were placed under guard. John D. Lee, still causing trouble, called Lieutenant Smith a "little wolfish tyrant."[41] According to William Coray, "Some messengers . . . brought an express from Kearny stating that the Mormon Battalion if they were not there within 8 days could not be fitted out for California."

Sat., Oct. 3, Ocata Creek, New Mexico, 7 miles plus 22 miles. Lieutenant Smith asked fifty men from each company to go ahead with the best wagons and teams at an accelerated pace to reach Santa Fe by the tenth. All others were to continue at a slower pace under Lieutenant George Oman. Again, there was opposition to being divided. The soldiers didn't like the division. Captain Hunter told Company B he felt sending the group ahead was the best move. Oman's group consisted of women, sick men, children, broken wagons, cannon, and the cattle. Dr. Sanderson, showing little concern for their welfare, made haste to go with the forward group, leaving the sick to follow the best they could. Everyone was in gloomy spirits. After passing a high ridge, the Oman group saw foothills and mountains in the distance. They were on the Santa Fe Trail.

> Lt. Smith . . . thought it best to take 50 men of each company—the capts, 2 Lts, 2 sergts, and 2 corps, and take a forced march to Santa Fe that they might claim the right to fit out for California. To this proposition they agreed unanimously. Accordingly we made ready and marched 22 miles this evening and left Lt. Oman in command of the detachment. We camped on a creek near a high rock. (William Coray, with advance company)

Sun., Oct. 4, Wagon Mound, New Mexico, 22 miles. Because they found good water and grassy lands for the animals, they called this place the

Valley of Hope (Oman group). "Traveled 22 miles and camped on a Creek. The road was very rocky in places. A large chain of mountains in sight in southwest. Game is plenty here, antelope and deer particularly" (William Coray, with advance company).

Mon., Oct. 5, Mora River, New Mexico. The Oman group traveled until midnight because so many men were ill and they had the weakest animals. Once when they were on high rocks they could see the advance company in the distance (Oman Group).

> Marched 30 miles to a Spanish village called Vegas, 5 miles from where we camped, there is a Missourian living in good style. The Spaniards are industrious in this Vegas, however not very wealthy. They came out by the wholesale to see us and trade with us. They seem to have plenty of mules, goats, sheep and cattle. They milk the goats as much as they do the cattle and more.[42] (William Coray, with advance company)

Tues., Oct. 6, 12 miles. Rested and washed clothes (Oman group). "Marched 12 miles to Barnett Springs. This day's march mostly through yellow pine, cedar & spruce. Our course was southwest mostly. As we went winding through the mountains going up some creeks and down others, it put me in mind of the Pennsylvania Mountains as I drove along" (William Coray, with advance company).

Wed., Oct. 7, La Junta, New Mexico, 18 miles. Traveled through irrigated cornfields and several Spanish settlements. The Catholic church had two bells (Oman Group). "Passed the town of San Miguel [del Bado], which contains a cathedral church and about 150 houses which were built of brick about four times as large as United States bricks. For the last 135 miles we were short of rations and marched at a very quick rate" (William Coray, with advance company).

Thurs., Oct. 8, New Mexico, 22 miles. Passed through Las Vegas and several valleys. Another long, hard day. The men complained that Lieutenant Oman was driving them too hard when so many were ailing. Lieutenant Luddington's personal wagon broke down and he left it (Oman Group).

Fri., Oct. 9, New Mexico, 20 miles. When Lieutenant Oman gave orders to march, Lieutenant Luddington, Company B, refused. He wanted to return to his wagon and repair it. Lieutenant Oman ordered Sergeant Hyde to take command of Company B and proceed, but Sergeant Hyde refused. Lieutenant Oman left with the other four companies while Company B stayed behind. A few men went back with Luddington to repair his wagon while the rest proceeded slowly (Oman group).

On the outskirts of Santa Fe the advance company fixed bayonets and drew swords. They marched to the public square, where they halted for fifteen minutes for inspection. Colonel Alexander W. Doniphan's men saluted the Mormons by firing blanks from the tops of the adobe houses.[43] While most of the American soldiers in Santa Fe appeared to welcome the Mormons, George Gibson was not impressed by their appearance: "They are well drilled, a shabby-looking set."[44]

There were two regiments, consisting of about sixteen hundred men in Santa Fe, one under Colonel Doniphan and the other under Colonel Sterling Price. The Mormons were pleased to see Colonel Doniphan because he had proved to be a friend to the Mormons previously. He ordered wood, feed, and other provisions hauled to their encampment northeast of the cathedral. Also there, as William Coray noted, was "Capt. Cooke, 1st Dragoons . . . awaiting our arrival to take command of us, being so ordered by Gen. Kearny. Santa Fe is 860 miles from Ft. Leavenworth."

Sat., Oct. 10, Pecos, New Mexico. The men in the rear group openly denounced Oman for long, forced marches. Oman did not wait for the men to come in with Luddington's repaired wagon. Luddington and Company B never did catch up all day. The church in Pecos was built 250 years earlier. Most of its walls were in a ruined state (Oman Group).

Sun., Oct. 11, Gold Dust. Struggled through Glorieta Pass and went about seven miles beyond to camp. Still no sight of Company B and Luddington (Oman group).

Crossing the Pecos River. Lithograph from Andrew Belcher Gray, *Southern Pacific Railroad: Survey of a Route for the Southern Pacific R.R., on the 32nd Parallel* (1856); courtesy of the California History Room, California State Library, Sacramento, California.

Santa Fe, New Mexico, ca. 1846–47. Lithograph from *Report of Lieut. J. W. Abert of His Examination of New Mexico, in the Years 1846–'47* (1848); courtesy of the Museum of New Mexico, Santa Fe.

CHAPTER THREE

Santa Fe:
Colonel Cooke Assumes Command

Mon., Oct. 12, Santa Fe, New Mexico. Lieutenant Oman and his four companies reached Santa Fe around noon. Company B, under Lieutenant Luddington, arrived at 6 P.M., six hours later. They camped in wheatfields behind the cathedral. The American flag was flying high in the air at Fort Marcy, located on a nearby hill overlooking the town. Colonel Alexander W. Doniphan, who had ordered a salute of one hundred guns from the house tops to honor the arrival of the advance battalion group on October 9, was commander of the post.[1] Doniphan and his regiment of First Missouri Mounted Volunteers had marched from Fort Leavenworth with Kearny's advance Army of the West to conquer New Mexico.

In Santa Fe differences between the battalion companies over being separated were forgotten and the Mormon troops rejoiced at being together again. When the wagons carrying the wives stopped, the Mexican women surrounded the women and shook hands with them. The natives were surprised to see women and children and were very friendly. They offered pine nuts, apples, peaches, pears, grapes, bread, onions, boiled corn, and melons for sale. Such a variety of food was enjoyed by the battalion.

The Mormons met Colonel Philip St. George Cooke, who was to be their new commander from Santa Fe to California.[2] Colonel Cooke told the officers he had been ordered to make a wagon road to the Pacific—something that had never been done before by a southern route.[3]

As Colonel Cooke took command, he noted the condition of the battalion and wondered what kind of an outfit was given him as a fighting force. He said the battalion

was enlisted too much by families; some were too old, some feeble, and some too young; it was embarrassed by many women; it was

65

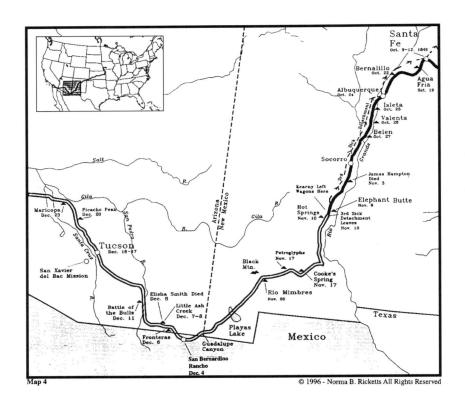

Map 4

1846-1847
Mormon Battalion Route
Santa Fe, New Mexico, to Tucson, Arizona

———	Mormon Battalion
═══	Blazed Wagon Road
▬ ▬ ▬	3rd Sick Detachment
– – –	States not in existence
▲	Camp Site

N

undisciplined; it was much worn by traveling on foot and marching from Nauvoo, Illinois; their clothing was very scant; there was no money to pay them or clothing to issue; their mules were utterly broken down; the quartermaster department was without funds and its credit bad; and mules were scarce. . . .

The battalion have never been drilled, and, though obedient, have little discipline; they exhibit great heedlessness and ignorance, and some obstinacy. I have brought road tools and have *determined* to take through my wagons; but the experiment is not a fair one, as the mules are nearly broken down at the outset.[4]

He decided the remaining women, children, and disabled men were to be sent back to Pueblo under Captain James Brown. Colonel Cooke wanted to send only disabled men along with the women and children. This caused grave concern among the men who did not want their families sent to Pueblo with only sick men to protect them.

Colonel Cooke began to show himself and to make arrangements for the Battalion to march. He was about at the point of giving an order that all the laundresses should go back to Pueblo with the sick and invalids of the Battalion, but Capt. Hunter chanced to hear of the calculation and informed Capt. Davis, Sgt. Brown and myself of it. We concluded to go over and make a contract with the Col. to let our wives go with us. To this he consented after some parleying, but said we must take them at our own expense, that they must be no detriment to the command. In the meantime the women were moaning and crying about the camp, thinking that they would in a few days be separated from their husbands and left in the care of sick men among savage tribes of Indians but many of our brethren swore in their rath they would not leave their wives, order or no order! I thought so myself. (William Coray)

Cooke reorganized the battalion staff. He appointed First Lieutenant Andrew J. Smith to be quartermaster and Second Lieutenant George Stoneman assistant quartermaster. Major Jeremiah H. Cloud remained as paymaster as did Doctor George B. Sanderson in his position and George P. Dykes as adjutant. All but Dykes were non-Mormons. Cooke also retained most of the Mormon officers. Jefferson Hunt, Jesse Hunter, and Daniel Davis remained captains of A, B, and E. Captain James Brown was assigned to take a sick detachment to Pueblo and First Lieutenant George W. Rosecrans was placed in charge of Company C. Second Lieutenant Sylvester Hulet was assigned temporary command of Company D, filling the vacancy created when Captain Higgins took the family detachment to Pueblo.[5] Cooke reduced to privates Joel J. Terrell,

David Wilkin, and Jabez Nowlin. In their place he promoted to sergeant Daniel Tyler and Edward Martin and to corporal Russell G. Brownell, William Squires, and John Fife. James Ferguson became the sergeant major, replacing James H. Glines, who went with Brown's sick detachment at the request of Captain Brown.

Tues., Oct. 13, Santa Fe. A message from General Kearny arrived with orders to proceed to the Pacific with sixty days' rations. Colonel Cooke and General Doniphan began organizing the detachment that was to go to Pueblo under Captain Brown and Lieutenant Elam Luddington. Cooke still favored sending the women without their husbands:

> Col. Cooke ordered the Dr. to discharge as many as he thought proper so they arraigned before the Dr. for examination. "Now," he said, "you are on your own, men, by God, take care of yourselves." The boys did not know what it meant at first but, being told that they were actually discharged, they began to feel quite sorrowful. The Captains no sooner heard this than they went to Col. Doniphan and got him to order it otherwise, and instead of being discharged they were put on detached service with the laundresses, to march back to Pueblo to winter. (William Coray)

Wed., Oct. 14, Santa Fe. John Steele talked to Dykes and Colonel Cooke, but they told him the husbands could not go. John Hess, who had been driving teams all the way, asked Captain Davis if his wife could continue with the battalion. Captain Davis wanted John to drive for him, but Emeline Hess, his wife, was to go with the sick detachment. Hess felt he "could not consent to" this arrangement and "retain his manhood," so he remonstrated with Captain Davis but to no avail. He said he would not continue on and leave his wife. This was a bold assertion for a private to make to his captain. John Steele and John Hess decided to talk to General Doniphan. They went to the general's quarters with their hats under their arms and called his attention to their business. He was very stern and said he had been informed that the twenty men who had wives along wanted to go on to California and let their women go back. The two men told them they had not been consulted in the matter. General Doniphan asked them to leave, remarking he had left his wife. Hess replied: "General, I suppose you left your wife with her friends, while we are required to leave ours in our enemy's country in care of a lot of sick, demoralized men."[6] This seemed to touch a sympathetic cord. Hess and Steele left as the general called for Adjutant Dykes.

In a few minutes, Adjutant Dykes climbed on top of the hind wheel of a wagon and shouted: "All you men who have wives here can go back with them. I have never seen men go about crying enough to melt the heart of a crocodile before, so I have arranged it."[7] General Doniphan had agreed to let the able-bodied soldiers go to Pueblo with their wives and the disabled men: "Finally the Col. for some purpose gave the men the privilege of going with their wives. The only cause of this tyranical move was that Cooke was striving for military glory and depended on the coming expedition to raise him up. By this time we began to find him out a little as you might suppose" (William Coray).

Colonel Cooke gave permission for five women to continue. Later in the day Adjutant Dykes read a bulletin stating Cooke was replacing Gully as quartermaster by Lieutenant Smith. This change came about when Cooke appointed his new staff. The soldiers liked Gully because he stood up for them and was not afraid to speak out in favor of the men. Levi Hancock was very upset by this turn of events. He talked about getting a petition and asking everyone to sign it so Colonel Cooke would know the men preferred Gully. Cooke requested the soldiers to participate with the Mexicans in a fandango to show respect and interest in their culture. Some of the men attended mass as the colonel suggested. Azariah and his father, Albert Smith, thought the statues in the Catholic church were beautiful and enjoyed the music. After attending the Catholic mass, Azariah commented: "After the me[e]ting I stayed to see the ladies, some of which looked very pret[t]y; others looked like destruction."[8]

William Coray did not think highly of the manners of the women at the fandango. The clothing of the Mormons looked shabby and drab compared to the bright colors of the Mexicans. The soldiers washed their white belts before going.

> The officers were requested to attend a party and bring their ladies with them. I was against the operation but I was finally persuaded to go for curiosity. Our accomodations were poor, and the whole affair sickened me. I saw them dance their waltz or what they called Rovenas. Their music was tolerable, but the ill manners of the females disgusted me. . . . I thought I would stick it out till supper but had I known before what I knew afterwards the supper would have been no object as it proved to be a grab game all the way round, and the man that waited for manners lost his supper. (William Coray)

Thurs., Oct. 15, Santa Fe. The petition to keep Gully was signed by nearly everyone. Hancock planned to give it to General Doniphan the next day. John Tippets noted, "It is interesting to see how the Spaniards turn the streams out of their course into little streams to water their crops. There is little or no rain in this country yet they raise very good wheat, corn and onions and have lots of goats, sheep, jackasses, cows, mules and oxen."[9]

Fri., Oct. 16, Santa Fe. General Doniphan received the petition and said he could leave Gully as he was, but as soon as the battalion moved out, he would be removed again. So Gully decided to resign. The men didn't want him to leave as he was not afraid to defend the Saints in any place and before any man. There was no money to pay the battalion, so checks were issued for one and one-half months. Locals charged to cash checks, so many decided to send their checks back with Lee as well as letters to their families. Azariah Smith wrote letters for several men who knew how to sign their names but not write.

During the night someone broke into Doctor Sanderson's trunk and stole his gold watch, valued at $300, and pilot Philip Thompson's watch worth $180. Two mules also were stolen. The doctor blamed the Mormons and insisted everyone be searched. Ten men from each battalion company were ordered to guard their comrades while the entire encampment was searched. The watches were not found.

Sun., Oct. 18, Santa Fe. Captain Brown and the sick detachment left for Pueblo. The parting was hard for both groups. Henry Bigler was sad to say good-bye to his sister, Emeline, and her husband, John Hess. Only five women and one small boy continued with the battalion at this time:

1. Lydia Hunter, wife of Captain Jesse Hunter, was pregnant.
2. Phebe Brown was the wife of Sergeant Ebenezer Brown. Her son, Zemira Palmer, was one of the young aides traveling with the battalion.
3. Susan Davis was the wife of Captain Daniel Davis, who had his six-year-old son, Daniel Jr., along. The boy's mother had died and his older brothers and sisters were left behind with family members.
4. Melissa Coray, wife of Sergeant William Coray, was a bride of three weeks when she began this historic trek with her husband.
5. Sophia Tubbs, wife of Private William Tubbs, was the fifth woman allowed to continue at this time. She did not go all the way to California. She and her husband were in the third detachment that went to Pueblo, under Lieutenant W. W. Willis.

The women who continued were transported in private wagons or walked. On occasion, they rode mules.

Colonel Cooke learned the rough terrain had forced General Kearny to abandon his wagons, so Colonel Cooke ordered pack saddles for the mules. Because the animals pulling the wagons were in such poor condition, baggage had to be cut down to reduce the weight in wagons. He ordered skillets and ovens to be left behind; each mess was allowed to take only one camp kettle.

Mon., Oct. 19, Santa Fe. John D. Lee and Howard Egan left for Council Bluffs with $2,447.32 in checks, currency, and coin from battalion

members. Samuel Gully, ex-quartermaster, and Roswell Stephens went
with them. Gully was unpopular with the non-Mormon officers because he
openly expressed opposition to the commanding officers. The Mormon
soldiers thought he was brave and loyal to them. With the words, "God
bless you, Brother Gully, and a safe journey," his comrades bid him good-
bye.[10] Roswell Stephens acted as a bodyguard for Lee and Egan with the
money they were carrying and as a courier with letters to families and
Mormon Church officials.[11]

The battalion left Santa Fe about eleven o'clock with the following:

25 government wagons
15 mule wagons, 3 mule wagons for each company for com-
    pany supplies, each pulled by 8 mules
6 large ox wagons for heavy equipment
4 mule wagons for the battalion command (field and staff,
    quartermaster, hospital department, paymaster)
5 company wagons, purchased by the men to haul their equip-
    ment so they wouldn't have to carry such heavy loads
12 private family wagons

With every effort the Quartermaster could only undertake to furnish
rations for sixty days with full rations of only flour, sugar, coffee and
salt; salt pork only for thirty days, and soap for twenty. To venture
without pack saddles would be grossly imprudent, so that burden
was added. (Philip St. George Cooke)[12]

Upon learning that rough terrain forced General Kearny to abandon his wagons, Cooke also took packsaddles for the mules. Colonel
Cooke found maps unreliable, so he hired two guides—Pauline Weaver
and Stephen Foster. (They would soon be joined by Antoine Leroux and
Jean Baptiste Charbonneau.)[13] Colonel Cooke ordered new messes of ten
men each.

As to my own circumstances, they were rather sorrowful. I had only
two poor mules to start across the great deserts with and no money
to get more with. I had laid over 60 lbs. of flour extra, some pork,
etc. We commenced our march to California, marched 6 miles
south and camped under the command of Lt. Col. Cooke. This
evening he learned by some means that five women were in his command and he forthwith ordered the adjutant to have them cast lots
which should go back and if they would not, the adjutant must do it
for them. As soon as the husbands of the women heard this they told
the adjt. their women should do no such thing for they had made a
contract with him to have them go and if he broke his contracts so
quick, they would not obey his orders. I was one of those gentlemen.

Sgt. Brown went to the Lt. Col. and reminded him of his contract and settled the trouble. (William Coray)

Tues., Oct. 20, Santa Fe, New Mexico, 15 miles. They followed an old Spanish trail south through the Galinas Valley that had been planted with corn. They camped along the San Marcos Arroyo. Cooke was upset when he learned there were no buckets for watering the animals. No grass, but cornstalks and fodder were obtained without difficulty. The men did not like to march behind the baggage wagons as ordered because of the dust. Cooke was very strict with everyone about obeying orders, including the officers. During the evening Colonel Cooke issued new regulations: Each company was to have its own quartermaster, rations were reduced to ¾ lb. of flour, ¾ rations of sugar and coffee, and ½ lb. beef per day. Public wagons could not carry muskets or knapsacks. The soldiers could not go more than a quarter mile from their company and could not fire muskets in camp. Anyone disobeying would be confined under guard. The men were very upset over the reduced rations:

> The Col. was closely watched. From the very onset we had taken a dislike to him. He ordered the baggage in advance of each company on the march. A circumstance occurred this morning which showed how particular the colonel was with us. Capt. Hunter, having lost one of his mules, left camp to hunt it without permission from His Excellency, for which cause he ordered him under arrest as soon as he arrived and made him march in rear of his co for three days without his sabre; But the Capt. being a humorous fellow, cared very little about it and appeared as well contented in rear of his company as in the front. The weather was very pleasant during the day but uncomfortably cold during the night. (William Coray)

Wed., Oct. 21, Rio Grande del Norte, New Mexico, 24 miles. Traveled on the hard sandy bed of the Galisteo River near present Cerillos. They followed along for eight miles before reaching flat land and entering the Rio Grande bottoms a mile from the San Felipe Pueblo near La Mesita. Guide Foster purchased twenty bushels of corn, so most were able to have parched corn for supper. The Indians had melons, apples, and onions, but wouldn't trade for dollars. They wanted clothes and blankets.

Thurs., Oct. 22, Rio Grande, 12 miles. The sandy roadbeds were too much for the weary animals, so the men helped push the wagons. "On this terrible, sandy road, down the stream, several oxen fell, and had to be rolled out of the road, they making no motion; the feet of others were bleeding" (Philip St. George Cooke).[14] Came to Galisteo. Again, the Mexican señoritas were surprised and curious about the five women with the battalion. Colonel Cooke couldn't purchase oxen or mules because the natives didn't like American rule and did not want to do anything to assist the Americans. The Mexicans had large flocks of sheep and goats. They wore leather with blankets around their shoulders and carried bows and arrows. They carried lances, made from long sticks with sharp spear points on the ends. It was a novel sight to the soldiers. The days were hot and dusty and the nights were freezing when the sun went down.

Fri., Oct. 23, Bernalillo, New Mexico, 11 miles. Colonel Cooke seemed to get more strict as the days passed. The battalion normally did not march before 9 A.M. Cooke decided not to waste any morning hours, so he set up a new schedule, starting out soon after daybreak. Cooke and many men were sick. Cooke thought several men had the measles. The road was extremely bad; it took them seven hours to travel eleven miles.

> Three days after leaving Santifee I was appointed commissary seargeant and my duty was to deal out the rations every day to the five companies. This released me from carrying my knapsack, cartridge box and gun, but I was under great responsibility in making my returns every night and morning to the Commissary Colonel and officers of the staff. This gave me much opportunity to learn things. (David Pettegrew) [15]

They met three companies of Colonel Price's Missouri Volunteers who had been on a march against Navajo Indians. Continued down Rio Grande Valley and camped near Albuquerque. Lots of irrigation and neat farms, orchards, vineyards, and large quantities of red peppers. They bought sweet grapes and other fruit from the natives. Many were sick with influenza, including Colonel Cooke, because of extreme temperature changes from hot days to cold nights. Passed more Spanish towns.

> The Col. by this time has become very severe and strict. The buglers blow the assembly and the drummers act immediately and play off reveille, not to exceed two minutes in all, and if the men are not in the ranks to answer to their names they are ordered on an extra tour of guard. Every man is to be in the ranks before the drum ceased. The teamsters must scamper for their mules and have scarce time to hitch up before the advance signal would be given, when every man must quit all, even his breakfast, and come in to ranks. (William Coray)

Sat., Oct. 24, Albuquerque, New Mexico, 15 miles. Quartermaster Stoneman exchanged thirty broken down mules for fifteen good ones. He paid forty dollars for ten others and bought twelve bushels of corn ears. The troops were surprised to see the Indian men in breech cloths and the women with red paint on their faces. The women rode horses sitting in front of the men, who put their arms around the women to hold the reins.

This was reverse from what the soldiers knew. Pioneer women always rode behind men on horses.

Heading west out of Albuquerque they crossed the Rio Grande in chilly water up to their knees to follow a branch of the Chihuahua Trail. Camped in the early afternoon on the west bank. Some paid the Mexicans five cents to take them across the river on mules. The men were very tired after dragging wagons through the sand. Colonel Cooke purchased twenty oxen and eight mules from Captain John Burgwin, who was camped nearby.[16] He also exchanged two heavy ox wagons for two pontoon wagons and a light cart. Melissa Coray sometimes rode in the Hunter wagon. She and Lydia Hunter enjoyed visiting and singing church hymns and other favorite songs like "Lucy Long" as they rode along. This ride sharing stopped when Captain Hunter said his animals were too poorly to pull Melissa's extra weight. A new guide, Jean Baptiste Charbonneau, arrived.[17] He was assigned to Colonel Cooke by General Kearny. A light rain fell in the evening.

Sun., Oct. 25, Little Island (Isleta), Rio Grande, New Mexico, 15 miles. Colonel Cooke told the captains before leaving camp that the men should take better care of the mules and gave orders how to care for them. He said sentinels caught sleeping would receive the death penalty. Sergeant Elijah Elmer, Company C, was reduced in rank because he didn't answer roll call on time. They crossed the river and camped near Isleta Pueblo in the sand.

> This was Sunday, but we continued our march, stopping for nothing . . . camped on the Rio del Norte. The Spaniards brought to us apples, grapes, corn, and wine for sale, though at an exorbitant price. They seemed much delighted at the sight of our women and would crowd before us in such multitudes that I could hardly press my way through. They would cry: "Mujer 'Mericana quiere manzana?"—and give them apples. (William Coray)

Mon., Oct. 26, Valencia, New Mexico, 18 miles. Broken irrigation ditches caused deep mud on the roads and made walking difficult for both men and animals. "The mules are getting sore shoulders. I called up the captains and gave them a lecture on the subject, as to fitting and cleaning collars, shortening harness, etc., and relieving mules, about to become galled" (Philip St. George Cooke).[18] Camped near Los Chavez and secured bushels of corn and a cartload of firewood. The natives said Indians had come the day before to their village and had driven off their sheep and goats.

Tues., Oct. 27, Belen, New Mexico, 12 miles. Walked along in the rain all day and saw snow far away on the mountains. Passed through Belen where there was a large Catholic church with steeple bells. Lots of goats, sheep, and hogs. Belen residents wouldn't sell the army any mules. The tents were pitched in a dry river bottom. Enough bread for a couple of days was baked at night. Phebe Brown collected any burned bread after each meal and gave it to her son, Zemira.[19] Colonel Cooke bought nearly a cord of wood for six dollars.

Wed., Oct. 28, Bosque, New Mexico, 10 miles. Cold rain slowed the morning departure. They left at nine o'clock and marched until four in the afternoon. The rain settled the sand and made the road better. All were wet and cold. As they walked along, they sang Levi Hancock's song:

> How hard to starve and wear us out,
> Along this sandy desert route.

Thurs., Oct. 29, La Joya, New Mexico, 12 miles. As they left La Joya, they marched into the sand dunes and crossed high bluffs and the Rio Puerco before camping in cottonwoods south of La Joya. The condition of the animals remained very poor. Because of the continuous rain, everything was wet and they could not build fires to cook supper. They ate the bread they baked the night before. Their clothes were damp and cold.

Fri., Oct. 30, San Acacia, New Mexico, 12 miles. They traveled in sand dunes that reached from the Rio Grande to the mountains. It took them two hours to cross the dunes and twenty men on ropes and double teams to get the wagons through only three hundred to four hundred paces. Traveled on a grassy bottom before Polvadera. Here they had to cross a large canal and used hoes and spades to make a road across it. Saw a cotton patch. Many Mexicans entered camp to barter. "Their land for cultivation is enclosed by ditches, hedges, & adobe walls. On account of the dry Seasons in this country, they have to irrigate all this farming land, all their vineyards and orchards, which is done by leading the water from the River through ditches through all their grain and everything else that is raised or produced" (Henry G. Boyle).[20]

Sat., Oct. 31, Socorro, New Mexico, 13 miles. The bluffs were so close to the Rio Grande it was difficult to travel. In one place the men stood in cold water to pull the wagons around a bluff. Camped south of Socorro in a green valley near some old ruins. They left worn-out oxen by the side of the road for about the last twenty-five miles. Colonel Cooke decided to return three heavy ox wagons to Santa Fe. He mustered and inspected the battalion in the evening. "Left the settlements this day and the road too except Genl. Kearny's trail" (William Coray).

Sun., Nov. 1, 15 miles. Cooke called the troops to parade in the morning. He was hard on them because he said his orders were not being followed. Adjutant Dykes was appointed in charge of Company D to replace Captain Higgins, now in Pueblo. Cyrus Canfield was named first lieutenant in Company D and Philemon Merrill, Company D, was made adjutant. This boosted the men's morale as they felt Dykes went against them to gain favor with the battalion officers. "Came out on parade, heard an order read accepting the resignation of Adjt. Dykes and appointing P. C. Merrill in his stead. The object of Dykes in resigning was, no doubt, to supplant Capt. Higgins and take the command of Co. D, supposing that Capt. Higgins would be court martialed for not coming back before his furlough ran out" (William Coray).[21] William Hyde and Samuel Miles sold their mule to Merrill, which he needed in his new position. More sandy hills and bluffs close to the river. Camped on the Rio Grande. During the evening Lieutenant Smith bought three hundred sheep and cattle from traders. The sheep were in poor condition and half were lambs. Camped near timber.

    Mon., Nov. 2, Paraje de Fra Cristobal, New Mexico, 15 miles. Continued in the river bottom and camped at a watering place. They found a sign from General Kearny which pointed southwest and said "Mormon Trail." Merchant wagons were camped around a bend in the river. Eighty sheep were purchased by Lieutenant Smith. Colonel Cooke hired three Mexicans as drovers to be in charge of the 380 sheep.

    Tues., Nov. 3, New Mexico, 15 miles. Traveled along the river and camped on a high plain covered with "gama grass" and trees growing on the bottom land. They pushed wagons all day through sand and crossed bluffs, sandhills, and broken country. Wagon wheels cut tracks from three to twelve inches deep in the sand. During the day James Hampton became ill and was unable to walk further. He was placed in a wagon but his condition worsened. They stopped at two o'clock for twenty minutes and he died. When they reached camp that evening, a grave was dug. "Early this morning at reveille the corpse was borne in silence before the lines; all was silent and we were standing on an elevated point on the banks of the river, the occasional ripple of the waters and the barren and desolate land around us made the scenery solemn and produced a feeling of solemnity in almost every bosom" (David Pettegrew).[22]

    James Hampton was rolled in his blanket and buried in a lonely grave. He left his family in Illinois because they did not want to join the Mormons and go west.

    Levi Hancock complained the sick couldn't ride in wagons unless they reported for sick call. Then it was calomel. He blessed the sick each day. Rations were reduced to 10 oz. of pork and 9 oz. of flour. These smaller rations made the men angry:

Following Kearny's trail. . . . Our rations were reduced . . . and the reason assigned for this, according to the report of our principal guide was that we were yet 90 days from settlements, with less than 50 days rations and less than ¼ the no. of mules necessary for such a trip. I considered this open abuse. We were only 3 days from settlements where there was plenty of mules and provisions for sale. Why did he not quiz the guide before it was too late? Because he wanted to disencumber himself of baggage train and he wanted to make California as soon as possible in order to raise his name in the world by performing a trip with less means and less humanity than any other man. It was well for the old culprit that he had Mormons to deal with. No body else would have borne what we did. . . . And such were the hardships of the soldiers that they became very dissatisfied with their commander. (William Coray)

Wed., Nov. 4, Crawford Hollow, New Mexico, 18 miles. Passed stoney hills and some arroyos before camping south of San Jose Arroyo. During the day they were divided into groups of fifteen to twenty men for each wagon to help the mules pull the wagons through the rocks and sandy bottoms. There was an adobe-colored rock about thirty feet high on a bluff behind the camp. It looked like a church. The men were hungry, cross, and angry. Not only did they laboriously help the animals to move the wagons forward, but they were bearing the burden of ammunition, blankets, and other equipment to lighten the animals' loads. Two men in Company D, Robert Stewart and Philander Fletcher, were tied cross-handed to the rear of a slow ox wagon with large, heavy ropes on their hands and their knapsacks on their backs with dust and the heat of the sun upon them. Lieutenant Dykes, officer of the day, said they didn't show proper respect when he passed their guard duty at midnight. At the end of the day, the two had to stand five and one-half hours guard duty. This treatment really upset everyone:

The appearance was that he [Dykes] regarded not the lives of his brethren as he was willing to report against them for the most trifling offence with a view as it appeared of trying to please those in charge. The present prospect seems to be that indignant feelings are arising in the bosoms of many in the battalion in reference to the course Lieutenant Dikes is pursuing, which will hardly ease.[23] (William Hyde)

Thomas Woolsey, clad entirely in buckskin, arrived in the evening, after traveling from Santa Fe. He reported Captain Higgins, who had taken the first sick detachment to Pueblo, had received orders in Santa Fe from Colonel Sterling Price to remain in Pueblo with the family detachment. This settled the question about a court-martial for not returning to the battalion. He said there were fourteen families from Mississippi at Pueblo.

Thurs., Nov. 5, Rio Grande, New Mexico. The soldiers had marched seventeen days straight with no rest. Animals and men were exhausted. In addition, they suffered the discomfort of very stormy weather. Colonel Cooke declared a rest day. They bathed in the cold Rio Grande. Soap was scarce so they used a root called arinola sold by the Mexicans, which made good suds. The day of rest provided time to clean their guns. Clothing, now threadbare, was mended where possible. An old ox was butchered for supper, but the meat was not good, mostly bone and hide.

Fri., Nov. 6, near Elephant Butte, New Mexico, 11 miles. Continued down the Rio Grande over rock hills and sandy valleys. Shrubs were green and beautiful but very thorny. The thorns caught on clothes and often tore the skin on the men's legs. "The shrubbery covering the hills is mostly green and beautiful and much of it is very thorny, though they are strangers to me by name. By sight they familiarize themselves much faster than I wish. The familiarity and annoying acquaintance they make with my legs every day keeps my clothes in rags and often penetrate the skin" (Guy M. Keysor).[24]

This was where General Kearny abandoned his wagons and continued on with pack animals. Colonel Cooke ordered the battalion to break a new road around the western bank of the Rio Grande. The battalion wagons cut tracks for the first time on this land. Camped at southern end of a horshoe bend. It took a cow and twelve lambs to make out the ration for the evening meal.[25] Fearing a surprise attack, the men slept with their muskets at their sides. "Our course has been very irregular. Sometimes we marched 10 miles to gain 5. Such is the case today. The Rio del Norte presses its way through mountains of sand running to the southwest and how the Col. expects to get to California coursing this river through the sand I cannot imagine, but he is our leader and follow him we will, life or death" (William Coray).

Sat., Nov. 7, Rio Grande, New Mexico, 10 miles. The heavy sand required twenty men pushing and pulling each wagon in addition to the animals. The mules were so worn out they no longer had to be staked at night to keep them from wandering. There were many strange plants, which the men had never seen before. Around the campfire that night, they complained strongly to Colonel Cooke about the reduced rations. Abraham Day was put under guard for firing his gun in camp.

> This day nearly all the mules gave out. The men nearly worn out pushing on half rations. Every man was willing to take 10 days' rations on his back if the Col would leave the wagons. He said if the road did not get better within several days he would leave them, for he knew if they did not gain ground faster they would perish in the plains of Sonora or Chihuahua. (William Coray)

Sun., Nov. 8, Horse Island, New Mexico, 8 miles. A cold rainy night soaked animals, men, and tents. Marching began at 9 A.M. over a very bad trail. They continued to push and pull the wagons along with the animals. Everyone was very hungry. There were large mountains in the distance. The men called this place Council Point because it was here they tried to convince Colonel Cooke to leave the wagons. Guide Antoine Leroux returned after going about fifty miles. He reported deep sand ahead, which would make it almost impossible for the wagons.

Mon., Nov. 9, Rio Grande, New Mexico, 10 miles. A long, difficult winding hill started the day. The country was desolate and lonesome. It made the men want to pass through as soon as possible. They were even more fatigued from pulling the wagons in the heavy sand. Many were so weak they had to ride in the wagons. Another group of fifty-four men, who were ill, and one woman were selected to go to Pueblo with Lieutenant Wesley W. Willis leading them. The last ox wagons were left for Captain Burgwin to take back to Santa Fe. They were filled with extra camp kettles, mess pans, tent poles, and tents. Colonel Cooke wanted to cut down the weight in the wagons because of the poor condition of the animals. With the departure of the sick detachment, it was necessary to rearrange the messes into nine men to each tent. The tent poles were left behind, so the tents were to be supported by muskets. Leaving so many wagons made it necessary to pack one hundred pounds of supplies and equipment on the mules.

John Tippets thought the landscape looked "lonesome and desolate, no insects to be seen, not so mutch as a bird of any kind . . . I should not think that any live thing would stay here no longer than it would take them to git away."[26]

Tues., Nov. 10, Rio Grande, New Mexico, 15 miles. Lieutenant William W. Willis and his sick detachment left in midafternoon. William Hyde felt dividing the battalion was like "cutting the threads of life."[27] Sophia Tubbs was the only woman in the Willis company. Her husband, William, returned to Pueblo with her.[28] That left four women to continue, plus one child, Daniel Davis Jr. The boys serving as aides to the officers also continued.

The Willis company took one wagon, loaded with sick men and provisions, pulled by two worn-out mule teams. The sight of the sick men stowed away in the wagon like so many "dead hogs" was not a pleasant one. Levi Hancock shook hands with Lieutenant Willis and asked him to take good care of his charges. Tears streamed down their faces as the two men shook hands and parted. Thomas Woolsey was assigned to pilot them to Pueblo. After they left, the men remaining packed the oxen and mules. The oxen created quite a stir since they had not carried baggage before. They "kicked up before and reared up behind, they bellowed, whirled, and jumped in every direction."[29] At night Captains Hunt and Hunter and several others went to the Willis camp to administer to the sick and to wish them Godspeed once again. They spent the night and returned to the battalion the next morning.

Colonel Cooke figured he gained eight days' rations for the battalion by sending the Willis detachment to Pueblo. The rest of the command was anxious to continue and left about three o'clock in the afternoon.

This does in reality make solemn times for us, so many divisions taking place. May the God of Heaven protect us all. A new organization of messes took place today . . . roads still very bad, having to labor almost incessantly, helping the wagons through the sand. . . . This is now the 10th day we have been on ½ rations. Some rumors of our going to take the town of Sonora in the District of Sonora, in order to get a fresh supply of provisions, as it is thought impossible to cross the mountains to the Pacific sea with as little as we have now. (Henry Standage)[30]

Nov. 11, Seco Creek, New Mexico, 15 miles. The soldiers used their muskets as tent poles for the first time. They set the breeches on the ground in front and rear of the tent and put a peg in the muzzle for the ridge pole. The back of the tents were split and a gore inserted. This gave the tents a low pyramidal shape, while making them more roomy. They were six inches lower, but slept nine instead of six.

I did not like another separation but we could do no better. We durst not rebel for fear of after claps coming on the church. I do not know but it is for the best for they were mostly invalids who went back. I was obliged to have Mrs. Coray ride on a mule. The captain's [Hunter's] team was giving out and he wanted his load lightened. She rode all this day [on the mule] and was very much fatigued at night. (William Coray)

Thurs., Nov. 12, Rio Grande, New Mexico, 16 miles. Traveled up a canyon where they camped on a bluff near the Rio Grande, near present Williamsburg. Catfish for supper was a treat. William Coray felt the tension over dividing lessened during the day even though their hardships were great. He thought men other than Mormons would not continue under these circumstances. Colonel Cooke ordered three additional men, all suffering from illnesses, to catch up with the Willis company.[31] The total number sent to Pueblo in the three detachments was 159 men, 29 women, and 43 children. There were 335 men remaining to go to California.

At night several of the brethren organized themselves into a debating club to pass the evening hours. They seemed to have a good time in their "polemic" session.

Camped on the Rio Norte. The face of the country has not changed, neither the timber or anything else. I discovered, as I was riding

along, that the face of the ground was covered with broken pieces of
earthenware. . . . All things go on in the battalion in good order,
although our hardships are great, such as any other people would
not stand, half fed, pushing wagons through deep sand. Lt. Dykes of
D Co. has settled down quietly in his office and contents himself
with being the object of odium and disgust in the battalion.
(William Coray)

Fri., Nov. 13, Foster's Hole, New Mexico, 20 miles. After following the
Rio Grande for several weeks, the troops took a last look at the river and
turned southwest toward the Pacific Ocean. Colonel Cooke found a note
on a pole from the guide Leroux giving directions for their route, which
had many miles of desert ahead. After a long difficult march, they
reached a water hole at the head of a canyon. The water was in a stone cis-
tern at the bottom of perpendicular rocks on three sides. To get to the
water, the men followed a narrow, winding course down. At the bottom
there were about twelve rock steps to climb down to the water. It had to be
dipped out and poured in holes below to water the cattle. This was a long,
tedious job for a group this size. They named it Foster's Hole after one of
the guides.[32]

Perhaps it would be well for me to record the history of every day
occurences. Our march was attended with very great fatigue. We had
to be up generally two hours before daylight to get breakfast. The
trumpet would be blown at the first appearance of day. This is called
the assembly, but the drummers and fifers would set in immediately
and play reveille, not at full length and the men must all be in ranks
before it ceased or receive an extra tour of guard. The first sergeants
called the rolls of the companies and detailed the guard under the
inspection of an officer. Within 15 minutes the sick call was made. 5
minutes before this the morning reports must be handed in to the Adjt.
30 minutes after sick call guard mounting must be attended to.
Immediately after guard mounting the signal was to the teamsters to
get up the teams. All hands laid to help them till we were ready to
start. Then the companies were divided into equal parts under the
superintendence of officers or N.C. officers to boost at wagons all
day. These were every day occurences. (William Coray)

Sat., Nov. 14, Jug Valley, New Mexico, 18 miles. On the way out of the
valley, they passed small hills before coming to a vast plain with a singular
round mound in its midst. There was gama and buffalo grass as far as
they could see. Mountains surrounded this trackless desert. They went
upstream on a creek to camp for night and discovered a rock foundation
of an ancient building with five rooms. Pottery shards were strewn about.

Azariah Smith's eyes were sore again, so his father stood guard for him part of the night.

> Here we are approaching rugged mountains searching out a route for wagons in an unknown region, a trackless desert—no one present having ever been here before. The pilots were very expeditious and spared no fatigue or pains to search out the road for us to go. It seemed that we must follow down the ridge of mountains which we are now butting against, running from north to south. Everything seemed to forbid our passing through and we must go at least farther down. This place is beautiful in the extreme, covered with grass, though it dries up in the winter it retains all its nourishment the year round. The weather changed quite cool toward night and commenced raining so that it was uncomfortable. (William Coray)

Sun., Nov. 15, White Ox Creek, New Mexico. A double rainbow appeared after sunrise and cold winds blew off the snow on the mountains. Rested here for the day. When Ephraim Hanks and his mess hunted antelope, they found white grapes in an abandoned vineyard. A small detail, including Daniel Henrie, was sent back for an old white draft ox that had been left behind to die. When they found the animal, they pulled bunch grass and hand-fed the ox. They put water from their canteens into Henrie's hat so the poor old thing could drink. Finally with much hoisting and coaxing, they got the emaciated animal to its feet and back to camp, where the quartermaster ordered it killed and rationed out to the men. The ox was so poor, lacking fat, that the meat was jellylike, which some men wouldn't eat. They named this place White Ox Creek. "Having to do so much duty when in camp & having to march nearly every day, I have but little time to write. Therefore, I cannot notice as much in my journal as I would be pleased to. I would like to describe the appearance of the Country I am passing through if I had time, but I have it not" (Henry G. Boyle).[33]

Mon., Nov. 16, White Ox Creek, New Mexico, 18 miles. After traveling a fairly level road through foothills, they reached a swampy water hole. A rock formation that looked like a fort wall was on a nearby hill. Charbonneau returned this evening and reported finding a pass through the mountains. Levi Hancock told the men not to whip their animals or swear so much. He said the meat would be better to eat when it was butchered if the animals hadn't been beaten. He suggested the men imitate Abraham Hunsaker, Company D, as he didn't whip much or swear any and had a mild spirit.

> Very cold this morning, quite winter weather. The wind blew from the snowy mountain's top. Though the sun shone bright upon us, it

chilled us through, the change being so great from the last 2 or 3 days. . . . I was told the Apache Indians often encamped here. One of the pilots returned and reported a pass through. . . . We were glad to hear this, as we feared it would cost us many days if we marched around it. (William Coray)

Tues., Nov. 17, Cooke's Spring, New Mexico, 6 miles. A clear, crisp morning. Passed through a rocky canyon and came to another spring. There were thirty-six cone-shaped holes cut into a large rock, which may have been used with mortars for pounding or to catch water. Several soldiers, who had done mining, thought the holes might have been used for extracting gold. They were six to ten inches across, and ten to fourteen inches deep. Nearby were many drawings on the rocks. There were animals, lightning streaks, circles, and other figures, all belonging to an ancient people. The men decided these drawings might have been made by the ancient people in the Book of Mormon. The men thought the streams were peculiar in this part of the country because they disappeared in the sand as they descended from their fountain. A large cache of antelope and deer skins, nicely cured and stored in some rocks near camp, was found, but was not disturbed. The skins were left as the men found them.[34] Brigham Young had counseled them to respect the property of others. In this case, it must have been hard with many of them needing covering for their feet.

We marched to the 6 mile spring which was in the midst of the mountains. Much curiosity was excited by the strangeness of this lonely unfrequented portion of God's creation, seen only by the wild Apaches and the fleety antelope, their prey. We could plainly see where the mountains have been rent from each other and thrown up at a tremendous height. There is one which Capt. Hunter, myself and our wives visited, (south which stands full 2,000 ft. high) split open at the top a good way down, leaving a large cavity through which the air sucks so that it is almost impossible to stand there. The vegetable kingdom seems also engaged in producing strange things to the traveler's astonishment, such as muscale and pedistol and other vegetables which I have not time here to describe. I can say that while others fancied the flesh of wild animals I feasted upon the beauties of nature and thus passed away the time in the Mountains of Chihuahua, New Mexico. (William Coray)

The first California partridge was observed. They are rounder, smoother, and have longer necks than ours, with a beautiful plume to the head, and are slate colored. Also a cactus of hemispherical form, fifteen to eighteen inches in diameter with ridges armed with horny hooks three inches long. (Philip St. George Cooke)[35]

Wed., Nov. 18, Indian Ruins, New Mexico, 20 miles. Started at daybreak and traveled over a rolling prairie toward a river. After several hours they finally saw the Mimbres River but had to continue eight miles to reach its banks. Men and animals were worn out. Food and water were scarce. All day they seemed to misjudge distances. William Coray said ascending ground made objects seem farther away, while descending land made objects seem much closer. They camped on the west bank of the river, surrounded by cottonwood trees. Just below their camp the river disappeared into the sand. Guide Foster returned to report water was twenty-five miles ahead.

Thurs., Nov. 19, Rio Mimbres, New Mexico, 18 miles. Although starting at 7 A.M. it took nearly two hours to cross the river. A broken wagon caused the delay. They finally reached a small, stinking water hole. Cooke increased rations to 10 oz. flour and ¾ lb. of fresh meat. The mules were worn out. Camped near some abandoned copper mines. Although the grass was dry, its stalks were juicy and the mules and cattle seemed to like it.

Fri., Nov. 20, Rio Mimbres (Cow Springs), New Mexico. The guides couldn't find a trail westward. None of them had been on this route before. Cooke and the guides climbed to the top of a high mound and built a fire as a distress signal. Within a few hours two Mexican traders came galloping in, each carrying lances. The Mexicans sold dried beef to a few of the men. Then several Apache Indians came. They all had seen the distress signal. The Indians explained the trails and sold Cooke eight good mules. The Mexicans told of a trail that ran south from Cow Springs to Janos in northern Sonora. Cooke had been ordered to find a practicable wagon route. After talking to the Mexicans it seemed the southeasterly route, known to have both fodder for the animals and settlements with food for the men, seemed the best route to follow. Later in the day Cooke summoned the company officers to explain his decision to go to Janos. The colonel said the provisions were disappearing. Captain Hunt told him the men were very hungry and rations were insufficient. As a result, rations were increased to 10 oz. flour and ¼ lb. of poor beef per man, still an inadequate diet. David Pettegrew thought Cooke might be leading the battalion into Mexico to get whiskey and tobacco, so in the evening he and Levi Hancock visited each tent and asked everyone to pray that Cooke would not lead them into Mexico.

We remained here on the 20th by order of the commander in consequence of the pilots finding no water ahead so they made it a day of council and raised a smoke signal which is a signal of distress to the Indians. . . . Within less than two hours Spaniards [and Indians] came to the signal to see what was the matter. These Spaniards . . . seemed to know the way some 200 miles. One of them was employed to go as a pilot as far as he knew the way. They said it was 300 miles to the Pima Village one way and 200 miles another. One way took them by Sonora, New Mexico, and the other took them to the headwaters of the Gila River through a trackless range of mountains. These traders reported that there was an army of men coming from Sonora on their way to Chihuahua and Santa Fe to retake that country from the Mexicans. After hearing the Spaniard deliberate upon the matter which was the best the Col. concluded that he would consult Capts. Hunt and Hunter upon the matter. They told him they would have nothing to say about it, that he must take the responsibility upon himself. (William Coray)

Sat., Nov. 21, Rio Mimbres, New Mexico, 12 miles. After marching a few miles southward toward Janos in Sonora, Mexico, Cooke stopped on a mound. When he saw the trail curving to the southeast, he told the men his orders from Kearny were to go to California. Then he ordered the bugler to blow orders to turn westward. When David Pettegrew heard the bugle, he shouted, "God bless the colonel." Most felt this was an answer to their prayers. Others thought Cooke wasn't as hungry as they were and so altered the course to avoid main settlements. In the evening Captain Hunt gave a talk and accused John D. Lee of interfering in battalion business. The men agreed Lee freely gave his opinion on different problems when he came to collect the soldiers' pay. Lee had left October 19 and was not there to defend himself.

There was a little difficulty in the camp this night arising from Nathan Young, Capt. Hunter's servant, buying meat from the quartermaster's negro in a secret manner and being caught at it. The negro denied selling the meat and said he [Nathan] stole it. So the Col. had him [Nathan] tied up to a wagon wheel all night and made to starve also. During the night he turned the wheel and laid down and the Col. put the sentinel under arrest for suffering it to be so done.[36] (William Coray)

Sun., Nov. 22, South of Black Mountain, New Mexico, 20 miles. Left midmorning with men walking double file in front of the wagons, just far enough apart to make a path for the wagon wheels. At the end of an hour, the lead company and teams halted to allow the next company to take its turn at breaking the road. This gave all an equal share of the burden. In the afternoon a smoke signal from guide Leroux told of water. It was too far away to reach before night. This was a day of suffering for the men and many teams gave out. To make it even more aggravating, during the after-noon sometimes they saw a lake that looked like a sea of water; other times it appeared to be a river, only a short distance ahead. They never could gain on it as it always remained about the same distance ahead. It was a mirage. Camped south of a black mountain. One pair of oxen was mired in the sand, so Samuel Rogers and others took the yoke off and one ox got out. When the men put a rope around the other ox, they broke its neck. This made a serious problem, so the men prayed and next morning there was a pair of steers with the oxen. To the desperate men, this seemed to be divine intervention in their behalf. Two batches of salt-rising bread were prepared. One man stayed up all night watching the risings so the bread could be baked the next morning. Since there was no wood, they cooked with weeds.

Charbonneau, the guide, came into camp, packing his saddle and pistols on his back. When he stopped to let his mule graze, the animal kicked him, and ran off. When he couldn't catch the animal, he shot the mule to save his saddle and pistols from falling into the hands of the Apache Indians.

Mon., Nov. 23, Black Mountain, New Mexico, 17 miles. A beautiful sun-rise appeared as they passed the black mountain. When they reached the water hole Leroux had signaled about, Cooke let his white mule and other staff animals drink first before the soldiers. This drained the pool, so the men had to lay on the ground lapping the water like dogs as it seeped out from the rocks. Others captured the water with their spoons or sucked it through quills. Captain Hunt was very upset about not having water for the men first and told Cooke in hard words. One of the pilots returned and reported water was thirteen miles ahead. Some remained here while others continued on, many fainting along the way. They had traveled about forty miles without water to this point. Camp was pitched by a spring next to a dry lake with Mexican traders nearby. The blanket wagon did not arrive, which meant a cold, uncomfortable night. A few sol-diers carried kegs of water back to their comrades who had fallen along the way. Several teams gave out. "Oh, how everyone suffered for water this day" (Samuel Rogers).[37]

Daniel Dennett cut narrow strips along both edges of his belt and chewed the leather, hoping to obtain a little nourishment as well as mois-ture in his mouth and throat. They learned that carrying a small stone in their mouths seemed to make them less thirsty. (Nearly sixty years later, when Melissa Coray died, her family found a small, round, smooth peb-ble, carefully wrapped in tissue, among her possessions. It was the stone she had carried at times in her mouth on her march with the Mormon Battalion. She told her grandchildren it seemed to help if they didn't think about how thirsty they were as they walked along.)

Tues., Nov. 24, Dry Pond, New Mexico. The men straggled in all night. Cooke purchased twenty mules from Mexicans they met. The men bought dried beef from them. Henry Bigler thought it was the best meat he'd ever eaten even though the men suspected it was horse flesh because it was so fat and oily. Stayed over for men and beasts to rest. Colonel Cooke hired a Mexican to guide the battalion. A mule in Company B failed. William Coray sold one of his for thirty dollars to replace it. The Mexicans said there were plenty of wild cattle at the San Bernardino Rancho. John R. Murdock, who drove the colonel's baggage wagon, became sick and could not drive the wagon further. "After so long and hard a tramp for 2 days without water, it was thought wisdom to stay here a day and wait for the men who are yet behind. They arrived in camp in good season safe" (William Coray).

Wed., Nov. 25, Playas Lake (Animas Range), 25 miles. Crossed the divide covered with pine and oak, close under a mountain peak of granite. It was long and narrow, and the mules and oxen broke down. Camped about sunset by a small stream in a sycamore grove. Two antelope and several deer were shot. The guide Charbonneau was a little ahead when he came upon three grizzly bears. He killed the most ferocious one and then was able to escape the other two by climbing on a rock. The bear was so big the men put it in a wagon to bring it into camp. With lots of wood available, they feasted on bear, antelope, and deer. They also saw a flock of quail with pretty top knots. Henry G. Boyle drank too much water upon arriving in camp because he was warm and very thirsty. He became violently ill. Since he was scheduled for guard duty, he had no choice but to report to Sanderson for the usual dose of calomel. Boyle spit it in the fire when he was out of the doctor's sight: "I attended Sick Call & was ordered by the Doctor to take a dose of Calomel & Quinine. I took the dose away with me, but did not take it in to my stomach."[38] Daniel Tyler and another soldier anointed him with oil and lay hands upon him with a blessing. He was well before the night was over. "The pass in the mountains was very difficult and the road somewhat impracticable; my wife rode a mule this day" (William Coray).

Thurs., Nov. 26, New Mexico, 22 miles. "We marched down the valley in a southerly direction. The country was rough in places and showed signs of being a rich mineral country. The gold blossom was to be seen in many places. The timber is yet scarce, what there is is nothing but scrubby oak. Our feelings were pretty well about this time, though the rations were scant indeed. The game was very plentiful such as antelope and deer" (William Coray).

Fri., Nov. 27, Bercham's Draw, New Mexico, 15 miles. The night was the coldest they had experienced since leaving Council Bluffs. They marched over flat tableland into a beautiful valley. Prairie dogs barked as they passed. At night they had a feast of antelope and a black-tailed deer, killed by Thomas Kirk, both roasted in a dug-out pit. Azariah stayed up until one o'clock in the morning baking bread. "While I am writing this I am comfortably seated in my tent while my wife is cooking supper by a fire made of brush in a pit, which we commonly dig to save wood" (William Coray).

Sat., Nov. 28, Cloverdale Springs, New Mexico, 6 miles. Traveled through a small gap in the mountains. After several miles across the Animas tableland, they reached a massive cliff that looked down into rocks and arroyos of the mountains. Camped back from the cliff and dug for water. Robert Bliss climbed a nearby hill and said they were "hemmed in by mountains" on all sides. The guides didn't know the way to the pass. A drunk Apache chief, brought in by Leroux, told them they were on the right trail. Cooke decided to go over the cliff. In the evening they baked bread. A light rain fell during the night. "There is considerable sickness in the camp at present. Capt. Davis was taken sick two days since and remains very ill up to this date. He is under the doctor's care. About sundown the pilots returned with two Apache Indians and informed the Lt. Col. that the place which we thought was impassable was the only way for us to go" (William Coray).

Sun., Nov. 29, Guadalupe Mountains, New Mexico, 8 miles. All provisions were taken out of the wagons and put on pack animals.

This was a fair day. By orders of Cooke nearly one hundred fifty mules were packed and sent on nine miles with Dykes' company as a detachment. These mules returned the same day. The object of this was to lighten the wagons that they might take them down the declivity after the way was prepared, which was done by adding 20 men to the Pioneer company under Lt. Stoneman, 1st Dragoons. By hard labor they made the way passable so that wagons could be taken down in the morning. (William Coray)

Mon., Nov. 30, Guadalupe Mountains, New Mexico, 9 miles. The wagons had to be let down by hand with ropes over the ledges. Two or four teams of mules pulled the wagons with fifteen men grasping the ropes tied to the rear axle to keep the wagons from going into animals. One wagon in Company A snapped and was abandoned, but the others made it through. Traveled until they caught up with their provisions and set up camp. Henry Bigler thought "No other man but Cooke would have attempted to cross such a place with wagons."[39]

After the tents were up, pilot Foster arrived and said he had found the pass about three miles away. Cooke became angry, said the guides were "ignorant of this country." Azariah bought a butcher knife from Samuel Rogers for 37½ cents.

The Pioneers marched early to commence on the road, 25 in number. The whole train followed soon and descended the declivity with

Guadalupe Pass, Cooke's Wagon Road. Sepia by John Russell Bartlett, courtesy of the John Carter Brown Library at Brown University, Providence, Rhode Island.

Pass of the Dome, San Bernardino Rancho, Mexico. Lithograph from Andrew Belcher Gray, *Southern Pacific Railroad: Survey of a Route for the Southern Pacific R.R., on the 32nd Parallel* (1856); courtesy of the California History Room, California State Library, Sacramento, California.

little accident, though it required 10 or 15 men in some places with ropes to keep the wagons right side up, with care, they being empty at that. They were till night from 8 o'clock going 9 miles where we encamped on a small rivulet in the midst of the mountains. In this hollow, the trees were as green as in spring. (William Coray)

Tues., Dec. 1, Arizona, 10 miles. Traveled in a westerly direction through evergreens, cottonwoods, and blue ash. The roadbed was rocky and sandy with large tufts of grass and thorny bushes. William Coray enjoyed the rugged beauty of the broken mountains and jagged rocks with green grasses and sycamores, colored brightly by the frost. In the evening they discovered herds of wild cattle nearby. The cattle had run wild since the Apaches drove the Mexicans from this part of the country. "The appetites of the men have become so sharp that they now eat beef hides, tripe, feet, heads and entrails, in fine, everything that can be eaten" (Samuel Rogers).[40]

Cooke climbed a hill and saw San Bernardino Valley. Henry Bigler had been ailing for several days. Yesterday he hired a messmate to do his duty because every muscle in his body was sore and felt like he had been beaten with a club. He still had some ginger he got at Ft. Leavenworth and made tea with it, hoping it would make him feel better. "Some of the brethren went out hunting; four laid out over night. One of them [John Allen] has not returned yet. We suppose he is lost" (William Coray).

Wed., Dec. 2, Guadalupe Arroyo, Arizona, 12 miles. Traveled northwest across a plain. There were four pairs of mules to each wagon. The air was cold and penetrating. They left the arroyo and climbed bluffs westward to San Bernardino Valley. Camped near ruins of an abandoned ranch. Indians, wearing plumes and feathers, came to camp with cooked roots to sell. The roots were baked underground with hot stones and were sweet and nutritious. They refused money, wanted to barter. Cooke offered a knife and a few yards of material, but they chose blankets, clothing, and buttons that some men cut off their shirts. Ephraim Green, reduced and weak from starvation, lost his reason. A tragic accident nearly occurred during the night when Lieutenant George P. Dykes, officer of the day, attempted to catch the night guards not attending to duty. He slipped inside the area where the guns were stacked. Henry Boyle, the sentinel on duty, thinking it was an enemy invader, cocked and loaded his gun. He was ready to pull the trigger when he recognized Dykes.

Marched . . . across a large plain of sand. Camped at San Bernardino, the deserted Spanish town. This place has been vacated 15 years. The Apache Indians drove them [Mexicans] away and scattered their cattle, which cattle are here running wild now in large herds to be seen at any time we choose to go out of the camp. The

Indians met us here with a few mules and some horses which they offer for a blanket each, but the Col. forbid us trading with them till the quartermaster has his supply, but the quartermaster did not get his supply because he wanted the animals for less than they were worth and the Indians know it well. This evening the lost man, John Allen, returned half naked and almost used up. He said he had wandered three or four days before he found track or trace of us, that the Indians robbed him of his gun and clothes and he finally got here safe, but very ill indeed. (William Coray)

Left the valley and entered a plain, traveled ten miles and camped at a deserted village in another valley. The place had been occupied by Mexicans who had been driven out by the Apache Indians. The place was called San Bernardino Ranch and was built like the other Mexican houses we have seen; this was the 31st day since we saw a house . . . wild cattle abound in this section, some hunters . . . returned bringing in the carcasses of 4 wild cattle . . . The Indians have brought in some mescal ready cooked, which is sweet and good. The Indians seem friendly, they are hearty, robust and intelligent. (Samuel H. Rogers)[41]

Thurs., Dec. 3, San Bernardino Ranch, Mexico. Stayed over to wash clothes, rest, and trade with Apaches, and to kill some of the wild cattle. The soldiers shot several wild animals and brought in choice meat for a feast. Cooke and his staff weighed the commissary provisions and found fifty-one days of rations remained. Current daily rations were 10 oz. of flour, 1fl lb. of meat, and 10 oz. of pork. "We remained at this place all day to give the hunters a swing among the wild cattle as we were quite scant in rations. It came in very good. In the evening they reported about 20 killed and brought 7 or 8 into camp" (William Coray). "We feel hungry all the time, we never get enough" (Henry G. Boyle).[42]

Fri., Dec. 4, San Bernardino Ranch, Mexico, 6 miles. The morning was spent drying a lot of wild beef. Frames were made from mesquite to jerk the beef. There was no salt, but the dry desert air helped. Suddenly Cooke ordered camp to move out at noon. More time was needed for the meat to cure. The men were upset by the sudden change of plans. When they left at 2 P.M., the guard didn't douse the fire well and the prairie burned behind them. Camped between two mountains, with plenty of wood and water. Cooke issued orders the soldiers were not to leave the column while marching or camp at night. Their muskets were not to be used to fire at game. No one liked these orders as the animals were wild, and if they charged, there could be serious consequences if they had no protection. Several Indians brought a couple hundred pounds of fat meat the men found to be delicious. Cooke learned today Company B had a private wagon that carried the men's equipment. When he was told it was a private wagon, he said he didn't give a "damn" and ordered the men to carry their own knapsacks and blankets. The soldiers were angry. William Hyde said it was a "small streak in the colonel, proportioned somewhat after the shape of his body, which was about six feet tall and about the size of a mud wasp at the waist."[43]

Whenever Robert Bliss didn't have any ink to write with, he poked his arm and used the blood to write in his journal. Oliver Workman watched him write with his blood and since then Robert's journal was referred to as the "blood journal."[44] William Coray used a quill pen and ink for his journal. He bought these writing supplies at Fort Leavenworth and kept them in a box in the baggage wagon.

> On the morning of the 4th Col. Cooke came out with another order, stating that we had wasted 6 days' rations and there was enough left to take us at 10 oz. per day, which statement was a lie indeed. We marched at 1 o'clock and gained 6 miles; the orders were to kill no more beef cattle till the 9th in consequence of there being so much on hand. This evening the Lt. Col. told the adjt. not to receive any on guard who had not their knapsacks on, neither should they ride if they had horses. This I called tyranny in the extreme. (William Coray)

Sat., Dec. 5, Agua Prieta, Mexico, 15 miles. Crossed low mountains and saw thousands of wild cattle. Then came a rocky climb up a large knoll. One wagon broke down, leaving fifteen government wagons. Went through a valley covered with desert scrub and wild cattle. Four bulls were killed. Captain Hunter told his wife, Lydia, they were young heifers so she would enjoy the meat. Because cattle were so plentiful, most of the carcasses were left and only the best cuts used. Camped by a spring. Daniel Tyler became ill but hid in the tall grass until the command all had passed to avoid going to see Dr. Sanderson. By this time Sanderson's calomel had given out and he was substituting arsenic.[45]

> Passed through another range of mountains and camped at a sulphur spring. There were many wild cattle here and Capt. Hunter, Lts. Merrill and Barrows [Ruel Barrus] and myself went out to kill a bullock or two for ourselves by permission of the Col. We succeeded in killing two and bringing the stake into camp though not till sometime after dark. (William Coray)

Sun., Dec. 6, Mexico, 16 miles. A miserable day cutting road through mesquite brush, pelted with a heavy, cold sleet. Mesquite and thorny bushes tore their skin and clothing. Camped on a little stream running through ash, oak, and black walnut trees, plenty of wood. Elisha Smith, a teamster, was very ill. Guards stood on nearby ridges to watch over animals and camp while large wolves roamed around sometimes only a few feet away, making the night frightful with their howls. They seemed to smell death in the camp. Very cold rain continued throughout the night.

Mon., Dec. 7, Little Ash Creek, Arizona. No traveling today. Stayed over to dry out and to allow the guides to go ahead and find a camping place. They washed clothes, mended garments, and smoked beef over ash and walnut fires.

As the teams were so fatigued, we laid by here the 7th and I went hunting again with Capt Hunter and Barrow [Ruel Barrus]. We saw nothing but bulls. We suppose the Indians had selected out the cows and calves as they were tender. When we got into camp, the soldiers were making preparation for an early march. The pilots had returned and said the San Pedro River was within 30 miles. The pilot, Weaver, professed to be acquainted all the way. After we got to the San Pedro we had some reason to entertain some fears from Sonora as we were drawing near her borders. We are now within 12 miles of a Spanish Garrison [Tucson] and one of the sheep drivers ran away on the night of the 6th being a Spaniard. We have some reasons to believe that he has gone to inform them of our approach and numbers. The Sonora army is nearly 5,000 strong. We could expect nothing less than capture if we go among them in their thickly settled country. (William Coray)

Tues., Dec. 8, Little Ash Creek, Arizona, 18 miles. Elisha Smith died during the early morning and was buried four rods north of Ash Creek. The men piled a lot of brush on top of his grave and burned it to keep hungry wolves and grave diggers away. A prayer was said and Levi Hancock sang a song he had composed previously. After the burial, they traveled on hard barren ground, which made a good road bed, and crossed a few small hills before reaching a broad valley. They walked into a stiff wind all day, which irritated their eyes and breathing. They were in sight of snow on the mountain. Camped at a dry river fork where there was no water. Wild horses, cattle, and one antelope were seen.

Wed., Dec. 9, San Pedro Valley, Arizona, 16 miles. The march began soon after sunrise. About noon they reached the San Pedro River which had fish in it and traveled downstream about six miles. The men were talking about reaching Tucson, a military garrison, and then the seventy-mile desert beyond they would have to travel to reach the Indian villages. The animals had improved on the dry, dead-looking grass and more water.

Thurs., Dec. 10, San Pedro Valley, Arizona, 14 miles. Traveled along the river and camped at an abandoned village, with only its walls standing. A few men left the column against the rules to hunt and fish. Fish hooks were hard to come by and cost a lot. Many bulls were neck deep in the brush. Albert Smith and John Lawson went after the meat of a wild bull killed earlier in the day. A cold, wet snow during the day caused much suffering.

> Camped on the same San Pedro. As the command passed along I struck off to the right in company with Bro. [William] Spencer to kill a fat bull if possible. We marched out of sight of the battalion and got among the cattle behind a mountain and gave them chase. After firing a good many shots, we killed one and by the time we got loaded up to start to the camp it was nearly night. I supposed the battalion 12 miles ahead, but luckily it hove in sight after we had passed over the first hill. Very much to my surprise I got home before dark. (William Coray)

Fri., Dec. 11, San Pedro River, Arizona, 12 miles. After winding through small hills for a couple of hours, they began going back down to the river bottom. As they neared the river some wild bulls got in with the cattle and were killed by the sheep drovers.[46] When the companies stopped at the San Pedro for water, other bulls, frightened at the smell of blood, charged into the soldiers. The rampaging bulls charged on and on. There was great confusion and fear. The bulls charged men, mules, and wagons. Albert Smith was trapped between a bull's horns. He was badly bruised and had three ribs partially severed from his backbone. One bull caught Amos Cox and gored his thigh before tossing him in the air. Levi Fifield had no wagon or tree for protection and threw himself flat on the ground when a bull charged him. The bull jumped over Fifield, leaving the soldier frightened but unharmed. Paymaster Jeremiah Cloud's pack mule was gored to death. Lieutenant Stoneman was reloading his rifle, when two bullets fell into a cylinder causing one ball to misfire. It ripped off the upper joint of Stoneman's thumb.

There was so much dust from the charging that it was difficult to see for a few minutes. When the dust cleared and the bulls had passed, three men were wounded and three mules were gored to death. Several wagons were tipped over and a couple were damaged from the charging. One bull charged Cooke, who was riding his big white mule.

> I saw an immense coal black bull charge on Corporal Frost, Company A. He stood his ground while the animal rushed right on for one hundred yards. I was close by and believed the man in great danger to his life and spoke to him. He aimed his musket very deliberately and only fired when the beast was within ten paces; and it fell headlong, almost at his feet. . . . We crossed a pretty stream which I have called "Bull Run." (Philip St. George Cooke)[47]

Cooke said Corporal Frost was "one of the bravest men he ever saw."

Henry Standage and Sanford Porter had stayed behind to fish for salmon. They arrived on the scene after the excitement was over. They counted nine dead bulls in one place, but it is not known exactly how many others were killed. After the stampede, it took a while to settle down and get the animals quieted. They traveled briefly up the river and camped.

Sat., Dec. 12, San Pedro River, Arizona, 15 miles. As they followed the river, the road got rougher. They could not use all the wild beef killed and there was not time to dry it. Albert Smith suffered greatly from his injury. Amos Cox could not walk due to his injury, but he declined going on sick report to avoid Dr. Sanderson's "cure-all." Guide Leroux returned with a report on Tucson, which was about thirty-six miles away. Leroux said there were two hundred soldiers stationed there. The battalion passed around the old Presidio of Santa Cruz de Terrenate, founded in 1775 and abandoned after four years because of hostile Indians and harsh weather.

Sun., Dec. 13, along San Pedro River, Arizona, 8 miles. After the nooning stop, Colonel Cooke ordered his charges to muster. The soldiers didn't drill to his liking and he swore at them profusely. Each man was given twenty cartridges to practice hitting targets. He also drilled them to go from a line to a column and back to a line. Even after additional drilling, he still wasn't satisfied with the results. Cooke told the men they were to go through Tucson in peace, that as soldiers they were to show justice and kindness to the unarmed. He also reminded them to hold property of individuals sacred.

Mon., Dec. 14, Santa Cruz River, Arizona, 20 miles. Reveille at 4 A.M. with an early start. Left the river and labored up bluffs before going down to a wash. They walked on firm sand covered with grass and prickly cactus, following a trail along an arroyo, camped near a distillery where Indians and Mexicans made cactus whisky called mescal: "Some of the men tasted the whisky and say it is poor stuff" (Henry W. Bigler).[48]

Encamped near the distillery. The pilots called it only 18 miles but I call it 20. We were met by seven Mexican Dragoons from the Garrison, who wanted to know our intentions, whether it was to kill, destroy and take prisoners or to pass through peaceable to which the Lt. Col replied that it was to pass through in peace, that we did not come to make war on Sonora though he was able to demand a surrender, he should not do so but wished to trade with them for provisions and mules as we were quite destitute. They said their citizens were leaving in fear and in haste, but the Col. desired them to detain their people which they promised to do, acknowledging their weakness and inability to compete with us in any shape. In the meantime, Dr. Foster was detained and we knew not why. (William Coray)

Tues., Dec. 15, Pantano Wash, Arizona, 15 miles. The Apaches had spread rumors that a large army was coming. The Mexicans at the distillery said this alarmed them and the Mexicans in Tucson. Cooke assured those at the distillery that they were friendly Americans. The Mexicans had corn and meal to sell. The distillery was a curious sight, consisting of animal-skin tubes and earthen jars. To the men it was a muddy, filthy place. The battalion continued to a spring and then climbed up to a plain covered with thousands of giant cactus with arms, which impressed Colonel Cooke: "Another extraordinary variety of cactus was seen which should be called *columnar;* a straight column thirty feet high, near two feet in diameter, fluted very similarly to the Corinthian column, only the capital wanting; some throw out one or more branches, gracefully curved and then vertical, like the branches of a candelabrum."[49] Mexican messengers arrived from Tucson asking the troops to march around, not through the town. Tucson was a Mexican outpost for protection against Indians. They camped about sixteen miles away from the garrison.

At 12 o'clock at night Foster came into camp. He had been confined ever since he went there as a spy, but they liberated him at the arrival of this messenger, whereupon we liberated the Mexicans. We traveled this day through the most prickly, prongly, thorny country I ever saw. The prickles were in every shape imaginable. And though the mules were nearly worn out with fatigue, when they came to these prickleys, many of them acted very badly indeed and threw their riders. (William Coray)

Wed., Dec. 16, Tucson, Arizona, 16 miles. The mules got loose during the night, so rounding them up caused a late start in the morning. They noticed the prickly pear cactus for the first time, in all sizes with round-shaped leaves and very thorny. Some were very wide, but not too tall. As the army approached Tucson, Cooke ordered the men to load their muskets. Before entering, Cooke reminded everyone again to respect private rights and property.[50] When they reached Tucson, most of the inhabitants and soldiers had fled, leaving only the old and sick:

After a heavy day's march we came to the garrison of Tucson. We found the town sacked. The troops with nearly all the inhabitants had fled, taking with them their property. Those few who remained entreated us to save the town and preserve their property and we assured them we would do so. This place is well situated in a valley that resembles the valley at Santa Fe very much. Fruit of various kinds we found here. Gardens were neatly laid out with beautiful

Tucson can be seen in the upper right background. St Augustine Catholic Church
and the two-story building, mentioned by Colonel Cooke, are in the foreground.
Pencil and sepia wash by John Russell Bartlett, courtesy of the John Carter Brown
Library at Brown University, Providence, Rhode Island.

irrigation for watering purposes. Their houses were built of dobies as in Santa Fe. The people were more enterprising and happy, but their troops were cowards and their acts spoke for them. The wagons arrived before dark and we encamped ¾ miles north of town. A strong guard was posted out this night. All was well and quiet. I was sent to town by the officer of the day with three men. We ransacked [patrolled] the town and found all well and returned. (William Coray)

When we arrived here today we were tired, hungry, and thirsty almost beyond endurance. After we had encamped a Short time a few individuals made their appearance from whom we obtained some bread & beans in exchange for shirts & various kinds of clothing. (Henry G. Boyle)[51]

Like Santa Fe, Tucson is not seen until very close by. Of course, its adobe houses are the same in appearance but inferior. There is a wall with abutments and battlements in bad repair, which surrounds the barracks; it is on the highest ground. The town . . . is a more populous village than I had supposed, containing about five hundred . . . Beside the very large stone church above [San Xavier, nine miles south of Tucson] and an adobe one here [St. Augustine] there is another, very large [two-story] adobe at a small Indian village close by. (Philip St. George Cooke)[52]

The battalion passed through and camped on an irrigation ditch north of Tucson. The Mexicans were friendly and brought the soldiers beans and flour. Against the blue desert sky the stars and stripes were raised. They thought it might be the first American flag to fly over Tucson. Christopher Layton, Company C, hoisted the flag.[53]

No private property was disturbed, but the colonel found a public storage of wheat and took as much as the wagons could carry. Mexicans used stones pulled by small donkeys to grind the wheat. The Mormons ate the wheat, but many later suffered with diarrhea. They had some quinces and pomegranates, both highly enjoyable. Three bushels of salt also were obtained. They had been without salt for almost the entire trip. Some men bought flour and hid it in their packs so the colonel wouldn't find out. The animals were so worn out the colonel didn't want more weight put on them.

Cooke left a note for Señor Don Manuel Gandara, governor of Sonora:

Your Excellency: The undersigned, marching in command of a battalion of United States infantry from New Mexico to California, has found it convenient for the passage of his wagon train to cross the frontier of Sonora. . . . Be assured I did not come as an enemy of the people whom you govern; they have received only kindness at my hands. . . . Meanwhile I make a wagon road from the streams of the Atlantic to the Pacific ocean, through the valuable plains and mountains of Sonora. This, I trust, will prove useful to the citizens of either republic, who, if not more closely, may unite in the pursuits of a highly beneficial commerce. with sentiments of esteem and respect, I am,

Your Excellency's most obedient servant,
P. St. Geo. Cooke, Lt.-Col., U.S. Forces[54]

Thurs., Dec. 17, Tucson, Arizona.

We laid by all day except a detachment of 50 men, volunteers, who were called for some purpose. I among the rest stepped into the crowd and went along, not knowing where or what for, but heard it whispered that it was to pursue the enemy and get their field pieces and mules. We [the detachment of fifty men] marched 4 miles when the Col. ordered Stoneman to come back and tell us to load our guns, that we would undoubtedly have a fight and divided the company into 3 divisions, giving Lts. Canfield and Clift command of 2 divisions and myself command of the other. He told every man to stand for himself in a rout as that was the way. At the time I expected to fight certain and sure, but the good spirit showed the Col. his folly and we were ordered back just in time for we were then close to the enemy and we a handful and they a corps of 2 or 3 hundred. We seized the public wheat for horse and mule feed this afternoon, and took it to camp. After the usual ceremony we went to bed to be ready for a start in the morning. (William Coray)

During the night two of the guards, Albern Allen and his son, Rufus C. Allen, saw more men than the colonel's order allowed and fired warning shots. The entire battalion, under George Oman, officer of the day, quickly formed a line on both sides of the road. It turned out to be a false alarm:

About 12 o'clock at night a body of men came upon our picket guard advancing slowly and cautiously when Bro. Allen of Co. A. hailed and fired. The next to him fired also and ran to camp as soon as they could and informed Capt. Hunt of the fact. My tent being near enabled me to hear the whole story and I thought surely we must fight now. The alarm was given soon public, then the assembly beat and all the men were into ranks in one devil of a hurry, I tell you, though perfectly calm and without frustration. The battalion was fronted towards the enemy eagerly looking for them. As they did not come, the Lt. Col. ordered Co. A to march down to town and see if the enemy had approached that far, but no enemy came, being afrighted at the firing of guns by the sentinels and turned back. The guard was made doubly strong and the battalion dismissed with loaded pieces. I slept sound till morning being very fatigued. I could not help thinking of Mrs. Coray while I was in ranks wondering what she would do if the battle commenced, but this was one of the places where a trust in God was necessary to reconciliation. (William Coray)

Fri., Dec. 18, Santa Cruz River, Arizona, 30 miles. From Tucson, it was seventy miles across a desert to the Pima villages. They traveled through deep sand over flat land and camped without water. Quite a few were lame, with badly-worn shoes. Straggling, worn-out, famished men came in all through the night. The rear guard reached camp at daybreak. Elijah Allen was so ill he was put in a wagon. Henry Bigler and a messmate slipped out during the night to search for water. They found some and filled their canteens, arriving back in camp just before daybreak. "The morning we left Tosone [Tucson] the Colonel gave me the key of the public store and I went with the men and loaded the mules with wheat. I suppose there were fifteen or twenty thousand bushels in the pile. We made us of what public property we wanted, wasting none" (David Pettegrew).[55]

Sat., Dec. 19, Santa Cruz River, Arizona, 32 miles. The day started at 6 A.M. and ended at 11 P.M. with no water. Men were scattered all along the way. They traveled through baked clay and had to help pull wagons in the sandhills in several places. Some walked only two or three miles at a time all night trying to keep up. They arrived in camp by morning just in time to start out once more. Again, many were left by the road in groups of two or three without blanket, fire, or tent. Company C was in the rear and Lieutenant George Rosecrans left his men and rode into the hills to find water. He took some of his command to the water, where they all filled their canteens. Riding back to the famished men, they gave them the water they had carried. The suffering this day was severe. The men were strung out for miles. Azariah was so lame he could hardly walk. Many others were in the same condition. When Dr. Sanderson checked to see how Elijah Allen was, he wasn't in the wagon. He had crawled out during the night and had been left behind. A couple of soldiers were sent back to find him.

There was still greater suffering. We marched . . . over the parched ground and found no water yet, save a small mud pond which was drunk up by Co. C. We were from 6 o'clock till 11 at night before we encamped leaving men all along the road over night. Capt. Hunter observed to the Col. that the mules suffered. Said the Col "I don't care a damn about the mules, the men are what I'm thinking of." He told the men to get provisions where they could regardless of measurement and stop till morning if they chose to do so. I was much pleased at this expression. It was the first humane word I had heard from him. Here we were and harsh words would not do at such a time. (William Coray)

None but ourselves will ever know how much we suffer.[56] (Henry G. Boyle)

Sun., Dec. 20, Signal Peak, Arizona, 18 miles. Azariah arrived in camp in the morning just as orders to start for the day were given. His feet were painful. The men found Elijah Allen and brought him to camp. He was very sick. They camped by a pond of new rain water where the mules had to be held back to keep from drinking too much. The men were not allowed to dip water so as many as possible could have a drink. They had to lay down on their stomachs and suck the water there was so little of it. They ate fried pork and parched corn cooked in stagnant muddy water. William Hyde thought the men appeared to be over ninety years old. Colonel Cooke remarked he wouldn't have come this way if he had known how bad it was. He thought another company might have mutineered under these conditions. When they camped about noon, several groups took mules and canteens back to those fallen along the way. From here the command would follow the Gila River to southern California.[57]

Village of the Pima Indians, River Gila. Watercolor over pencil by Seth Eastman, Museum of Art, Rhode Island School of Design, Providence, Rhode Island; gift of the RISD Library; photography by Del Bogart.

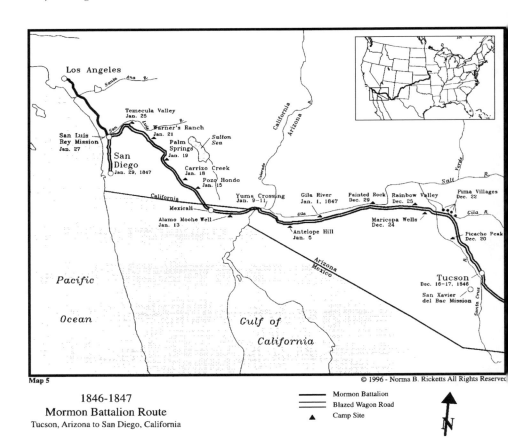

Map 5

1846-1847
Mormon Battalion Route
Tucson, Arizona to San Diego, California

CHAPTER FOUR

Pima and Maricopa Indian Villages

Mon., Dec. 21, Sacaton Mountains on Gila River, Arizona, 15 miles. On the road at sunrise. The mountains were covered by tall saguaro cactus with arms. After crossing the cannon tracks of General Kearny, they reached the Gila River and camped on grass under trees. A great many Pima Indians came to trade corn, wheat, flour, pumpkins, and beans, a welcome feast for the soldiers. The Pima showed interest and curiosity at the sight of the army wagons, the first wagons they had seen. Amos Cox's leg had improved from the bull goring, but he still was not able to walk. The mules were forty-eight hours without water; the men marched thirty-six consecutive hours, twenty-six of which were without water. They covered sixty-two miles in a little more than two days. No meat rations were issued on one day. "From the point where Gen. Kearny left the Rio Grande, about two hundred and twenty-eight miles below Santa Fe, and where our routes diverged, near the Pimo village, I made a map and sketch of my road; I had the aid of no instrument but a compass" (Philip St. George Cooke).[1] (Cooke's Wagon Road, now called the Gila Trail, became a major artery of westward migration with the discovery of gold in California. Once the gold rush was over, the Gila Trail remained a main corridor of travel and communication between California and the rest of the country.)

Tues., Dec. 22, Pima Villages, Arizona, 10 miles. About four thousand Pima Indians lived in small villages scattered for twenty-five miles along the Gila River. The women, most of whom seemed to carry babies, made their blankets and cloth by hand. Adults and children had happy countenances. "One little girl particularly, by a fancied resemblance, interested me much; she was so joyous that she seemed very pretty and innocent; I could not resist tying on her head, as a turban, a bright new silk handkerchief, which I happened to wear today; the effect was beautiful to see—a picture of happiness" (Philip St. George Cooke).[2]

103

They [Pimas] . . . farmed for a living, raising wheat, corn, beans, pumpkins, melons, cotton. The cotton is used by the Indians for making a kind of blanket or sheet with which they wrap themselves up . . . I saw one weaving. He had four stakes driven in the ground, one at each corner of the blanket, then two cross pieces were fixed and the thread passed from one to the other; he then had some thread around a stick, with this he interwove the thread fastened to the cross pieces and made a kind of blanket. . . . they are a noble race of Indians, uncorrupted by missionaries and no cross bloods. (David Pettegrew)[3]

Colonel Cooke talked to the chief. The soldiers traded buttons from their clothes for cakes, old clothes for corn, beans, meal, squash, and molasses. Even their ragged shirts were in great demand. The men tasted the Indians' stewed pumpkin and enjoyed the watermelons. Colonel Cooke was impressed with this area and spoke with "two senior captains of the battalion on the subject of their settling near here: They seem to look upon it favorably. Captain Hunt asked my permission to talk to the chief on the subject, and I approved of it."[4]

Walter [Barney] had bought some beans from the Indians and gave them to the cook to prepare for supper. When the cook announced that supper was ready they all looked at the kettle of bean soup. The camp kettle was standing in the middle of the mess camp. Barney stepped back about ten steps, pulled off his overshirt and hat and yelled, "Stand back, boys, while I make a dive to the bottom of that kettle to get a bean!" (James V. Williams)[5]

The Pimas filled a ditch with water for the battalion. Their huts were made of straw, sticks, and mud in a beehive shape. They were tall with black hair hanging down their backs, braided or coiled around their heads. All were naked to the waist.

It was truly surprising to see the multitudes of women and children; the women looked very baudy indeed, with nothing but a breech cloth. Many of them were singularly formed. Their bubbies was nearly 18 inches long and looked unnatural. They flocked into our camp in great multitudes, gazing at everything they saw. . . . They told Mr. Weaver, the pilot, that the Sonorarians had tried to hire them to capture us, but they refused the proposal. These Indians have a chief who exerts great influence over his people. (William Coray)

Wed., Dec. 23, Maricopa Wells, Arizona, 21 miles. Colonel Cooke left a parting gift for the chief: "I decided to add to their comfort and welfare by introducing sheep among them, by giving him for the ultimate use of his people, three ewes with young, which was the best I could do."[6]

After traveling all day they came to a Maricopa Indian village. Three guides arrived from Kearny to direct them to Warner's Ranch. They reported that the country was in a state of rebellion and that Kearny wanted the battalion to continue as fast as possible. The Indians were curious about the four women traveling with the soldiers.

Thurs., Dec. 24, Maricopa Wells, Arizona. A no-traveling day to rest and wash clothes. Camp was crowded with Indians, who stole several items. The Indians displayed their pottery, baskets, and woven blankets. Their homes looked like a round top hat, with a hole in the center of the top to let smoke out. Colonel Cooke ordered no more provisions were to be put in the wagons because the animals were not able to haul additional weight. Any purchases individuals had made were to be carried or left behind. This seemed to be harsh since the soldiers were on less than half rations and starving, yet some had to leave food on the ground because they were too weak to carry it. The company captains intervened without the colonel's knowledge and did not leave all behind. The captains took as much as they could in the company wagons. Cooke decided to take the desert route. Several men in Company E boiled and ate public corn, a fact reported to the commander by Lieutenant Dykes. The commander ordered the beef due Company E that day to be fed to the mules. This order was carried out, but the beef was left on the ground. The mules refused to eat it.

Fri., Dec. 25, Rainbow Valley, Arizona, 21 miles. After leaving the village, they traveled uphill before camping without water. Cold beans, pancakes, and pumpkin sauce made up their Christmas feast. William Hyde remembered Christmas with his family and contrasted it to "parched lips, scalded shoulders, weary limbs, blistered feet, worn out shoes, and ragged clothes" he was experiencing at this time. Guy Keysor remarked they had no sleigh bells or families to say "Merry Christmas," but he hoped for better days to come. The treat for the day was eating watermelon. Horace Alexander worried about his wife. She was with child when he left in July and the baby was due about this time. He wondered if the baby was born and if he had a son or daughter. "The weather was pleasant today. The task we had before us was heavy. We were to cross a desert of two days' journey without water and forced to leave the river to save 60 miles travel, it being that much farther around. We started at 10 and marched 21 miles by 9 o'clock at night" (William Coray).

Sat., Dec. 26, Gila River, Arizona, 26 miles. They traveled through a pass in a ridge of mountains and camped at dark on the Gila River with little grass and brackish water. Cooke ordered the loads to be lessened by leaving a cache of three hundred mule shoes and sixty pounds of nails. This lightened the load of the animals considerably.

Sun., Dec. 27, Gila River, Arizona, 8 miles. They traveled down the river, sometimes on sandy bottom and sometimes in quicksand. The men worked hard helping pull the loads in the sand. The sheep and oxen had so little flesh the meat didn't provide adequate sustenance. For the men, eating dry corn and boiled beef day after day caused constipation. Occasionally two spoons of flour for each man was added to beef water to make soup. "This evening we were met by some Spaniards from California making their escape. They reported California in a perfect state of rebellion and said a battle had been fought and many killed on both sides and that the war was by no means over" (William Coray).

Mon., Dec. 28, Gila River, Arizona, 11 miles. Traveled over a plain of clay to camp near the Gila. Hunger and thirst were big problems. When an animal was killed, the entire carcass was used. It was divided among the men in an unusual way. After cooking, the meat was separated into lots. One man turned his face away while another pointed to a lot and asked, "Who shall have this?" The man with his head turned away said a name and the lot was given to the man just named. Another lot was pointed to and the question was repeated. This procedure was followed until each man had a portion. Thus, it was by chance a participant either got a good portion of meat or a less desirable one.

Tues., Dec. 29, Painted Rocks, Arizona, 12 miles. It was a very chilly morning. They saw huge rocks covered with pictures of men, animals, birds, and snakes.[7] They passed a coal black rock bluff and trudged through sand, rocks, and hills. Camped in a river bottom among brambly willows and cottonwoods. Lieutenant Stoneman went ahead with several men to build a road. "We marched . . . over a very rough road. All well save with me. There was a report put into circulation by the Lts of B Co. to injure me, which was false and I proved it so. It seemed there was some jealousy existing for a long time and I know not why. In this Wm. Hyde was my friend and told me" (William Coray).

Wed., Dec. 30, 16 miles. Several bad hills today. Again wagons had to be pulled by men with ropes through the sand. The animals were too weak to do it alone. A cool north wind blew. Shoes were worn out. The men wrapped their feet in burlap, pieces of wagon covers, and animal hides for protection from rocks and the cold.

Thurs., Dec. 31, Gila River, Arizona, 9 miles. Colonel Cooke mustered the troops at dawn for inspection. They marched on hard ground, which made traveling somewhat easier. Grass was scant so the animals fared badly. They camped by a pond of salt water one-half mile from the river and found shards of crockery.

1847

Fri., Jan. 1, Gila River, Arizona, 12 miles. Four mules and several sheep were found dead in the morning. New Year's Day was greeted with corn or wheat cakes. Colonel Cooke talked about making a boat of two wagon bodies and floating supplies down the river to lighten the load of the animals, already in bad shape. The men didn't like the idea at all. They felt supplies were so scarce no risk should be taken for either the boat or the supplies to be lost. They found more shards of crockery. Camped on the Gila River near a bluff. New Year's supper was bread, coffee, and flour gravy. They met two families camped nearby, who were on their way to Sonora. The couples had left California with a small, insufficient supply of food and had been living on horse flesh for several days. The principal man was William Money. Mrs. Money had given birth to a child two days before. Because of her condition, they stopped over for a couple of days. Money was a Scotchman and liked California. He gave the soldiers general information in regard to California and the war and reported Kearny was about to make his way through the pass into San Diego. Money and his group had heard the firing of guns before leaving California and supposed a battle was being raged. An Indian told Money of a big battle and great loss. Money also reported that over two hundred Mormons from New York, who came by sea to San Francisco under Samuel Brannan, were well situated.[8] (Details on this colony are given in chapter 9.)

Sat., Jan. 2, Gila River, Arizona, 12 miles. Pursuing Cooke's idea, the troops tied two wagon boxes together to make a pontoon boat. Cottonwood logs were tied together for the wagon beds to rest upon. The pontoon boat then was loaded with 2,500 lb. of provisions for men and animals, tools, and baggage. It was to float down the river and be moored near camp each night. On the first day, the boat caught on a sandbar shortly after starting and didn't arrive at camp. The command continued along the river bank to a high bluff, where they stopped near a stoney mound.

Sun., Jan. 3, Gila River, Arizona. They passed the big bluff and camped near the river. Again, the boat did not catch up with the battalion by evening. Several provisions on the boat were abandoned so the boat would float off the sandbar. Colonel Cooke was very cross, perhaps because his boat idea wasn't working and provisions were so low. The men cut bark from cottonwood trees for the mules and cattle to browse on, since there was no grass.

Mon., Jan. 4, 8 miles. The soldiers filed over a bluff and camped by a volcanic peak about five hundred feet high. They took the animals to river bottom to graze with guards posted to keep them from wandering away. No news was received on the boat, which did not arrive at camp as planned. Loss of the boat flour would cause serious suffering. Azariah, his father, Albert Smith, and several more climbed a nearby peak in the evening and rolled huge rocks down and watched them as they crashed loudly down the hillside. The nights were very cold. Those who slept in buffalo sacks didn't notice the cold as much.

Tues., Jan. 5, Antelope Hill, Arizona, 12 miles. Left Kearny's trail and traveled through bramble-covered bottoms toward the mountains. Camped quite a distance from the river. Daily rations were reduced to 9 oz. of flour and 8 oz. of pork per person. Guide Foster arrived and reported the provisions in the boat were left about twenty miles upstream on banks and on sandbars.

Wed., Jan. 6, Gila River, Arizona, 14 miles. Several men fainted during the day's travel. Rations were reduced by 1 oz. more. The boat arrived empty. They followed the river over sandy and stoney washes, surrounded by thorny bushes. Several men were detailed to go back for the supplies left by the boat. Dr. Sanderson wouldn't let the sick ride and forced them to take his medicine. David Rainey was very ill. He hid among the provisions in the mess wagon. When an officer approached, the driver gave a certain whistle so David wouldn't groan until the officer had passed. Charles Hancock became ill during the day. The medicine he was given only made his distress more acute. George Hancock slipped behind the wagon after dark, took his brother in his arms, and carried him out of sight of the camp. He cradled his sick brother in his arms all night. In the morning Charles was recovered sufficiently to continue. A few of the enlisted men thought the colonel ate heartily while the soldiers grappled on half rations. Lack of clothes was a real problem. Raw skin protruded through their worn garments. Most had traded their second shirts for food long ago; many were already shirtless, covered only by a blanket, which made the soldiers' appearance approach the Indian mode of dress. "The provisions [on the boat] which had been left would have been lost altogether had not the Capts. been cunning enough to send men with pack mules after it contrary to the Col's. order. The Col. cares not for our suffering, as he had plenty. There was only 7 days' half rations and we were more than 15 days from settlements" (William Coray).

Thurs., Jan. 7, Devil's Point, Arizona. When the remaining food supplies were checked, only four days of provisions remained. It was a short day of travel because they had had to build a road over rocky points and gullies. Towering peaks reached high into the sky and were so close to the river in some places it was difficult to pass with a wagon. The landscape was barren. Levi Hancock said it looked as if this land had been tossed upside down and stirred around. The mules had to swim across the river to eat grass and cottonwood bark on the opposite bank. The men didn't return with the boat provisions. A government wagon was abandoned.

Fri., Jan. 8, Gila River, Arizona, 18 miles. When the guards crossed the river to bring the mules back, the animals had icycles on them. During the day Adjutant Merrill was in charge and led the battalion over hills to a

Junction of the Gila and Colorado Rivers. Colonel Cooke described the meeting of
these two rivers with these words: "A vast bottom; the country about the two rivers is
a picture of desolation; nothing like vegetation beyond the alluvium of the two
rivers; bleak mountains, wild looking peaks, stony hills, and plains fill the view."
Pencil and sepia wash by John Russell Bartlett, courtesy of the John Carter Brown
Library at Brown University, Providence, Rhode Island.

plain near Devil's Point. They struck tents near the mouth of the Gila River, surrounded by black mountains and stoney hills. Robert Bliss thought it was remarkable that the men were preserved when the animals failed continuously and possessions were left behind. Six oz. of sugar and 4 oz. of coffee were issued. This was the end of these supplies.

David Rainey's mule died. Because it belonged to him, he was given his choice of the animal to eat when it was cooked. David chose the heart and liver because he thought they would be tender and more edible. After the animal was all divided up, the men scraped the hide, and cut it into strips to chew as they walked along. The men are nearly starving for bread already. There are great prices offered for a morsel. The beef which is the only means for sustenance at this time is of the poorest quality. A man would have been fined in any place but this to have sold such beef. Notwithstanding the intense suffering of the men, there was not much grumbling after all. (William Coray)

Sat., Jan. 9, Colorado River, Arizona, 10 miles. Forty men were assigned to gather mesquite seeds to feed the animals. All seeds were not given to the animals. Seeds were ground in the coffee mills and used in different ways: mixed in flour for bread, made into pudding, roasted, or eaten raw. When ground, the seeds looked like meal, were slightly sweet and pleasant to taste, but caused constipation.

We marched very early. The wagons were 6 hours reaching the crossing of the Colorado. About half the road was bad, sand or soft clay. The mules are weak and their flagging and failing today in 10 miles is very unpromising for the 100-mile stretch, dry and barren before them. Colorado or Big Red River is one of the boundaries of California. It is one year this day since I was in the Temple at Nauvoo. I little thought of being here at this time, I am certain. On the opposite of this river the brush is so thick that it is almost impossible to pass through. The pilots fired it and it is now in flames. (William Coray)

Sun., Jan. 10, Colorado River, Arizona. The men were ferried over the river in the boat all through the night. They were tired, hungry, and thirsty. While John Borrowman was on guard, he felt very faint for want of something to eat. Sergeant Albert Smith, who was injured severely by a wild bull, was ordered by the Colonel to ford the stream, although, by virtue of his office, he had the right to ride in any wagon of his company. The water, in places, was up to Smith's neck.

Mon., Jan. 11, Colorado River, Arizona, 15 miles. Ice was one inch thick along the edges of the water. All men were across the river by late morning.

Two mules drowned while being driven across; wagons were floated and pulled by mules. There were 20 cattle and 130 sheep to cross. Each trip took about one and one-half hours. Cold air, high wind, and wet, hungry men caused a lot of bickering and swearing. By noon everything was in California. Two more wagons were left here. They proceeded southwest around sand dunes. Mules had a bad time pulling the wagons as the tar on the wagon wheels remained stiff from freezing river water and cold air. When army mules collapsed, Colonel Cooke took all private animals except those belonging to men with wives. Another wagon was left behind during the afternoon. They reached a dry well that had a dead wolf in it. Lieutenant Oman dug a new well nearby, but quicksand kept filling it in. Captain Davis's wife, Susan, had a washtub they had hauled all the way from Nauvoo. Lieutenant Oman wanted to put it in the bottom of the hole to keep quicksand out. Susan refused to part with her tub. Colonel Cooke ordered the tub taken over her objections, and holes were made in the bottom for water to seep in. It didn't work, so the entire bottom was knocked out. The tub was put inside the well hole and a little water seeped in and then stopped. The tub didn't solve the problem.

> When the quicksands were entered, it [the well] caved in, so as to render it impossible to make the hole more than two or three inches deep. Many expedients were discussed. It was concluded our only hope was in a washtub belonging to a captain . . . Lieutenant Oman reported to me, to my utter astonishment, that they were unwilling to give up that valuable article, almost our lives depending on it, it seemed to me. I had it taken. The well, after a long time, seemed to work pretty well and promisingly. Then it failed again. And then I had the tub taken up, and the bottom, which had been bored, knocked out; then it worked better. (Philip St. George Cooke)[9]

Lieutenant Oman dug a third well ten feet deep in muddy clay and found enough water that it could be dipped with a camp kettle. Finding water cheered the men. The water seeped in so slowly it took several hours to water the animals. They called this place Cooke's Well. Colonel Cooke complimented Lieutenant Oman for finding water, but there is no record of his saying anything to Susan Davis about the loss of her tub. "We were in a desert; no water, no grass, no provisions for ourselves but beef and a little flour. . . . The mules are giving out fast. We leave 5 or 6 every day. . . . Many of our men were so tired they did not come up" (William Coray).

Tues., Jan. 12, Colorado Desert, Mexico, 16 miles. Two more wagons were abandoned and the supplies they carried were put on pack mules. Only seven army wagons were left of the twenty-five they had when they started. They traveled under cloudy skies over a desert of sand and gravel. With no water at their campsite, they used their canteens. The mules ate yellow grass close to their camp. Thomas Morris remarked he has been thirsty for the last one hundred miles. Daniel Dennett was so hungry and thirsty he cut all the leather he could from both edges of his belt to chew as he walked along.

Wed., Jan. 13, Alamo Mocha Well, Mexico, 10 miles. The weather was hot and cloudy and the road was crooked and covered with heavy sand. When they reached Alamo Mocha Well, they found four dead wolves in it and little water. Lieutenant Oman went ahead and cleaned out two wells and dug a third one. The water was warm and had an unpleasant taste. It took eight hours to water the animals and there was no grass for them. The animals were so pitiful that Colonel Cooke abandoned two more government wagons, leaving only five army wagons. General Kearny had told Cooke to make a wagon road and Cooke seemed determined to succeed in this order. "J. [Jeremiah] Cloud [paymaster] proffered to lend me a horse for my wife to ride to the settlements, which I accepted, though with some reluctance" (William Coray).

Thurs., Jan. 14, California, 20 miles. A few soldiers left early to go ahead and dig wells at Poco Hondo. Haversacks and broken guns were buried: "Lt. Stoneman went ahead with 20 men in search of water. By order two wagons were left and a great many harnesses cached. This morning the baggage wagon of Co. B was left on the ground. The mules were sold to the highest bidder because the mules could not draw the wagons any farther" (William Coray). They left camp at noon and traveled until nine at night with no water. The battalion traveled over sandy road and saw sea shells along the way. The soldiers thought the ocean had covered this land a long time ago. "Some difficulty arose between Lieut. Oman and [Robert] Boyd Stewart. This caused Stewart to be tied to a stock of guns three hours in the morning of the 14th and under a guard for several days after" (David Pettegrew).[10]

Fri., Jan. 15, Pozo Hondo, California, 10 miles to dinner plus 20 miles after. A beautiful rainbow appeared in early morning. They arrived at Pozo Hondo where guide Tesson was waiting with thirty-three fresh mules and twelve cattle. The new mules were wild and Tesson hired four Indian drovers to handle them. It took the Indians four hours to lasso the mules, choke them until weak, and then trip the beasts to put on the harnesses. They cooked a beef and rested. Water was so scarce each man could have only 1½ pints. "This [water] was muddy and bad-tasted, yet we were glad to get it for we were very thirsty" (David Pettegrew).[11] Started again at 4 P.M. and continued until 11 at night. Many men stayed by the side of the road, thirsty and exhausted, most without shoes. Thirty miles of desert were still before them.

Sat., Jan. 16, Carrizo Creek, California, 25 miles. Started again at 1 A.M. It was cold and dark, with no moon but very bright stars. Half naked, the men suffered for lack of clothing. A tropical sun during the daytime and winter cold at night was detrimental to both men and animals. Continued to Carrizo Creek, surrounded by frog ponds, salt grass, and barren mountains. They had completed a march of nearly sixty miles in forty-eight hours over the worst stretch of desert without water.[12]

> The Col. ordered the officer of the day to call up the musicians at one o'clock to beat an assembly and we would move on for water. No feed yet for the mules, and it is a sin the way they are dying off. Part of the command did not get to the camp during the day, such was the extreme suffering of the Mormon Battalion. Three days without water and if the fresh beef had not met us nothing could have saved our lives but the unseen hand of Almighty God. . . . we had passed a large desert the worst place we had encountered since we left the states. (William Coray)

> We were all weary & fatigued, hungry, nearly naked & barefoot but our burning thirst drowned every other suffering. At the Summit of every hill . . . how eagerly did we look forward and around us for the long expected watering place, but were as often disappointed. (Henry G. Boyle)[13]

Sun., Jan. 17, Carrizo Creek, 20 miles. The past five days seemed the hardest of the trip to date. John Lawson's mule, loaded with his clothing, blanket, gun, and other supplies, disappeared. Many, many men had no shoes. They wrapped rawhide around their feet and tied it in place. When an ox was killed, some of the men cut a ring around the leg above the joint. The skin was peeled off without cutting it lengthwise. The lower end was sewed up with sinews. The natural crook of the hide shaped it somewhat like the foot. Thus, after several days' wearing, it was like a short boot.[14] Others wrapped clothing around their feet for protection against burning sand in the daytime and freezing cold at night. The men were used up from thirst, fatigue, and hunger; there was no talking. Some could not speak at all, their tongues were so swollen and dark. Many had scurvy. The men used their last 4 oz. of flour; there had been no sugar or coffee for weeks. Sixteen more mules gave out. Only five government wagons and three private wagons remained, and no company wagons. Many men carried water from Carrizo back to those lying along the way. Levi Hancock remarked the great Mississippi would be lost in this ocean of sand. He thought living here would be worse than a prison. Heavy clouds and a cool wind made traveling easier. They marched close together during the afternoon in case of an attack by Californians. They reached Palm Springs and saw palm trees for the first time. The men were in such bad condition, they remained here for a short while to rest. "More mules died this day than any day before and the men gave out. They seemed weaker than before they came to water, by overeating and drinking, I suppose. The Indians live along here in the mountains upon muskeet" (William Coray).

Mon., Jan. 18, Palm Springs, Vallecito Creek, California. They arrived at Vallecito midmorning and learned Kearny had defeated the Californians in the South. During the rest stop, they washed clothes and cleaned guns. Some amused themselves by rolling large boulders down the mountain that shook the earth and made a loud noise like peals of thunder, shaking the earth. Colonel Cooke didn't understand how the men were suddenly so energetic. An Indian from a nearby village brought a letter from the alcalde in San Diego welcoming the battalion to California. In the early evening they were paraded and inspected. There was some uneasiness in camp about seven men who went back more than ten days ago after the boat flour but still had not returned.

In the evening singing and fiddling and a little dancing cheered their spirits. Someone stowed a fiddle in a captain's wagon when they left Council Bluffs. Occasionally, after a hard day's march when the battalion was all together, the fiddle was brought out and a lively dance followed. Some boys took the girls' side and a jolly time was had by all. It was a good way to rest after a hard day and the men said they felt better than if they sat all evening. Each company had several fiddlers and they took turns with the fiddle, which provided a variety of tunes and styles of fiddling. "We have nothing but beef and very small rations of that. I was glad today to go and pick up the pork rinds that were thrown away by the Colonel's cook, although they were in the sand"(Henry Standage).[15]

Tues., Jan. 19, 10 miles. The soldiers were ordered to march in front today with the wagons in the rear in case of attack by the Californians. Nothing but beef to eat and not enough of that. They crossed through a mountain where they had to use crow bars, picks, and axes to hew a passage through the rock. The sides of the canyon were of solid rock and the width of the canyon was one foot too narrow for the width of the wagons. The wagons were emptied. One wagon was taken apart and carried through. Other wagon bodies were lifted and carried through sideways. The last two light wagons were pulled through by mules without unloading. After carrying all supplies through the narrow canyon and reloading the wagons, they continued along an arroyo for a short distance. They ascended a ridge where they camped without water.

Wed., Jan. 20, San Felipe Valley. The night was cold and miserable. Traveled about three hours before breakfast. Crossed a rocky hill where men with ropes helped animals pull wagons. Charbonneau returned from San Diego. He reported meager supplies were there. He suggested the battalion should go to Warner's Ranch. After a noon rest, they continued up a valley and camped at dusk with green grass and oak trees. Colonel Cooke ordered a drill this night. Jerome Zabriskie, one of the men who had gone back on January 6 to get the supplies from the boat venture, arrived in camp. He reported there were 400 lb. of flour at Vallecito, but the mules were so broken down they could not carry their loads any further.

Thurs., Jan. 21, San Felipe Valley. Crossed through Warner's Pass and camped on Buena Vista Creek, in sight of Warner's Ranch. These were the first houses they had seen in California. Jonathan Warner had several cabins and herds of cattle scattered over the range. The view was a welcome sight to the weary, fainting soldiers. They had their first full meal since the rations were reduced near Tucson. They ate beef, without salt, and pancakes bought from Indians. Cattle and horses were cheap since they were so numerous. Warner sold beeves for $3.50 but kept all hides. They were thankful to arrive here:[16]

> Warner's Rancho is in a beautiful valley. There is a hot spring here not quite boiling but hot enough for suds. Mr. Warner pretends to own nearly 15 leagues, equal to 40 miles square, a pretty good farm. It lies between the mountains and the climate is very different from that on the coast. "It is," says Mr. Warner, "not uncommon for snow here in June on the hills." Winter wheat can be sown here any time from September to March and comes to maturity, producing from 30 to 50 bushels to the acre. Mr. Warner had cattle brought up by the Indians and killed here. We saw a performance that beat anything entirely. The Indians on horseback throwing the lassoes and catching cattle by the head and legs and throwing them and holding them down by having the reata wound round and round the segerhead of the saddle, their skill beat anything I ever saw. They throw with so much certainty. Well, the beef tasted good as we were nearly starved. (William Coray)

Fri., Jan. 22, Warner's Ranch. The men enjoyed bathing in the hot springs, downstream a little where the water was not too hot. The Indians cooked food by placing baskets in the boiling water of the spring. On cold nights the Indians lay in the stream with their heads on the bank where the water was just warm. Although daily rations were increased to 4 lb. of beef a day, there still was no salt or anything to go with it. William Coray, William Hyde, and Nathaniel Jones bought a hog from Warner. William and Melissa Coray thought they never had tasted anything so good. Hard rain fell during the night. Colonel Cooke decided to go to Los Angeles instead of San Diego:

> We laid by this day to rest. Heard some news from Genl. Kearny which we could not dispute or credit importing that peace was

declared, but the Col. concluded to go by the way of Pueblos de Los Angeles and assist Genl. Kearny if he needed any assistance, instead of going to San Diego as he was directed, thinking perhaps he might meet some of the rebels eloping to Sonora and cut off their retreat. I might mention here that my sufferings were relieved partially by buying a hog of Mr. Warner. I can say candidly that I never ate anything that tasted as good before, but the brethren's wants were not supplied and it hurt my feelings to see them beg for food. Some of them were nearly naked also. (William Coray)

Sat., Jan. 23, Warner's Ranch, 25 miles. After leaving Warner's Ranch, they proceeded northwest on a steep road surrounded by mountains and camped at dusk. Chief Antonis and his Indians asked Colonel Cooke if they could travel with the soldiers. After a severe wind storm blew down tents, hard rain put fires out and continued into the night. William Muir and the other men arrived with about 400 lb. of flour, little more than a pound per man saved from the boat. They had been gone since January 6. Several mules died. The men were upset that Cooke decided to go to Los Angeles instead of San Diego.

Sun., Jan. 24, 4 miles. Everything was soaked—blankets, guns, supplies, and their clothes. Levi Hancock called the men to repentance, saying that God seemed to open the heavens with wrath on the Mormons. He said since church authorities had promised they would not die in battle, he thought they would be spared in spite of their sins. Marched several miles down Temecula River and camped in a forest which provided shelter and wood. Weather cleared at sunset. The mud was so soft and deep that when the men lay down, their bodies sank halfway in. It was soft enough to mire a blanket. William Coray and several others developed coughs, chills, and fever from being wet so much.

This morning all awoke wide awake in a storm which had continued all night and blew over many tents, mine among the rest and wet me and Mrs. Coray and everything we had. It was with hard pleading that we could gain admittance into the public wagon because the boys knew it disturbed them so much as to wake them out of their warm nests though we should perish with the cold. They remonstrated against our coming in, we however prevailed. No roll was called this morning. We marched 4 miles in the rain and camped. The rain continued all day and ceased in the night. (William Coray)

Mon., Jan. 25, Temecula Valley, 11 miles. A messenger arrived from General Kearny with instructions to proceed to San Diego and he would meet them there. This cheered the troops considerably. When they stopped near an Indian camp, the Indians were burying their dead, who had been killed in a recent battle with the Spaniards. The Indians were pleased to see the soldiers.

> We . . . encamped in the most beautiful valley I had ever seen, the soil very rich and fertile indeed above anything yet. It filled all my expectations of California at once. I must relate the circumstance of our camping. Before we were in sight of the camp ground we saw the smoke ascend from many fires. It had the appearance of an army very much but we still were unconcerned. Directly we came in sight of the place and we could plainly see a company of men formed in a line of battle. I thought to myself, surely we will have to fight now, and I knew there could be no better place in the world than the place which we were then in. But we found upon closer examination that it was a body of friendly Indians. (William Coray)

Tues., Jan. 26, 16 miles. Passed through a valley with high grass and plenty of wild mustard and white clover. Cooked, these mustard greens were a treat to go with beef. There were problems in crossing the river because of quicksand and swift, high water from late rains. Every officer got a complete soaking except the colonel. The whole battalion was wet through to the skin. Thousands of wild cattle, geese, ducks, and other small animals roamed freely. The men were relieved with the decision to go to San Diego instead of Los Angeles. There was a feeling of thanksgiving to God for his protection and the promise by Brigham Young that the battalion would not participate in battles. Rations were increased to 4 lb. of beef a day, but still no flour or other food to go with it.

Wed., Jan. 27, San Luis Rey, California, 20 miles. About noon they passed a beautiful mission, made of brick, on a small rise of ground. The porches and railings were white and gave it a look of splendor. Just as the sun was sinking, they saw the Pacific Ocean for the first time. There was silence as they viewed the long-awaited site; no tongue spoke. After twenty minutes absorbing the view, they continued on. Cheer filled their souls. They had sung about the "great Pacific Sea" since leaving Nauvoo and here they were marching to it. The sight was more beautiful than they had imagined. It was so calm, it looked like a mirror:

> I never Shall be able to express my feelings at this enraptured moment. When our colums were halted every eye was turned towards its placid surface, every heart beat with muttered pleasure, evry Soul was full of thankfulness, evry tongue was silen[ce]d, we all felt too ful to give Shape to our feeling by any expression. . . . The Surrounding hills are covered with wild oats & grass nearly a foot high, green & luxuriant as mid-summer and how Sweet and refreshing is the breeze that is winging its way from the ocean up this fertile

valley which Stretches itself from the Shore back to the "Sieras."
What an expansive view! How bright & beautiful every thing looks!!
(Henry G. Boyle)[17]

The sun was sinking. . . . so placid was the sea that it shone a vast
space of seemingly transparent light, which, by contrast, gave to the
clear sky a dusky shade. What a strange spectacle was that! The earth
more aerially clear and bright than the cloudless heavens. (Philip St.
George Cooke)[18]

They continued into a valley that was out of view of the ocean.
Sunlight and shade, birds calling together with the sound of the waves on
the rock-bound shore, all joined in an impressive welcome to the weary
soldiers. The men had trouble sleeping so loud was the ocean roar.
"Passed through the San Luis Valley down the river to San Luis Rey. It is
well supplied with gardens on either side with a variety of shrubbery and
fruits of various kinds. The Col. ordered the Indians to drive into the
drove a quantity of fat cattle this day" (William Coray).

Thurs., Jan. 28, San Dieguito Valley, California, 19 miles. The springlike
weather was pleasant, as they marched down the coast in sight of the
ocean. Wild oats, grass, and mustard were plentiful along the way. Their
journey was nearly over. They lost cattle during the night, but the colonel
said to gather more from the wild herds instead of hunting the lost ones.
Indian scouts brought several hundred cattle into camp. They stopped
near several pools of water.

Fri., Jan. 29, San Diego, California. Crossed into a valley, then traveled
through hills soggy from recent rains and camped on a flat below the old
mission, about four miles from the seaport of San Diego. The mission, surrounded by gardens and vineyards and a plaza in front, was several miles
from town. The burial ground was on the east and the church on the west.
The rooms were dark and damp with brick floors. There were olive trees
and a large wine press. General Kearny was in San Diego waiting for a ship
to go to Monterey, since hostilities in this area seemed to be over. Colonel
Cooke went to San Diego in the evening to report to General Kearny that
a wagon road "of great value to our country" had been opened to the
Pacific Ocean. (Cooke did not know that gold would be discovered in
California one year later and that Cooke's Wagon Road would become one
of the major overland routes to the West.) Five government wagons and
three private wagons had come all the way. The march of the Mormon
Battalion to the Pacific Ocean was completed: "We have endured one of
the greatest journeys ever made by man, at least in America, and it is the
faith and prayers of the Saints that have done it" (Robert Bliss).[19]

Sat., Jan. 30, San Diego. They began cleaning the dilapidated and
dirty buildings of the mission. They washed clothes, rested, and enjoyed

the view. In the evening a few dragoons came to quarter in the mission too. The troops had no food except beef, salt, and mustard greens. All clothes were in terrible condition and very few had shoes. San Diego was a small Mexican settlement with no place for the men to replace their clothing.

The building is about 14 rods in front and 11 rods in width with a plaza in front and is over one story high. The walls are of unburnt brick whitewashed the outside and inside. The building is covered with concave tile which are laid on and last fast. . . . The church is nearly two stories high. The front has a rude representation of a steeple. This building is constructed upon the same principle as the building at New Mexico having a square in the center. The square here was nearly three quarters of an acre with one tally port or entrance on the west end in the rear of the church. (Nathaniel Jones)[20]

Laid by as we supposed for good . . . this mission as a station for us. . . . I went down to Diego with one or two others. Saw Genl. Kearny. He is a very good-looking man, graceful in his appearance and sociable to all. (William Coray)

Sun., Jan. 31, San Diego. Most remained in camp, trying to clean the fleas out of the mission rooms. Others visited the port. In the evening orders were issued to proceed to San Luis Rey to hold that position in case hostilities should begin again.

Genl. Kearny and Commodore Stockton are at variance for some cause which took place in the Pueblo Angelos. When Pueblo [Los Angeles] was retaken they joined their forces together and gave the Genl. the command, as he was a land officer and Stockton was a naval officer. After it was taken the Commodore gave the govt. into Frémont's hands contrary to order or policy. This troubled the General as he was appointed before he left the states sole governor of California. The General set sail for Monterey this morning in the *Scion,* a sloop of war. (William Coray)

Mon., Feb. 1, en route to San Luis Rey Mission, 16 miles. The battalion was on its way back to Mission San Luis Rey. The dragoons went with them.

We took up the line of march again for another port according to orders. There was no clothing to be held at San Diego or any other place in California at present. I was told so by many who ought to know at least which made it hard traveling, the boys without shoes, etc. We marched 16 miles and camped. I went to Lt. Col. Cooke and told him the men had not rations enough and he ordered more immediately. It was only beef and that very cheap. We thought we ought to have enough to eat after starving 4 or 5 months. Upon the head of this he ordered that the fleshy part of the beef must be boiled, that the bones might be boiled too. (William Coray)

We have now been one hundred and three days from Santa Fe. We started with . . . sixty days rations and we lost several hundred pounds of flour on the Gila. Thus, we traveled under greater embarrassments than it is possible to realize except by passing through them. We have opened roads through impassable mountains and trackless deserts, without wood, water, or grass, and almost without provisions. We now find ourselves without clothes and worn down with fatigue. For nearly thirty days we have had nothing but beef and not enough of that all the time. (Nathaniel Jones) [21]

Tues., Feb. 2, en route to San Luis Rey Mission, 22 miles. "Camped on a beautiful plain. We passed the hill on which General Kearny had been hemmed in and was obliged to eat mules and they gave it the name Mule Hill. Lieutenant Merrill told around this day that he intended to resign his adjutancy and come back into the company" (William Coray).

Wed., Feb. 3, San Luis Rey Mission, 12 miles. Arrived in San Luis. Levi Hancock wrote a poem about this country:

> I now can tell a better story
> Than I could about Sonora
> For the soil is a little wetter
> And the land a little better.
> I think 'twill bring corn and potatoes
> Beans and cabbage and tomatoes
> Raise all things to suit our notion
> Along by the Pacific Ocean.

The buildings at the mission were all connected, including the church. They formed a square around several acres of land. The church was in the southeast corner. It had six bells and a lot of statues. In the front there was a row of pillars supporting an arch. The men thought it was a beautiful place. The square resembled a fort. In the center were orange trees. Nearby there were vineyards, another orange orchard, and pepper and cocoa trees. There was a great view of the ocean.

They found plenty of feed here for their animals. They had never seen several trees before: coconut, olive, and fig. A peach tree was in bloom. Wild beans, peas, and cabbage plants grew by themselves, since the mission was deserted. There were lots of grapes, most of the raisin kind. Battalion members felt blessed to be in such a productive country.[22]

Thurs., Feb. 4, San Luis Rey. Eighty men were assigned to clean up the square and others tried to rid the mission rooms of fleas. They were required to drill for several hours during the day and were given orders to keep all garrison duties strictly. Their clothing was ragged; most men were without a change of clothing.

Colonel Cooke read congratulations to the men for successfully arriving at the Pacific Ocean and completing the long march from Fort Leavenworth. He said the wagon road would be of great value to the country and that the men exhibited qualities of veterans.[23] The men threw their hats in the air and cheered the colonel when he finished. His remarks pleased the men considerably. Colonel Cooke then ordered a general cleanup: arms, clothes, shaving, haircuts. The men, who had beards and hair a foot long, wanted to show their wives, but Colonel Cooke said, "No, shave the beards and cut the hair."[24] He also ordered all private mules and horses be disposed of by February 15. "We cleaned up our quarters and the Col. read an order to the battalion . . . concerning our long march and said it had not a parallel in the world" (William Coray).

Fri., Feb. 5, San Luis Rey. Cooke's order praising the men, which he read the day before, started a feeling of gratitude and good will between the men and Colonel Cooke. It seemed to erase some of the misunderstanding between the commander and his men:

> From the commencement of this march until we arrived in California . . . commenced a succession of hardships and privations by long marches without water and scanty food which only the most robust could endure. Had it not been for the cool headedness and sagacity of our stern commander, . . . we must have all perished before reaching our destination. There is no doubt in my mind but what Colonel Cooke was one of the ablest officers then in the Army . . . he appreciated our services to the cause that he was engaged in and which he expressed to the battalion. (John J. Riser)[25]

Sat., Feb. 6, San Luis Rey. Even after the cleanup and repair of quarters were completed, they still were bothered by fleas. Levi Hancock met with the seventies, one of the divisions of the Mormon priesthood, and warned against using God's name in vain and suggested the men wash each other's feet as in ancient times. He visited various quarters during the evening. The men washed their wide, white belts preparing for an inspection the next day. Some also tried washing their clothes. Many had no extra clothing to wear while washing. "Went into the garden and washed my shirt and a pair of pants, which I had made out of an old wagon cover—all the clothing I had" (Henry Standage).[26] John Borrowman was on guard duty.

Sun., Feb. 7, San Luis Rey. All men and quarters were inspected. They were divided into ten-man squads with daily duties starting immediately.

Colonel Philip St. George Cooke. Sketch from *Harper's Weekly*, June 12, 1858.

The men generally were worn out after living on beef and nothing else for so long. Thomas Morris could only carry a pail of water a rod at a time without resting because of his weakness. This was typical of the physical condition of the men:

> Last night [while on guard duty], being worn down with sickness and our long journey on half rations and having nothing but beef to eat, I was so weak I could not well stand my two hours at a time and sat down to rest a little on a square built of brick . . . and before I was aware I was caught asleep on my post by the sergeant of the guard who reported me and put me under guard so that I am this day in guard quarters a prisoner. (John Borrowman)[27]

> By this time everything began to look like a regular garrison. The strictest discipline was enforced. Five men were put into the stocks for passing through the Colonel's hall and other like offenses. As we are now stationed in California I shall cease writing a daily journal and only note the particular incidents which accrue and which I like to preserve for the future. My only object in keeping a daily journal on the way was more to ascertain the distance than anything else, and while I was noting the distance, it came very handy to record other items, which may be a satisfaction to me in future expecially if I should ever retrace my steps. (William Coray)

Mon., Feb. 8, San Luis Rey. Colonel Cooke started daily drill with the officers in the early morning. They then taught the maneuvers to the enlisted men for one hour in the morning and one hour in afternoon. Azariah remarked that it was the first time he'd been taught how to turn around in formation. It was the same for many others. "The brethren soon became very playful and happy, fiddling and dancing nearly every night. Still they were without sufficient clothing to hide their nakedness and living on beef mostly. The Lt. Col. said there was a prospect for flour within 7 or 8 days and we were contented till it came" (William Coray).

Tues., Feb. 9, San Luis Rey. The troops were ordered to turn in all cartridges by 10 A.M. Colonel Cooke was very abusive to the men during drill. James Pace, an officer in Co. E, wrote a letter to Colonel Cooke complaining about Cooke's treatment of the battalion. Levi Hancock held a meeting and many of those attending asked for forgiveness of sins. Colonel Cooke sent Lieutenant Oman and ten men with fourteen mules to San Diego for flour. Indians brought them corn, which they ground for a fine supper.

Wed., Feb. 10, San Luis Rey. More corn was ground. A daily routine was established:

Roll call	Daylight
Sick call	7:20 A.M.
Room cleaning	
Breakfast	8:40 A.M.
Morning drill	10–11 A.M.
Afternoon drill	3 P.M.
Roll call	Sundown
Tattoo	8:30 P.M.
Taps	9 P.M. (lights out and silence)

Thurs., Feb. 11, San Luis Rey. Lieutenant Oman and his group returned from San Diego with 2,100 lb. of flour. The men cleaned their guns and prepared for a general inspection in three days.

Fri., Feb. 12, San Luis Rey. Drills were held as usual. The men talked about the authority of certain men to preside over them.

Sat., Feb. 13, San Luis Rey. There was a heavy, disagreeable mist all night. Drills as usual. "I am still under guard and have to spend my time the best way I can, sometimes reading the Bible and other times speaking with the guard" (John Borrowman).[28]

Sun., Feb. 14, San Luis Rey. A general parade and inspection was held after which Adjutant Philemon Merrill read the military law to the soldiers. Religious meetings were held during the afternoon and evening. Captain Hunt asked George Dykes to preach, which offended some who thought Levi Hancock should make religious assignments. Dykes talked from Daniel 2, followed by remarks from Captain Hunt, who reminded the men of their duty to God and to each other. It was the first church meeting since they arrived in California. "Some of the brethren . . . would not stay to meeting because Capt. Hunt gave out the appointment. After service was over, he [Hunt] gave out the appointment for another sermon on the following sabbath" (William Coray).

Mon., Feb. 15, San Luis Rey. Drills were held for an hour in the morning. They carried arms while drilling in the afternoon. In the evening Levi Hancock, who had been chosen by the men shortly after leaving Fort Leavenworth to be their spiritual leader, called a meeting:

Levi Hancock held a meeting at Lt. Dykes' quarters in which he stated that he hated to be under the necessity of telling the brethren his rights. Said he, "The spirit of God should do it. Men have tried to take away my rights (meaning the captains) but I won't give them up to any man." He said that a number of the battalion brethren had met together and washed each other's feet, and annointed each other with oil, and that the Spirit of the Lord had testified to them that it was right. "In regard to preaching Bro. Tyler is the man to preach to this battalion. I know it for it was revealed to me." . . . After casting many insinuating remarks about the captains taking the lead when it was not their place, etc., he concluded by taking an expression of the congregation whether Brother Tyler should preach next Sunday or not. Thus, I conceived he got up an opposition to Capt. Hunt, who had given out an appointment on the same day. Whether this was intentional or not, I do not know. Wm. Hyde arose, stating that he had but little to say, but what he should say would be at the risk of all hazard, which was that Levi Hancock was his file leader and that he would obey his counsel, let the circumstances be what they may. And farther, if he had done anything, he wanted forgiveness, but, he knew he had not done anything wrong for he sought to do as his officers told him all the time and his file leader also who had not profaned the name of the Deity, but had carried himself perfectly straight.

In the meantime I sat still and listened to all that was said, but said naught myself. I found that Brother Levi and the captains were at variance. The captains being present at the time considered themselves insulted by having their appointment taken up before their faces. I went home and concluded to keep dark as I knew not which was right and did not know but they were both wrong. This variance had existed a long time between the parties, the fact of it was Bro. Levi thought he had the most authority and the Capts. thought they had the most authority and so it went. As to myself, I have but little to say in favor of my good deeds. Neither have I very many grievious errors to charge myself with. Upon the whole I claim to be nothing more than a middling sort of fellow at the best or worst. Lest I should forget what my sentiments were at the time in regard to the captains and Bro. Levi, I will here record them so that when I get to the Church I may know if I guessed right.

When the Battalion was about ready to start as I was one of them, I wanted to know if any man would be sent along to be our counselor or not. I asked Bro. Willard Richards if there would be any. He said, "No, your officers will be your counselors." After that Bro. Brigham and others of the Twelve met the officers, commissioned and non-commissioned, to give them instructions at which place President Young said, "Brethren, go and be faithful. Hearken to your officers who shall be over you. Let it be said of you that you are the best men that ever entered the service." Speaking to the officers in particular, he said, "Be as fathers to the soldiers and counsel them, for you are their counselors and if I hear of your dancing or playing cards, that it will be right if you control it. You must have control over everything and all will be well." There was never anything said about Levi or Wm. Hyde presiding or dictating in any way. Notwithstanding, Bro. Levi Hancock is first counselor to Joseph Young and President of the Seventies and I could do no more than acknowledge his authority over me in spiritual things, but still I thought the course he pursued an improper one in getting up an excitment against the officers and destroying their influence with the men whom they should control according to Pres. Young's instruction. Neither could I justify the officers altogether because some of them set very bad examples and were somewhat tyranical. Not so with all, but as little differences should not be aggravated, but rather forgotten, I will say no more on this subject. (William Coray)

Tues., Wed., Feb. 16–17, San Luis Rey. Drilled again as yesterday. Nathaniel Jones and Lewis Lane were talking to each other about not understanding why the battalion was still on such short rations when beef was so plentiful and cheap. Lieutenant Dykes overheard their conversation and reported the men to the commander. "This day I have been quite unwell and very lonesome. I wish very much to be tried that I may know what my sentence will be and that I may be delivered from my imprisonment and from the hands of our Gentile commander. I am very uncomfortable here as I have no bedding but my blanket and a cold, damp, brick floor to lie on"(John Borrowman).[29]

Thurs., Feb. 18, San Luis Rey. After tattoo a meeting was held in Azariah Smith's room. All present took turns washing and anointing each other's feet. Daniel Tyler, appointed by Levi Hancock, preached on remembering covenants. Everyone seemed to be thinking more about religion and families now that the hard conditions of travel were past.

Sergeant Jones and Corporal Lane were reduced in rank to private. Dykes said they were guilty of insubordination and conduct unbecoming a non-commissioned officer when they discussed short rations the day before. Their comrades thought this was an unfair charge, since there was no neglect of duty. It was merely a private discussion between the men with no attempt to arouse other soldiers to action: "He [Dykes] carried false reports to the colonel, and through his false reports broke me of my office, which he had purposed to do from the beginning and had boasted of it" (Nathaniel V. Jones).[30]

Fri., Feb. 19, San Luis Rey. Flour and beans arrived from Warner's Ranch. Lieutenant Oman returned from San Diego with 2,100 lbs. of flour. Regular drills were executed. "This day has passed away more pleasantly than I expected. Mr. Clark has been very kind and allowed me the privilege of the guard room most of the day" (John Borrowman).[31]

Sat., Feb. 20, San Luis Rey. Rations issued—10 oz. of flour, beans for five days, with 2 lb. of beef for three days. Regular drills.

Sun., Feb. 21, San Luis Rey. Inspection at 9 A.M. Adjutant Dykes read rules and regulations at an 11 A.M. mustering. Levi Hancock presided at afternoon services and called on Daniel Tyler to preach. Tyler spoke again on the "necessity of the brethren remembering their covenants," emphasizing strongly against swearing and other vices. "This day there was preaching in the quarters, but I did not get to hear. I am alone today, my fellow prisoner having been released at guard mounting this morning" (John Borrowman).[32]

Mon., Feb. 22, San Luis Rey. Drills as usual. "I am well but weary . . . [wish] very much to be released" (John Borrowman).[33]

Tues., Feb. 23, San Luis Rey. Drilling in the morning and afternoon. The colonel received word that a vessel from the Sandwich Islands arrived in San Diego. He sent several teams and wagons forthwith for supplies.

Wed., Feb. 24, San Luis Rey. Three men—Isaac Peck, John Mowrey, and Ebenezer Harmon—were arrested for stealing and butchering an Indian's cow. Dress parade was held in the afternoon. The battalion performed well and the colonel seemed pleased.

Thurs., Feb. 25, San Luis Rey. Captain Hunt and Lieutenants Oman and Clift heard John Borrowman's court-martial. He had been under guard since February 7: eight days. Borrowman was sentenced to six days in the guard house with three hours a day in the cell and a three-dollar fine. Peck, Mowrey, and Harmon were sentenced to ten days, two hours each day for five days, and fined $2.50 each to repay the Indian for his cow.

Fri., Feb. 26, San Luis Rey. The wagons returned with pork, flour, sugar, coffee, soap, candles, and other needed supplies. Dress parade was in the evening. "I was called on to hear my sentence read which was to be confined three [six] days in guard quarters and three hours each day in the cell and three dollars of my pay stopped which was disapproved of by the Colonel and I was released and this is in answer to my prayers" (John Borrowman).[34]

Sat., Feb. 27, San Luis Rey. General washing of clothes and cleaning belts. Wagons were sent to San Diego for more supplies.

Sun., Feb. 28, San Luis Rey. Colonel Cooke sent eleven men under Lieutenant Samuel Thompson back to the Colorado River to get the supplies and wagons left there. The colonel gave a very close inspection during a general muster.

Mon., Mar. 1, San Luis Rey. Drills continued. The wild oats were headed out and the men thought it seemed like midsummer.

Tues., Mar. 2, San Luis Rey. An Indian child died from a rattlesnake bite. The funeral was held in the church. All six bells rang for nearly an hour, accompanied by lots of weeping. Azariah and others went into the church and thought the inside was very nice. He said there were twelve statues.

Proceedings of A Battalion Court martial
Convened by virtue of following order in

Orders }   H^d D^r morm Batt
N° 21 }   San Louis Rey Feb 25

— A Battalion Court Martial to consist
of Capt. Hunt. 1st Lieut. Oman 2^d Lieut
Cliff. members. will convene this Morning
At 11 O'Clock for the trial of such
Prisoners as May be Brought before it
        By order of Lt. Col. Co
        P. C. Merrill Adgt

Orders }   H^d Dr Mormon Batt
N° 22 }   San Lus Rey Feby: 26/47

I, Before the Battalion court Martial
Convened by orders N° 21. of the 25 inst
and of which capt Hunt President were
Tried 1st Private John. Borroman of Com^y
B Mormon Battalion charged with Sleeping
On post to which charge the prisoner pleald
Guilty the court fined the prisoner guilty as
Charged and Sentence him to six days
Confinement in charge of the guard three
hours each day in the cells also to A Stopage
of three dollars of His pay 2^d 3^d & 4th
Privates J. Peck John Mowery and F. Harm
mon of Comp^y C mormon Battalion each

The court-martial record of John Borrowman. Archives, Historical Department,
Church of Jesus Christ of Latter-day Saints, Salt Lake City, Utah; used by permission.

Wed., Mar. 3, San Luis Rey. More provisions arrived from San Diego. Drills as usual.

Thurs., Mar. 4, San Luis Rey. Drills in the morning and dress parade in the evening. Sugar, coffee, beans, and flour for four days were issued. Cold winds were very disagreeable.

Sat., Mar. 6, San Luis Rey. After daily drill, Ephraim Green was reduced to ranks for not learning the drill. David Rainey was promoted to sergeant and Horace Alexander to corporal. Elijah Allen and John Borrowman went a mile to the Indians' tents to trade for corn and milk. A dress parade was held in the evening. The cool weather was more noticeable because of the scarcity of clothing.

Sun., Mar. 7, San Luis Rey. The battalion was drilled in firing without their muskets and in wheeling. Colonel drilled Company A afterwards. He was upset with them and finally walked away. The men were assigned back into messes of six again.

Mon., Mar. 8, San Luis Rey. Colonel Cooke was not pleased with drill. Several non-commissioned officers were reduced in rank for not learning the drills.

Wed., Mar. 10, San Luis Rey. Morning drill dismissed due to rain, but was resumed in the afternoon when the rain stopped.

Sat., Mar. 13, San Luis Rey. At a full battalion drill, the soldiers practiced firing, wheeling, and other military maneuvers. This was the first day they had drilled with their muskets.

Sun., Mar. 14, San Luis Rey. Colonel Cooke received orders to send one company to San Diego and the rest to Los Angeles. General inspection. James Park and William Evans were put under guard for washing under the spout, which was contrary to orders. "Up until now we had [not] been receiving many orders. Today Co. B was ordered to march to San Diego and the remainder to Pueblo de Los Angeles except the sick who [will] remain at San Luis Rey under Lt. Oman" (William Coray).

Mon., Mar. 15, en route to San Diego, 15 miles. Company B, under the command of Captain Jesse Hunter, left for San Diego with two hours notice. The other four companies were to leave for Los Angeles in a few days. Most men in Company B had no shoes at all, only a few had moccasins. Lieutenant Stoneman went with Company B. The men looked forward to more food once they arrived in San Diego. Robert Bliss talked about having oysters and fish. Lieutenant Robert Clift, Company C, who was assigned to work with the alcalde in San Diego, went with Company B. He also was to serve as commissary assistant for Company B under Captain Hunter.

San Diego, ca. 1847. Courtesy of Theodore W. Fuller.

CHAPTER FIVE

San Diego:
Company B Makes Friends

Although the Mormon Battalion reached San Diego January 29, 1847, without firing a single shot at the enemy, it would be another year before the war ended officially with the capture of Mexico City. But in California the conquest was complete; there would be no fighting. The battalion served in peacetime garrisons in San Diego and Los Angeles.

All was not peaceful, however. For several months Stockton, Frémont, and Kearny bickered over who was the supreme American authority in California. Stockton refused to acknowledge Kearny's authority and withdrew navy and marine detachments from the general's command. General Kearny and Lieutenant Colonel Frémont met in Los Angeles on January 17. Because he had accepted Commodore Stockton's commission appointing him governor of California the previous day, Frémont refused to obey Kearny's orders. Kearny asked Frémont to cease reorganizing the civil government; Frémont refused, insisting he was under Stockton's orders.[1]

Frémont made Los Angeles his capital and stationed his troops, the California Volunteers, at San Gabriel, about eight miles northeast of Los Angeles. Exasperated, General Kearny wrote to Adjutant General Roger Jones in Washington relating Frémont's refusal to obey his orders and explained, "as I have no troops in the country under my authority, excepting a few dragoons, I have no power of enforcing them."[2]

From advance scouts, General Kearny learned the battalion would reach Los Angeles by the end of January. Kearny sent orders to Colonel Cooke to lead his troops to San Diego. Assured of the battalion's loyalty, he left San Diego January 31 and arrived at Monterey February 5.

While in northern California, Kearny met Commodore Branford Shubrick, who replaced Commodore Stockton January 22. Shubrick immediately agreed to accept Kearny's authority in California. Both men decided to ignore Frémont's governorship in southern California until they received official dispatches from Washington.[3]

Colonel Richard B. Mason brought the dispatches from Washington to Kearny in San Francisco. Written by General Winfield Scott, the dispatch ordered Kearny to assume command as senior officer of the land forces, to be the legal governor of California. Scott directed Colonel Frémont's California Volunteers were to be mustered into the regular army. Scott also advised Kearny to return east when California appeared tranquil, leaving Colonel Mason in command.

Colonel Cooke, the strict, orthodox disciplinarian, was shocked at the military situation in California: "General Kearny is supreme—somewhere up the coast; Colonel Frémont supreme at Pueblo de los Angeles; Commodore Stockton is commander-in-chief at San Diego; Commodore Shubrick, the same at Monterey, and I, at San Luis Rey; and we are all supremely poor; the government having no money and no credit; and we hold the Territory because Mexico is poorest of all."[4]

Captain Henry S. Turner, serving as adjutant general, reached San Luis Rey on March 14 with the important documents. He had a circular dated March 1, issued jointly by General Kearny and Commodore Shubrick, announcing that General Stephen W. Kearny formally assumed command as the governor of California. Colonel Cooke was to send one battalion company to San Diego and take the other four companies to Los Angeles.[5]

Turner then proceeded to Los Angeles to deliver a copy of Order Number 2 to Frémont, also in Los Angeles, which contained the following orders by Kearny:

1.   Frémont was to forward all public documents to General Kearny in Monterey.
2.   The California Volunteers who desired would be mustered into the regular army.
3.   Colonel Philip St. George Cooke would assume command of the Southern Military District, which included the Mormon Battalion, Company C of the First Dragoons, and the California Volunteers.

Frémont refused to obey General Kearny's orders because he considered the countryside unsafe. He expected there would be more Spanish uprisings. Frémont left Los Angeles March 22 for Monterey.

The story of Company B is resumed as the company arrived in San Diego. (The details of the other four companies in Los Angeles continue in chapter 6.)

Wed., Mar. 17, San Diego, California, 8 miles. When Company B arrived in San Diego, Captain Hunter was the ranking military authority.

They found a small town, consisting mainly of a plaza surrounded by a church and several buildings.[6] It was the only port south of San Francisco. Two American flags were flying over the fort the marines had started. In the harbor was the ship *Congress*. Dr. John S. Griffin, the ship's doctor, was not impressed by the appearance of the battalion:

> The Californians have no great idea of their soldier-like qualities and in action would not dread them much—this arises in a great measure from their dress, carriage, etc., which is as unlike any soldier as anything could possible be. Yet I think if brought into action they would prove themselves good men as I am told they are generally fine shots and they drill tolerably well. They are bear footed and almost naked.[7]

The men dug until very late at night trying to find water. They were so emaciated and dehydrated, eating was a serious problem when they first arrived. Daniel Dennett put grains of sugar on his tongue while sipping small amounts of water until his stomach could tolerate food.

Thurs., Mar. 18, San Diego. William Hyde and eighteen men were sent to the fort, located on a hill one-fourth mile east of San Diego overlooking the town and countryside. The fort was constructed by digging a trench around the summit of this hill. A row of large logs were put around the inside of the trench. Gravel and rocks were thrown up against the logs, forming a barricade. Seventeen pieces of artillery were positioned strategically against the logs.[8] Several battalion soldiers went down to the sea and bathed their feet in the salt water for the first time. They gathered clams at the beach and took them to camp for supper. Lieutenant Stoneman took the dragoons up to San Luis Rey, where they were ordered to stay so the other four battalion companies could go to Los Angeles.

Fri., Mar. 19, San Diego. All marines in San Diego went aboard their ship, the *Congress*. Company B took command of the fort on the bluff. The company was drilled in the afternoon.

Sat., Mar. 20, San Diego. Azariah Smith and several men went on the ship *Congress*. The crew was sociable and showed them different areas of the ship. They gave Azariah a few potatoes.

Mon., Mar. 22, San Diego. Azariah and his father went to the ocean to bathe. While there the ship *Savannah* came round the point. It was a sight to see. Lydia Hunter, expecting a child soon, was not well. Mussels and oysters were the fare for supper. Azariah boiled his potatoes, the first tasted since Fort Leavenworth.

In Monterey a tense meeting was held by Frémont and Kearny. Frémont offered to resign, but Kearny refused to accept the resignation. He asked Frémont directly if he would obey his orders. After a short deliberation, Frémont responded he would.

Tues., Mar. 23, San Diego. Robert Owen, John Lawson, John Borrowman, and Azariah Smith went to the ocean after more mussels. Azariah caught twenty-three fish weighing about one pound apiece.

Fri., Mar. 26, San Diego. When the *Savannah* left, the sailors fired her guns, which made the air ring. Philander Colton and John Stoddard built forms to make mud bricks.

Sun., Mar. 28, San Diego. Mr. Warner's child was buried just at dusk. Two Indian women carried on their heads the body on a platform decorated with ribbons. Girls, one on each side, held lighted candles. Two men played instruments with strings. After the body was in the grave, both men and women threw handfuls of dirt and then left. Death didn't seem to frighten them, as they were quite cheerful.

Mon., Mar. 29, San Diego. Azariah and his father, Albert Smith, went to the ocean and ran races, jumped, and sang songs. He said it was the first time since they left Nauvoo. Francis Brown was sick. He had not regained his strength from the march. There were daily military drills, but not much else to occupy their time, so they looked into other activities to occupy the long, empty hours. Captain Hunter gave permission for them to work for the citizens of San Diego. Samuel Miles helped the alcalde by keeping his records and making out his reports. He also helped with administering the American law at the Mexican alcalde's request. Without enough to do, everyone thought about their families and church. Thomas Dunn said these were the most "lonesome days he ever saw, with nothing to interest the eye and but little the mind."[9] Azariah wrote poems, one of which follows:

> Oh, my home, when shall I see thee,
> And the friends I love so well?
> I do not like this barren country
> But glad would bid it long farewell.
>   Let me hasten
> To the home I love so well.
>
> My heart feels sad I can't forget thee
> While I love thy scenes so well,
> Haste kind heaven and restore me
> To the home I love so well.
>   Let me hasten
> To the home I love so well.

Tues., Mar. 30, San Diego. Lydia Hunter, who expected her baby any time, was still not well. No regular meetings were held. There was much prejudice against Mormons from rumors spread by dragoons and Missouri soldiers before the battalion arrived.

Wed., Mar. 31, San Diego. Two wagons arrived from Los Angeles for groceries. Except for the morning drills and guard duty, few military orders were issued. "Here our company fared well while the other companies [in Los Angeles] had to drill every day twice until they commenced the fort and then they had to work all the time while we lived at our ease" (William Coray).

Thurs., Apr. 1, San Diego. A light refreshing rain fell during the morning. The men thought more and more about discharge and joining their families. They organized a Young Men's Club for the purpose of lecturing, debating, and reciting poetry to have something to do. Azariah was very lonesome to see his mother and sisters, but was comforted to know only three more months remained until discharge. William Coray's bad cough continued.

Fri., Apr. 2, San Diego. Although there were rumors that a great battle between General Taylor and General Santa Anna had taken place, with fourteen hundred Mexicans and five hundred Americans killed, the soldiers believed they would not have to go to battle because of Brigham Young's promise.

Sun., Apr. 4, San Diego. William Hyde preached an "excellent" discourse. Many sailors, officers, and citizens were present at the meeting. There was general satisfaction among those attending.

Thurs., Apr. 8, San Diego. The ship *Barnstable* arrived from San Francisco bringing forty barrels of flour and a letter from Colonel Cooke telling Captain Hunter to resume full rations of flour and 1½ lb. of beef per day per soldier. Azariah and Thomas Dutcher went swimming in the ocean and a fish stung Thomas on the foot. The stinger was in the fish's tail. His pain was very severe for several hours. John Lawson built a blacksmith forge.

Wed., April 18, San Diego. A sailor named Beckworth, from the ship *Congress,* was baptized in the ocean, probably the first Mormon convert in California. He was baptized by William Garner of Company B. Some cut up their tents to make shirts and pants, which Captain Hunter didn't like.

Fri., Apr. 16, San Diego. A shooting today resulted in a local man being put in irons when he shot at a Spanish man. It caused excitement for a while. The first regular mail arrived from San Francisco in seven days, establishing a mail route. The round trip would take fourteen days.

Tues., Apr. 20, San Diego. Lydia Hunter had a baby son, named Diego, seventy-eight days after arriving. Traveling and carrying a baby on the long journey was hard on her. She was pregnant the entire trip from Ft. Leavenworth. Diego was the first child of American parents to be born in San Diego.

Wed., Apr. 21, San Diego. Samuel Rogers and his mess built an oven for baking bread and meat. Lydia's condition continued to be very grave.

She had an attack of severe rigors and had great difficulty breathing, together with a high fever.

Fri., Apr. 23, San Diego. Lydia continued to have attacks of rigors about eleven each morning along with cramps and nervous twitchings. It affected her mind.

Sun., Apr. 25, San Diego. Lydia remained delirious since the day before. She suffered greatly. Dr. John Griffin from the ship *Congress* attended her.

Mon., Apr. 26, San Diego. Lydia Hunter died at 10 P.M. in great pain. Juanita Wrightington, a local lady, who had helped during Lydia's confinement, agreed to take care of the week-old infant. Lydia's death touched the hearts of the soldiers. The guide, Charbonneau, was very kind and helpful to Captain Hunter during this sad time.

Tues., Apr. 27, San Diego. Lydia was buried in the old cemetery on Point Loma.[10] William Hyde preached her funeral sermon. A feeling of sadness prevailed. He told of her bravery on the whole journey and remembered her as a "very estimable lady," a faithful member of the Mormon Church, who would be missed. With Lydia's passing, Melissa Coray was the only woman with Company B in San Diego. The other two women, Susan Davis and Phebe Brown, were in Los Angeles with their husbands.

Wed., Apr. 28, San Diego. A pitiful cripple came into San Diego begging. He said he'd been hiding in the mountains for a long time, was one of Frémont's men, and was a member of the mob at the Haun's Mill massacre.[11] Horace Alexander, Company B, knew him. Azariah baked a light bread, similar to flap jacks, which his comrades enjoyed. David Rainey baptized John Borrowman, Elijah Allen, and Thomas Dunn for the remission of sins.

Sun., May 2, San Diego. Quite a few went to the Catholic church to see a mass for the first time. It was a Catholic holy day and Christ's funeral procession was reenacted.

Tues., May 4, San Diego. Major Cloud arrived with six months' pay. Privates drew $42. The money came at a very good time because it provided money to outfit for the trip east to rejoin families and church.

Wed., May 5, San Diego. The beggar was caught stealing a knife. He begged the Mormons to forgive him for his role at Haun's Mill. The locals were becoming more friendly as they realized the soldiers of the battalion were different from what they had been told. As the soldiers became acquainted with the Californios, they found the natives to be friendly and intelligent, living like gentlemen with many Indians as their servants. Drills were held as usual.

Thurs., May 6, San Diego. A steady rain made the men feel wet and uncomfortable. John Borrowman was on mule guard when he found a nest with eight duck eggs in it. They made a good supper for his mess.

Sat., May 8, San Diego. The men bought wild mares for $3; those broken to ride were from $6 to $12; horses unbroken, $6 to $8; broken to ride, $10 to $20. Mules were double the price of common horses. Albert Dunham was very ill. John Borrowman bought a pocket knife and some linen to make garments, special underclothes worn by faithful Mormons.

Mon., May 10, San Diego. The men were ready to burn the bricks they had made. Azariah, Ephraim Green, Israel Evans, Jesse Martin, and Hyrum Mount went eight miles to cut wood for the kiln. Albert Dunham's condition worsened. An Indian was whipped in the square for getting drunk and trying to kill his mother.

Tues., May 11, San Diego. Albert Dunham died. The doctor said he had an ulcer on his brain. He suffered terribly. He was buried beside Lydia Hunter on Point Loma. Azariah and others made shoes from skins. Some earned extra money by ocean fishing and cutting wood for locals. They received two dollars per cord. Word was received that General Doniphan was successful in two battles.[12]

Thurs., May 13, San Diego. Sergeants William Coray and Ephraim Hanks left for Los Angeles.

Sat., May 15, San Diego. A large bell was hung, which was to ring every night at eight o'clock. Ammunition for their guns was issued to be ready in case of an uprising. Henry Bigler found the skeleton of a whale, bleached white, on the beach. The ribs were about nine feet long and ten inches wide. He took two of them to the fort for seats. Francis Brown had never recovered from the physical demands of the journey and was still sickly. He married an Indian girl, Magell Mancheeta, who was good to him and took care of him. A Mexican child was buried in the evening. The body, all decorated, was carried on boards on their heads by several women. An Indian man followed carrying the coffin, then came two men fiddling, and last was the priest. There were two men behind the procession who kept firing rifles over their heads.

Sun., May 16, San Diego. Mail arrived from Los Angeles. The carriers from Fort Moore brought the news that General Kearny and Colonel Cooke planned to leave Los Angeles for the East and would take fifteen men from the four battalion companies in Los Angeles as guards. Ephraim Hanks, Company B in San Diego, and Bill Casper, Company A, one of the mail carriers from Los Angeles, borrowed horses and performed an unorthodox bull fight, much to the enjoyment of their comrades.

Mon., May 17, San Diego. John Borrowman cut out a garment and sewed part of it. He had never made garments before.

Tues., May 18, San Diego. Captain Barker, whose ship was in the harbor, was married to a Californio lady by the Catholic priest. Cannon from the ships in harbor and muskets were fired. Feasting and dancing went on all night. Borrowman continued to work on his garment.

Thurs., May 20, San Diego. Melissa Coray finished a garment for Samuel Rogers and he paid her fifty cents. William Coray and Ephraim Hanks returned from Los Angeles with four good mares and two fine horses.

Sun., May 23, San Diego. Troops were inspected in the morning. The weather continued to be ideal, and the men's thoughts turned more and more to home. They performed various jobs to earn extra money and to keep busy. They made adobe, burned bricks, built houses, dug wells, and did various mechanical labor. Baking, tailoring, reading and fishing occupied many hours and kept the men busy. They bought mules and horses and scarce clothing items preparing for the trip. About thirty Indians came to town at night.

Mon., May 24, San Diego. John Borrowman cut out another pair of garments and began sewing them.

Tues., May 25, San Diego. Samuel Rogers picked up another garment Sister Coray made for him and paid her fifty cents. John Borrowman couldn't sleep because of the fleas.

Sun., May 30, San Diego. William Bush, John Borrowman, and Nathan Young borrowed a boat from Captain Henry Fitch, the alcalde, and went to an island in the bay. They saw a deer and two hares. Henry Bigler said the fleas were taking over the fort.

When the mail arrived, several men in Company B received letters. Horace Alexander learned his wife died in January. He was heartbroken. He had worried about her the entire trip. He had such a hard time leaving her. The letter didn't say if the baby lived or not, or if he had a son or daughter. The men were buying mules and horses—$5 to $15 each—and some were breaking them. They also learned many of the *Brooklyn* Saints were settling around San Francisco and that Sam Brannan, their leader, had gone to meet Brigham Young and the pioneers to tell them about California. The *Brooklyn* passengers had planted 145 acres of wheat and several acres of corn and potatoes at New Hope.

Tues., June 1, San Diego. Robert Bliss reminded everyone that in one and one-half months "we bid good-bye to Uncle Sam, having it to say, 'You are the most exacting Uncle we ever had.'"[13] John Borrowman finished his garments.

Fri., June 4, San Diego. The mail brought official word General Taylor had beaten General Santa Anna in the Battle of Buena Vista on May 22–23, which ended the Mexican resistance in northern Mexico. Colonel Cooke ordered a salute of twenty rounds by cannon to celebrate the news. The Catholic church had a few less glass windows than before when the men ceased firing.[14] Colonel Cooke had come to San Diego to catch a ship to San Francisco to meet General Kearny for the trip to Fort Leavenworth.

Tues., June 8, San Diego. The men were busy getting supplies, live-stock, and clothing to leave. Azariah's coat was stolen.

Sun., June 13, San Diego. Albert Smith's mare ran away. Azariah and Thomas Dutcher went after wild oats growing on nearby hills. Since Colonel Cooke was going to Fort Leavenworth with General Kearny, a new commander, Colonel Jonathan D. Stevenson, arrived and was intro-duced to the soldiers.[15]

Fri., June 18, San Diego. An Indian child, dressed neatly with colorful ribbons, was buried. The corpse was carried from the house to the grave by two women. Music was played upon stringed instruments, with muskets fired as fast as they could be loaded. At the grave the corpse was taken from the shoulders of the women and placed on the ground. Then it was put into a coffin and lowered into the grave. Both men and women filled the grave with handfuls of earth, after which the whole group left singing accompanied by instrumental music.

Tues., June 22, San Diego. Stephen St. John and Elisha Averett came from Los Angeles and reported the companies there generally were in good health and that a quorum of seventies had been organized to regu-late Mormon Church business. St. John was quorum president.[16]

Wed., June 23, San Diego. Colonel Stevenson addressed the company, expressing high satisfaction with Company B in San Diego. He spoke of their good reputation among the Californians. He wanted the men to reen-list for another year, especially the young single men.[17] Captain Hunter spoke and offered to reenlist for six months on condition of being paid travel pay back at the end of the term. Not many were in favor of reenlist-ing. The men wondered what Levi Hancock, whom they considered their spiritual leader and who was in Los Angeles, thought about reenlisting. Only thirteen from Company B indicated a willingness to sign up. Sergeant Hyde and Corporal Horace Alexander were opposed to reenlisting. They went with Captain Hunter and Colonel Stevenson to Los Angeles. When the foursome arrived at Fort Moore, they learned David Pettegrew believed the men had served their commitment and should return to their families.

Thurs., June 24, San Diego. Lieutenant Robert Clift, Company C, was appointed alcalde, replacing Captain Henry Fitch, who resigned. Clift had been assigned to assist Captain Fitch and had traveled to San Diego with Company B from San Luis Rey.

Fitch, a long-time resident of San Diego, married a native lady in the morning. After the wedding by the priest, several battalion boys fired guns too close and broke several windows in the church. The wedding fandan-go, which was scheduled to last several days and nights of feasting and drinking, was said to cost Fitch five hundred dollars.

Sat., June 26, San Diego. Henry Wilcox was sick and unable to stand guard, so he paid John Borrowman fifty cents to take his duty.

Mon., June 28, San Diego. William Garner and Henry Bigler dug a well and lined it for Captain Fitch. The wedding celebration continued.

Tues., June 29, San Diego. Henry Bigler and others cleared the first yard for moulding brick in San Diego. The labor was performed for Juan Bandini, a prominent Californian. Philander Colton and Rufus Stoddard burnt the kiln. George Taggart made pack saddles for their trip to their families after discharge. The wedding revelers seemed to be winding down.

Wed., June 30, San Diego. Company B was mustered for the last time in San Diego. They were to be discharged in Los Angeles with the other four companies.

Sun., July 4, San Diego. This was the seventy-first anniversary of America's birth. Five cannon and small arms were shot off at sunrise. After that James Sly led a group of men around to the officers' quarters and some of the friendly Californios' residences, shooting their muskets and giving the local residents cheers and a hearty salute. The town people were pleased and brought out wine and brandy. Some of the boys were drunk by the end of the festivities. Mrs. Juan Bandini, an important lady in town, gave a short, touching speech saying they didn't want the Mormons to leave. She said they should take the American flag flying in the town square when they left. When Captain Hunter, William Hyde, and Horace Alexander returned from Los Angeles in the evening, the men shouldered their pieces again and marched to the arrivals' quarters and gave them a hearty cheer. Robert Bliss wrote this poem about leaving:

A few days more and we shall go
To see our wives and children too
And friends so dear we've left below
To save the Church from overthrow.
Our absence from them has been long
But, oh, the time will soon be gone
When we shall meet once more on earth
And praise the God who gave us birth.

Mon., July 6, San Diego. While here the soldiers had dug about twenty wells and walled them with bricks. They also laid brick sidewalks and built chimneys. Carpenters finished the insides of several houses. Fences and buildings were whitewashed. Philander Colton, Henry Wilcox, Rufus Stoddard, and William Garner stated they burned forty thousand bricks that were used in buildings, chimneys, wells, and walkways. Sidney Willes built a windlass and bucket to haul fresh water up from the bottom of the well. John Lawson opened a blacksmith shop. Captain Hunter produced adobes for a wall, the jail, and a corral at twenty dollars per thousand. An oven for baking bread and meat was built. George

Taggart opened a tannery. Samuel Miles helped the alcalde administer the common law in force in California.[18] He also kept the alcalde's court records and made reports for the military governor. They worked a coal mine on Point Loma, but it was not too successful.[19]

All of these things won the friendship of the residents, but perhaps the thing that impressed the natives most was having wells. Before the battalion arrived, they had to go quite a distance for water of very poor quality in wells about a foot deep. The wells the soldiers dug were thirty feet. deep. After Willes rigged the windlass and bucket, the residents were astounded. As soon as breakfast was over, the native men went to the well and sat around, smoking their cigaritos, while one of the party kept drawing up a bucket of water. They called the soldiers Mormonitos. The residents sent an express to Colonel Cooke asking for another company of Mormonitos to replace Company B. The citizens found the men to be peaceful, quiet, industrious fellows, who had improved their town greatly. They had been told the Mormons would steal everything and insult their women, but that had not been the case.

Thurs., July 8, San Diego. Brick masons Philander Colton, Rufus Stoddard, Henry Wilcox, and William Garner, finished the house they were building, which was the first brick house in San Diego. It was to be used for both a courthouse and schoolhouse. While the brick workers took a bath in the ocean after finishing their work, the citizens set out a table in the square and invited everyone to help themselves.

Fri., July 9, San Diego, 10 miles. Good-byes were said and Company B took up the line of march for Los Angeles to be discharged. As they left, the natives clung to them like children.

Sat., July 10, en route to Los Angeles, 21 miles. Traveled twenty-one miles and camped.

Sun., July 11, 10 miles. Azariah Smith's mare, apparently startled by something, jumped stiff legged and Azariah fell, hitting his head on a rock. He suffered greatly with a terrible headache. Camped by the old Flores Mission.

Mon., July 12, 24 miles. Camped by San Juan Mission.

Tues., July 13, 24 miles. Camped by a spring and a grove of trees in a very large valley. They passed thousands of bullocks, besides hundreds of horses and other cattle.

Wed., July 14, 22 miles. Azariah did not complain, but continued to suffer with a severe headache.

Thurs., July 15, 10 miles. Company B arrived in Los Angeles. The five companies were pleased to be united again.

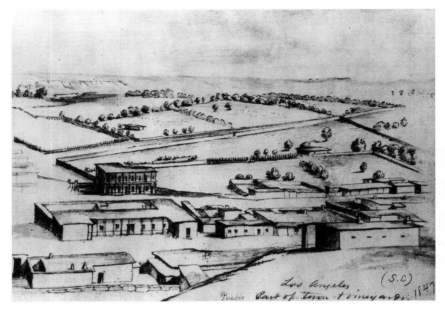

Los Angeles (S.C)
Pueblo Part of town & vineyards. 1847

Panoramic view of Los Angeles, 1847, showing the plaza area and vineyards.
Security Pacific Collection, Los Angeles Public Library, California.

CHAPTER SIX

Los Angeles: Building Fort Moore

After Company B departed for San Diego, the other four companies stayed in San Luis Rey for three days before leaving for Los Angeles March 19. Lieutenant Oman and thirty-two men who were ill remained at the mission.

The experiences of the four companies in Los Angeles were different from those of Company B in San Diego. Pueblo de Los Angeles was much larger than San Diego and there was not the interaction between citizens and the soldiers on helpful, constructive projects in Los Angeles. The soldiers had spare time daily and many recorded how they walked about town. By contrast, the soldiers in San Diego asked for permission to hire out and help the natives by digging wells, making bricks, and performing other odd jobs. Also, in Los Angeles there were other soldiers besides the battalion—the regular army and the First Dragoons—as well as more natives, all of which presented exposure to the very temptations the Mormons had been warned against. Many activities around them simply did not fit in with the moral code of their church. Some succumbed to the temptations surrounding them. In San Diego the men formed a debating society when not working and read literature and recited poetry. In Los Angeles there is no evidence of this type of activity. Azariah Smith told of going to the ocean and running in the sand along the San Diego beaches while singing with his father. Los Angeles had no calming beaches for the young men to work off extra energy.

In Los Angeles there also were differences between the officers and the enlisted men on a variety of subjects. Some of this tension went back to the beginning of the march when Lieutenant Colonel James Allen died. The men still did not understand why the officers voted to let Lieutenant Smith lead the battalion without giving the privates a chance to vote. This resentment festered over on several occasions during the journey, the last of which was in Los Angeles. By contrast, the men in Company B liked their leader, Captain Hunter, and seemed to get along well with each other. There also was resentment in Los Angeles that the men in San Diego could hire out for pay while they toiled building a fort without the opportunity to earn extra money. A study of the companies during their four months in Los Angeles reveals general discontent, inactivity, and boredom. They began looking forward more and more to returning to their families and church. Their story is picked up in San Luis Rey after the departure of Company B for San Diego.

Tues., Mar. 16, San Luis Rey. Regular drills, and everything as usual.

Wed., Mar. 17, San Luis Rey. Four days of reduced rations were issued. Instead of 12 oz. of flour, they received 8 oz. Instead of ¾ lb. of pickled pork, they received ¾ lb. of salt beef. There was talk among the companies of refusing to do duty until more food was furnished. The country abounded in beef and there were supplies in San Diego. Several in Company D were put under guard for voicing their feelings. William Maxwell, Company D, was put in the stocks for refusing to drill.

Thurs., Mar. 18, San Luis Rey. Drills were dispensed with so preparations could be made to leave for Pueblo de Los Angeles. Many were barefooted. Henry Standage wrapped raw hides around his feet as did others.

Fri., Mar. 19, San Luis Rey, 20 miles. Lieutenant Oman and thirty-two sick men were left to garrison San Luis Rey while the rest of Companies A, C, D, and E left for Pueblo de Los Angeles. Camped close to the ocean at night. The colonel increased rations of beef at suppertime.

Sat., Mar. 20, 13 miles. Tents were struck at sunrise. They traveled along the beach for ten miles before going up a fertile valley to San Juan Mission. It was a large stone building, damaged by an earthquake years before. They found many fruit trees such as quince, pear, apple, orange, fig, olive, pepper, and date and a large vineyard. The men who wrapped their feet in rawhide suffered greatly because the animal skins hardened and cut into their feet and ankles. There were many painful blisters.

Sun., Mar. 21, Foster's Range, 23 miles. The men were very tired in the morning. They crossed a large plain with thousands of cattle roaming, but not a house in sight. There were many flowers of different colors, but no timber or water. The troops were generally very worn out.

Mon., Mar. 22, San Gabriel River. They struck the tents early and continued across the large plain. They passed cattle that covered the landscape as far as the eye could see. Several men dropped behind because of fatigue and hunger and did not reach camp until night. This was where General Kearny and Commodore Stockton were victorious in the Battle of the Mesa with the Mexicans.

Tues., Mar. 23, Pueblo de Los Angeles. After crossing the San Gabriel River in the morning, they arrived in Pueblo de Los Angeles about noon. It seemed, upon arriving, to be a pleasant place with much cultivated land along the San Pedro River. They learned they were in the middle of the trouble between General Kearny and Colonel Frémont. Having served under General Kearny, they were loyal to him. Frémont claimed he conquered the country and should be the governor. Because some of Frémont's troops were from Missouri where anti-Mormon sentiment ran high, there was immediate distrust and concern by the Mormon soldiers about camping in such close proximity. "After arriving at Los Angeles we were halted and required to stand in ranks ready at a moment's notice. We were in this position for about two hours while the two generals [Kearny and Frémont] discussed the matter, but we were finally allowed to sit down or stand at ease" (Zadock K. Judd).[1]

When they arrived in town, there were no quarters, so they camped about a mile away in a beautiful green area near an Indian village. They were given "stinking" meat by the colonel, who stayed in town with the dragoons. The City of the Angels was situated a few miles from the coast. There were about five thousand Mexicans and Indians, a few foreigners, and one thousand buildings surrounding a central plaza. The buildings were small and inferior with walls of adobe and roofs of tar and leaves. They were one story high with flat roofs. Acres of vineyards and fruit-bearing orchards and vegetable gardens surrounded the pueblo. Thousands of cattle roamed the countryside. There were many grog shops and gambling houses.

> There are a number of tar springs in the vicinity. It has the smell of stone coal and boils up out of the earth. It is used by most of the inhabitants for covering to the houses. When exposed to the sun it melts and becomes soft, but in case of a storm it is a perfect barrier. The roofs are flat and when made a layer of cane or small sticks are laid on the poles. After this the tar is broken up from the springs where it becomes hardened when exposed to the sun, drawn in carts and put on the roof. It is there melted down in the process of time and the roof becomes flat. (David Pettegrew)[2]

Wed., Mar. 24, Pueblo de Los Angeles. Several battalion officers and privates went into town. The Indians brought corn, bread, and liquor to camp for sale. Colonel Cooke and Doctor Sanderson went to San Gabriel, where two hundred of Frémont's California Volunteers were quartered in the mission under Captain Owens. The soldiers appeared polite and friendly, but when Cooke explained his new authority as commander of the Southern Military District, Captain Owens, on orders from Frémont, refused to move his troops from San Gabriel. He also refused to turn over any public ordnance to Cooke. Colonel Cooke was upset particularly because Owens would not relinquish two field pieces Kearny's dragoons had hauled from Santa Fe to California. Despite Owens' refusal, Cooke did not use force, but rather returned to Los Angeles. He expressed his outrage in his official report:

> The general's orders are not obeyed? . . . To think of a howitzer brought over the deserts with so much faithful labor by the dragoons; the howitzer with which they have four times fought the enemy, and brought here to the rescue of Lieut. Colonel Frémont and his volunteers, to be refused to them by this Lieut. Colonel Frémont and in defiance of the orders of his general! I denounce this treason or this mutiny.[3]

Thurs., Mar. 25, Pueblo de Los Angeles. Henry Standage was detailed for mule guard, starting at 8 A.M. The company officers tried to make arrangements for the battalion to obtain clothing. A three-mule team left for San Diego for supplies.

Fri., Mar. 26, Pueblo de Los Angeles. The night guards were relieved at 8 A.M. They had no supper before going on guard duty and no breakfast in the morning until 11 A.M. when they received 1 lb. coarse flour, no sugar, no coffee, and only 1¼ lbs. of beef.

Sat., Mar. 27, Pueblo de Los Angeles. The battalion moved up the San Pedro River one mile to a pleasant camping ground, still in sight of town, but separate from all other troops.

Sun., Mar. 28, Pueblo de Los Angeles. Jeremiah Willey preached at a meeting. The dragoons under Lieutenant George Stoneman returned. They killed four Indians, who had been attacking the Mexicans. "The Dragoon horses came back with feet so worn as to make the most of them lame and useless. I shall tomorrow commence the introduction of horse shoes in California, at least in this southerly part" (Philip St. George Cooke).[4] George Dykes, Cyrus Canfield, and others preached in the evening.

Mon., Mar. 29, Pueblo de Los Angeles. Captain Davis made arrangements for leather for his men so they could make shoes. Drills were at four o'clock.

Tues., Mar. 30, Pueblo de Los Angeles. Colonel Cooke visited the Mormon camp. He brought news their money was coming and they would be paid soon. Everyone was destitute for clothing. Colonel Frémont arrived from the North. Captain Hunt preached in the evening and related again the circumstances connected with Lieutenant A. J. Smith's taking command of the battalion. Hunt tried to show he was not to blame and the prejudice of the battalion against him was ill-founded. Levi Hancock and Philemon Merrill also made a few remarks.

Thurs., Apr. 1, Pueblo de Los Angeles. Word was received that David Smith died in San Luis Rey. Drills as usual.

Fri., Apr. 2, Pueblo de Los Angeles. Some washed clothes. Drills continued.

Sat., Apr. 3, Pueblo de Los Angeles. Regular drills were held.

Sun., Apr. 4, Pueblo de Los Angeles. At four o'clock Captain Hunt called a dress parade. Many mistakes were made because Captain Hunt was not familiar with leading drills. Twenty ladies, dressed in rich, fancy clothing, were present with their attendants. They came to visit Captain Davis's wife, Susan, and Sergeant Brown's wife, Phebe.

Mon., Apr. 5, Pueblo de Los Angeles. The wagons returned from San Diego filled with coffee, sugar, soap, candles, and other needed supplies. The drivers of these wagons reported the reason David Smith died was that he was killed with calomel administered by Dr. Sanderson in San Luis Rey. He was speechless two days before dying. Colonel Richard Mason arrived at the mouth of the San Pedro in a ship and brought a letter to Captain Hunt from General Kearny in Monterey. Mason had been sent by Kearny to discharge Colonel Frémont's California Volunteers. Mason met with Frémont with orders to muster the volunteers and demanded delivery of all government artillery, arms, supplies, and horses. Once more, the California Volunteers refused to be mustered into the service of the United States, so Mason ordered Frémont to discharge his men immediately. The ordnance pieces received from Frémont's troops were secured and placed under the Mormon Battalion at the fort the Mormons were building on the hill overlooking the town.

Tues., Apr. 6, Pueblo de Los Angeles. Two wagons were sent to San Pedro for supplies from a newly arrived ship.

Wed., Apr. 7, Pueblo de Los Angeles. The wagons returned from San Pedro loaded with fine flour and clothing for the regulars. Two cannon were brought from San Gabriel Mission, which had been in charge of Colonel Frémont's men. The Mormons started a petition requesting discharge from the army, since the fighting with Mexico appeared to be over in this area and there seemed to be no further need for the battalion. Captain Daniel Davis and Lieutenants James Pace, Andrew Lytle, Lorenzo Clark, George Dykes, and George Rosecrans were against the petition.

Thurs., Apr. 8, Pueblo de Los Angeles. Several teams sent to the San Gabriel Mission returned with seven more cannon. Colonel Mason sent his orderly to Colonel Frémont's headquarters with a written request for the military and civil records. Three times the orderly presented himself to Frémont's headquarters and three times Frémont's orderly turned him away.[5] The battalion had drills as usual.

Fri., Apr. 9, Pueblo de Los Angeles. Drills as usual for the battalion. Frémont finally appeared at Mason's quarters. Mason demanded

Frémont account for the large herd of horses which his topographical party had taken from the United States. Frémont walked out without accounting for the horses and challenged Mason to a duel. When General Kearny heard of the proposed duel, he demanded that it be postponed indefinitely.

Sat., Apr. 10, Pueblo de Los Angeles. Lieutenant Sylvester Hulet asked to resign and be relieved from army service. Henry Standage thought Hulet's release showed the officers' hearts were softening and were more willing to listen to the men's petitions.[6] No drills.

Sun., Apr. 11, Pueblo de Los Angeles. Lieutenant James Pace and Company C were ordered to post guard at Cajon Pass. Several Mexicans came into camp.

Mon., Apr. 12, Pueblo de Los Angeles. The morning was very foggy, but it cleared away by noon. Lieutenant Pace and Company C left for Cajon Pass. Henry Standage sold coffee in town for thirty-seven cents a pound in exchange for saleratus at fifty cents a pound. General Mason of the First Dragoons visited the Mormon camp and gave them praise for "being the best volunteers of any he had ever seen in the manual of arms."[7]

Tues., Apr. 13, Pueblo de Los Angeles. Lieutenant Oman and the detachment from San Luis Rey arrived today and were quartered with their comrades. A few of Oman's company still were not well.

Wed., Thurs., Fri., Apr. 14, 15, 16, Pueblo de Los Angeles. Drills as usual.

Sat., Apr. 17, Pueblo de Los Angeles. Sergeant Daniel Browett went to the different companies and advised them that a "Mass Quorum of Seventies" would be organized the next day at 11 A.M., three-fourths of a mile from camp.

Sun., Apr. 18, Pueblo de Los Angeles. The seventies met as scheduled. After singing, Stephen St. John spoke on the evils arising in the battalion: drunkenness, swearing, and other sins. A vote was taken to have the seventies unite to use their influence in stopping these vices. The vote was carried unanimously.[8] St. John was voted senior president of the quorum, and James Pace, Andrew Lytle, Daniel Browett, Jonathan Holmes, Fredrick Fauney, and Jeremiah Willey, were the seven presidents of the seventy. Each of the presidents spoke, followed by Cyrus Canfield, who talked about the impropriety of some in camp. John Allen was excommunicated unanimously for drunkenness, swearing, and other vices.[9]

While on guard duty Lieutenant George Oman told Henry Standage that Levi Hancock's course with the men would have amounted to insurrection had he been left to pursue the same and had not been checked.

Mon., Apr. 19, Pueblo de Los Angeles. Received more tents left by Frémont's men at San Gabriel Mission. Frémont's California Volunteers were discharged.[10]

Tues., Apr. 20, Pueblo de Los Angeles. Rumors from various sources were that Colonel Frémont and Colonel Mason were not friendly. Drill as usual.

Wed., Apr. 21, Pueblo de Los Angeles. Paymaster Jeremiah Cloud of the battalion staff returned from Monterey with gold for the battalion. Drills continued.

Thurs., Apr. 22, Pueblo de Los Angeles. A detail of twenty-four men, eight each from Companies A, D, and E, was made to relieve Company C at Cajon Pass. This detail was ordered to town to receive pay, each receiving $42. In the evening David Pettegrew and Levi Hancock preached. Captain Hunt called the meeting on "the necessity of keeping ourselves from being polluted and remembering our covenants." Hunt told those who had sinned to sin no more.

Fri., Apr. 23, Pueblo de Los Angeles. Colonel Cooke sent word to move to a green meadow one- half mile below town as the Missouri Volunteers were threatening to "come down" on the Mormons. The battalion packed and moved to be safe.[11]

Sat., Apr. 24, Pueblo de Los Angeles. Company A received six months' pay.

Sun., Apr. 25, Pueblo de Los Angeles. Company A moved into town to start building a fort. At night they were ordered to load their guns and fix their bayonets. Colonel Cooke heard that Frémont's men might attack the Mormons, so he sent word to be ready.

Mon., Apr. 26, Pueblo de Los Angeles. Frémont's men had been trying to prejudice the Mexicans and Indians against the battalion by telling them the Mormons would insult their wives. This caused excitement throughout the area. Frémont's men didn't come during the night as expected. Companies D and E received pay of $42 and were ordered to town. They camped on the hill where Company A was building the fort.

Tues., Apr. 27, Pueblo de Los Angeles. A report was received that the Mexicans attacked Lieutenant Pace and Company C in Cajon Pass. They left Los Angeles April 11.

Wed., Apr. 28, Pueblo de Los Angeles. As soon as the night guard was relieved in the morning, they were ordered to work on a ditch and to assist in building the fort.

This is the closest place we have been in yet, to stand guard through the night and then to be obliged to work on the fort through the day 10 hours, parade at retreat with our accoutrements and do our own cooking, and especially as we can see no use of crowding business this close. The fact is if our Battalion Officers who profess to be our brethren would act as fathers to us we could have easier times but they seek to please the gentiles and to gain favor at our expense. Our officers will even find fault with us even in these times, for not having our guns in good bright condition when it was impossible for us to do in consequence of our being tented out and crowded 9 into a tent calculated at first for only six. Being compelled to leave our guns outside the tent or lay them on the ground in the night time. This evening Company C and Lt. Pace came back. The reports we had of them being attacked were false. (Henry Standage) [12]

Thurs., Apr. 29, Pueblo de Los Angeles. Twenty-eight men of the First New York Volunteers came in from Santa Barbara and brought cartridges for the battalion. This regiment, commanded by Jonathan A. Stevenson, was composed of immigrants and others who wished to settle in California after the war. [13]

Fri., Apr. 30, Pueblo de Los Angeles. David Pettegrew preached to the battalion on drunkenness and drinking in general. General Kearny notified Colonel Cooke that the sutler with Frémont's volunteers had a full assortment of clothing and the battalion could have them at a reduced price.

Sat., May 1, Pueblo de Los Angeles. A bakehouse was opened this morning. The soldiers were to be issued bread instead of flour. Henry Standage was assigned to the bakehouse.

Sun., May 2, Pueblo de Los Angeles. Henry Standage walked around the Pueblo and was not impressed with what he saw:

I have been more or less through the city of Angels and must say they are the most degraded set of beings I ever was among, professing to be civilized and taught in the Roman Catholic religion. There are almost as many grog shops and gambling houses in this city as there are private houses. Only 5 or 6 stores and no mechanics shops. A tolerable sized Catholic church, built of unburnt bricks and houses of the same material. Roofs are made of reeds and pitched on the outside (tar springs close by or I may say pitch). Roofs flat. There are some 3 or 4 roofs built American fashion and covered with burnt [tile] English fashion. The Spaniards in general own large farms in the country and keep from one to 20,000 head of cattle, horses, mules, sheep, goats, etc., in abundance. The Indians do all the labor and the Mexicans are generally on horse back from morning till night. They are perhaps the greatest horsemen in the known world, and very expert with the lance and lasso. They are in general a very idle, profligate, drunken, swearing set of wretches, with but very few exceptions. The Spaniards' conduct in the Grog shops with the squaws is really filthy and disgusting even in the day time. Gambling is carried to the highest pitch, men often losing 500 dollars cash in one night or a thousand head of cattle. All kinds of clothing is very cheap and cattle and horses very cheap. Horses from 5 to 25 dollars and the very best of mares from 1.50 to 10 dollars; mules equally cheap. Cattle from 5 to 6 dollars. [14]

Mon., May 3, Pueblo de Los Angeles. The bakeshop was busy all day.

Tues., May 4, Pueblo de Los Angeles. Before Frémont's California Volunteers left for Santa Barbara, an order was read offering them the privilege of being discharged and enlisted in the dragoons for a period of five years. The offer, holding no interest for Frémont's men, was refused.

Wed., Thurs., Fri., May 5, 6, 7, Pueblo de Los Angeles. Work continued on the fort and in the bakehouse.

Sat., May 8, Pueblo de Los Angeles. An express arrived from Santa Fe, telling of an Indian uprising. Colonel Sterling Price and the army units at Santa Fe had fought Indians for three days in Taos before suppressing them. Twenty-eight dragoons and a number of Price's volunteers were killed. Governor Charles Bent was murdered in his home in Taos. (Details of this battle are told in chapter 12.) The companies in Los Angeles wondered about their comrades in the Pueblo detachments and hoped they were safe. Express mail from Nauvoo, Council Bluffs, and other places in Iowa was welcomed by recipients in the battalion. Lieutenant Samuel Thompson and twenty men took rations for three days and went to the Williams Ranch near the mountain to quell an Indian uprising.

Sun., May 9, Pueblo de Los Angeles. General Kearny arrived in Los Angeles and received a twenty-one-gun salute. Colonel Stevenson and other officers came with him. Colonel Stevenson was appointed commander of the Southern District, relieving Colonel Cooke so he could go with General Kearny to Fort Leavenworth. General Kearny visited the Mormon camp and gave them good advice. Teams were sent to San Pedro for supplies.

Mon., May 10, Pueblo de Los Angeles. General Kearny inspected the battalion in the morning. After inspection they closed ranks and the general made a few remarks, thanking them for their good behavior and work. He also asked the single men to reenlist. Fifteen men were detailed to accompany him to Fort Leavenworth as guards for John C. Frémont, who was to be court-martialed for not obeying military directives in California.

Wed., May 12, Pueblo de Los Angeles. One hundred and twenty New York Volunteers belonging to Colonel Stevenson's regiment came in from Monterey.

Thurs., May 13, Pueblo de Los Angeles. Twelve of the guards selected to go with General Kearny left by land for Monterey. The other three Mormon escorts were to go by ship with the general and Colonel Cooke. Originally the plan was to take three battalion men from each company, but since Company B was in San Diego, all were taken from the four companies in Los Angeles.

Lieutenant Samuel Thompson and his party surprised a small band of Indians in the mountains, killing six of them. Two of his men, Benjamin

Mayfield and Samuel G. Chapin, were wounded slightly by arrows—
Mayfield in the groin and Chapin under the eye. One of the Mexicans
who accompanied them was wounded. A second Mexican, also with
Thompson's party, slipped out among the dead Indians, scalping them
and cutting off their ears. Under California rule, a premium was paid for
Indian scalps. Thompson and his men were disgusted at this atrocity. This
barbaric custom was abolished immediately and the alcalde was instructed
not to pay any bounty on these six scalps or any in the future.[15]

Lieutenant Pace again left for Cajon Pass with twenty-six men to
guard the entry to the area, since the Indians still were troublesome.

Fri., May 14, Pueblo de Los Angeles. General Kearny, Colonel Cooke,
and three Mormon escorts left for Monterey by ship.

Fri., May 21, Pueblo de Los Angeles. Lieutenant Stoneman of the First
Dragoons came in with his detachment from the mountains.

Sat., May 22, Pueblo de Los Angeles. The men were busy rigging up
their bridles, saddles, and purchasing horses in preparation for their discharge. The bakeshop continued to bake bread daily.

Sun., May 23, Pueblo de Los Angeles. A meeting was held today.

Mon., May 24, Pueblo de Los Angeles. The men continued to ready
themselves for discharge.

Tues., May 25, Pueblo de Los Angeles. Captain Daniel Davis returned
from a trip to the country. He went to look at the ranches and farms and
gave an excellent report of the valleys he visited.

Wed., May 26, Pueblo de Los Angeles. Work continued on the fort.

Fri., May 28, Pueblo de Los Angeles. Work on the fort continued.

Sat., May 29, Pueblo de Los Angeles. The battalion soldiers were busy
buying horses. Many used cut rawhide to make lariats or long halters and
rigging on new saddles.

Mon., May 31, Pueblo de Los Angeles. Henry Standage had a tooth pulled.
News came that a battle with Mexicans was being fought in the South.

Tues., June 1, Cajon Pass. The small detachment of Company C
assigned to guard Cajon Pass against the Indians held its own religious
services while in the mountains: "On arrival here, finding ourselves separated from the gentiles, we retired to a grove and cut poles and prepared
a place to hold meetings in, and here we have a meeting once each
Sunday, and prayers morning and evening. Edward Martin, one of the . . .
Seventies has taken the lead of our meetings" (Henry G. Boyle).[16]

Wed., June 2, Pueblo de Los Angeles. The men continued to work on
rigging their saddles and going into town. The inhabitants began sweeping the public square.

Thurs., June 3, Pueblo de Los Angeles. The locals continued sweeping
the square getting ready for a church festival the next day, celebrating St.
Mary's birthday.

Fri., June 4, Pueblo de Los Angeles. In the morning the inhabitants erected four stages with altars in each corner of the square. They decorated the stages with green boughs, roses, and strips of white cloth. They put serapes, an outside covering thrown around the men while on horseback, on the ground. This celebration commemorated St. Mary's birthday and was one of many holy days observed by the Catholics.[17] Services began at ten o'clock. Colonel Stevenson ordered one cannon brought into the square and one company of New York Volunteers to be there as guards. The colonel wanted the Californios to know they were protected in their rites and ceremonies. After mass was performed inside the church, the priest and a long line of attendants walked in the square, where the priest performed rites at each of the four altars. The band of the New York Volunteers played as the procession went from corner to corner. As the priest passed, the inhabitants threw costly garments on the ground for him to walk on. The cannon was fired at intervals as the procession moved from place to place.

Sat., June 5, Pueblo de Los Angeles. Henry Standage bought a four-year-old mare for $5.50, well broke. Dogs roamed the streets at will; some were mad and had bitten three men, one of whom died. Colonel Stevenson asked several New York Volunteers and eight Mormons to kill all the stray dogs they could.[18]

Sun., June 6, Pueblo de Los Angeles. The dog killing continued with good success. By order of Colonel Stevenson and the alcalde there was horse racing today. Several Mormons rode their horses along the river and bathed in it.

Mon., June 7, Pueblo de Los Angeles. The guard at the calaboose in town had a little excitement. Henry Standage and several other Mormons were on post about dusk when one of the prisoners, an American, put on an Indian woman's clothes and passed out the jail door. Standage hailed him and discovered what was going on. He ordered Dancing Bill, as the American was called, back to the jail at the point of the bayonet and requested the corporal in charge of the jail to lock him up in another room. While this was being done, Dancing Bill made many threats and curses upon the Mormons.[19] It was cloudy all day. Many horses were purchased.

Tues., June 8, Pueblo de Los Angeles. All animals had to be tied up so they spent the day hunting for *saccate* (grass) for their animals.

Wed., June 9, Pueblo de Los Angeles. Lieutenant Thompson assigned the men the job of digging the ditch around the fort. The men told him they would work on the ditch only the usual time, no longer. Leonard Scott spent the afternoon trying to break his horse to carry grass.

Thurs., June 10, Pueblo de Los Angeles. A detail of men was sent to San Pedro to guard the military store. Several men hired Indians to make them Spanish halters for their horses.

Fri., June 11, Pueblo de Los Angeles. An express came in from Monterey with letters from the Mormon soldiers who went as guards with General Kearny. Horses, mules, saddles, and other items were much dearer in Monterey than in the Pueblo. The general left Monterey for Fort Leavenworth on May 31. Orders were read by the sergeant major from Colonel Mason, now governor of California. One of the orders related to John Allen, formerly of Company E, who had been in the calaboose for several weeks for desertion of his post as a picket guard. His sentence was to have half of his hair shaved and to be drummed out of town.

Sat., June 12, Pueblo de Los Angeles. John Spidle was thrown from his horse and was hurt severely. A detail of men was sent to the mountains for two long poles to make a "liberty" pole to raise a flag at the fort.

Sun., June 13, Pueblo de Los Angeles. During the morning Colonel Stevenson conducted a general inspection of arms, quarters, and grounds. Leonard Scott and Henry Standage went after grass for their animals. Henry's horse was scared by a Mexican woman. Henry was thrown and was injured in the fall. Several soldiers were on detached duty at the Williams ranch. They were working to obtain grain, which would be converted into flour for use on the journey home. Although cutting grain was the principal work at the Williams ranch, they also dug a race to get a small mill going.

Isaac Williams had one thousand acres of wheat to cut. He had been a resident of this area for many years. He also had a large vineyard to make wine. Before the war broke out, he had fifteen thousand head of cattle but did not know how many horses he had at this time. Williams killed a large number of cattle each summer for the hides and tallow. The meat was left to rot on the ground. He had a kettle ten feet deep and ten feet in diameter, which was filled with meat and left to simmer down. The grease was dipped off and poured into a bin about twelve feet square and the meat was thrown away. A kind of earth was added to the grease instead of ashes or lye to make soap. The Indians did this work.[20]

Mon., June 14, Pueblo de Los Angeles. Work continued on the fort in the morning. In the afternoon John Allen had half his head shaved and was discharged dishonorably from the army. A corporal marched Allen between four sentinels until he was out of town. The drummers and fifers were in the rear. He was marched through town at the point of a bayonet while the musicians played the *Rogues March*. Allen was not to return during the present war. If he did, he was to be kept in irons until the close of the war.

Tues., June 15, Pueblo de Los Angeles. Heavy morning dew, warm noontimes, cold nights, and high winds caused many to have colds. In the evening the journal of an emigrant from Missouri was read which told of great suffering in deep mountain snows of the Donner Party. The emigrants were forced to eat their animals and the hides. Some died and those remaining ate the bodies of the dead.[21]

Wed., June 16, Pueblo de Los Angeles. Many continued to suffer from colds. Horses were purchased daily by the battalion, all preparing to go home. John Allen was found in town and was put in the calaboose.

Thurs., June 17, Pueblo de Los Angeles. The detail returned from the mountains with the two large pine logs, each ten feet long. Cutting and hauling them to Fort Moore cost $100. With only a month until discharge, the men were getting anxious. An order was read from the colonel at night asking for volunteers for another six months, but none enlisted. The New York Volunteers were few in number and very discontented. The colonel thought Los Angeles would be poorly guarded when the Mormons left.

Fri., June 18, Pueblo de Los Angeles.

> They cannot in reason expect us to enlist again and especially when they know the treatment we have received, receiving no pay to go home and no ammunition to be given to us with our guns, etc. and no pay for our back rations, although we have paid out much money on the road when our rations were kept back or in other words when the Col might have procured full rations at Govt. expense . . . hard has been our fare as soldiers. (Henry Standage)[22]

Sat., June 19, Pueblo de Los Angeles. The battalion worked on the ditch around the fort and mixed mud until noon. Many still were unwell with colds. Several washed clothes in the afternoon, others read in their tents. "Some fears entertained . . . fearful of our being pressed into service for another year. The Col. very stingy. Officers generally very strict and seem to bear down on the Battalion in particular" (Henry Standage).[23]

Sun., June 20, Pueblo de Los Angeles. John Allen escaped from the calaboose by digging through the adobe wall. David Pettegrew and Levi Hancock held an evening meeting with remarks by Lieutenant George Oman and others. There was rejoicing that the end of army service was fast approaching.

Mon., June 21, Pueblo de Los Angeles. Nightly guard duty was continued. Henry Standage put away thirty-eight rounds of ball and buckshot cartridges for going home.

Tues., June 22, Pueblo de Los Angeles. Guard duty continued.

Wed., June 23, Pueblo de Los Angeles. The men were busy erecting the "liberty" pole at the fort. Colonel Stevenson left for San Diego to visit Company B.

Thurs., June 24, Pueblo de Los Angeles. This was St. John's Day, a Catholic celebration, with little work being done. There were horse races, bull fights, and gambling. The Mexicans were great horsemen. It was nothing for them to ride one hundred miles a day. It did not appear to require any extra effort to ride that long distance. They rode one hundred miles, using two or three horses, like the Americans rode fifty miles. Their exploits with the lasso in catching wild horse and cattle were astonishing to the soldiers:

> The lasso is a very strong rope usually made of raw hide and is about sixty feet in length, at one end of which there is a noose, which is thrown upon the neck of the horse or horns of the cattle, while the other end is firmly attached to the pummel of the saddle . . . they will on full gallop pick up a piece of money without halting or dismounting. They are never on foot only when entering a house. . . . I saw a game played by these Spaniards: A cock was buried in the sand save his head only. The Spaniards rode by in turns on a full gallop trying . . . to pick up the cock, several being successful. . . . These horses are much better trained for the saddle than ours. They endure fatigue much better than American horses. (Henry Standage)[24]

Fri., June 25, Pueblo de Los Angeles. Guard duty while work on the ditch and the fort continued.

Sun., June 27, Pueblo de Los Angeles. Elisha Averett and Steven St. John returned from San Diego. They reported Company B was able to work for the citizens for pay when off duty.

Mon., June 28, Pueblo de Los Angeles. Henry Standage and a small group were detailed to build an oven in town. Colonel Stevenson returned from San Diego, accompanied by Horace Alexander, William Hyde and Captain Jesse Hunter. Thirteen men in Company B had agreed to sign up for another six months under certain conditions. "I told them the contract was made by the highest authority on earth that the officers and men were called out for one year and no longer, and if one year would not satisfy twenty would not, and if they were for a further enlistment I was not with them" (David Pettegrew).[25]

Tues., June 29, Pueblo de Los Angeles. All were ordered to remain in camp for an assembly at 8:30 A.M. Colonel Stevenson spoke on the necessity of keeping the troops here until more could be transported from the United States. He said he had orders to try to keep the whole battalion or at least one company. He knew the men with families were anxious to be discharged, but thought the single men might volunteer for the extended duty. He promised they could elect their own lieutenant colonel and would be discharged in February with a year's pay. He praised their good behavior.[26] The men were dismissed into the hands of their company officers for a meeting to consider the subject of reenlisting. At ten o'clock they met one-fourth mile from camp. Captain Hunter spoke first and said he believed the battalion should enlist for another term. Captain Hunt agreed with Captain Hunter on the matter and endeavored to show the advantages gained during the year of service in the army. Captain Hunt said that if anything happened to Governor Mason or to Colonel Stevenson, the Mormon commander, being third in command, would rise to higher power. Captain Daniel Davis agreed to everything that had been said, followed by Cyrus Canfield, who felt it would be the best thing to do. He said he had not decided whether he would reenlist or not. Lieutenant George Dykes then spoke and told the men they should sign up for another six months. David Pettegrew believed they had accomplished what they signed up for and that they should return to their families. The meeting then was adjourned to a large tent because of the hot sun. About twelve o'clock the meeting began in the tent, where it was agreed to appoint a committee to draft an agreement stating the terms on which reenlistment would take place.

Captain Hunter, Captain Davis, and David Pettegrew were chosen for the committee. As soon as the writing was finished, the group met together again and several short speeches were made, including one by Sergeant William Hyde, who favored returning to families and the church, saying that their offering for the past year was acceptable, that all were satisfied with their efforts, and he believed God was satisfied. David Pettegrew favored returning. James Ferguson, Captain Hunt, Captain Hunter, and others spoke in favor of reenlisting. Lieutenant Canfield confirmed his belief that they should sign up for another six months. Levi Hancock, speaking from the door of the tent, said he had never influenced the men against the officers, either publicly or privately. Captain Hunter said someone had been trying to set the men at variance with the officers. Lieutenant Lytle also denied ever using influence against the officers. The meeting ended with sixteen saying they would sign up. The decision and terms were taken to Colonel Stevenson, but the proposal and terms were rejected.

Wed., June 30, Pueblo de Los Angeles. General inspection at 10 A.M. No work on the fort today.

Thurs., July 1, Pueblo de Los Angeles. George Hancock and three others raised the liberty pole without incident. There was planning for the celebration of independence.

Fri., July 2, Pueblo de Los Angeles. Standage purchased a horse, well broken, for seven dollars. More preparations for the celebration.

Sat., July 3, Pueblo de Los Angeles. General policing and getting ready for the celebration the next day.

Sun., July 4, Pueblo de Los Angeles. Independence Day was celebrated by all the troops at Pueblo de Los Angeles when the whole command was paraded within the fort at sunrise. The New York Volunteers played the

"Star Spangled Banner" as the flag was being raised, followed by nine cheers by the men. After the song "Hail Columbia," the First Dragoons fired a general salute of thirteen guns. At eleven o'clock they were called again to arms. Marching to the music of the regimental band, the troops paraded within the fort, with many Spaniards and Indians present. Lieutenant Stoneman, First Dragoons, read the Declaration of Independence, followed by "Hail Columbia" by the New York Volunteers band. Colonel Stevenson gave a short address and officially named the new fort—Fort Moore after Captain Benjamin D. Moore, one of Kearny's First Dragoons killed in December 1847 in the Battle of San Pasqual. Cuidad de Los Angeles Band played "Yankee Doodle." Levi Hancock of the battalion sang a patriotic song he had composed, followed by a march played by the band. Guns were shot twenty-eight times, once for every state in the union. Wine was passed to the soldiers before they marched to their quarters. In the evening a number of the battalion soldiers walked around town.

Mon., July 5, Pueblo de Los Angeles. The battalion was invited to attend the funeral of one of the army regulars who died in the hospital the previous night. They appeared with their side arms at 10:30 A.M. The procession continued to the burial grounds of the Catholic church, since the deceased was a Roman Catholic. The First Platoon of Regulars walked in front, followed by the corpse carried by some of the regulars. His horse came next, covered with black velvet and carrying the uniform of the deceased, arms, sabre, vallas, etc. His boots were turned backwards and put into the stirrups. Then followed the rest of the dragoons, the regimental band of the New York Volunteers, the New York Volunteers, the Mormon Battalion, and the staff. In the rear were a large number of citizens who also attended the funeral. The band played slow marches as the procession moved along to the grave site. The platoon of dragoons fired three shots over his grave. A quick pace was followed back to quarters.

Tues., July 6, Pueblo de Los Angeles. Several men were killed in fights the day before and on the fourth. None belonged to the battalion. No work today as everyone was preparing to leave.

Wed., July 7, Pueblo de Los Angeles. One of the New York Volunteers and one of Frémont's men were taken in on suspicion of being involved in the murders on July 4 and 5.

Thurs., July 8, Pueblo de Los Angeles. The paymaster arrived from San Pedro. Guards were on duty by the liberty pole. The natives began cleaning the square again.

Fri., July 9, Pueblo de Los Angeles. No work was done on the fort for several days. In preparation for another Catholic celebration the next day, the whole town was illuminated. The battalion was armed as there was a rumor the Mexicans would use this festival as an opportunity to recapture the town. Several more brass cannon were brought in from San Pedro.

Sat., July 10, Pueblo de Los Angeles. This was a special festival for the Catholics. The musicians, consisting of two tenor and a bass drum, two violins, and two flutes, went around to all the principal houses and serenaded them. During the past week the Mexicans and Indians erected a large corral around the exterior of the square. Outside this rail fence they erected circular seats rising one above another to the height of twenty or thirty feet like an amphitheater and sufficiently strong to accommodate many people. It was an arena for bull fighting.

The bull fights seemed cruel and barbaric to the Mormons. Pio Pico, the late commander in this area, and all the principal officers in the Spanish army were present, along with priests, all mingling together. General Pico went in on horseback several times to fight the bull with a short spear. Other fighters fought bulls throughout the day. One horse was gored.

Sun., July 11, Pueblo de Los Angeles. The bull fighting began again. It was dangerous to be in town. Several horses were gored in the combat. Two were hurt seriously. One bull broke out of the enclosure and caught Captain Davis's little boy, Daniel Jr., with its horns, tossing him about twenty feet in the air. The six-year-old boy was bruised and scared. The fights continued until late in the evening. General Pico took an active part again during the day. He was very richly attired as were the other Californios.

Mon., July 12, Pueblo de Los Angeles. The bull fights continued until evening when they broke up.

Tues., Wed., July 13, 14, Pueblo de Los Angeles. Regular guard duty. Much preparation for traveling.

Thurs., July 15, Pueblo de Los Angeles. This was the last full day in the service of the United States and there was much rejoicing among the battalion. Company B arrived from San Diego to be discharged with the four Los Angeles companies. What remained of the battalion finally was all together once again.

Fri., July 16, Pueblo de Los Angeles. There was no morning roll call and no guard mounts. At three o'clock in the afternoon, 317 men of the Mormon Battalion assembled by company in Los Angeles at Fort Moore. Company A was in front, Company E in the rear, leaving a few feet of space between each company. Lieutenant Andrew J. Smith of the First Dragoons marched down one line and back on another. When he finished, he returned to the front and said in a low voice, "You are discharged." There was no other ceremony and no one from the regular army command spoke.

After being discharged, the Mormons gathered around their company leaders for brief remarks by Captain Daniel Davis, James Pace, Andrew Lytle, Levi Hancock, and David Pettegrew. At the conclusion, three cheers were given. The men left with their animals and other belongings for a camp three miles up the San Pedro River where they planned to organize for the return trip.

The Mormon Battalion was no more—the men were all mustered out. They were given their arms with twenty-one rounds of ammunition and accoutrements as promised by General Kearny. So it was that, one year after marching away from their families, the men were on their way back. They did not know where Brigham Young and the pioneers were, but they were on their way to find them.

CHAPTER SEVEN

General Kearny's Escort to Fort Leavenworth

When the Mormon Battalion arrived in California in January 1847, a highly charged political drama was unfolding. Brigadier General Stephen W. Kearny and Commodore Robert F. Stockton had seized Los Angeles January 10 on orders from Washington, D.C. The Californians, led by Andre Pico, fled northward from Los Angeles and surrendered to Lieutenant Colonel John C. Frémont, commander of another United States force in northern California. Frémont had been appointed temporary governor of California by Commodore Stockton. Under Pico's signature, he and Frémont entered into what has been called the "Cahuenga Capitulation," a treaty dated January 13, 1847, which essentially ended the fighting in California.

When Kearny arrived claiming to be the new governor, Frémont refused to accept Kearny's claim. A query to Washington clarified the confusion. Kearny was to be the governor of California. Frémont refused to acquiesce to Kearny. He would not turn his troops over, and he subverted the work of his superior. Finally, Kearny decided the only thing to do was to begin court-martial proceedings against Frémont. This meant Frémont would have to be taken east for the trial. (Details of the Frémont-Kearny conflict are given in chapters 5 and 6.)

General Kearny was commander of the U.S. Army of the West. As such, the Mormons had received their original orders to serve from him and had served under Kearny's command throughout their service in the battalion. The battalion was loyal to Kearny. In recognition of their loyalty, he ordered fifteen men to accompany him and his detachment as escorts when he took Frémont to Fort Leavenworth to start court-martial proceedings.

The original plan was to take three men from each of the five battalion companies. However, Company B was in San Diego, so all fifteen men

were selected from the four Los Angeles companies. Hulet was a lieutenant and Jones was a sergeant. All others were privates.[1]

Kearny's Escorts

Gilman Gordon, Co. A	William W. Spencer, Co. D
Joseph Taylor, Co. A	Sylvester Hulet, Co. D
Charles Y. Webb, Co. A	Nathaniel V. Jones, Co. D
Jeremiah Willey, Co. A	Amos Cox, Co. D
Thomas C. Ivie, Co. C	Matthew Caldwell, Co. E
Ebenezer Landers, Co. C	John W. Binley, Co. E
William F. Reynolds, Co. C	Samuel G. Clark, Co. E
Elanson Tuttle, Co. C	

Monterey in northern California was designated as the rendezvous
for all those going with Kearny. Kearny went by boat, leaving San Pedro
Bay aboard the USS *Lexington* on May 15, dropping anchor in Monterey
Bay on May 27. Three battalion soldiers, including Jeremiah Willey, went
with him.

The other twelve escorts, traveling with pack mules, under the command of William Tecumseh Sherman followed the El Camino Real, staying
overnight in six missions en route.[2] They arrived in Monterey about noon
May 25, 1847, two days before Kearny, and quartered in the southern part
of town in a building formerly occupied by Colonel Stevenson's regiment.
Kearny arrived in the evening of May 27, 1847. When the detachment was
assembled, there were sixty-four men under his command:

Lt. Colonel Philip St. George Cooke; Willard P. Hall, member-elect
to Congress; George B. Sanderson, former surgeon of the Mormon
Battalion; Lt. Col. John C. Frémont; Major Thomas Swords and
Capt. Henry S. Turner, two witnesses for the future court-martial; Lt.
William Radford, U.S. Navy; nineteen members of Frémont's former
topographical party; the fifteen-man battalion escort; J. C. Quigley,
bugler; and servants, citizens, guides, and discharged Dragoons.[3]

Kearny took no wagons. He wanted to reach Washington, D.C., by
the end of August. They had 172 public horses and mules plus a large
number of private animals.

Riding government horses and mules, the detachment left
Monterey May 31, 1847, after being issued pack mules and rations for seventy-five days. As they left, Joshua S. Vincent watched them leave and
described the scene in his diary: "It was a fine sight to see the long train of
horses and mules winding around the margin of a little lake a short distance from town."[4]

Kearny and his group traveled from Monterey to the San Joaquin Valley on the way to Sutter's Fort. They made a boat of hides to carry the men and provisions across the Stanislaus River. Part of the provisions were transported to the other side. While the boat was returning through the slough, a band of Indians approached the provisions on the opposite bank. Colonel Cooke asked the men if they could swim. Jeremiah Willey and three others said they could. Cooke ordered them to the other side to guard the supplies. The river was high and the water was very cold. When Jeremiah was a short distance from the bank, his arms became numb and he nearly drowned. They stopped the Indians from taking the supplies while the rest of the company came across in boats and swam the mules.

When they crossed the Stanislaus River, they were six miles up the river from New Hope, where Brannan had sent a few men from the ship *Brooklyn* to establish a colony.[5] For several days they passed many "digger" Indians, so called because they lived on grass, seeds, and roots. The "diggers" were naked except for a wisp of grass tied around their waist.

When they reached New Hope June 11, the soldiers learned Brannan and C. C. Smith had gone to meet Brigham Young and the Saints to tell them about the riches of California with its fertile valleys and ideal climate. Brannan volunteered to pilot Young and the pioneer company across the mountains to California, an offer not accepted by Brigham Young.[6]

The battalion saw a field of corn planted by the *Brooklyn* men at New Hope and were impressed with the potential of the San Joaquin Valley. That evening Thomas Rhoades visited their camp. Rhoades had arrived in October 1846 with his large family and had settled on the Cosumnes River.

They stopped a night with Alcalde John Sinclair, who lived on the American River about a mile and a half from Sutter's Fort. There were twenty-five soldiers at Sinclair's settlement.

John Sutter received the Kearny contingent hospitably and provided needed supplies and horses so every man had a horse. Sutter was a Swiss quixotic who arrived at the confluence of the American and Sacramento Rivers eight years before and began New Helvetia. Traders and immigrants referred to it as Sutter's Fort. Kearny's contingent purchased dried beef, flour, and pork. Corn did not grow well in the Sacramento Valley unless it was watered. Mechanics wages were high due to the shortage of skilled labor. Sutter was expanding his empire in several directions and needed laborers badly. As a result wages were high whenever he could find workers. Land was twenty-five cents per acre and wheat was one dollar per bushel.

Kearny's group left Sutter's Fort June 15 late in the afternoon as they were packing their supplies and effects most of the day. After traveling two days they reached Johnson's Ranch on Bear Creek, forty miles from Sutter's Fort. While here Edwin Bryant and a servant joined the company, making sixty-six in Kearny's company.[7] Frémont's group generally marched a mile or two in the rear of Kearny's detachment and made a separate camp at night. Kearny, his officers, and other travelers were in the lead, followed by the battalion escorts.

They left Johnson's Ranch on the morning of June 18 and reached snow in the mountain tops two days later. Spring vegetation had just started. They rested in Bear Creek Valley, where they found a cabin with many things left in it. When they reached Truckee Lake (now Donner Lake) June 21, they camped near the head of the lake. John Binley was shoeing his horse when he was kicked by the horse, injuring his back severely and breaking several ribs.

They descended down to the lake and found the cabins used by the Donner party the winter before. Many of the Donner group starved to death. The soldiers had been told one man lived four months on human flesh, that he sawed heads open, ate brains, and mangled up bodies in a horrible manner. They called this place Cannibal Camp. Kearny called a halt and detailed Major Thomas Swords and a party of five Mormons to bury the bodies lying around. After they buried the bones of the dead, they set fire to the cabin.

As we were the first ones there, after the horrible death of these people, we . . . cleared out an old cellar . . . and put the bones of 150 persons [the Donner party consisted of eighty-one people, thirty-six of whom perished from starvation and exposure] into it and covered them as best we could. This was the most awful sight that my eyes were ever to behold. There was not a whole person that we could find. (Matthew Caldwell)[8]

At this point, Colonel Frémont and his party passed. It was the first time the Mormon escorts had seen him since leaving Sutter's Fort.[9] While stopped for the gruesome task, J. C. Quigley, the bugler, shot himself accidentally in the shoulder below the collarbone.

One mile beyond was another cabin and more dead bodies. General Kearny did not order them buried. They passed this chilling scene with disbelief at what they saw but without disturbing it.

Kearny's advance group had cached a wagon filled with supplies for those following. However, when the Mormon contingent reached the wagon, they found it dug up by the Indians, with everything wasted. Quigley's condition worsened as they traveled along.

They passed an Indian village of about two hundred Washoe Indians, with both men and women naked. Many ran to the mountains and others hid in the brush as the soldiers arrived. A few came out later after camp had been made.

By June 27 they arrived at the hot springs on the Humboldt River. The steam was thrown out in a solid column four feet high, sometimes higher, and could be seen three or four miles off. It would discharge one barrel in one minute. The ground all around seemed to be crusted and hollow underneath and was hot. A mule broke through this crust a half mile from the spring and the steam came up very hot.

While crossing the Nevada desert, an order was issued that no horses were to drink at a watering place until all the men had drunk and filled their canteens. General Kearny also changed the daily travel routine. The soldiers would start marching before daybreak and travel about fifteen miles before stopping for breakfast. During the afternoon heat the men could rest before finishing the march in the early evening. There were immediate results for they traveled thirty-one miles on the new schedule and twelve miles on the old one.

> On one occasion Uncle Amos [Cox] was guarding a water hole and before the men all had time to get their water, Gen. Kearny rode his horse up and started to water it. Uncle Amos warned him away. He paid no attention until Uncle Amos pulled his gun and threatened to shoot him unless he took the horse away until all the men had all drunk and filled their canteens. Gen. Kearny then departed but afterwards he had Uncle Amos court martialed and strung up by the thumbs for pulling a gun on his superior officer. (Sylvester Hulet)[10]

When they camped on the Humboldt, they found the river sank into the sand at their campsite. They had no wood, only a little grass and salty, bitter water. A few mules and horses gave out.

On July 4, a man named Minek (not in the battalion) was too ill to keep up and was left behind. He finally reached camp during the night. The next day Western Shoshone Indians stole four horses. Although the men went after the horses, they did not recover them. On July 10, they camped at Goose Creek. Colonel Frémont, who had been traveling immediately behind the Mormon escorts, caught up and traveled with the Mormons for a few days.

On July 13 they reached the fork where the Oregon Trail turned left. Kearny's company crossed the fork and traveled eight miles without water. Two groups of Oregon-bound emigrants passed during the day— one with forty-three wagons in the morning and another large group in the afternoon.

When they reached Fort Hall on July 15, they obtained bacon and continued on in the afternoon for sixteen miles, passing Oregon emigrants along the way. While camped on the banks of a small stream in Bear River Valley July 16, the Mormons remembered it was the anniversary of the year of their enlistment. Traveling along the Bear River, they found twenty Indian lodges. The Shoshone Indians had a great many horses.

They reached Green River in present Wyoming July 22, where they met Orlando Strickland, an old friend of Nathaniel Jones and others. They left Green River about five in the afternoon and traveled all night. Since travel was not difficult in this area, Kearny's group covered about twenty miles or more each day. They found considerable game—buffalo and antelope—which improved their daily menu considerably. After a forty-mile day, they reached Independence Rock July 27.

Mormon emigrants were camped at Independence Rock, waiting for another emigrant company to catch up. This western-bound company was under the leadership of Charles C. Rich. In it were Orville and Elvira Cox and their children. Sylvester Hulet was overjoyed to meet his niece Elvira and her family. Since the battalion's year of enlistment was up, Hulet asked General Kearny to be released so he could return west with the Rich company. His request was granted. Orville Cox had sad news for his brother, Amos Cox, one of Kearny's escorts. Amos's little daughter, Loenza, was dead.[11] Saddened, Amos continued with the detachment of guards to Council Bluffs. John Binley still suffered from his injury.

Nathaniel Jones and several escorts asked for permission to ride ahead to meet another approaching company. Twenty miles east of Fort Laramie, they met the second group. These two companies were part of the big company—a large group of pioneers who had left Winter Quarters in June and were on the trail before Brigham Young's company reached the valley in July. Various divisions of the big company began arriving in the valley in September 1847. By early October more than fifteen hundred persons reached Salt Lake Valley. The arrival of this large number made the work (tending crops, building the fort and homes) of the persons who arrived first in the valley important to their survival.

The Mormon escorts knew many of the emigrants and learned of their families and other news. Nathaniel Jones received a letter, dated June 6, from his wife Rebecca, the first he had received since he left Fort Leavenworth a year before.[12] Jones and his companions camped that night with the emigrants. General Kearny and the rest of his company caught up the next day.

On August 4, 1847, Captain H. S. Turner, First Dragoons, a member of Kearny's command, recorded meeting these Mormon emigrants: "Past the whole Mormon Emigration, numbering as follows: 800 men—750 women—1,556 [children] under 16 years of age—4,530 head of cattle—142 horses & mules—344 sheep—685 wagons."

They proceeded early the next morning, traveling forty miles in the rain before stopping at Scott's Bluff. The rain continued as they traveled another forty miles to Ash Hollow. Colonel Frémont's men killed two buffalo. Quigley, the bugler who shot himself in the collarbone, was too ill to ride his horse, so Matthew Caldwell, Charles Webb, and William Spencer, hospital steward, were detailed to stay behind and help Quigley. Their rations were left with them as well as one animal apiece and two pack animals.[13]

On August 8, the escorts struck camp at sunrise and traveled across the plain, leaving the North Platte River. They camped on an island in the South Platte and killed several buffalo, which were in innumerable herds. On August 14 they left the Platte and traveled thirty miles to the Little Blue Creek. They arrived at Big Blue on August 18 at noon and stopped to rest. On August 19 they left the Wolf River and traveled twenty miles. In the morning they overtook a man named Davenport, who was a Mormon traveling with Oregon emigrants. In this group was a Mormon missionary named Littlejohn. Nathaniel Jones bought a horse from the Oregon group for twenty dollars.

The Mormon escorts had very little food for breakfast on the morning of August 21. They were hungry as they began their trek for the day. At noon they struck the road and followed it to Independence Creek, which they reached late at night. All were very hungry. Major Seward of Kearny's command gave them a little flour for supper.

On the morning of August 23, they traveled eighteen miles to Fort Leavenworth.[14] They turned over their public property in the afternoon and received only $8.60 for their extra service. On August 24 the thirteen remaining guards were given an issue of clothing and seventy-five dollars severance pay; they were discharged with the good feelings of their officers.[15]

At Fort Leavenworth, General Kearny as commander of the Army of the West, ordered Colonel John C. Frémont put in irons and in that condition took him to Washington, D.C., for trial. Frémont was convicted by court-martial of mutiny and other charges and was dismissed from the service by the court. President Polk approved the sentence but removed the penalties due to the long period of service Frémont had rendered to the United States and due to the many hardships he had endured. His trial, which was quite lengthy, created much excitement and was a subject of national interest.

The thirteen discharged veterans started at noon August 24 for Weston, Missouri, immediately after completing their business. Because they had turned in their army-issued horses and mules, the discharged veterans had to walk the last two hundred miles to Council Bluffs, Iowa. After traveling sixteen miles, the men stopped at dark at a hotel, operated by a former associate in Nauvoo named Green. They saw the wife of Sterling Davis, who was still in California.

Their next stop was St. Joseph, Missouri. More travel brought them to Waldon's Ferry, where they crossed the Missouri River and stayed with another friend named Colton in Savannah. The escorts continued walking to Council Bluffs, completing a four-thousand-mile round-trip in mid-September 1847. Matthew Caldwell described the last portion of this remarkable journey: "This [last] two hundred miles on foot after being used to riding all summer was very hard on us. But as usual, we took it as we had done through the whole of the battalion journey—as best we could." Caldwell also painted a vivid picture of the men's appearance: "Webb and Spencer had the raggedest pants that I had ever seen. My antelope breeches had been wet and dry so much that they drew up to my knees. Our shirts were gone except the collars and a few strips down the back. I was entirely barefoot."[16]

These were the first men of the battalion to return. They brought the initial firsthand accounts of the battalion's exploits to the families still waiting to go west. It would be December before any more soldiers reached their families. Brigham Young, Heber C. Kimball, and others were en route east, but they did not arrive in Council Bluffs until October 1847, a month later.

CHAPTER EIGHT

After Discharge

The five companies of the Mormon Battalion, U.S. Army of the West, were discharged officially at Fort Moore in Los Angeles on July 16, 1847, one year after their enlistment. There were 317 men who lined up for the brief ceremony. After discharge, it took several days for them to receive their final pay and to complete arrangements for their journey. Henry Standage went to Lieutenant A. J. Smith to get his pay for working in the bakery, but Smith refused, saying he was unable to pay without an order from Colonel Stevenson. When Standage went to Colonel Stevenson, he signed the order and Standage was able to get his money from Lieutenant Smith.[1]

Each man received $31.50, but no transportation allowance for traveling back as promised. When the companies were paid, they purchased animals and supplies for the return journey. Several men noted that the price of horses increased when the Mormons began buying so many. Quantities of flour and salt were purchased.

Seventy-nine men from the battalion signed up to reenlist for another six months. They were called the Mormon Volunteers and were assigned to garrison duty in San Diego. (The activities of the Mormon Volunteers are detailed in chapter 13.)

Five men—Horace Alexander, Newman Bulkley, Abraham Day, Philander Colton, and Dorr P. Curtis—left immediately to go to their families by the southern route they had traveled six months earlier. Nine-year-old Charles Colton, who had served as an officer's aide on the western trip, traveled with his father. Four ex-soldiers chose to remain in California: Jesse Hunter, William Hunter, Francis Brown, and Elijah Allen. Six men contracted to build a mill for Isaac Williams at his ranch east of Los Angeles: Joseph Bates, Calvin W. Moore, Christopher Layton, Walter Barney, Albert Knapp, and Shadrack Holdaway. Two others, John Borrowman and James Park, left San Diego August 17 by boat and

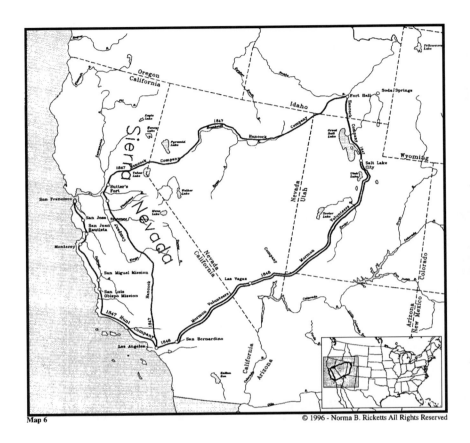

Map 6

1847-1848

Mormon Battalion

After Discharge

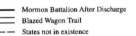 Mormon Battalion After Discharge
Blazed Wagon Trail
States not in existence

N

reached San Francisco at noon September 23. The two men stopped briefly in San Francisco before continuing to Sutter's Fort to meet their counterparts, who traveled north through California's central valleys. This left 223 men preparing to leave Los Angeles under the direction of Levi Hancock. David Pettegrew noted, "A happier set of men I never saw."

Since military authority no longer existed, Levi Hancock, as the highest Mormon Church officer in their midst, took charge. The men were divided into hundreds, fifties, and tens, as was the practice of the church when traveling. Hancock appointed Andrew Lytle and James Pace captains of the two hundreds; William Hyde, Daniel Tyler, Reddick Allred, and Jefferson Hunt were chosen to lead the four fifties. Not all names of the captains of tens are known. Only Levi Savage, Luther Tuttle, Foster Curtis, and Elisha Averett have been identified as captains of ten. Elisha Averett and his ten were assigned as scouts to travel ahead to locate the best route and water.

The pages that follow attempt to identify the movement of the soldiers after discharge. The Hancock company was well defined as it left the San Pedro camp near Los Angeles. As this group separated into smaller units, no rosters were made. Only by searching individual diaries can one glean an occasional name as the writer identified a traveling companion. When additional research is done, these smaller groups, no doubt, will be identified further. For now, this is a place for new research to begin.

The Hancock company, consisting of 223 men, did not remain in the San Pedro camp long. Captain Jefferson Hunt and his group of fifty-one, including William and Melissa Coray and Philemon Merrill, left the San Pedro camp July 22 and went north along the coast to San Francisco.[2] They followed the well-established route, El Camino Real, an old Spanish road connecting California's missions. They passed through Santa Barbara, San Luis Obispo, and over the coastal range to San Miguel on the Salinas River, arriving in Monterey August 13. The group split in Monterey, with a few remaining in Monterey, and others proceeding to San Francisco. Hunt did not remain long in San Francisco, but continued on to Sutter's Fort with about twenty-five of his original group. At the fort they joined their comrades when they arrived from southern California.

One fifty, commanded by Reddick Allred, left Los Angeles July 23 and traveled twenty miles to General Pio Pico's ranch, where they camped. They found two large gardens and vineyards. There was no grain, but plenty of fruit such as grapes, figs, pears, apricots, cherries, plums, peaches, apples, black pepper, olive, date, and palm trees. The two groups of fifty captained by Daniel Tyler and William Hyde arrived at Pio Pico's ranch July 27.

When the Allred-Tyler-Hyde fifties left Pio Pico's ranch in the San Fernando Valley, they traveled with their beef cattle in front. As they passed over the rugged mountains of the Sierra Madre, they lost eighteen head of beef cattle over several nights. The men decided to stop and kill the remaining beef cattle and dry the beef. Averett and his scouts went ahead to look for Walker's Pass while others remained in camp caring for the meat.

The company continued through Tejon Pass and crossed the Tehachapi Mountains. As they entered the 500-mile-long central valley, the August heat was unbearable even for the seasoned travelers. Once again, exhausted men fell by the side of the trail for lack of water. Their companions, as before, returned at night with water and helped them into camp.

> On the 7th of August we had a hard day's travel among the hills. After supper the camp was called together by the sound of Captain Averett's fife and a meeting was held in charge of Father Pettegrew and Levi W. Hancock, who exhorted the . . . camp to be faithful in keeping the commandments of God. They succeeded in settling some misunderstanding that existed in camp. (Henry Bigler)[3]

They reached the Kings River on August 11 several miles east of present Fresno. Canteens were filled and sent back to fallen comrades. They sent Averett and his scouts up the Kings River to find Walker's Pass over the Sierra Nevada to the Great Basin. The pass was named for Joseph Walker, trapper and guide. When the travelers had not located Walker's Pass by August 13, they decided to continue north to Sutter's Fort and follow the Truckee route over the mountains at Donner Pass.

On August 21 they came to the Stanislaus River near present Ripon and New Hope, consisting of twenty families from the ship *Brooklyn*. New Hope was the communal farming settlement Samuel Brannan was building near present Stockton, hoping Brigham Young and the Mormons would settle in California.[4]

They continued until they arrived in the Cosumnes Valley August 24 where Martin Murphy Jr. and Thomas Rhoades and his large family settled on the Cosumnes River in 1846. The Rhoades family was converted to the Mormon faith in Ohio and experienced the persecution in Missouri. It is probable that Thomas Rhoades knew some of the discharged battalion while in Nauvoo and during the exodus from Illinois. While stopped here, C. C. Smith, who had traveled to Green River (Wyoming) with Samuel Brannan, arrived and told the ex-soldiers that Brigham Young and the pioneers were settling in the Great Salt Lake Valley. This was the first news the battalion had heard about church movement since the Arkansas crossing.[5] David P. Rainey, Reddick N. Allred, Luther T. Tuttle, Alpheus Haws, Elisha Averett, and Daniel Dennett went to Sutter's Fort to arrange to purchase provisions.

While still camped on the Cosumnes River near the Rhoades, the men held a meeting on the evening of August 25 as they had done frequently since being discharged. They learned from Thomas Rhoades that John Sutter needed laborers. Men with poor outfits wanted to remain and work for Sutter until spring. The wages were good because labor was scarce. Others thought they might go to San Francisco to find work where there was the colony of Mormons who had sailed from New York on the ship *Brooklyn*. Levi Hancock made appropriate remarks on the unity that existed among the men and thought it would be alright for a few to remain and labor until spring. Hancock then asked for a vote that if any did remain, they should have the prayers and blessings of those who continued on. All voted in the affirmative. Several others expressed positive remarks on the same subject. Those who decided to remain in the area expected to receive wages from twenty-five to sixty dollars a month. How many made this choice is unknown, but it probably did not exceed a dozen.

The men also learned firsthand from John P. Rhoades, Thomas's son, about attempts to rescue members of the Donner Party. John and his brother, Daniel Rhoades, were in the first rescue team; John returned several times into the mountains to bring out the stranded emigrants.[6] Jefferson Hunt and his party arrived from San Francisco en route to Sutter's Fort.

After traveling twenty miles, they camped on an existing ford on the north bank of the American River, two miles east of Sutter's Fort. This crossing is between present town of Brighton and Sacramento State University. Jefferson Hunt and his party left the fort and started over the mountains August 26. When Hunt left Los Angeles, he had orders from Colonel Stevenson to ask the church authorities to recruit five more companies of Mormons for the army. Because he was carrying this official communication, he was anxious to be on his way: "Jefferson starts out I understand with recruiting orders [to raise] five companys from the Mormons. we think he cant come it. he is gone ahead of all with his picked company of officers, the old fathers as the soldiers call them" (Levi Hancock).[7]

Many men were sick with chills and fever, what they called ague. The animals were shod at Sutter's Fort for one dollar per shoe. They purchased unbolted flour at eight dollars per hundred. One group of four tens left Sutter's Fort on August 27 and traveled about eighteen miles, from which point their course changed from north to east. Captains of these tens were Elisha Averett, Levi Savage, Luther Tuttle, and Foster Curtis.

The groups reassembled at Johnson's Ranch on Bear River on August 28.[8] William Johnson was an American sailor who had settled on the river in 1845. He employed Indians on his ranch, which was the first settlement in the western foothills of the Sierra Nevada. More horseshoeing was done. Levi Hancock bought a pack saddle and lasso from Johnson for fifteen dollars.

They left Johnson's Ranch August 29 and followed General Kearny's trail. Wild huckleberries were plentiful and were a treat as they walked along. Grass was scarce, but water was plentiful and cold. "We traveled only a short distance, made an early camp and held a prayer meeting" (Henry Bigler).[9] James Pace's company moved ahead, usually keeping a day or two in the lead. The narrative, unless otherwise indicated, follows from here on Andrew Lytle and his men, who trailed behind.

After their second day of travel, a severe summer storm with high winds, thunder, lightning, and rain kept the men from sleeping. The seasoned travelers had walked many times in wet clothing during their long journey west and splashing along soaked through was little more than a slight inconvenience. However, being wet so often and for extended periods of time caused illness among the men.[10] They watched dark clouds above the mountain tops, but there were no clouds over the valley below. The constantly melting snow kept the Bear River deep and swift so it was impossible to ford in some places. By bracing well they crossed the river several times, frequently with the water up to their chests.

On September 1 they camped twenty miles from Bear Valley among pine trees, good water, and grass. While here the men thought about the contrast to where they were the previous year on this date. A year ago they had been in the Mormon Battalion under Lieutenant A. J. Smith, marching toward Santa Fe on a swift, forced march. Then they had to carry their arms and cartridge boxes, clothes, and knapsacks, as well as stand guard when sick or take calomel and be sicker. This year they could do as they pleased—ride or walk, hurry or take their time, and they had enough to eat.

Henry Hoyt had been ill with hepatitis since leaving Sutter's Fort. His condition worsened, so it was decided to have Captain Allred's ten travel at a slower pace with Hoyt for a time to see if his condition improved. Men in Lytle's group made tea for Henry Hoyt out of watermelon seeds before traveling on. He would agree to stopping for short periods, but then insisted on continuing. Several times he fainted and had to be taken from his horse to recover from the sinking spells. A short time before his death, Captain Allred asked him if he would like to stop and rest. Hoyt replied, "No, go on." Those were his last words. As they traveled slowly on, he grew weaker and was helped from his horse by Captain Allred and his other companions. They put him in the shade of a tree where he died a few minutes later. They wrapped him in his blanket and buried him in a shallow grave because they had no tools to dig a deeper grave. Tree limbs and brush were piled on top of the grave to hide it from the wolves. They carved his name on a tree halfway between the grave and the trail: "Henry P. Hoyt died on the 3rd of Sept. 1847 after 9 days' illness with jaundice, 80 miles from Sutter's Fort."

Meanwhile, the Lytle group had continued over terrain that was up and down in hollows and steep mountains. At Mule Springs they found the names of their comrades who had escorted Kearny's company carved on an oak tree, dated June 19, 1847. On the other side was the date Captain Pace and his group had been there: "Capt. Pace with 50 men camped August 31–1847." Levi Hancock noted, "We have a company as large under Capt Andrew Lytle who camps here to knight Sept 2–1847."[11] Pace and Lytle were captains of hundreds, but some had stayed at Sutter's, Hunt and others had gone ahead, Allred's ten were behind, and the men spread out as they traveled, so groups of fifty men were noted at Mule Springs. Evidently only fifty soldiers camped together on these two occasions.

When they left Mule Springs, they were near the crest of the Sierra Nevada. Its central ridge appeared to be a thousand feet high. As they traveled downhill, it was like coming out of the clouds. They thought this was the best timber they had seen in California. One tree was 10 feet in diameter and 150 feet high. They boiled pine needles to make a refreshing drink. The boiling process eliminated the hemlock taste. The group decided to wait for Captain Allred and his party. Allred and the men who had stayed behind with Henry Hoyt caught up with the Lytle group September 4 with the news of Hoyt's death and burial: "We . . . morn the death of Brother Henry Hoit [Hoyt]" (James Pace).[12]

They continued over very rough terrain and camped on the west side of the mountain near present-day Soda Springs. Traveling over the stony hills with sharp-cornered rocks cut the horses' feet and made them very sore.

Samuel Brannan came into camp on his way to San Francisco. He was returning from Green River (Wyoming), where he met Brigham Young and the pioneers and traveled with them to Salt Lake Valley. He thought he could persuade Brigham Young to settle in California. After an unsuccessful attempt, Brannan left Salt Lake City in company with Captain James Brown, who had taken a sick detachment to Pueblo. The three Pueblo detachments had reached Salt Lake Valley a few days after Brigham Young and the pioneer company arrived there. Captain Brown was en route to Monterey to get the mustering-out pay for the Pueblo detachments. Before leaving Salt Lake City, Brigham Young had given Brown a letter for the battalion members in California. Brannan thought the letter should have been given to him since he was the presiding elder in San Francisco. From the beginning of the journey, Brannan and Brown did not get along. Brannan no longer traveled with Brown and had no kind words to say about him. Neither did he think much of Brigham Young's decision to remain in Salt Lake Valley when the fertile fields of California beckoned.

Brannan told the ex-soldiers that Captain Brown was a day behind. Arriving with Brannan was David Rainey of the advance Pace company. Rainey came back to tell Captain Lytle to bring his group forward so they would be together when James Brown arrived with the letter from Mormon Church officials. Richard Sessions was sick with fever and chills.

After Samuel Brannan left early the next morning. Captain Lytle and his group hurried forward to catch the Pace contingent. They came together near Truckee Lake. Captain James Brown arrived midmorning and told an entirely different story than Brannan. At one point the two men actually had a physical confrontation. Brown called on John Fowler and William Squires, who were traveling with him and several others, to witness that what he said was true. Both verified that he told the truth. The sick detachments had wintered in Pueblo and then proceeded to Salt Lake Valley, arriving July 29, 1847. Brown had come to California at the request of Mormon Church leaders, with a power of attorney, to collect the final pay of the soldiers.[13] He brought letters for a few men from their families. Levi Hancock was one who received a letter. His wife Clarissa wrote she had borne a son on the first day of February in Mount Pisgah and named the baby Levi. Henry W. Bigler received a letter from George A. Smith, one of the apostles, telling of the arrival in Salt Lake Valley of Brigham and his pioneer company and the detachments of the battalion from Pueblo. Smith also stated that Brigham Young was going to return to Council Bluffs and that John Smith, patriarch, would preside until the church officials returned the next season.[14]

Brown delivered the letter from the church leaders, dictated by Brigham Young and addressed to "Capt. Jefferson Hunt and the officers and soldiers of the Mormon Battalion." It was dated August 7, 1847, Valley of the Great Salt Lake. Brigham Young and the pioneers had been in the valley only two weeks when he wrote the letter to the battalion. Already they were in destitute circumstances in the valley, and Brigham Young's concern about an influx of people and the resulting strain and hardships it would make on the meager resources of the pioneers in the valley was understandable. A week after writing the letter, Young and two groups of men left to go east for the families waiting across Iowa.[15]

The letter recommended that those men with adequate provisions proceed to Salt Lake Valley. Others were asked to remain in California to labor until spring, then bring their provisions and earnings with them: "Brigham Young . . . counsiled all that had no famlyes to stay and work one year in California as thare was but A small company coming thrue to

Salt lake that fall & it would be an imposibility for them to have any provision . . . to Spare" (Albert Smith).[16]

> At a proper time the attention was cald to hear the Epistle from the Twelve which was chearing nuse to us. The spirit of the Epistle bore testamony to us from whence it came and that not withstanding the hardships we had undergone, attended with all the privations that could be expected from sutch a trip, they had not forgotten us. neither had they slacked their hands But with all diligence saught a location for the Saints No moore to be thrown down we hastily congratulated them in their success & in the work they had accomplished Being satisfied that we had born an humble part & that it was a prevaledge even to become a scape goat in time of Trouble . . . we had a quit[e] time of rejoising. (James Pace)[17]

After hearing the letter from Mormon Church authorities, the group divided, with approximately half, who may be called the Hancock-Sierra company, continuing on and half returning to Sutter's Fort to find employment: "About one hundred of us went on for Salt Lake over the high mountains where the perpetual snow was plenty" (David Pettegrew).[18]

The organization of hundreds, fifties, and tens established in Los Angeles was disrupted when half the men returned to Sutter's Fort. There is no evidence any attempt to reorganize was made at this time. They seemed to continue with the same companions they had traveled with since leaving Los Angeles but in smaller groups. Hunt's group continued to be the lead company. Philemon C. Merrill wrote that he traveled with Jefferson Hunt and seven others.[19] Hunt had about twenty-five men before the division.[20] The principal leaders—Hancock, Lytle, and Pace, Hyde, Tyler, and Allred—continued east. The exact breakdown of these companies is uncertain at this time.

The Lytle party continued through the mountains in an easterly course and reached the first campsite of the Donner party, where General Kearny's company had buried the bodies.[21] At sundown they reached the second "cannibal camp" just east of Donner Lake, where General Kearny had not had his men bury the bodies. The men were horrified at the sights—a skull covered with hair, mangled arms and legs with the bones broken. In another place, they found a whole body covered with a blanket and parts of other bodies scattered in all directions. There was one man's body lying above them in a hollow. His flesh was mummified and the body had been dragged about by wild animals. The soldiers thought it was a scene of intense suffering as well as fiendish acts and were relieved to leave the tragic camp.

They continued along the Truckee River over huge boulders and high steep hills. One day, they crossed the swift river, with its round, slippery rocks, five times. The canyon bottoms were narrow. They passed a large area of wet, marshy land and had to pass through much of it to get across. They camped at the foot of the hill where there were rushes and grass. In the evening the officers called all hands together and expressed their feelings concerning pushing forward, which all agreed to. Many of the swift travelers wanted to go ahead with the prayers and good wishes of their comrades. If they left immediately and if their families were not in Salt Lake Valley, they would have time to go to Council Bluffs this year. Before the meeting ended, the officers asked forgiveness if they had hurt anyone's feelings.

At this reorganization, it was determined those who could travel at a faster pace were to go ahead with Lieutenant Pace, while all others were to travel with Lieutenant Lytle. Pace and his group, including Elisha Averett, started across the forty-mile desert. There was usually only a day or two between the two companies. Pace's group left occasional notes for those following. Levi Hancock was in Lytle's company. The Hunt party continued to travel ahead of both these two groups.

Lytle and his men traveled thirty miles along the Humboldt River on September 15.[22] From the beginning of this last portion of their journey, the Indians had been troublesome along their route, stealing horses and mules. Captain Lytle found a note from the Pace company and read it to his men:

Capt. Lytle, sir:

Capt. Pace & Co arrived at this place of encampment at 12 o'clock this day. Since our arrival the company has been called together and it is in the minds of all after having taken into consideration the scarcity of feed and the convenience of traveling in small companies and that we now are where there is no danger of Indians and to travel on and if we should get to the forks of the road before you overtake us and should we conclude to take Hastings Route across the desert we will leave signs and my camp are generally well & hope all is well with you and yours.

With respect Capt Pace, D. Pettegrew, E. Averett, W. Hyde.

The groups continued to travel separately. By September 20, Captain Lytle's men and animals were worn down. Because of the continuous harrassing by Western Shoshones, they decided it would be better to travel together and decided to try to catch the advance Pace company.

Robert Bliss, who was in the advance Pace company, wrote:

Lay in camp Still hoping Bro. Gardner [William Garner] would be better so as to travel as soon as the last camp Should come up; he has the Chills every day & this is the 3d day we have lay by & our Brethrin do not come up Yet; if we felt safe in traveling alone we should go on a few miles every day before Bro. Gardner is sick but it probably will be wisdom for us to wait for our Brethrin to come up before we go on; we are lonesome but employ our time as well as we can; we are a long distance from Salt Lake Yet & have been on the Road about two months since our discharge without tents or anything to Shield us from the Storms but our Blankets; but traveling has become a kind of Second Nature to us so we do not complain.[23]

On September 24, Captain Lytle found a note from David Pettegrew in Pace's group, stating they caught up with Captain Hunt September 20. Lytle and his company passed the Hastings Cutoff on September 26 and saw horses' tracks and thought the advance groups had gone that way.[24] Lytle's group camped a little west of the hot springs.

When they reached the hot springs, they learned Captains Pace and Hunt did not go on the Hastings route and were only slightly ahead. Lytle's group passed the backbone ridge between the Humboldt River and the hot springs.[25] They saved several animals left behind by the companies traveling in front. Meanwhile, William Hyde and Luther Tuttle, both with the Pace group, had gone ahead to Fort Hall to secure bacon if possible.

The Lytle soldiers reached Goose Creek September 29 and found water and good grazing for their animals. By the time they reached the Raft River, both men and animals were tired. At the Oregon Trail turnoff, there were several undisturbed graves with no identification.[26] They traveled up the Snake River to American Falls and reached Fort Hall October 6, where they were able to buy bacon and buckskins.

All three groups were together at Fort Hall. Captain Pace and ten men left Fort Hall on October 7. The Pace and Hunt groups reached Salt Lake Valley about noon on October 16. Lytle and his comrades arrived a couple of days later. A few were overjoyed to find their families. Others were disappointed to learn their families had not yet arrived. Brigham Young and Heber C. Kimball had left in August to go east to bring other companies to Salt Lake Valley.

The ex-soldiers were destitute for clothing. John Taylor, acting president of the Mormon Church in Young's absence, and Edward Hunter, also a church official, collected needed articles, whatever could be spared, from the settlers, who also were in difficult circumstances. They had been in the valley only two and a half months. Everything donated was used. Nothing went unused. Anything that would cover the nakedness of the men or help keep them warm was acceptable. When wearing this mismatched and ill-fitting clothing, the men presented a rather motley appearance. But comfort to them was the first consideration and they were thankful to get any article of clothing.

Two days after arriving thirty-two men from the Hancock-Sierra company, whose families were not in Salt Lake Valley, left on October 18 to go east. The names of twenty-six men in this group are known:

Reddick N. Allred	Andrew Lytle
Elisah Averett	William Maxwell
Jeduthan Averett	Levi H. McCullough
Robert Bliss	James Myler
Edward Bunker	George W. Oman
Augustus Dodge	James Pace
John Martin Ewell	David Pettegrew
Levi W. Hancock	David P. Rainey
Robert Harris Jr.	Alonzo P. Raymond
Abraham Hunsaker	George W. Taggart
William Hyde	Luther T. Tuttle
Charles Jameson	Daniel Tyler
Hyrum Judd	Joseph White

In his autobiography, sixteen-year-old William Pace, who was traveling with his father, describes the beginning of this journey to Council Bluffs:

> Provisions being scarce in the valley, we were told we could get supplies at Fort Bridger and at Laramie reasonable, and it would be a great help to the people if we would leave our provisions and replenish on the road. Having a common interest we unloaded our supplies, taking only what was supposed enough to do us to Fort Bridger. . . . Arriving at Fort Bridger we found that they had not anything to sell. Here we were as it was over 400 miles to Fort Laramie and nothing to eat, a council was called, consisting of a committee of the whole [party]. much time was taken up in trying to decide whether the party in Salt Lake who advised us to leave our supplies and depend on getting more on the road acted from sinister motives, whether we were to go back to Salt Lake and fight it out during the winter with the others, or go ahead without anything to eat, however no one thought for a moment but what we could get what we wanted at Fort Laramie so it was unanimously decided to go ahead and depend on game.[27]

They reached Fort Bridger in a severe snow storm and learned the supply of flour they had planned to purchase had been bought by emigrants going to California and Oregon. While at Fort Bridger, Luther

Tuttle bought a buckskin shirt from an old Indian woman, and it was both a shirt and coat on the cold journey.

They killed two buffalo bulls before reaching Fort Laramie and jerked the best of the meat. They ran out of the flour they brought from Salt Lake Valley and existed on buffalo, beef, small game, and an elk.

The supply situation—no flour available—was the same when they reached Fort Laramie on November 10. Captain Lytle bought one pound of crackers for twenty-five cents. The trader advised them not to kill any more buffalo, for it would offend the Indians.

Twelve miles after leaving Fort Laramie, they found an Indian trader on the south side of the Platte River. Some of the men crossed over and bought one hundred pounds of flour for twenty-five dollars. With five hundred miles to go, they decided to use the flour (about three pounds to the man) only to make gravy or to thicken soup.

They were out of meat in seventy miles. Since there were many buffalo around, they decided to kill them as needed for food and risk upsetting the Indians. They killed a bull and a calf. While skinning the bull, they saw smoke and discovered Indians on the opposite side of the river from where they were. The men discussed what to do with the meat. Captain Allred said it would be useless to try to flee because of their worn-out animals, so it was decided they would do nothing. They acted casual as they dressed the beef and returned to their camp on the river. The Indians disappeared after dark without molesting them.

One hundred fifty miles below Fort Laramie the men encountered a snow storm that left twelve inches of snow. From here to Winter Quarters, about 350 miles, they broke trail through snow from one to two feet deep. Once again led by Pace, two groups traveled some distance apart.

Lytle's men found the head of a donkey. It was supposed to have belonged to Sergeant David P. Rainey. Captain Allred took an axe and opened the skull and he and his comrades had a supper of brains. Near this same point, Martin Ewell opened the head of a mule also killed and left by Captain Pace's company, with the same results.

When the Pace company arrived at Loup Fork River, several of the weakest horses drowned while trying to cross the river. They saved the carcasses and ate the drowned horse meat. The Lytle group caught up with Pace's company at Loup Fork just as Pawnee Indians were threatening to attack Pace's men. The two groups of armed men apparently caused the Indians to leave without attacking. They ate the last of their food, which consisted mainly of rawhide "saddle-bags" they had packed their provisions in from California. Their next food was a young mule of Captain Lytle that gave out.[28]

The cold became so extreme that the Loup Fork River began to freeze over. They had to wait nearly a week for the floating ice to get solid and thick. It was here that Abraham Hunsaker, in the hope of procuring corn from an Indian field across the river, took his frying pan full of coals from the fire and started across the ice on his hands and knees. He used two long sticks as skis and pushed his frying pan ahead of him. When near the other shore, he broke through the ice and went under, frying pan and all. He poured the water off the coals in an attempt to save his fire. The fire was his main concern. Abraham quickly slid the frying pan across the ice to the river bank and then began his fight to get out of the freezing water.

Since the ice would not hold him up and since his feet could scarcely touch the bottom, it was extremely difficult from there on to break the ice and fight his way out, inch by inch, as he was forced to do in the icy water.

He finally reached the opposite shore, almost frozen. There he saw in front of him an old rotted stump of a tree he felt Providence must have provided. He gathered slivers from the stump and laid them over the coals in his frying pan, which showed no sign of life. He blew until his breath was almost exhausted, then he rested and blew again. Finally he saw a faint glow among the coals and soon had a roaring fire. He dried his clothes and warmed himself.

Later he filled his frying pan again with coals and went into the Indian corn field. He saw no Indians, for which he was thankful. By diligent searching, he succeeded in finding a few ears of corn, enough for a feast as it seemed to him at that time. This he carried to an abandoned Indian wickiup, where he renewed his fire and parched the ears of corn. He ate until he was satisfied.

That night he slept in the abandoned Indian hut. The following morning he went again to the corn field, this time to gather corn for his friends. He had just returned to the hut with a few ears when three Indians appeared looking very forbidding and warlike. As they stood in front of him, he thought, "This is probably the end." Abraham stood tall and tried to look fearless. The Indians looked at him, grunted, and, with a look of disdain on their faces, turned and rode away:

> Perhaps they [the Indians] thought such a skeleton of a man could not long survive anyway, why bother with him. Yet I know if I had tried to escape from them, or had shown in any way the fear I felt, they would have taken my life, then and there. Again my Heavenly Father had overruled in my behalf. (Abraham Hunsaker) [29]

The cold continued so intense the river finally froze over and Abraham returned to his group, to be welcomed by his companions, who were near death from starvation and cold. They had given him up for dead. The corn Abraham carried to the men eased their hunger enough to continue. [30]

On the morning of the sixth day of waiting, the weary travelers decided the ice was strong enough to hold them. The crossing was treacherous with the ice cracking, but all reached the other side safely. From this point on the Pace and Lytle groups traveled together.

During the last ten days before they reached Winter Quarters, the only food they had was mule meat Captain Lytle had saved, to be eaten without salt. They arrived at the Elk Horn River December 17, 1847. Winter Quarters was only thirty miles away.

The next morning they left early and arrived in Winter Quarters about sundown December 18. They had made the journey from Salt Lake Valley to the Missouri River in two months. Some of the company found their families in Winter Quarters, while others were in Council Bluffs or Mt. Pisgah. The soldiers, although respectable, were unavoidably dirty and ragged, yet they found a warm welcome from the people and Mormon authorities.[31] Their four-thousand-mile journey was over.

When Levi McCullough, who was in this group, reached Winter Quarters, he was informed by a friend that his wife and two-year-old daughter had died. His other children were living with different families. McCullough and his two traveling companions were offered food and shelter for the night by the friend. Later that evening one of McCullough's sons arrived and, looking at the three men, asked: "Which one of these ragged men is my father?"[32]

San Francisco in 1847. Lithograph from Owen Cochran Coy, *Pictorial History of California* (1925); courtesy of the California History Room, California State Library, Sacramento, California.

CHAPTER NINE

Monterey, San Francisco, and the Brooklyn

The Hunt fifty divided in Monterey with some remaining and others going on to San Francisco with him. Hunt did not stay long in San Francisco but lost several more of his traveling companions. He continued to Sutter's Fort with about twenty-five of his original Los Angeles company. He joined with the Hancock company to cross the Sierra Nevada. William and Melissa Coray stayed in Monterey because of her advanced pregnancy: "At this place [Monterey] I considered all things and concluded to stop for a season, expecting my wife to be confined any day. I rented a room and went to work with my team. . . . Business became very dull with me and I worried more and more about the Church, hearing nothing only that Capt. Hunt with a part of his company had gone on to meet them"(William Coray).[1]

Other ex-battalion men in Monterey were Elijah Elmer, Samuel Thompson, Thomas W. Treat, and Zadock Judd. The first three worked at odd jobs as carpenters and roofers on various structures and the custom house. Elmer worked for Thomas Larkin, a successful American businessman. By February they had earned $1,883. Judd opened up a tailor shop.[2] William Coray used his team and wagon to freight.

The *Brooklyn* passengers, under the leadership of Samuel Brannan, arrived in California July 31, 1846, a year before Brigham Young and the pioneers arrived in Salt Lake Valley. Yerba Buena (later San Francisco) was an obscure Mexican outpost, occupied mainly by Californios, Indians, a few sailors of the *Portsmouth* in the harbor and a handful of adventurers. Two weeks before the Mormons sailed into the harbor, the United States Navy had secured Yerba Buena and raised the American flag. The *Brooklyn* members were the first colonists in California under American rule. Their 24,000-mile journey around Cape Horn also made them the first colonists to come by sea. For a brief time Yerba Buena was a Mormon settlement. Both the ex-soldiers and the 238 *Brooklyn* passengers met regularly in religious services with Samuel Brannan as the presiding elder.

Brannan hoped Brigham Young and the body of the Mormon Church would continue to California. With this in mind Brannan sent twenty men and their families to New Hope (near present-day Stockton) to plant crops and to build cabins, anticipating Young's arrival in California. Unlike the battalion, the *Brooklyn* immigrants had not been directed to leave California.

Brannan left California on April 4, 1847, to find Brigham Young and tell him about the wonders of California as a settling place for the church.[3] Three men, C. C. Smith and two others, went with him. They left Sutter's Fort April 26, 1847, and continued to Green River (Wyoming), where they met Young and the pioneer company June 30.[4]

Brannan traveled with these pioneers into the Great Salt Lake Valley. Unable to convince Brigham Young that California was the place for the Saints and, after several days of watching Brigham Young establish the final stopping place for the Saints, Brannan left for California August 9. He arrived at Sutter's Fort September 10 and reached San Francisco September 17. Disillusioned, Brannan continued for a while to fulfill his duties as presiding elder. After his return, it seemed Brannan had other things on his mind besides building up the Mormon Church.

Amasa Lyman, one of the Twelve Apostles, was sent to California by Brigham Young to collect tithing.[5] The Mormons in Monterey and San Francisco gave their tithing to Lyman, and their names were on the tithing list Lyman submitted to Brigham Young upon returning to Salt Lake Valley.

When Melissa's time for delivery arrived in Monterey, William Coray found two Mexican women to help. Although they did not speak English, they assisted in the birth of a baby boy on October 2, 1847: "My wife was delivered of a fine boy and I named him William after myself as he was my firstborn."[6] On October 11, 1847, William wrote to a comrade, James Ferguson, in San Francisco: "I am the biggest man in all Israel. I have the greatest boy you ever want anywhere, and I am coming up to show him just as soon as the woman gets well enough."

The Corays decided to move to San Francisco, where William could find more freighting. Before they left Monterey, their infant son died. William made a small pine coffin and Melissa dressed the baby in his best clothes. They buried him in the Monterey cemetery, where William read a few scriptures and Melissa said a prayer before placing wildflowers on the tiny grave.

The Corays had difficulty finding a place to live in San Francisco but finally managed to obtain a single room in back of a store with stables in the yard where William could keep his team. "San Francisco is a beautiful place, a fine ship harbor perfectly secure from storm, also very healthy. The place at this time was improving rapidly, lots selling at a great price, and it was all stir and speculation and money-making both by the Mormons and the worldlings" (William Coray).[7]

On Sunday, October 24, 1847, John Borrowman recorded in his journal: "Had preaching by Elder [William] Cory and by Elder [Addison] Pratt in the evening."[8]

Francis Hammond, a non-Mormon, set sail from the Hawaiian Islands on Oct. 1, 1847, arriving in San Francisco twenty-three days later:

> When we entered the Golden Gate leading into one of the finest harbors in the world . . . there were no docks or wharfs to which ships could approach and discharge their passengers and cargoes. This was done by means of lighters, or large flat-bottom scows. So after we had come to anchor we hoisted out our yawl boat, and the captain and three men passengers besides myself, got in and were pulled to shore. I was in the . . . front part of the boat, and as we struck the beach I made a good spring and jumped ashore without getting my feet wet. On our landing we found quite a few men with drays, a kind of a low, two-wheeled, one-horse cart, with a kind of platform extending quite a distance in the rear of the wheels and raised but little from the ground. One of these persons stepped up to me and saluted, and asked me if I wanted my baggage taken to a hotel. I replied that I did. He asked me to which one. I replied I was a stranger and told him to take me to any respectable place.
>
> This man was Bro. William Corey as I afterwards learned, a sergeant in the ever-memorable Mormon Battalion. By this time it was nearly dark, and after going over a rough road quite a distance, he stopped at a Mormon boarding-house kept by William Glover. (Francis Hammond. Glover had come on the ship *Brooklyn*.)[9]

Battalion men seated at the supper table when Hammond arrived that night were John White, Orlando F. Mead, Thomas Dunn, Meltiar Hatch, Orin Hatch, Boyd Stewart, and James Ferguson. Hammond bought the cook's galley, twelve by fourteen feet square, that had been on the ship *Brooklyn* and used it as a place to live and a shop for his shoemaker's trade. He hired two ex-soldiers, John White and Orlando Mead, to work for him.

On Thursday, December 2, 1847, the San Francisco branch of the Mormon Church was organized with Addison Pratt as president. This was the first branch of the church in California. Meetings were held regularly on Sundays—one in the morning and another in the evening. There also were midweek meetings. Although Francis Hammond had been warned by friends in Hawaii about the "awful Mormons" in San Francisco, he was baptized on December 31, 1847, by Robert Petch in the San Francisco

Bay and was confirmed by Samuel Brannan. His was the first conversion in San Francisco and the second Mormon baptism in California.[10]

Before leaving New York City, items necessary for colonization were packed aboard the ship *Brooklyn* by Brannan, including agricultural and manufacturing tools, dry goods, hardware, candles, wheat, vegetables and grass seeds, bibles, school supplies, and a library of 179 volumes. Also on board were two grist mills, carpenter tools, sawmill irons, a printing press, a supply of newsprint and all the necessary type to begin a newspaper. Brannan named the paper while still in New York City and had the wooden masthead made there in December 1845. The first edition of *The California Star* reached the streets of San Francisco January 7, 1847. It was the city's first newspaper. The early editions carried the story of the tragic Donner party stranded in the Sierra. After a plea in its column for assistance, $1,500 cash and clothing donated by *Brooklyn* Saints, battalion members, and other local residents were sent to John Sutter in Sacramento for supplies to aid the starving Donner company and the rescue parties.

The ex-soldiers met in San Francisco on January 26, 1848, to begin plans to go to Salt Lake Valley. On Sunday, March 19, there was a heavy rain all day and no meetings were held. However, in the evening Henry Dalton, Company B, married Elizabeth Kittleman of the *Brooklyn*. It was a festive occasion for the Bay Area Mormons. One diarist gave a glowing account of the wedding food, without listing the names of the bridal couple. There were other weddings between battalion men and *Brooklyn* women.[11]

The merchants of San Francisco believed the city was not growing fast enough. They asked Brannan to publish a special edition of *The California Star* extolling the virtues of the city and state. Two thousand copies of *The Star* were to be carried across the country and would, they hoped, attract colonists to California.

The type for this special edition of *The California Star* was handset, letter by letter. Usually only four pages, eighteen by twenty-two inches, this enlarged edition had six pages with four columns on each page. The paper was ready to print except for a couple of empty inches on an inside page when news of the gold discovery in Coloma reached San Francisco. (The story of the discovery of gold is given in chapter 10.) This important historical happening rated only a brief paragraph on the inside page and that without a proper headline, probably for two reasons. First, the magnitude of the gold discovery was not realized by the editor. Even those who knew about finding gold in Coloma didn't realize what a rich find it was. It took another month for the news to affect lives in San Francisco. Second, if he did recognize it, it would have been too tedious to reset the letters by hand.

The papers were bundled and labeled for major cities through which the riders would pass. Nathan Hawk remembered one bundle being addressed to the "reading room of the National Library in the City of Washington." They carried single copies to give to travelers they met en route. Perhaps the paper would cause emigrants to choose California instead of Oregon to settle. The men also carried letters for fifty cents each and papers for twelve and a half cents.[12]

Ten men—six battalion men and four non-Mormons—known as *The California Star* Express riders, were hired by Brannan to carry the papers east. Of the ten *Star* Express riders, only the names of the six Mormons are known: William Hawk, Nathan Hawk, Silas Harris, Richard Slater, Daniel Rawson, and Sanford Jacobs, captain. The Mormons were delighted with the chance to earn money and to have supplies furnished while returning to their families. In addition to the papers and mail carried, each of the Mormon riders took extra supplies, pack mules, and horses. They left San Francisco April 1, 1848. John Sutter noted their arrival upriver: "Work going as usual, a strong southerly breeze. The *Dice mi Nana* arrived with Mr. Brannan, Mr. Hawk, the express Mail carrier, and a few others."[13]

The men left Sacramento April 15. Brannan rode with them as far as the foothills beyond Sacramento. After Brannan left, they went a short distance when their pack animals stampeded and scattered their provisions over the ground. Three days later they reached snow three and four feet deep. This deep, soft snow was another challenge. They traveled the Truckee River over the California Trail. The Truckee was very high and swift, with a rocky dangerous bottom, but the men crossed it numerous times safely although the freezing waters resulted in much discomfort.

Indians caused the little group a lot of problems, continually harrassing them and stealing horses. One night shortly after leaving Sutter's Fort, Indians stole seventy-five horses, but all were recovered.

When they reached Salt Lake Valley, Daniel Rawson rented a small piece of ground and planted corn and other seeds he had brought from California so he could harvest the crops when he returned with his family after delivering the newspapers. Only five of the Mormon express riders continued—Silas Harris remained in Salt Lake City.

The express riders met Brigham Young and several large companies on their way to Salt Lake Valley:

We met Brigham Young . . . in the Black Hills. We stopped and talked with Brigham Young for quite a time. He was very anxious to find the conditions in the country we had traversed. I showed him the gold and asked if he would go on to California. He replied: "No! I hope they will never strike gold in the country where we [are] located, for I do not want my people to go digging for their God." . . . I forgot to tell you that the gold I took with me across the

plains . . . was dug out by myself and three or four others of my comrades at Mormon Island. (Nathan Hawk)[14]

High water presented problems all the way to the Platte River in
Nebraska. Near Grand Island, the Pawnee Indians stole eighteen horses.
While trying to recover the animals, William Hawk was struck across the
forehead with the Indian's bow. William was stunned for a moment and
carried the mark on his forehead for a long time.

Their contract was to deliver the newspapers to Missouri and the
express riders completed their journey successfully by late July. The bun-
dles of papers for the East coast cities were sent on: "My party arrived safely in Missouri where my family resided. My companions [the other riders]
went to different sections. . . . The papers of Brannan that I put in the
mails and sent on [to] their destinations soon spread the news and were
the cause of heavy immigration West in 1849" (Nathan Hawk).[15]

One copy of this overland special edition found its way to the offices
of the *New York Herald,* where an astute reporter went through *The Star,*
picking out a paragraph here and there until he had a two-column story,
but the gold discovery item was his leading paragraph. On Saturday,
August 19, 1848, the front page headline in the *New York Herald* read
"Gold Discovered in California." The story included the following:

The gold mine discovered in December last [actually January 24,
1848], on the south branch of the American Fork, in a range of low
hills forming the base of the Sierra Nevada, distant thirty miles from
New Helvetia, is only three feet below the surface, in a strata of soft
sand rock. From explorations south twelve miles, and north five
miles, the continuance of this strata is reported, and the mineral
said to be equally abundant, and from twelve to eighteen feet in
thickness, so that, without allowing any golden hopes to puzzle my
prophetic vision of the future, I would predict for California
Peruvian harvest of the precious metals, as soon as a sufficiency of
miners, &c, can be obtained.

That *The California Star* Express riders were successful in distributing
the papers they carried is evidenced by articles that appeared during
August in other eastern newspapers.[16] Among the places where they
appeared were St. Louis, Missouri, August 8; Baltimore *Sun;* New Orleans
Daily Picayune; New York *Journal of Commerce;* and the Philadelphia *North
American,* September 14. Since these newspapers published stories during
August 1848 (except the Philadelphia paper), it is assumed they were
taken from *The Star.* The Philadelphia story also probably came from *The
Star* because other communications had later arrival dates and the *North
American* contained phraseology similar to that used in *The Star.*

It did not take long for the news to arrive from other sources. President Polk made an official proclamation about the discovery of gold during his annual message to Congress, December 5, 1848. He had received the news from an official communiqué from Governor Mason of California.[17] The president's declaration that gold had been found gave a legitimacy to what previously had been rumors. From all over the United States, wagons and ships began wending their way west. The gold rush was on. Other correspondents in California, including Alcalde Walter Colton, San Francisco, and U.S. Navy Agent Thomas Larkin of Monterey sent letters telling about the gold placers, which were quoted in New York City and Washington, D.C., papers during September 1848.

The California Star Express riders were part of two important happenings. First, the papers they carried gave the world its first written news of the gold discovery in California. Second, the mail they carried was the first mail to go overland, from West to East, under private contract.

On Sunday, April 30, Samuel Brannan spoke on the "disaffection that existed in the branch and called for those who found fault with him to bring forth their charges." Brannan's dissatisfaction with the Mormon Church was apparent to members who questioned his financial transactions and moral decay.

> [Brannan] would play billiards and drink grog with the greatest blacklegs in the place. . . . However, he seems to have taken his position as a Mormon leader seriously up to the time the Saints were established in California. He demanded the saints keep the Sabbath and conduct themselves honestly and morally. He lectured regularly on board the ship and in Honolulu and in California after the Saints arrival here.[18] (William Coray)

Edward Kemble, editor of *The California Star,* was very cautious in writing about the gold discovery. No doubt he did not comprehend its importance, but he may have played it down to give Samuel Brannan a chance to get his stores established in the mining region. Brannan called a meeting on Wednesday evening, May 10, and informed the San Francisco Saints a rich vein of gold had been discovered at Mormon Island and advised all present to go to the gold fields.[19] Although rumors of the gold discovery reached San Francisco in April, it is interesting that the *Brooklyn* passengers seemed to ignore the rumors until after Brannan's May 10 announcement. The mass exodus of other residents to the gold fields did not start until about this same time. When the news finally sank in, San Francisco almost became a deserted city.

The planned departure date of the battalion soldiers to leave California was mid-June. The ex-soldiers in San Francisco, already preparing for the rendezvous, may have left the bay city a little earlier than planned because of Brannan's news. The *Brooklyn* Saints also rushed to the gold fields. During their brief months in San Francisco the battalion men and the *Brooklyn* passengers made a significant contribution to the development of the young city. Merely the fact that they were there so early gave them the opportunity to take part in many "firsts."[20]

Not all were impressed by the golden discovery. To some, families and church were more important: "We saw them washing out the gold with pans, but we did not stop there long. We were anxious to come to Salt Lake"(Melissa Coray).[21]

CHAPTER TEN

Sutter's Workmen

After meeting Captain James Brown in the mountains, the men returning to Sutter's Fort gave most of their supplies and animals to those continuing to Salt Lake Valley. Samuel Miles wrote, "This caused about half our company to return."[1]

> So the company divided right where we met each other. Some went on to Winter Quarters, some to the valley and some turned back. I being one of that number. Daniel Browett, [Richard] Slater, [John] Cox, Levi Roberts and myself turned back to Sacramento and went to work for Mr. Sutter who treated us very kindly. The rest of our mess, Robert Harris, Hiram Judd, Jedit [Jeduthan Averett] and Bro. [Edward] Bunker went on to Winter Quarters with Lieutenant Little [Andrew Lytle] and company. I sent a mule to my wife with Bro. Harris, which she got. (Robert Pixton)[2]

When approximately one hundred ex-soldiers returned to Sutter's Fort after the Sierra meeting with Brown, they joined their comrades who had remained behind. About twenty continued to San Francisco to find employment. The rest were put to work immediately by Captain John Sutter, who wrote in the fort log after the Mormons had returned, "I employed about 80 of them."[3]

Sutter and the Mormons entered into a contract for various work throughout his growing empire:

> Captain John A. Sutter being desirous of building a flour mill some six miles from the fort, and a sawmill about forty-five miles away, proposed to hire all the men either by the job or month at their option to dig the races. Twelve and a half cents per yard and provisions was finally agreed upon, the men to do their own cooking. Their animals were also to be herded with the Captains, free of charge.

SUTTER'S FORT - NEW HELVETIA.
Published by C. S. Francis & Co. N. York.

Sutter's Fort, ca. 1847. The small building in the left foreground is where Samuel Brannan had his store with C. C. Smith. Courtesy of the California History Room, California State Library, Sacramento, California.

Captain Sutter advanced one half of the prospective cost in gentle work oxen. A portion of the men obtained plows, picks, spades, shovels and scrapers and moved up to the designated place for the sawmill while the balance went to dig the race for the grist mill. The former commenced labor about September 17, clearing $1.50 each the first day. They subsequently earned more. (Daniel Tyler)[4]

Records kept by Sutter's clerk reveal the Mormons worked as carpenters and laborers, dug ditches, made shoes, tanned hides, built granaries and a grist mill at Natoma. Others split shingles and clapboards. There were farms to be cultivated and cattle and sheep to be tended. Thomas Weir was a tanner and curryer. Levi Fifield and Samuel Lewis were blacksmiths. John S. White, foreman, Jonathan Holmes, Orlando Mead, Francis Hammond (a recent convert in San Francisco), and six others were shoemakers in a room at the fort. Holmes's journal entry of September 4, 1847, told of making five pairs of "stogy at one dollar per pair." Daniel Henrie opened up a meat market, bought and slaughtered cattle, and sold the meat to the settlers. Working on the grist mill were Samuel H. Rogers, Jonathan H. Holmes, Daniel Q. Dennett, James Douglas, Daniel Browett, Joseph Dobson, and David H. Moss. The Mormons provided much-needed labor for Sutter's expanding empire.

Six Mormons were hired to help build the sawmill in the mountains. The following arrived at Coloma September 29 and began working under the direction of James Marshall: Henry Bigler, Azariah Smith, Alexander Stephens, James S. Brown, William Johnstun, and William Barger.

Henry Bigler described the Coloma Valley well:

We arrived on the twenty-ninth [September]. The country around the mill site looked wild and lonesome. Surrounded by high mountains on the south side of the river, the mountains were densely covered with pine, balsam, pionion pine, redwood, white oak, and low down live oak, while on the north side there was not so much timber. The mountains were more abrupt and rocky, covered in places with patches of chamisal and greasewood. The country was infested with wolves, grizzly bears, and indians.[5]

The men began work immediately, with tasks assigned according to individual skills. "The week past I with two others pin[n]ed the pla[nks] on the forebay. . . . Home keeps running in my mind, and I feel somewhat lonesum especially Sundays, but my heart leaps with the expectation of getting home in the spring . . . I keep up as good courage as I can"(Azariah Smith).[6]

Work progressed on the sawmill until December 18 when Marshall went to Fort Sutter to make models for the mill irons. Levi Fifield, a

Sutter's Mill, Coloma, California, 1848. Drawing by William M. Johnson from Norma B. Ricketts, *Mormons and the Discovery of Gold* (1966).

Mormon blacksmith, had been hired to make them. Samuel Lewis assisted Fifield. An entry by Sutter is noteworthy: "Today the sawmill crank has
been commenced and will be finished tomorrow as the iron is good, this
is the heaviest kind of blacksmith work which ever has been done here,
and give Fifield great credit as a good workman."[7]

John S. White was in charge of a dozen men making shoes in a small
rear room at Sutter's Fort. The shoemakers asked Sutter if they could prepare Christmas dinner for him and his guests. Sutter approved the idea,
but no record has been found that reveals the menu.

Winter rains brought high, swift water to the American River, which
threatened the sawmill. The men saved it by working all day and continuing through the night. When the flood waters receded and work was
resumed, it was determined the tail race needed to be deeper. Early one
morning Marshall was at the end of the race, where most of the digging
had been done, when he saw his first gold flakes. Later Marshall could not
remember the date but thought it was around the nineteenth of January.
California recognized the nineteenth for several years. It was not until
Henry Bigler's journal came to light and was studied that the actual discovery date of January 24 became established.

The journal entry that preserved this historic moment for California
was the following: "This day some kind of mettle was found in the tail of
race that looks like goald."[8] Bigler stated further on the same date that
gold was "first found by James W. Martial, the boss of the mill."

Bigler's journal settled two questions with these brief sentences.
One, who discovered the first gold, and two, the actual date of the discovery. When Azariah Smith wrote in his diary at the end of that week, on
January 30, 1848, his entry confirmed Bigler's date: "This week Mon. the
24th, Mr. Marshall found some pieces of (as we suppose) Gold, and he
has gone to the Fort, for the purpose of finding out."[9] These are the only
first-hand accounts of the gold discovery that were recorded contempora-
neously with it. They establish without a doubt the date of the initial discovery of gold. Only five of the Mormons were at the mill site on January
24. William Johnstun was at Sutter's Fort with a team and wagon for supplies and missed the excitement.

Sutter asked Marshall and the workers to keep the discovery a secret
until he could secure the land. There is no record that the Mormons told
outsiders, but they did tell each other: "I wrote to Jesse Martin, Israel Evans
and Ephraim Green (three mess mates of mine while in the Battalion) who
were at work on Captain Sutter's flouring mill, and informed them that we
had found gold at the saw mill, but had to keep it to themselves unless it
would be to someone who could keep a secret"(Henry Bigler).[10]

It wasn't long until curious comrades visited their friends in
Coloma. Such was the case on February 27 when Sidney Willes, Wilford

Monday 24th this day some kind of mettle was

discoved was found in the tail race that that looks like goald first discovered by Jam.s Martial, the Bos of the mill.
Sunday 30 clean & has been all the last week our metal has been tride and prooves to be goald it is thought to be rich we have pick up more than a hundred dollars woth last week

February. 1848
Sun 6th the wether has been clear

Henry Bigler's journal entry for January 24, 1848. Courtesy of the Marshall Gold Discovery Park, Coloma, California.

Hudson, and Levi Fifield arrived at the mill with their guns and blankets on their backs. Hudson asked Marshall for permission to prospect in the tail race the next morning, which permission was given readily.

The three men remained in Coloma several days. On the return trip, Henry Bigler and Fifield went to the fort by the road, while Willes and Hudson followed the river. Bigler later returned to Coloma. When Willes and Hudson reached their comrades scattered around Sutter's Fort, they told of finding gold particles on an island in the American River, halfway between Coloma and the fort. Several days later, at the urging of Ephraim Green and Ira Willes (Sidney's brother), Sidney Willes and Wilford Hudson returned to the island and showed the others where they found the gold particles previously. The Willes-Hudson strike became known as Mormon Island and turned out to be the second major gold strike, one with very "rich diggings."[11]

It was not long until many of the ex-soldiers and men from the ship *Brooklyn* gathered on Mormon Island to search for gold. They marked off plots of five square yards for each man and worked five men together. The Mormons were situated ideally, being on site at the beginning of the gold rush, working with friends before the onslaught of Forty-niners. The atmosphere was one of openness and trust. They tossed their daily golden findings into containers on their plot and left their tools out at night. One group divided $17,000 at the end of one week.[12] Mormon Island became a very busy place, with about two hundred ex-soldiers and *Brooklyn* men all panning for gold. There were scores of tents and brush shelters, a store, and several "boarding shanties." On April 12, Henry Bigler wrote that "the Willes boys . . . met with Sam Brannan and let him in on the secret."[13]

John Borrowman and others from the San Francisco area arrived at Mormon Island late on the evening of May 17: "Got there about sunset and found Brother Willis [W. Sidney Willes] weighing the gold that had been dug today. . . . there was one man had 128 dollars." Borrowman and William Wood worked together and dug seventeen dollars on their first day, May 18.[14] The next day, they "Worked at washing gold and made 22 dollars but as Brannan & Co. requires thirty per cent my share only came to $8 as Brother Wood and [I] are in company."[15]

They used different methods to find gold: flat pans, baskets, rockers, and knives. Benjamin Hawkins, formerly with Company A, found a rocker that floated down stream to where he and Marcus Shepherd and three others were working. Using the rocker, they washed out over $3,000 in one day.[16]

> It was mining in a primitive way. We had no pans, no lumber to make rockers, and so we used Indian baskets to pan with. The Indians made a water-tight willow basket that answered the place of

a pan. When we would get panned down to the black sand we would dump the gold on a flour sack which we had spread out upon the ground. In order to weigh our gold, we made a balance with two chips, a stick and a string. We imitated the scales held by Justice. We placed the gold on one chip and Mexican or Spanish gold coins on the other until they balanced. In that way we could pretty closely estimate the value of our day's work, which averaged about $20 to the man. (Nathan Hawk) [17]

When Samuel Brannan visited the gold fields to collect tithing, payment of tithes became a topic of discussion. Brannan asked for thirty percent—ten percent for tithing, ten percent for rent to Willes and Hudson for finding gold at Mormon Island, and ten percent to build up the kingdom. Other times Brannan's statement was contradictory with the last ten percent going to build a temple or to obtain cattle for the Mormon Church. The men thought this assessment was too high. John Borrowman said he was against paying "rent" as he thought it was an imposition. Others questioned if Brannan actually gave their tithes to the church or if he kept the money himself.

While at the mines I had very good luck. I gathered nearly $300.00, which makes me worth in all about $400.00. The most I made in a day after the toll was taken out was 65 dollars, which was 30 out of 100, this percentage going to Hudson and Willis [Willes], who discovered the mine, and Brannan, who was securing it for them. . . . While there Mr. Brannan called a meeting to see who was willing to pay toll, and who was not, most of the men agreed to pay, while others refused. (Azariah Smith) [18]

When Addison Pratt, the president of the San Francisco branch of the Mormon Church, journeyed to the gold fields prior to leaving California, he was asked directly about paying tithing to Brannan:

Soon after we went to Mormon Island . . . on our arrival there we learned that Brannan had entered into an agreement with the brethren there, to the effect that all who dug gold there should pay a tax of 30 per cent of all they found. The claim was that this percent should go to the Church, and from that means obtained, that young cattle should be purchased in California and sent to the valley. I had seen enough of Brannan's tricks to convince me that the Church would never see any cattle bought in this manner and considerable dissatisfaction existed among the brethren who had come up from San Francisco over this matter. Many asked me if I intended to pay the per cent asked. I told them that I considered the demand unjust, and yet if the Church could get the benefit of the money I had no objection to paying it. I saw at once that if I refused to pay the tax most of the brethren would follow my example. And as Brannan had already collected some means in this manner I foresaw clearly that his low cunning would naturally lead him to send what means he had already collected to the Church and then report that if I had not come out against him he would have been able to send more. (Addison Pratt) [19]

Governor Richard Mason and William Tecumseh Sherman toured the area and visited Mormon Island. Sherman recorded the following incident in his memoirs:

As soon as the fame of the gold discovery spread through California the Mormons . . . turned to Mormon Island, so that in July 1848, we found about three hundred of them there at work. Sam Brannan was on hand as the high priest, collecting his tithes. [William S.] Clark, of Clark's Point, one of the elders, was there also, and nearly all of the Mormons who had come out in the Brooklyn . . . I remember that Mr. Clark was in camp talking about matters and things generally when he inquired, "Governor, what business has Sam Brannan to collect tithes here?" Clark admitted Brannan was the head of the Mormon Church in California, and he was simply questioning as to Brannan's right, as high priest, to compel the Mormons to pay him the regular tithes. Colonel Mason answered, "Brannan has a perfect right to collect the tax, if you Mormons are fools enough to pay it." "Then," said Clark, "I, for one, won't pay it any longer." [20]

Azariah Smith understood it to be a tax for Willes and Hudson for discovering the claim and Brannan for securing it. Pratt thought it was tithing with the additional ten percent for buying cattle for the Mormon Church. John Sutter thought it was for still another purpose: "The Mormons were being assessed to build a temple to the Lord. Now that God had given gold to the Church, the Church must build a temple." [21]

No record has been found that any of the tithes collected by Brannan were turned over to the Mormon Church. Brannan benefited in another way from the gold the men found. He operated a store just outside the front gate of Sutter's Fort with C. C. Smith. Estimates place Brannan's earnings from his store, C. C. Smith and Company, at $36,000 grossed between May 1 and July 10, 1848. [22] Brannan also had a store at Coloma and grew rich from the earnings of both stores, making a 300 to 500 percent profit. Samuel Rogers recorded numerous purchases from the store during May 1848 and revealed the rate of exchange. Typical of the transactions made by the men are the following purchases of Rogers. [23]

[May 12, 1848:] I washed enough so . . . I have seventeen dollars and fifty cents after paying thirty percent rent [tithing] of what I dug.

[May 19, 1848:] I bought a bolt of blue drillings . . . for 4 dollars and 62 cents.

[May 21, 1848:] I bought a small mare from John Eager for 20 dollars. I paid in gold at 16 dollars per ounce. I also bought one hickory shirt, price one dollar and seventy-five cents.

[May 29, 1848:] I went to the fort, bought a buckskin $1.50. I also bought a mare of mister Ni [Nye], price 20 dollars—10 in specie and 10 in gold at 14 dollars per ounce.

The Coloma mill was in regular operation by the end of March; the Mormons' contract to finish the mill was fulfilled. By April, news of the gold discovery began to spread in California. A steady stream of people from San Francisco, Sonoma, San Jose, Monterey, and other parts of northern California made their way constantly to the mines. A meeting was held by the ex-soldiers at the fort on April 9 "to talk over matters and things in regard to making arrangements for going up to the Great Salt Lake and come to some understanding when we should make the start."[24] Brannan attended this meeting where it was decided not to follow the established Truckee route because of crossing the river so many times. Daniel Browett was appointed to inform Sutter of their decision to leave and to obtain wages, cattle, and other articles. He also was to make arrangements to purchase two cannon from Sutter.

Even with the discovery of gold, most ex-battalion soldiers still planned to go to the church and their families. They remembered the letter from church authorities the previous August advising them to work until spring to obtain needed supplies, a plan which they seemed determined to follow. As the departure date approached, journals indicate a longing to be united with families and the Mormon Church. Azariah Smith wrote he was very lonely, especially since his father, Albert, had gone ahead with the Hancock-Sierra company. The men made several trips to Sutter's Fort for their pay for the work they had done, but Captain Sutter was unable to settle. His books were not up-to-date since his bookkeeper, like others, was in the gold fields. Sutter apparently attempted to settle his accounts with the battalion workers on April 18, 1848, when he wrote, "A very buissi day to settle accts with some of the Mormons."

Also, by this time California was experiencing the arrival of the first gold seekers, who appropriated Sutter's cattle, sheep, and crops at will. Henry Bigler noted, "We observed the Sabbath like Christians and for the first time we were visited by gold hunters."[25] By the end of May all work on the grist mill at Natomas had stopped. The sawmill, after cutting only a few thousand feet of lumber, was shut down. The shortage of labor closed all of Sutter's projects.

> After the discovery of gold was known, it began to spread like wild fire all over California. . . . all my plans and projects came to naught. One after another of my people disappeared in the direction of the gold fields. Only the Mormons behaved decently. . . . They were sorry for the difficulties in which I found myself, and some of them remained to finish their jobs. (John Sutter)[26]

The soldiers bartered for pay "in kind." Sutter gave them wild horses, mules, cattle, oxen, wagons they had made for him, plows, picks, shovels, iron, seeds, plant cuttings, and other items that would be useful when they reached Salt Lake Valley. "Paid off all the Mormons which have been employed by me in building these mills and other mechanical trades, all of them made their pile and some of them became very rich and wealthy but all of them are bound to the Great Salt Lake and [will] spend their fortunes there to the glory and honor of the Lord"(John Sutter).[27]

Captain Sutter had two small brass cannon he purchased from the Russians when the Russians closed Fort Ross in northern California. They were small, decorated, parade cannons, one a four pounder and the other a six pounder.[28] The men decided to buy them and take them to the leaders of the Mormon Church. Daniel Browett, acting as agent, collected gold flakes from the men and paid Sutter for the cannon. On May 7, Sutter again recorded in the *New Helvetia Diary:* "Delivered to the Mormons the two small brass pieces." They were placed on runners and hauled in a wagon to Salt Lake Valley by the Holmes-Thompson company.

Nine pioneers chosen to find a trail over the mountains were Daniel Browett, captain, Ira J. Willes, James C. Sly, Israel Evans, Jacob G. Truman, Ezra Allen, James R. Allred, Henderson Cox, and Robert Pixton. They decided to follow the ridge between the waters of the Cosumnes and the American Rivers. It took them three days to reach Iron Mountain, where the snow was piled so high in the passes travel was impossible, so they returned to camp.

Henry Bigler, John S. White, and Jacob M. Truman set out on the morning of June 17, 1848, to "select a place of gathering." They found "a nice little valley forty or fifty miles east of Sutter's Fort," which they named Pleasant Valley.[29] They brought supplies, wagons, and animals to the site but continued to hunt for gold up to the time they left California. More men arrived during the next two weeks. They began felling pine timbers to build a corral. Others came intermittently to the rendezvous. On June 21 a group brought loose horses. Twenty wagons, mostly drawn by oxen, had arrived by June 22. Eight or nine herdsmen were hired to take charge of the loose stock from 4 A.M. until 8 P.M. This allowed the men time to prospect for gold. Daniel Browett was elected president of the company.[30]

Browett, Ezra Allen, and Henderson Cox left to scout a road over the mountains. Their companions did not want them to go, but the three men were very anxious to get started and went ahead against advice. Browett, Cox, and Allen each had a riding animal, a pack mule, a saddle, his army musket, and any gold he may have found.

Everyone mined for gold while waiting for the three scouts to return. James Brown and Henry Bigler used a unique method. They spread a cotton sheet near a hole of water, slanting a little downward. Then they put pay dirt on it and threw water on it with shovels. This washed away the dirt and left the gold sticking to the cloth. They thought it was better than the wooden bowls they had been using.

When the three scouts did not return, the group decided to continue. Later known as the Holmes-Thompson company, they left Pleasant Valley July 3 on the last segment of their epic journey.[31] This was the first of several small groups of men who worked for John Sutter and in the San Francisco Bay area to leave California during the summer of 1848. They had worked a season as instructed; now they were going to their families and church. Other companies followed, but the Holmes-Thompson company led the way.

CHAPTER ELEVEN

Journey's End

From the "half" who turned back to California in September 1847 to work for a season (Sutter's workmen), small groups of battalion ex-soldiers left California during the spring and summer of 1848. These men arrived in Salt Lake Valley from September through November 1848.

As they left California on the last portion of their history-making journey, members of the Holmes-Thompson company did not know they would pioneer two more wagon roads before arriving in Salt Lake Valley. They took the first wagons over Carson Pass and built the road that became a major entrance into California for thousands of gold seekers. Later on their journey they made the first wagon tracks over the Salt Lake Cutoff. Because of the importance of these two roads, a daily account of this last phase of the journey as experienced by the Holmes-Thompson company continues.

Mon., July 3, on the divide, 10 miles. The main company moved out. Henry Bigler, Addison Pratt, and a handful stayed behind to round up stray oxen. The advance company consisted of 45 men, 1 woman, 2 small cannon, 17 wagons, 150 horses, and the same number of cattle. Each man had his army musket. Some also had six-shooters and other handguns.

Tues., July 4, 10 miles. Despite half-broken draft animals, they made good time on their first day of travel. The wagons had only minor problems. Keeping loose stock together was difficult. The stock has to be corralled at night under armed guard to keep the Indians from taking them and to keep the animals from straying.

In the morning they fired two rounds with the six-pound cannon to celebrate America's independence. They were relieved to be on their way at last. They had chosen this new, untried route because they wanted to avoid crossing the Truckee River so many times. They also hoped the Carson route would be shorter. They traveled about ten miles and

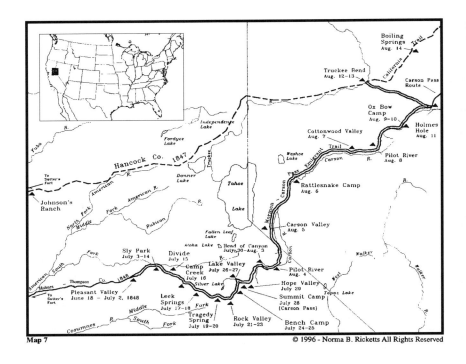

Map 7

1848
Holmes-Thompson Company
Mormon-Carson Pass
Emigrant Trail

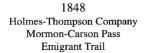

——— Holmes-Thompson Company
═══ Blazed Wagon Road
--- Truckee-Donner Route
▲ Camp Site and Nights Stayed

camped near a beautiful meadow they called Sly Park, named after James Sly, Company B, who found it. There was a stream and plenty of grass for the stock.

Thurs., July 6, Sly Park. There was great concern about the three scouts who had not returned. Ten days before three scouts—Browett, Allen, and Cox—went ahead to find a route through the mountains. A party of ten left in the morning to see if they could locate the three missing men. Those who remained in camp worked on the road, repaired wagons, harness, and equipment. Bigler, Pratt, and others who stayed behind in Pleasant Valley reached the camp in Sly Park. They planned to stay until the ten men returned with news of the three scouts.

Sat., July 9, Sly Park. The camp gathered at night to plan for their trip. One of the matters discussed was which way would be best to hold prayers—by messes or by the group as a whole. Since they were on their way home, they felt prayers were "needful for the prosperity of us all on our way home" (Elijah Elmer).[1]

Tues., July 11, Sly Park. The men built two corrals in the meadows for the cattle and horses. The weather was good. They had prayers in camp.

Wed., July 12, Sly Park. The search party returned without finding the missing men. However, they located a pass that would be a difficult wagon road even with considerable work. There was great anxiety for the three scouts who had not returned. Addison Pratt, the branch president in San Francisco, and John Eager from the ship *Brooklyn* joined the company.

Thurs., July 13, Sly Park. They remained in camp, packing and organizing to go over the mountains.

Fri., July 14, Sly Park, 8 miles. From the green meadows of Sly Park, they began the ascent to the top of the ridge, where they camped. Bigler, Hammond, and two others went ahead each morning to cut brush and roll rocks out of the way, returning each night to camp. Addison Pratt had fever and ague. He and John Eagar were not experienced in driving a team and wagon. Azariah agreed to drive their outfit while Pratt was given a horse and was assigned to watch the loose cattle when his health improved.

Sat., July 15, on ridge, 8 miles. The country was rougher than first reports indicated. The brush and rocks gave the wagons considerable difficulty in passing through. They continued on in a southeasterly direction following the high, timbered mountain and camped at Log Springs.

Sun., July 16, Log Springs, 10 miles. They reached Camp Creek after a short journey. Bigler and his group cleared ten more miles.

Mon., July 17, Camp Creek, 10 miles. They camped for the night by springs which the men called Leek Springs because of the wild onions that grew here. They stayed over a day to find strayed cattle.

Tues., July 18, Leek Springs. Bigler, Samuel Rogers, James Sly, Francis Hammond, and the road crew went ahead and cleared ten miles. They found a spring and a dead campfire. Nearby was a newly made mound that looked like a grave. As soon as James Sly saw it, he exclaimed, "Our brethren are in that grave."[2] On the way back to camp they passed several Indians and thought one of the Indians was wearing a vest belonging to a missing scout. When the road crew reached camp, they told their companions about the grave and what their fears were. They held a meeting to reorganize since Daniel Browett, their leader, was one of the missing scouts. Jonathan H. Holmes was appointed president, with Samuel H. Rogers and Addison Pratt as counselors.[3] Samuel Thompson was selected captain of the tens.

Wed., July 19, Leek Springs. The entire company left Leek Springs. Travel was slow with hard, heavy pulling and pushing due to rocks and a steep grade. Jonathan Holmes's wagon broke down going through a snow bank. They traveled only six miles until they reached the grave. When they arrived, the grave was the center of attention as there was evidence of a terrible struggle. Tools were taken at once from the wagons and the grave was opened. It was a shocking sight. There lay the three brethren, naked and brutally murdered. An ax or hatchet had been sunk into Browett's face and a shot had penetrated one of his eyes. Allen was lying next to him with Cox underneath. All were in a shallow grave. Bloody arrows, some broken, were strewn all around. Blood-stained stones with locks of hair adhering to them were located. Allen's pouch of gold was found lying under a bush with $120 in it. It was a double pouch with a long buckskin string attached so he could carry it around his neck and let it hang inside of his shirt. His messmates had seen him make it. There was blood on the pouch. The men thought that as the murderers took Allen's clothes off, the bag probably slid into the bushes undiscovered. Others thought that as he was hit in the back of the head the string had been cut and the pouch had fallen unnoticed into a nearby bush where it was found. Their animals, supplies, and guns were gone. All three were carrying gold. Melissa Coray thought, "In all my journey with the battalion, this was the worst night."[4]

Before they went to bed, a prayer was given. During the prayer something startled the horses and cattle, causing a stampede. The ground shook like an earthquake as the cattle ran away. They thought Indians might be lurking nearby. Lieutenant Thompson ordered the men to "limber up a cannon and let her speak once." A guard was posted and, although the rest of the night was quiet, no one slept much.

Thurs., July 20, Tragedy Spring. In the morning it was discovered one-third of the stock was missing. Three of the tens went through the timber in different directions to see if there were any Indians and to drive the horses and cattle together. The fourth ten stayed in camp, repaired wagons, and made a new grave for their fallen comrades. They dug a deeper

Friends of the three men buried here at Tragedy Spring hunted to find the rounded rock at the top of the grave for a headstone. The bronze marker listing the names of the men was placed by the International Society, Daughters of Utah Pioneers, in 1967.

The blaze on this stump from Tragedy Spring, carved on a stately fir about ten feet in diameter, preserved the identity of the three men and the location of their grave. For many years no one knew who the men were or how they happened to be buried in the common grave. When the stump was taken to Sutter's Fort in 1931, eighty-three years later, a passing traveler recognized the names as members of the Mormon Battalion. The stump now is located in Marshall Gold Discovery Park, Coloma, California. The park association recently injected a hardening material into the stump to keep it from deteriorating further.

grave and then built a wall of rocks about three feet high and about eight feet square around it. Then they filled in the center with dirt up to the top of the wall. The grave was covered with more rocks. Finally, after searching, a rock rounded on one end was placed upright at the top of the grave as a headstone. "We fixed the grave as well as we could. It was a solem time when it was ascertained that these men had been murdered & in so shocking a manner. It was a time of solemenity and morning to think that the man that was to be our Leader [Daniel Browett] to Salt Lake was now lying Dead. He was like a father to me & we morn his loss" (Jonathan Holmes).[5]

Nearby was a tall fir about three and one-half feet in diameter. Wilford Hudson took his ax and chopped the bark away on one side. Then he carved the names of the three men on the bare tree: "To the Memory of Daniel Browett, Ezrah H. Allen, Henderson Cox, Who was supposed to have Been Murdered and Buried by Indians On the Night of the 27th June 1848."[6] Hudson, a close friend of Allen, said he would take the gold pouch to Allen's wife in Council Bluffs. Browett's cow was to be taken to Salt Lake City for his widow if she was there. Sadness permeated the nightly campfire. They named this place Tragedy Spring.

Fri., July 21, Tragedy Spring, 4 miles. About fifty animals were missing in the morning. All were found but three. One of those not found was James Diamond's pack mule.[7] After setting up camp, the men built a corral. Thompson and Wilford Hudson killed a deer for the evening meal.

Sat., July 22, Rock Creek, 7 miles. Fifteen men worked road to the top of the mountain. From the top they could see several small lakes. They passed over snow more than two feet deep and saw banks of snow perhaps fifteen feet deep. Henry Bigler gathered flowers with one hand and snow with the other. A donkey was buried completely in a snow bank except for his ears sticking out. One of the men grabbed the animal's long ears and dragged him out. Someone remarked now they knew why donkeys have large ears.

Sun., July 23, Rock Creek. The camp laid by to observe the Sabbath, but some of the men went ahead to work on the road. Samuel Rogers wrote a letter to Captain John Sutter in Sacramento telling him about the murder of their three scouts. He left it on a tree for someone to find and take to Sutter. They melted snow for water.

Mon., July 24, Rock Creek, 7 miles. The wagons continued to break down and were hard to guide. The large hind wheels passed over the stumps, but they were not sturdy like the smaller front wheels. Samuel Rogers's wagon tipped over twice. Another wagon had every other spoke replaced with what the veterans called "red pine." Wilford Hudson, who was a wagonwright, daily repaired or replaced broken reaches, felloes, hounds, tongues, and axles. The blacksmith kept busy welding broken king and queen pins, bolts and chain links, which was very difficult to do in the mountains because the winds blew smoke and ashes into his eyes. Also, it was hard to tell when the correct temperature for welding was reached using an improvised forge. With only manzanita bushes as fuel, his skill was sorely tested.

Tues., July 25, Summit Creek. After reaching the summit they laid over, camping on the north side of the mountains. Many spent the day mending wagons while the road builders worked on the road down into the valley.

Wed., July 26, Summit Creek, 3 miles. Moved down steep mountain slopes and camped near a frozen lake. The scouting party could not find an opening through the mountains. There were several small lakes nearby. Azariah packed his mules and traveled with William Coray's pack horses. Ten men left during the afternoon to explore the road ahead. Two more wagons broke down and two overturned. There was plenty of trout for supper.

Thurs., July 27, Lake Valley. Fifteen men went ahead to work the road, returning in the evening. They melted snow for water. The scouts returned and reported the road was passable into the valley, about twenty miles away.

Fri., July 28, Lake Valley, 4 miles. After camping about one quarter of a mile from the top of the mountain, they built a corral by felling timber and cutting brush. They called this place Summit Camp because it was the highest they thought they would camp. Azariah called it the backbone of the mountains.

Sat., July 29, Summit Camp, 2 miles. The men worked and made a road across the mountain. These were cliffs with sharp drops. The wagons and the cannon were maneuvered over these steep drops with great difficulty and were let down by block and tackle, using ropes and chains wrapped around tree trunks at the top for safety. They camped at the head of a level valley filled with thick brush and trees close together, with plenty of grass for the animals. They called this place "Hope Valley" as they began to have hope of getting through.

Sun., July 30, Red Lake, 8 miles. After traveling down Hope Valley, they camped at the head of a canyon by a river. The boys caught trout and killed four mountain chickens and two ducks. Addison Pratt still was not well, so he was not expected to do heavy work but was asked to fish. He caught thirty-five trout.

Mon., July 31, Pass Canyon. More mountain chickens and ducks made fine pot pies. The roadbuilders said it was impossible to build a road through this canyon with rocky walls that reached several hundred feet high on both sides. It was a very cold day with ice two inches thick on a bucket of water. Azariah made a pair of pantaloons.

Tues., Wed., Aug. 1, 2, Pass Canyon. Work continued on the road, but was not finished. Steep rock cliffs, from eight to ten feet high on either side with enormous rock in between made any progress extremely slow and difficult. This six-mile Carson Canyon on the West Fork of the Carson River was one of the worst stretches on the trail:

> We had no hammers nor drill with which we could do anything with the stones. It seemed almost an impossibility to go farther. Finally someone suggested that we build a fire on the rocks, and as there was plenty of dry logs and brush near, there was soon a good fire blazing on each rock that lay in our way. When the fire had died down and cooled off a little, we found that as far as the heat had penetrated the rocks were all broken in small pieces, which were soon removed with pick and shovel and another fire built with the same result. After building three or four fires, we found that the rocks were not much in our way and we soon had a good wagon road right over them. (Zadock Judd)[8]

Thurs., Aug. 3, Pass Canyon. Work continued on the road, accompanied by rain and a light snow.

Fri., Aug. 4, Pass Canyon, 5 miles. It took seven days to cut a wagon road through the canyon, about seven miles at a mile a day. They traveled through the canyon filled with sharp rocks, which made the mules lame, and stopped at nine o'clock in the evening. The Holmes party was overtaken by fourteen Mormon Battalion boys with pack animals, who had left the mines five days before. Samuel Miles and Thomas Dunn from Company B were with these packers.

Sat., Aug. 5, Pass Creek, 12 miles. In the morning several men killed a beef while others went back to get a wagon left behind yesterday. At nighttime they camped in a beautiful valley four miles miles south of the hot springs where many antelopes were seen. Indians visited camp.

Sun., Aug. 6, Carson River, 10 miles. They continued down Carson River and passed a hot spring. Addison Pratt killed a rattlesnake. They named this place Rattlesnake Camp. At night they saw one hundred Indian fires flickering all over the mountains. The Indians were a big problem. They shot arrows and threw rocks at the travelers when they crossed streams. The Indians also stole their animals at night.

Mon., Aug. 7, Carson River, 15 miles. Four horses and an ox were missing in the morning. They camped on the river.

Tues., Aug. 8, Carson River, 11 miles. They crossed the river twice before stopping for the night. The fourteen packers, who had arrived August 4, went ahead. Ten men from the Holmes-Thompson company, including Zadock Judd, Francis Hammond, and William Muir, went ahead with the packers.

Wed., Aug. 9, Ox Bow Encampment, 15 miles. They camped on a short bend in the river, which they called Ox Bow encampment. The Indians came during the night and stole several choice saddle horses. Ten men chased them and recovered all horses except one, which belonged to George Pickup. The men said it was the most tiring chase on the entire journey. One Indian shot James Diamond in the breast but it was not serious. When the cows were driven in at night, they found a calf which had been shot with an arrow.

Thurs., Aug 10, Carson River, 12 miles. Departure was delayed to hunt for animals stolen during the night. After following Carson Valley and the foothills northeast, they camped at the bend where the Carson River approaches its sink and lake (near present Silver Springs, Nevada). They began preparation for crossing the desert.

Fri., Aug. 11, Holmes Hole, 12 miles. They left the Carson River traveling northwest, with no water or feed for the animals except what they were carrying. The spring was so hot the men made coffee by putting water in a kettle with the coffee. Under a bright moon, they started across the desert at eleven o'clock and traveled all night.

Sat., Aug. 12, Truckee River, 25 miles. They had left the Pilot (Carson) River about three miles east of Silver Springs and traveled northwest. When they camped where the Truckee River turned north toward Pyramid Lake, they learned they had traveled a considerable distance out of their way.

Sun., Aug. 13, Truckee River, 25 miles. While they stayed over to let the cattle's feet rest, the men cut grass to carry for the cattle when they continued as it would be many miles before they would have water or grass. They struck the Truckee route of the California Trail (at present Wadsworth, Nevada), where the packers left to travel ahead.[9] Several men preached in a meeting. They set out again at night.

Mon., Aug. 14, Boiling Spring, 25 miles. They came to a boiling spring below the sink of the Humboldt. When a little dog belonging to the camp fell in, it was dead in less than two minutes. They fed the cattle the grass they carried with them and saw their first mountain sheep. No corrals were built since they stopped only to rest. Guards were posted around the cattle until eleven o'clock. They journeyed for the rest of the night at a rapid rate. They were now on the California Trail.

Tues., Aug. 15, Humboldt Sink. They traveled until sunrise. It was hot and they spent the day lying in the shade of the wagons sleeping. They had been two nights and a day crossing the desert. Sixteen wagons from the States going to California passed, headed by James Clyman. Hazen Kimball, an apostate Mormon, was with them. Kimball and his family had wintered in Salt Lake Valley. He said the people in Salt Lake were plowing and sowing wheat and had put in eight thousand acres of grain.[10] They did not know gold had been discovered at Coloma. When they saw the gold dust the Mormons carried, an old man traveling with Clyman, Lambert McCombs, jumped to his feet, threw his hat in the air, and shouted, "Glory Hallelujah, thank God, I shall die a rich man yet."[11]

Wed., Aug. 16, Mary's (Humboldt) River, 20 miles. They traveled up the Humboldt River and camped on a stream with willows along its banks. The Indians were very bold because they could hide behind the willows. Several horses were shot with poisoned arrows and died. Twenty-five more wagons passed going to California.[12]

Thurs., Aug. 17, Humboldt River, 15 miles. In their camp on the Humboldt River one of their horses was shot with a poisoned arrow. Three Northern Paiutes rode into camp, carrying bows and arrows. The injured animal was shown to the Indians. An elderly Indian wept at the sight of the wound. He jumped off his horse and, putting his hands beside the wound, sucked several times and drew out the poison. The Indians were kept under guard all night.

Fri., Aug. 18, Humboldt River, 10 miles. In the morning the Paiutes were given breakfast and their bows and arrows were returned to them. When they learned they were free to leave, they were pleased and left with good feeling. At the nightly camp, there was little food for the animals and no timber, only small brush. The country was dry, dusty, and barren.

Sat., Aug. 19, Humboldt River, 15 miles. Daniel Browett's cow was so lame it couldn't walk, so it was killed and the meat was divided. Two more horses were shot by Indian arrows, one in the flank and the other in the foreleg. The men on guard saw two Indians and shot at them but didn't know if they hit them or not. They camped on the river bottom where grass continued to be very scarce, even though they were in an area of meadows.

Sun., Aug. 20, Humboldt River. The company laid by so the wounded mares could recover. It was hard to stop as all thoughts were turned to their families and the men were anxious to reach Salt Lake Valley.

Mon., Aug. 21, Humboldt River, 30 miles. It was dark when camp was called on the bank of the river at nine o'clock. They crossed the river twice.

Tues., Aug. 22, Humboldt River, 10 miles. A horse was left behind to die. They traveled along the Humboldt, crossing it just once today.

Wed., Aug. 23, Humboldt River, 20 miles. The Indians continued shooting their animals. They traveled up the river and found a grassy campsite near the fork of the Little Humboldt.

Thurs., Aug. 24, Humboldt River, 18 miles. Camp was made on the bank of the Humboldt.

Fri., Aug. 25, Humboldt River, 16 miles. Azariah's horse was missing in the morning. It was the one he paid seventy dollars for. He and three friends went back to find it but were unsuccessful. Seven Indians came into camp and promised they would stop shooting the horses.

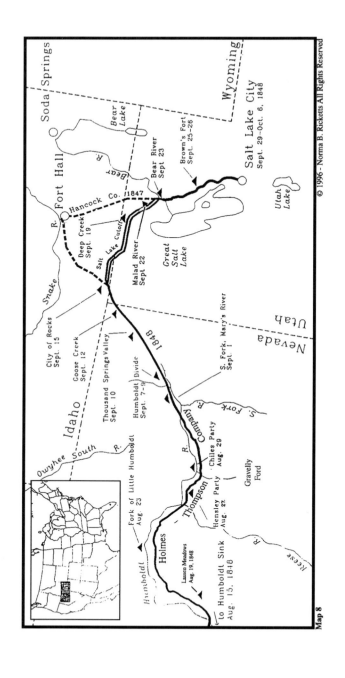

Wyoming

Soda Springs

Bear Lake

Fort Hall

Bear R.

Bear River
Sept. 23

Brown's Fort
Sept. 25-26

Salt Lake City
Sept. 29-Oct. 6, 1848

Snake R.

Hancock Co. 1847

Deep Creek
Sept. 19

Salt Lake Cutoff

Malad River
Sept. 22

Great
Salt
Lake

Utah
Lake

Idaho

City of Rocks
Sept. 15

Goose Creek
Sept. 12

Thousand Springs Valley
Sept. 10

Humboldt Divide
Sept. 7-9

1848

S. Fork

S. Fork, Mary's River
Sept. 1

Nevada

Utah

Owyhee R.

South R.

Fork of Little Humboldt
Aug. 23

Company R.

Chiles Party
Aug. 29

Gravelly
Ford

Holmes Thompson

Hensley Party
Aug. 27

Humboldt

Lassen Meadows
Aug. 19, 1848

Reese R.

to Humboldt Sink
Aug. 15, 1848

Holmes-Thompson Company

Blazed Wagon Road

States not in Existence

Hancock Co. 1847

Camp Site

1848
Holmes-Thompson Company
Hensley's Salt Lake Cutoff

Map 8

Sat., Aug. 26, Humboldt River, 20 miles. A group of emigrants on the way to California passed today.[13] One was a Mormon named Levi Riter, who said grain, corn, and garden plants did well in Salt Lake Valley and that it was five hundred miles to the valley. Riter, a bishop in Salt Lake, was going to San Francisco to claim goods he and others shipped on the *Brooklyn*.[14] The ex-soldiers traveled along the river, crossing once before camping.

Sun., Aug. 27, Humboldt River. The company remained in camp for the day. Addison Pratt held a prayer meeting at his wagon in the afternoon. Just as the meeting was over, Captain Samuel Hensley and a company of ten packers arrived. He said it was about 380 miles to the Great Salt Lake if they took a cutoff he just had found.[15] Hensley stated the route was a good one and would save eight to ten days. Previously the Mormons had planned to go by Fort Hall. Hensley also said his route was nearer than the Hastings Cutoff. These packers spoke favorably about Salt Lake and its inhabitants.

Mon., Aug. 28, Humboldt River, 22 miles. When they camped on the river bank, Azariah caught trout for supper.

Tues., Aug. 29, near Gravelly Ford on the Humboldt River, 18 miles. They met a company of emigrants with forty-eight wagons bound for California, coming by way of Fort Hall. Joseph Chiles, captain, gave the officers a way bill showing a route he said was nearer than Hensley's route. These western-bound emigrants were anxious to talk to Azariah Smith because he was present when gold was discovered. The Mormons bought bacon and buffalo meat from this company and tried to get coffee unsuccessfully. They camped again on the bank of the Humboldt River.

Wed., Aug. 30, Humboldt River, 16 miles. They traveled through a canyon for some time over a hilly road before crossing the river to camp.

Thurs., Aug. 31, Hastings Cutoff, 15 miles. During the afternoon a cold north wind blew. About sundown the rain began. They traveled up the river, crossing it once, before passing through a canyon just below the Hastings Cutoff.

Fri., Sept. 1, Humboldt River, 18 miles. After traveling up the river, they crossed the river once before camping. It was cold, cloudy, and misty all day, leaving them wet for the night. The feed for the animals was very good.

Sat., Sept. 2, Humboldt River, 10 miles. Rain and snow fell most of the day and into the night, making traveling very disagreeable.

Sun., Sept. 3, Humboldt River, 20 miles. The weather cleared during the night, but the morning was very cold. The mountain tops were covered with snow. There was a heavy frost down in the valley. Several Western Shoshones came to trade buckskins for knives and clothing. They also wanted gun powder.

Mon., Sept. 4, Humboldt River. The company laid by to rest the teams and had a mess of fish for supper. Azariah and one of the boys were roughing it when he fell on a rock and hurt his shoulder.

Tues., Sept. 5, Humboldt River, 5 miles. They stopped after traveling five miles. Four men were sent ahead to find the "cutoff" Chiles had told them about. Lieutenant Thompson's horse died from eating or drinking something that gave him the sours. Azariah's shoulder was very lame, so he rode in a wagon. They left the Humboldt River here.

Wed., Sept. 6, 18 miles. After traveling several hours, they came to the head of a canyon and found a note from the four scouts, which told them to camp at this place for the night. Sage hens were killed for supper.

Thurs., Sept. 7, 12 miles. After traveling twelve miles through the canyon, they reached the scouts, who had not located the turnoff for Bear River. A council meeting was held to discuss the direction they would travel from here to Salt Lake. It finally was decided to continue to try to find the Chiles Cutoff.

Fri., Sept. 8, 12 miles. In accordance with their decision the night before, they continued up the canyon another twelve miles. Nine scouts went ahead. They were to send a smoke signal if they found water. At sundown seven scouts returned with no sight of the Chiles trail or water. Later that evening James Sly and James Diamond, who had gone in another direction, returned saying they had found neither the trail nor water.

Sat., Sept. 9, Humboldt River, 15 miles. During a morning meeting, it was decided to turn back and take the Fort Hall route until they found the Hensley Cutoff. They hitched up their animals and returned to the place where they camped two days before. The Humboldt River came out of the ground here. They caught numerous trout for supper. Low mountains surrounded them, providing plenty of grass and a beautiful scene.

Sun., Sept. 10, Boiling Springs, 18 miles. After they had gone fourteen miles, the scout came back and told them there was water four miles ahead, but no feed. They continued past a hot spring and then stopped where there was grass for the animals.

Mon., Sept. 11, Warm Springs Valley, 14 miles. When they reached Warm (or Thousand) Springs Valley, they camped at the wells, which were a curiosity. Cattle frequently fell into them and could not get out without help. A light rain fell in early evening. There was good grass for their animals.

Tues., Sept. 12, Thousand Springs Valley, 17 miles. The camped at the headwaters of Goose Creek, a tributary of the Columbia River, with plenty of trout. The grass was not good.

Wed., Sept. 13, Goose Creek, 16 miles. They continued along Goose Creek and had another fine supper of small trout. James Brown traded a horse for a mule with a Shoshone Indian. They passed several undisturbed graves, the first they had seen that had not been looted by the

Indians for clothing and other valuables, or disturbed by animals. There was no identification on the graves. Otters were along the creek. Goose Creek increased in size, caused by small tributaries running into it, as they traveled along its banks.

Thurs., Sept. 14, Stone Creek Mountains (near Granite Pass), 14 miles. Samuel Thompson, Ephraim Green, and Sidney Willes went ahead to find the cutoff. The company walked seven miles down the creek before leaving it. They stopped at a spring three miles further to wait for news from the scouts. Samuel Thompson returned and advised them to continue four miles to a cold spring. They had to go up steep hills and did not get camped until dark. Later that night James Sly arrived and said he had located the Hensley turnoff eight miles ahead. There was a total eclipse of the moon.

Fri., Sept. 15, City of Rocks, 15 miles. They reached a chain of mountains with two towering rocks on the left. Addison Pratt called them the Twin Sisters. This place was known as the City of Rocks. They continued seven miles, leaving the old Fort Hall road. When they reached the Hensley Cutoff, they found only a pack trail. There were no wagon tracks and they realized they were making a new wagon road through the sage brush and boulders.[15] They camped at the head waters of Cassia Creek(Raft River). Everyone was in good spirits. John Borrowman suffered greatly from an infected ankle and leg, which he had scratched on the bushes and a poisonous vine.

Sat., Sept. 16, Cassia Creek, 10 miles. After going in an easterly direction and crossing the creek three times, they camped again on Cassia Creek in a notch in the mountains. They saw eleven Shoshone Indians on horseback. There were lots of trout in the creek.

Sun., Sept. 17, Clear Creek, 10 miles. They left the creek and traveled east on the pack trail through sage brush. They camped at a spring surrounded by birch trees at the bottom of a mountain. Addison Pratt went to a stream in the mountains and caught many trout. There was plenty of grass for the animals and cedar timber.

Mon., Sept. 18, Emigrant Spring, 18 miles. They traveled through a pass in the mountains and when they reached the other side they saw the Great Salt Lake for the first time. They were on the opposite side of the lake from where the city was being built.[16]

Tues., Sept. 19, Deep Creek, 15 miles. After descending the mountain, they crossed a dry sage plain and camped on Deep Creek, named by Samuel Hensley because it was so deep he had difficulty crossing. Many Shoshone Indians on horseback came to trade and camped with them for the night. Members of the company bought buckskins from these Indians. Plenty of grass for the animals.

Wed., Sept. 20, Deep Creek Valley, 15 miles. They followed Deep Creek for five miles before leaving it. After going ten miles further, they camped by a mountain spring in a deep valley between two high mountains with plenty of good grass and cedar wood.

Thurs., Sept. 21, Hansel Spring Valley (Blue Springs), 14 miles. They camped at Blue Springs in a valley with a number of warm springs nearby, but the water tasted and smelled like sulphur. The country was uneven. Here an old cow was lost. Although the men searched half a day, they never found her. The cow had been a lot of trouble because she was a slow traveler. Jacob Truman broke a horse for Samuel Rogers for $2.50. "We settled the cannon account. We paid 172 dollars for the work of Browett [before he was murdered], which makes the whole cost 512 dollars"(Samuel Rogers).[17]

Fri., Sept. 22, Blue Springs, 23 miles. After a dark, rainy night, a hard day's journey brought them to the Malad River, which was three miles from Bear River. There was no wood. The men caught fish as fast as they threw their hooks in the water. There was much rejoicing. Everyone was talking and singing. Daniel Dennett promised a new song for the next night.

Sat., Sept. 23, Malad River, 9 miles. Crossing the Malad River was difficult because of the mud, steep banks, and water up to the wagon beds. One wagon broke down but was quickly repaired. They traveled another four miles to the east side of the Bear River before stopping. They found old wagon traces here that led toward the Salt Lake settlement. Theirs had been the only wagon tracks on this cutoff to this point. They camped by a spring with plenty of grass for the stock. They realized they were nearing the end of their journey and there was excitement and anticipation in camp. Several friendly Indians arrived. A light rain shower didn't last long and didn't dampen their spirits. The men all gathered wood for a common fire. After supper and prayers the camp enjoyed singing songs and telling "yarns" and jokes on each other. Daniel Dennett sang his new song. Samuel Rogers donated $150 to be given to Daniel Browett's widow.

Sun., Sept. 24, Bear River Valley, 18 miles. They traveled down the Bear River through a valley with tall mountains on the left and Salt Lake and the Bear River on their right. They crossed a beautiful, clear water creek and camped by deep wells. Many of their calves were tenderfooted.

Mon., Sept. 25, Bear River Valley, 20 miles. The cannon wagon broke down and it was decided to leave it and continue on. Three other wagons broke down, causing further delay, but they finally reached Captain James Brown's settlement on the Ogden River in a beautiful valley. Brown was captain of one of the sick detachments that wintered in Pueblo. Subsequently, he had taken a small group of battalion veterans to California to obtain the mustering-out pay of the sick detachments. He had been asked by Mormon Church authorities to purchase Miles Goodyear's Fort Buenaventura with a portion of that mustering-out pay. There were half a dozen families at the fort, who sold the travelers cheese for ten cents a pound, a real treat. They were only twenty- five miles from the Great Salt Lake.

Tues., Sept. 26, Brown's Fort. The animals were rested for a day while a small group went back ten miles to get the cannon they had left behind. Wagons were mended, clothes were washed. The men trimmed their hair and beards. Everyone was busy and in good spirits. They especially enjoyed eating roasting ears of corn and melons. Jonathan Holmes, Samuel Thompson, and several others, who learned their families were in Salt Lake, left on horseback to get there as soon as possible.

Wed., Sept. 27, Brown's Fort, 18 miles. They left Brown's settlement and camped at Herd Creek. Most of the horses were driven loose. They met James Park driving his wagon. He told Addison Pratt his wife had arrived in Salt Lake the week before. Pratt said his heart was "filled with gratitude" for God's "preserving care" over him and his family while they were separated. It had been five years since he had seen them because of his mission to the Pacific Islands.[18] Other men, anxious to see their families, mounted their horses and rode ahead with Pratt. They planned to reach Salt Lake the next day. Azariah went with them. They left their loose horses and cattle in care of Jacob Truman and James S. Brown, who agreed to herd them to the valley for one cent per day per head.

Fri., Oct. 6, Salt Lake Valley. The remainder of the Holmes-Thompson company, with its wagons and animals, reached the valley. Soon after arriving the ex-soldiers paid a visit to Brigham Young to pay their tithing. This record of faithfulness is preserved in Young's Gold Account. Typical of those whose names appear in this account was Azariah Smith. He brought more than $500 in gold from California. Two days after arriving he visited Young: "Went to Pres. Brigham Young, and paid my tithing, also donating some for the poor and one dollar each to the twelve."[19]

Jonathan Holmes had been elected president to replace the missing Browett, with Samuel H. Rogers and Addison Pratt as his counselors. They had organized in the same manner the Mormon Church had used in the East and as they had when discharged in Los Angeles. This smaller group of forty-five men and one woman required only one captain of fifty and four captains of tens. Lieutenant Samuel Thompson, as captain of fifty, was in charge in case of any fighting with Indians. There were four captains of tens: James C. Sly, Ephraim Green, Elijah Elmer, and William Coray:[20] "This evening the company is organized in tens. There being four of them. Samuel Tompson, captain of the tens, and Jonathan H. Holmes, captain of the whole" (Samuel Rogers).[21]

The pack train, which went ahead on August 8, had arrived in Salt Lake September 24, 1848. The last of this group, including wagons and animals, arrived October 6, 1848. Several diarists mention there were forty-five men and one woman in this company, traveling with seventeen wagons. The following list, researched from many sources, attempts to identify this vanguard group as it left California. The names of thirty-nine battalion soldiers are shown. Since the journalists were reporting the number in the company leaving Pleasant Valley, one assumes they did not include the three scouts, absent at the time and later found to be murdered. Combining the thirty-nine soldiers and five known non-battalion men provides a total of forty-four names known to be in this company.

Mormon Battalion Veterans Leaving Pleasant Valley in the Holmes-Thompson Company

G. Wesley Adair	George Kelley
James R. Allred	Jesse B. Martin
Henry Bigler	Daniel Miller
James S. Brown	Miles Miller
Richard Bush	David Moss
William Coray (Melissa, wife)	William S. Muir
John Cox	George Pickup
Daniel Dennett	Robert Pixton
Joseph Dobson	Samuel H. Rogers
James Douglas	James C. Sly
Elijah Elmer	Azariah Smith
Israel Evans	Alexander Stephens
William Garner	William C. Strong
Ephraim Green	Samuel Thompson
Meltiar Hatch	Jacob M. Truman
Orin Hatch	Thomas Weir
Jonathan H. Holmes	Ira J. Willes
William Holt	W. Sidney Willes
William J. Johnstun	O. G. Workman
Zadock Judd	

The three men who were murdered were Ezra Allen, Daniel Browett, and Henderson Cox. The five non-battalion men in this company were James Diamond, non-Mormon; John Eagar, from the *Brooklyn*; Francis A. Hammond, the new San Francisco convert; Addison Pratt, a returning missionary; Philo M. Behunin, a twenty-year-old Mormon whose parents were in Salt Lake. It is not known how or when he reached California.

The next group to leave California was the Ebenezer Brown company, which left Pleasant Valley August 10, 1848. They followed the Holmes-Thompson company by about six weeks but made better time, benefiting from the road-building efforts of the advance group.

This company included ex-battalion members and families from the ship *Brooklyn*. There were forty-one men, including twenty-five ex-soldiers plus the men from the *Brooklyn*. Phebe Brown and her son, Zemira Palmer, traveled with her husband, Ebenezer. She was the last of the three women who traveled the entire trip from Fort Leavenworth to San Diego, to leave California.[22] The Browns went to the gold fields after he was discharged from the Mormon Volunteers in San Diego in March 1848.

Members of this party also were successful in their search for gold. Even though some were not in the gold fields long, they left California with bags of gold nuggets. Joseph Bates, who had worked at the Williams ranch after discharge, was in the mines only four weeks and washed out $1,800.[23] John C. Naegle (Naille) had $3,000 when he left the mines.

After the Brown company crossed the Sierran crest in the Carson Pass on August 26, eleven men, who were packers, decided to go ahead. They left August 27 and arrived in Salt Lake Valley October 7, 1848:

Joseph W. Bates	Benjamin Stewart (Came to
William Beers	California with James
Benjamin Brackenbury	Brown)
Levi Fifield	John R. Stoddard
Orlando F. Mead	Miles Weaver
Calvin W. Moore	John Reed (Came on *Brooklyn*)
Orrice Murdock	

As some of the brethren who were with us were packing they wished now to go on by themselves and leave us as they could go on much faster that we with waggons. So we stopt this day and killed a beef that we had along with us and the women baked sweet buisket and the men roasted the ribs of an ox and we had a general tea party and time of rejoicing. This was done that since we had to part we might part with good feelings. (John Borrowman)[24]

Ex-Battalion Soldiers and Families in Brown Company

Ebenezer Brown, Captain	Montgomery Button
Phebe Draper Palmer Brown	Joseph Clark
(Wife of Ebenezer)	James Ferguson
Elijah Thomas, 2nd Captain	Lucy Nutting Ferguson (Wife
James Park II, 3rd Captain	of James; *Brooklyn*)
Joseph Bates	Levi Fifield
William Beers	William A. Follett
John Borrowman	Timothy Hoyt
Benjamin Brackenbury	Albert Knapp

Orlando F. Mead
Calvin W. Moore
Orrice Murdock
Zemira Palmer (Son of Phebe
Brown)
William C. Prows
Benjamin F. Stewart
John Rufus Stoddard

Franklin Weaver
Christiana Rachel Reed
Weaver (Wife of Franklin;
Brooklyn)
Miles Weaver
William Wood
Phineas Wright

Passengers from the Ship *Brooklyn* with the Ebenezer Brown Company

Julius Austin
Octavia Lane Austin (Wife of
Julius)
Louise Marie Austin (Child of
Julius and Octavia)
Newton Francis Austin (Child
of Julius and Octavia)
Edward N. Austin (Child of
Julius and Octavia)
Newell Bullen
Clarissa Atkinson Bullen (Wife
of Newell)
Andrew Bullen (Child of
Newell and Clarissa)
Herschel Bullen (Child of
Newell and Clarissa)
John Joseph Bullen (Child of
Newell and Clarissa; born in
San Jose after arrival)
Charles Clark Burr, (Brother
to Nathan)
Sarah Sloat Burr (Wife of
Charles)
John Atlantic Burr (Child of
Charles and Sarah)
Nathan Burr Jr. (Child of
Charles and Sarah; born in
California after arrival)
Nathan Burr (Brother to
Charles)

Chloe Clarke Burr (Wife of
Nathan)
Amasa Burr (Child of Nathan
and Chloe)
Charles Clark Burr Jr. (Child
of Nathan and Chloe)
John S. Hyatt
Emmaline Lane
John Philips
Christiana Gregory Reed
(Widow)
John Reed (Child of Christiana)
Hannah Reed Jamison (Child
of Christiana)
John Jamison (Grandson of
Christiana)
Isaac R. Robbins
Ann Burtis Shin Robbins (Wife
of Isaac)
Wesley Robbins (Child of Isaac
and Ann)
Joseph Robbins (Child of Isaac
and Ann)
Margaret Robbins (Child of
Isaac and Ann)
Isaac R. Robbins (Child of
Isaac and Ann)
Orrin Smith
Mary Ann Daud Hopkins
Smith (Wife of Orrin)

Eugene Smith (Child of Orrin and Mary Ann; born in California)

Elizabeth Ann Smith (Child of Orrin and Mary Ann; born in California)

Eliza Smith (Child by Orrin's first wife, Werthy)

Henry M. Smith (Child by Orrin's first wife, Werthy)

Francis (Frank) Smith (Child by Orrin's first wife, Werthy)

Amelia Smith (Child by Orrin's first wife, Werthy)

Ellen Maria Hopkins (Child by Mary Ann's first husband, Andrew B. Hopkins)

Emily Marilu Hopkins (Child by Mary Ann's first husband, Andrew B. Hopkins)

Daniel Stark

Also in the Ebenezer Brown company was Daniel P. Clark, who came to California with Company B, New York Volunteers, in March 1847. This wagon group with its animals arrived in Salt Lake October 10, 1848.

The Marcus Shepherd company was the third group to leave the gold fields during 1848. After discharge, Shepherd did whip sawing in southern California before going to the gold fields. He was captain of a company of twelve men who left California in October 1848. He had a pack animal, nine horses, five mules, a stock of groceries, and clothing.

The names of his twelve companions are not known. There were four men, however, whose arrival date in Salt Lake Valley coincides with Shepherd's arrival, so they may have traveled with him: James Bailey, James C. Owen, John Roylance, and William Kelley. Thomas Tompkins (of the *Brooklyn*) went to Utah in the fall of 1848. He could have been in either the Ebenezer Brown company or the Marcus Shepherd company.

Shepherd traveled by way of Carson Valley and the Humboldt River to Ruby Valley, then across the desert and around the south side of the Great Salt Lake, in other words, by way of the Hastings Cutoff. He had an uneventful journey except for one encounter with the Indians: "Indians to the number of two or three hundred formed across the road, ten to twelve deep, so we made a charge as fast as the packs could go, with myself and another ahead. We drove them from the ground without a shot"(Marcus L. Shepherd).[25] Shepherd's was the last of the known companies to leave California in 1848

When the Mormon Volunteers were discharged in San Diego in March 1848, thirty-five went the southern route to Salt Lake Valley and the "rest" (maybe as many as forty-two) went to the gold fields. Although the names of the Volunteers are known, the breakdown into these two groups at discharge is not recorded.[26]

Also, men from the Pueblo sick detachments went to California after stopping for a while in Salt Lake Valley. At least one of the Kearny escorts returned. These late arrivals complicate the picture. With the gold rush frenzy starting at this same time, it may not be possible to identify these men and their companies further. It may be enough to have followed the members of the original battalion until they were on their way home or until they reached their families.

Levi Riter, the bishop who went to San Francisco to get the household goods he had shipped on the *Brooklyn,* returned to Utah in 1849 in a company consisting of several men from the battalion and *Brooklyn* passengers. Thomas Rhoades traveled to Utah with his four youngest children in 1849 in a group known as the Rhoades company. The makeup of both the Riter and Rhoades groups is not known. Daniel Henrie also went to Utah in 1849 as did Jerome Zabriskie (volunteers).

Brigham Young recorded the following statement in his journal on September 28, 1849: "Fourteen or fifteen of the brethren arrived from the gold country, some of whom were very comfortably supplied with the precious metal, and others, who had been sick, came back as destitute as they had been when they went on the ship 'Brooklyn' in 1846."[27] These men to whom Young referred could be the Rhoades-Riter-Henrie-Zabriskie group mentioned above.

A group of Mormon Church members from the Alameda–Santa Cruz area left San Francisco for Salt Lake Valley on August 28, 1857, in response to Brigham Young's request for all church members to come to Utah. Zacheus Cheney was captain of this group, which consisted of fourteen wagons, sixteen men, seven women, and fifteen children. Several were passengers from the ship *Brooklyn.* Among Cheney's company were the following:

Zacheus and Amanda Evans Cheney and children
Hannah Evans (mother of Amanda) and four children
John Cheney
E. Rinaldo Mowry, captain of the guard, and his mother, Ruth Mowry
Chapman Duncan, wife and children
Matthew F. Wilkie, clerk of company

Isaac and Catherine Smith Harrison and children
Harrison Blair and family
Carlton Blair
Tarlton Blair
Daniel Sill
Lewis Booth
Henry Wilkins
Sister Goodfellow of San Francisco
Jean Bautiste

The day before their departure, August 27, they held a meeting at which George Q. Cannon spoke and there was a "unity of feeling." Only Zacheus Cheney and Isaac Harrison in this group were members of the Mormon Battalion. Cheney had remained in California after discharge and had married Mary Ann Fisher of the *Brooklyn*. After Mary Ann died in 1851, he married Amanda Evans, another *Brooklyn* woman. Isaac Harrison reenlisted in the Mormon Volunteers and went to the gold fields after being discharged in San Diego in March 1848. He married Catherine Smith of the *Brooklyn* in San Francisco after her husband Robert died. Cheney's company arrived in Salt Lake Valley November 3, 1857.[28]

By 1857 only a handful of battalion soldiers remained in California. Perhaps a footnote to the battalion story is the surprising number of important historical events that occurred during their stay. Without realizing the significance of their contribution and, certainly, without meaning to do so, the Mormon Battalion filled a few pages of early California history.

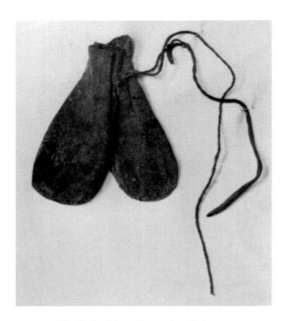

Ezra Allen's double gold pouch still shows
blood stains and where the common thong was
cut in back. It was returned to his widow Sarah
by his fellow ex-soldiers. A priceless heirloom
for descendants of Ezra Allen and Sarah Allen
Ricks, its present custodian is Preston P. Nibley.

CHAPTER TWELVE

Detached Service

In January 1845 there was a flourishing colony of Mormons in Mississippi. Brigham Young sent word to them that men were needed to build the Nauvoo Temple. Seven men—John Brown, William Crosby, John Bankhead, William (Billy) Lay (non-member), Daniel M. Thomas, James Harmon, and James Harrison—left from Monroe County, Mississippi, on March 14. They worked on the temple for three months and left Nauvoo June 3 to return to Mississippi. By August John Brown and William Crosby were on their way back to Nauvoo with their wives, where they continued to work on the temple until it was completed and they received their endowments.

During the winter of 1845–46 when the Saints were leaving Nauvoo, John Brown was instructed by Brigham Young to return again to Mississippi and to lead the Saints who were ready to the Platte River, where they were to meet the main body of the Mormon Church. Brown was accompanied to Mississippi by William Crosby and William Mathews. Crosby and Brown took their wives back to Mississippi.

Brown's instructions were to enter the prairie at Independence, Missouri, and meet the Nauvoo Mormons somewhere in the Indian country. In accordance with Young's instructions, Brown led fourteen families out of Monroe County, Mississippi, on April 8, 1846.[1] He was joined by five other men who went along to assist: William Crosby, Daniel M. Thomas, William (Billy) Lay, John D. Holladay, and George W. Bankhead. The wives of these men did not go west at this time. These six men, charged with the responsibility of piloting the fourteen families west, formed a mess with one wagon. They planned to return to Mississippi for their own families after seeing the fourteen families reach their destination safely. They crossed the Mississippi River at Iron Banks, advanced through Missouri and, after completing a 640-mile march, reached Independence May 26, 1846.

At Independence they were joined by a party of thirteen adults and numerous children, including the Robert Crow family from Illinois and the William Kartchner family, who had moved from North Carolina to Mississippi. The combined group then consisted of twenty-four men, women, numerous children, and nineteen wagons. William Crosby was elected captain with Robert Crow and John Holladay counselors.[2]

From Independence, Missouri, they followed the Oregon Trail to the Platte River, where they expected to find the main body of Mormon emigrants. On their journey they suffered from lack of water. Several times their animals stampeded. They also encountered a band of Cheyenne Indians as John Brown recorded in his journal: "On the 19th of June 12 Indians came into camp. They were Shians. We made them a feast & gave them some presents. Next day we came to their village. They received us kindly & made us a feast which consisted of stewed buffalo meat. We traded some with them and they appeared to be well pleased with our visit."[3]

After waiting a week in mid-June for the Nauvoo Mormons, they continued on the Oregon Trail on the south side of the Platte River. From Grand Island, the party traveled westward until the Platte River forked. The Oregon Trail led them along the North Platte toward Fort Laramie.

In July they met a group of travelers near Chimney Rock, which was about halfway to the Rocky Mountains. From these travelers they learned "there were no Mormons on the trail ahead" of them.[4] Some of the Mississippi group wanted to turn back, but they decided to continue to Fort Laramie.

A few miles below Laramie we met Mr. John Reshaw. He was going for supplies and to trade skins. He was camped in Goshen hole. He said that he heard the Mormons were going up the South fork of the Platte. We held a consel & concluded to go no further west but find a place for the company to winter on the east side of the Mountains. Reshaw said that the head of the Arkansaw River was the best place to go since there was some corn growing there & it being near the Spanish country the company could get Supplies. He was going to Pueblo in a few days with two teams. there being no road & he being acquainted with the route we concluded to stop and go with him. We moved over to his camp. (John Brown)[5]

John Richard (pronounced Re-shaw) was a Frenchman who ran a fur-trading post, Fort Bernard, eight miles east of Fort Laramie. He was going to Taos to take skins and to get supplies. Richard suggested they winter at Fort Pueblo, Colorado, on the upper Arkansas River, which was in a valley sheltered somewhat from winter storms. The mountain men and trappers who lived there with their Spanish and Indian wives had surplus corn. Also, supplies were available from the nearby Spanish communities. Richard agreed to guide the Saints to Fort Pueblo. On July 10 the Mississippi Saints turned south toward the head waters of the Arkansas, as John Brown recorded: "On the tenth of July we started for Pueblo. Mr. Reshaw proved faithful to us and rendered us all the assistance he could among the indians & on the plains."[6]

At one point a number of friendly Cheyenne Indians traveled with them. They came across a band of wild horses and both the Indians and the Mormon men chased the horses. A band of Indians appeared from the opposite direction and began rushing toward the camp of mostly women and children:

> Some were badly frightened, but it was useless to run. The Indians were well mounted. Our Indian was a good way off after the wild horses and as soon as he saw what was going on he came with all possible speed. He met his countrymen within one hundred yards of us. We did not know whether they were hostile. They reached out the hand for the usual howdy do which was a very pleasing sight to us. This kind of approach for friendship was new to us. Mr. Reshaw was with us & I watched him all the time to see if he was alarmed but he betrayed no fear. He was well acquainted with their chief whose name in English was Slim Face. His form very much resembled Andrew Jackson. (John Brown)[7]

The Saints met the entire tribe the next day near Cache la Poudre River. They feasted together and exchanged gifts. Under Richard's guidance they passed near the present-day site of Denver, where the trail left the south fork of the Platte. On July 27, after crossing the south fork, they found a wagon trail, which they followed the rest of the way. They continued until they reached the Arkansas Valley. The Mississippi Saints arrived at this small mud-walled settlement at the eastern base of the Rocky Mountains on August 7, 1846.

> The Arkansas ran along the valley below, among the woods and groves, and closely nestled in the midst of wide cornfields and green meadows, where cattle were grazing, rose the low mud walls of the Pueblo. . . . most primitive of construction, being nothing more than a large square enclosure, surrounded by a wall of mud, miserably cracked and dilapidated. The slender pickets that surmounted it were half broken down, and the gate dangled on its wooden hinges so loosely that to open or shut it seemed likely to fling it down altogether. (Francis Parkman)[9]

Fort Pueblo had been built on the Arkansas River in 1842 by fur trappers and mountain men as a winter rendezvous. Because it was located in a protected valley, winters were not so severe. They grew corn and with game plentiful, hunger was not a problem. The fort was adobe, sixty yards square. Several well-known trappers lived at Fort Pueblo during its existence, including Kit Carson, James Waters, John Brown Sr., Rube Herron, and the black scout James Beckwourth. Usually there were between fifteen and twenty men and their wives at the fort during the winter.[8]

During the years that followed trappers, mountain men, and traders needing protection from the severe weather spent the winter months at Pueblo. The Mormons stopped about a mile below the fort. They began felling trees in the bottomland and built several cabins.

Upon arrival at Fort Pueblo the Mississippi Saints voted to stay until spring and organized a branch of the Mormon Church with Absalom Porter Dowdle as presiding elder. They erected log houses from cottonwoods on the bottomlands, a short distance below Fort Pueblo on the north side of the river. Here they planted pumpkins, melons, and turnips and prepared fields for planting wheat and other crops in the spring. Flour was obtained in Taos. They dropped "Fort" and called their little settlement "Pueblo."

On September 1, John Brown, William Crosby, Daniel M. Thomas, George W. Bankhead, John D. Holladay, and William Lay left to return to their families. They felt they had assisted the Pueblo contingent as much as they could and that their responsibility to the Mississippi Saints in Pueblo was fulfilled:

> We counseled the brethren to prepare for winter to build them some cabins in the form of a fort. The mountaineers said they would let them have their surplus corn for their labor & those of us who had left our families stopped here until the first of September. We organized the company in the form of a branch. We instructed them and gave them such counsel as the spirit dictated, telling them to tarry there until they got word where to go. They were much disappointed expecting to have got with the body of the Church. We comforted them all we could and left our blessing with them. We bid them adieu on the morning of the first of September & started home following down the Arkansaw River to the Santafe trail. (John Brown)[10]

John Brown and his companions followed the Arkansas River for three days to reach Bent's Fort, where they learned Colonel Price and his teamsters were ahead. They hastened on so they could travel with Price through Indian country. Unexpectedly, on September 12 they met the California-bound Mormon Battalion at the Arkansas River. Brown and his company told the soldiers about the Saints and the branch of the Mormon Church in Pueblo. Brown described the meeting with the battalion: "[It] gave us the greatest pleasure, for we were well acquainted with a great many of them."[11] It was this chance meeting with John Brown that later gave Lieutenant A. J. Smith, commander of the Mormon Battalion, the idea of dispatching Higgins and the family detachment to Pueblo.

The Higgins family detachment left the battalion at the last crossing of the Arkansas River on September 18. The order of Lieutenant A. J. Smith to Higgins was that he and Quartermaster Sebert Shelton were to escort the Mormon families to Pueblo, where they would find a winter refuge with the Mississippi families. After settling the company in Pueblo, they were to rejoin the battalion in Santa Fe. It was the first division in the ranks of the Mormon Battalion and was not a popular move among the soldiers. The detachment included eleven men (counting the officers), nine women, and thirty-three children. Tippets and Woolsey acted as couriers and returned to the battalion. "I wanted it distinkly understood that it did not agree with my feelings for it was told to us that we must hold together, not to devide but it must be done they said and we must take the simerone [Cimarron] route" (Levi Hancock).[12]

Higgins Family Detachment

Soldiers:

Nelson Higgins, Captain
Gilbert Hunt, Corporal
James P. Brown
Montgomery Button
James Hendrickson
Dimick B. Huntington
Milton Kelley

Nicholas Kelley
Harley Mowrey
Norman Sharp
Sebert C. Shelton
John H. Tippets, Courier*
Thomas Woolsey, Courier*

Women and children:

Eunice Reasor Brown (James Polly Brown)
       Children: Neuman, Robert, Sarah, Mary Ann
Mary Bittels Button (Montgomery Button)
       Children: James, Jutson, Louisa, Samuel
Sarah Blackman Higgins (Captain Nelson Higgins)
       Children: Almira, Alfred, Driscilla, Heber, Nelson, Carlos
Celia Mounts Hunt (First wife of Jefferson Hunt)
       Children: John, Jane, Harriet, Joseph, Hyrum, and twins
       Parley and Mary

———————

*Not included in count of members of the detachment as they returned to the battalion.

Fanny Maria Allen Huntington (Dimick Huntington)
     Children: Lot, Martha Zina, Clark Allen
Malinda Allison Kelley (Milton Kelley)
Sarah Kelley (Nicholas Kelley)
     Child: Parley
Martha Jane Sargent Sharp (Norman Sharp)
     Martha's sister: Caroline Sargent
Elizabeth Trains Mayfield Shelton (Sebert C. Shelton)
     Children: Caroline, Cooper, Thomas, Maria, and, from
     Elizabeth's first husband, Jackson Mayfield, John
     Mayfield, and Sarah Mayfield

Higgins and his group traveled up the Arkansas River for four days during which Norman Sharp accidentally shot himself in the arm. The wound was severe. He was taken to a nearby Indian village for assistance. The medicine man was friendly and thought he could cure the injured soldier. He burned a fire near Sharp day and night for three days when complications set in. Sharp's wife, Martha Jane, and her sister, Caroline Sargent, and Thomas Woolsey were with him when he died September 28. Martha Jane had just passed her twentieth birthday on September 24; her husband was thirty-eight. She was expecting their first child. Woolsey and an Indian woman buried Sharp. Martha, Caroline, and Woolsey hurried to catch up with the detachment, which had stopped to set wagon wheels.

Without further incident the Higgins group arrived at Pueblo in early October, where they found the Saints from Mississippi already settled for the winter.

Pueblo is hundreds of miles from any settlement and poorly protected, but it was the best refuge that could be obtained. The men who were able to work set about strengthening the fortifications. Insufficient food and clothing occasioned much sickness among the men, women and children. The number of graves in the little cemetery gradually increased as the population of the place decreased, and but for the tender nursing of the women in the camp, many more would have been added to the city of the dead. (Nelson Higgins)[13]

They began building winter quarters for the families. There were nine wives and thirty-nine children to be cared for. When the shelters were completed, Captain Higgins, Sebert Shelton, and a few other able-bodied men left Pueblo to return to the battalion as instructed by Lieutenant Smith. Upon arriving in Santa Fe, they learned Colonel Philip St. George Cooke, the battalion's new commander, had led the battalion southward out of Santa Fe along the Rio Grande River.

Higgins and his group were told by Colonel Alexander Doniphan to return to Pueblo to take care of the families. One reason Doniphan approved of this plan was that the battalion's supplies had been sent to Bent's Fort. Now that the battalion was not going through Bent's Fort, Doniphan decided it was better to have the supplies used for the families instead of having the Mormons go to Fort Leavenworth or stay in Santa Fe. Higgins and his group were to continue on detached service status. The men, except Thomas Woolsey and John Tippets, turned around and went back to Pueblo. Tippets and Woolsey followed the battalion route on the Rio Grande and finally caught up with their comrades on November 4 at Crawford Hollow, New Mexico. When Higgins and his men did not return to the battalion in the thirty days allowed, there was discussion about a court-martial for them. Woolsey's report on his return quieted this talk.

The Brown detachment, which left the battalion in Santa Fe on October 18, made good time traveling to Pueblo, considering the poor state of the teams and the feeble condition of the men. The detachment consisted of ninety-one soldiers, Dr. McIntire, seventeen wives, two other women, and ten children. They reached their destination in four weeks. The teams were so weak they could not pull the loaded wagons up hills or on sandy or unusually rough roads, so the men, women, and children had to walk at those times. This forced walking was very difficult for them. There were about twenty able-bodied men in this contingent who received permission to go because their wives were being sent to Pueblo. James H. Glines was assigned to this company to make the reports.[14] On their third day of travel several fresh oxen were obtained, which really helped in their travels.

One rainy night near Las Vegas, New Mexico, the baggage wagon never arrived. The unhappy, rain-soaked travelers spent the night on the muddy ground without even a blanket for protection.

At the fork of the Santa Fe Trail, the company veered northward along the main trail to the Arkansas River. They passed scattered, friendly settlers along the way. Joel Terrell, who purchased dinner from an American settler from Carolina, wrote, "I took about 3 pints of milk, 2nd time I eat milk since I left Missoura. I paid 25 cts for it and then give 15 cts for another pint and 2 cakes and took with me for supper."[15]

The Mormons were impressed with the fertile valleys and lakes as they traveled along. They reached the settlement of Cimarron on October 27, 1846. The Santa Fe Trail turned northeast toward Raton Pass. Milton Smith died October 27 and was buried the next day near a tributary of the Canadian River. He was wrapped in tall grass and cane before he was buried. His grave was covered with large stones to keep the wolves away.

The weather turned cooler with intermittent snow. They crossed the high mountains of Raton Pass on November 1 and 2. Here they were able to kill several fat, wild turkeys which provided much-needed food for the weary soldiers. They struck the headwaters of the Purgatoire River and followed it out of the mountains. They traveled across plains on November 3 along the south bank of the Purgatoire for about eight miles, when they crossed the river. Abner Chase died about noon November 3 and was buried that evening on the right side of the road looking west. He was buried in his robes with a bed of grass below and above him and large stones over the grave.

On November 4 they left the river traveling across a barren prairie to reach Willow Springs on Timpas Creek November 6. They were so exhausted they thought they could go no further. Animals collapsed and the men broke down. Suddenly the guard detail drove thirty head of oxen into camp. They belonged to a company hauling provisions to Santa Fe for the army. Brown distributed the oxen among his failing teams. Later when two teamsters rode into camp inquiring about the oxen, Captain Brown replied:

[If there were] any cattle in his company they could take them out. They replied that each teamster only knew his own team. After examining our teams they claimed and took out four of the thirty stray oxen, this still left us with the thirteen yoke of fresh cattle which we considered a divine interposition from the kind hand of God in our behalf, as it seemed about the only chance of deliverance from starvation. (John Hess)[16]

Not all soldiers agreed with Brown's handling of these animals: "the rest we brought along and after we came to Pueblo the Captain took four yoke of them and the rest were divided among the favorites of the Captain" (John Steele).[17]

They reached the Arkansas River November 9 seven miles above Bent's Fort. While the company camped here, Captain Brown and a few men went to the fort for supplies. At the fort Brown obtained rations for sixty days of pork, flour, rice, beans, coffee, sugar, vinegar, soap, and other supplies and returned to his charges.

The detachment crossed the river November 10 and continued until November 15, when they stopped four miles from Pueblo so the officers could go ahead to make necessary arrangements for them. Two days later the Brown group entered Pueblo. During the five days of travel up the Arkansas River to Pueblo, they enjoyed full army rations supplemented by rabbits and wild turkeys. They reached Pueblo about two o'clock on November 17, 1846, and pitched their tents near the cabins of the Higgins detachment and the Mississippi Saints. It was a happy reunion between comrades, friends, and families. Daniel Tyler described their reception: "The greetings which occurred . . . when the two detachments met was quite touching. A thrill of joy ran through the camp which none but those living martyrs can fully comprehend."[18]

All men who were able chopped wood to use as timbers in building eighteen one-room log cabins, fourteen feet square. It was agreed those who were ill should be the first to occupy the finished cabins. There was an urgency in this undertaking because they were facing cold winter months. The log cabins were ready for occupation by early December. The view of Pike's Peak, crowned with snow, was a reminder about the cold months ahead. Next they built a thirty- by twenty-foot meeting house opposite the row of houses, situated in a grove of large cottonwood trees. The first house of worship in Colorado was a rustic building of cottonwood logs, located next to the Arkansas River.

Once the large building was completed, it became the center for both religious services and social activities. George Ruxton, a British army officer who passed through Pueblo in 1847, described the scene well:

> In a wide and well-timbered bottom of the Arkansas, the Mormons had erected a street of log shanties, in which to pass the inclement winter. These were built of rough logs of cottonwood, laid one above the other, the interstices filled with mud, and rendered impervious to wind or wet. At one end of the row of shanties was built . . . a long building of huge logs, in which prayer-meetings and holdings-forth took place. [19]

Joseph W. Richards was a young man serving as a musician in Company A. He originally became ill on the first part of the trip between Council Bluffs and Fort Leavenworth. His health improved for a time, but the long days of forced marching to reach Santa Fe were too much for him and his health failed again. Celia Hunt, wife of Jefferson Hunt, often comforted him and took nourishment to him as he grew weaker. She visited him and gave him his last food a few hours before his death on November 21, just four days after arriving in Pueblo. He was seventeen years old. Celia Hunt said he was among the most noble young men she had ever met. His comrades thought highly of him. James Ferguson, sergeant major of the battalion, stated he "was noble, generous, and brave and never complained." One of his messmates in Company A wrote a letter to Joseph's brother, Franklin D. Richards, telling of his death:

> We had become very much attached [on the journey]. . . . as his health seemed to fail . . . he placed himself entirely in my care. On

the sad night of his departure, while I was endeavoring, at his request, to render him some assistance, after grasping me with a hug which almost took my breath, he gradually sank down and in a few moments expired in my arms without a struggle or a groan, but quietly passed away like a child going to sleep. (Caritat C. Rowe)[20]

Brown Sick Detachment

Soldiers:

James Brown, Captain
Joshua Abbott, Co. D
Orson B. Adams, Co. C
Franklin Allen, Co. B
James T. S. Allred, Co. A
Reuben W. Allred, Co. A
Jeduthan Averett, Co. D
William E. Beckstead, Co. C
Erastus Bingham, Co. B
William Bird, Co. B
Mervin S. Blanchard, Co. A
Alexander Brown, Co. C
Jesse S. Brown, Co. C
John Buchannan, Co. D
James W. Calkins, Co. A
John Calvert, Co. C
Isaac Carpenter, Co. C
William H. Carpenter, Co. C
William Casto, Co. D
Abner Chase, Co. D
John D. Chase, Co. B
George Cummings, Co. E
James Davis, Co. D
Ralph Douglas, Co. D
Francillo Durphee, Co. C
James C. Earl, Co. A
David Garner, Co. A
Philip Garner, Co. B
William B.Gifford, Co. D
Luther W. Glazier, Co. E
James H. Glines, Co. A
John C. Gould, Co. C

Samuel Gould, Co. C
William Gribble, Co. D
Ebenezer Hanks, Co. E
John W. Hess, Co. E
James Hirons, Co. D
Elijah E. Holden Co. A
Charles Hopkins, Co. E
Henry Hoskins, Co. E
Schuyler Hulet, Co. A
Charles A. Jackson, Co. A
Henry Bailey Jacobs, Co. E
Jarvis Johnson, Co. C
Thomas Karren, Co. E
Lorin E. Kenney, Co. D
Barnabas Lake, Co. A
Lisbon Lamb, Co. D
Thurston Larson, Co. C
David Laughlin, Co. D
Elam Luddington, Co. B
Peter I. Mesick, Co. D
Daniel Miller, Co. E
Jabez Nowlin, Co. C
James Oakley, Co. D
Melcher Oyler, Co. A
William A. Park, Co. E
David Perkins, Co. C
John Perkins, Co. C
Harmon D. Pierson, Co. B
Judson A. Pierson, Co. C
Jonathan Pugmire Jr., Co. E
Joseph W. Richards, Co. A
Benjamin Roberts, Co. D

Caratat C. Rowe, Co. A
William Rowe, Co. D
Henry W. Sanderson, Co. D
Abel M. Sargent, Co. D
James R. Scott, Co. E
John Sessions, Co. A
Albert Sharp, Co. D
Andrew J. Shupe, Co. C
James Shupe, Co. C
John G. Smith, Co. E
Milton Smith, Co. C
Richard Smith, Co. C
John S. Steele, Co. D
Lyman Stephens, Co. B

Arnold Stevens, Co. D
Clark Stillman, Co. D
William Dexter Stillman, Co. B
Myron Tanner, Co. D
Joel J. Terrell, Co. C
Solomon Tindell, Co. C
William Walker, Co. B
Almon Whiting, Co. D
Edmund Whiting, Co. D
David Wilkin, Co. C
Thomas S. Williams, Co. D
Charles Wright, Co. B
John P. Wriston, Co. A

Dr. William McIntire, command staff, probably was with this large group.

Women and children:

Ruth Markham Abbott (Joshua Abbott)
Susan Smith Adams (Orson B. Adams)
Eliza Manwaring Allred (James T. S. Allred)
Elzadie E. Ford Allred (Reuben W. Allred)
Agnes Brown (Edmund L. Brown)
Harriet St. John Brown (Daniel Brown)
Mary McCree Black Brown (Captain James Brown)
 Children: George David Black, Mary's son by first husband; unnamed child of James and Martha Stephens
Jane Wells Cooper Hanks (Ebenezer Hanks)
Emeline Bigler Hess (John Hess)
Mary Ann Jameson Hirons (James P. Hirons)
Matilda Nease Hunt (Second wife of Jefferson Hunt)
 Brother: Peter Nease; Sister: Ellen Nease
Mary Eliza Clark Luddington (Elam Luddington)
 Children: Angeline A. and one other
Mary Emeline Sessions (John Sessions)
Sarah Prunty Shupe (James W. Shupe)
Catherine Campbell Steele (John Steele)
 Child: Mary
Isabella McNair Hunter Wilkin (David Wilkin)
Albina Merrill Williams (Thomas S. Williams)
 Children: Caroline, Ephraim; Albina's sister: Phoebe Lodema Merrill

Rebecca Smith, whose husband Elisha Smith was a teamster
   but not a member of the battalion and died en route to
   California
Lena M. Luddington, traveling with her son, Elam, and his
   family

On November 10, while camped on the Rio Grande River, Colonel
Cooke decided to send the remaining sick men back to Santa Fe under
Lieutenant William W. Willis. Cooke ordered the battalion quartermaster
to issue rations for twenty-six days, allowing 10 oz. of flour per day. The
soldiers' ration at this time was 18 oz. a day. This decision not only eliminated fifty-four sick and ineffective men but increased the rations for
Cooke's remaining troops by several days.

Preparations began immediately after the order was given for the
departure of the Willis detachment. Fifty-four men (including scouts
Woolsey and Tippets), one woman, one big government wagon, four yoke
of poor cattle, five days' rations, and two dressed sheep started out. Three
other sick soldiers would later catch up and increase that number to fifty-
seven. In the wagon they placed clothing, blankets, cooking utensils, tents
and tent poles, muskets, equipage, and provisions plus all the invalids
unable to walk. With great persuasion Willis also obtained a spade and a
shovel, but he had no medicine or other necessities for the sick. Through
a mistake when loading the wagon, the rations ordered by Colonel Cooke
for twenty-six days were not packed. As a result, the group faced three
hundred miles of travel with only five days of rations.

They left the battalion on November 10 at the Rio Grande River in
New Mexico and traveled just two miles before camping. "Such a sight I
never saw. They was stowed away in the wagon like so many dead hogs. No
better way could be done so it was said. I went to the Lieu and asked him
if he would see that they was well taken care of when he had it in his
power to do it and gave him my hand. He gripped it and I could say no
more, neither could he. Many gave me their hand and wept" (Levi
Hancock).[21] That evening the Willis group was visited by Jefferson Hunt,
Jesse Hunter, and others, who spoke words of comfort and encouragement. Hunt administered to those who were sick according to the ordinance of the Mormon Church. Hunt and his party returned to the
battalion the next morning.

John Green died during the night of November 12. They were
camped at the same place where James Hampton had died nine days earlier when the battalion passed. Green's grave was dug beside that of his
friend—the two fallen comrades were buried side by side.

John Tippets wrote, "The days passed of lonesome and melancoly.
The men are feeble and we git along slow and we have no way to make

them comfortable."[22] Three soldiers, all suffering from various ailments, joined Willis and his charges. Because of their condition, including one with measles, Colonel Cooke ordered them to catch the sick detachment and continue with them.

Elijah Freeman became very ill during the night of November 15. The next day he lay in the wagon and, as they walked along, his groans could be heard by the entire column. They stopped over the next day because of Freeman's illness. It was very cold and snowed during the day. Travel was resumed on November 18, but was stopped a short time later when Freeman died. After a twenty-minute stop they continued until evening when they buried him four miles south of Socorro, New Mexico, between the bluff and the Rio Grande. Robert Bliss said Freeman was one of the best men he ever knew, faithful in all that he did.[23] That night Richard Carter died and was buried beside Freeman. "At present it is our daily prayer that there will be no more deaths in our midst for truly it is grievous to see our brethren left by the side of the road" (John Tippets).[24]

Between Socorro and Albuquerque, the detachment passed through numerous Mexican villages. When possible they tried to spend the night in deserted Mexican houses, "but they wear stocked with gray backs or body lice. So there was no rest until our journey's end."[25] Abner Blackburn, an outgoing eighteen-year-old, told of an encounter with the Mexicans:

One evening camped close to a village and were awful dry for something to drink that was stronger than water. Saw an old Padre come out of kind of cellar with a large bottle of the needfull. Three of us went up to him and told him that we were dry and had not taken a sniff since we left Santa Fe. He says "nither nither no tengo Aguedente no tengo veno no no tengo." We pushed him up against the door of the cellar. He fumbled around in his pockets and raked an old rusty key and gave it to a servant who unlocked the door and we followed him in. The man took us back to the further end of the dungeon and lit a taper and showed us how to draw the good out of the cask with a hollow reed. You suck it full. Hold it over a vessel and let it run out. Then in our glory. We took our time, it was slow work. We filled up to the plimsol mark before we suspected anything wrong. Started back in the dark for the door. Groped around and found it locked. Well, the old devel had us in a trap. Went back to the cask to die happy. Took another bait of wine. Then scratched our heads in a deep studdy how to get out. Hunted for a soft place in the adoby wall and with our bayonets dug out in a short time. Slipped out and sneaked into camp as though nothing happened. The boys had been hunting for us for an hour. They went to the village and enquired for us but the Mexicans had not seen us. After things quieted down after dark we took the boys back, crawled through the adoby wall and with canteens and kettles cleaned the old sinner's cellar dry. The next morning our officer noticed something unusual with the boys. We made it all right with him by giving him a canteen of Nectar for the gods.[26]

Slow travel and long days followed. When Willis and his group of invalids reached Albuquerque, Captain John Henry Burgwin, First Dragoons, gave Lieutenant Willis five dollars cash and the opportunity to exchange the heavy wagon for a lighter one. Several diarists recorded infractions by Lieutenant Willis, saying he abused them verbally, withheld rations, threatened them constantly, and drank too much. Since Willis did not keep a journal, his side of the story is not known. He faced a difficult task because of the extremely poor condition of his charges and insufficient food. Winter was upon them. Perhaps this is why he threatened them if they fell behind or gave them extra duty for not keeping up.

Upon arriving in Santa Fe on December 1, 1846, Colonel Sterling Price, commander of the post, ordered Willis to continue on to Pueblo. Willis had been told by Colonel Cooke to take the sick company to Santa Fe for further orders. The prospect of continuing the extra three hundred miles over mountains in the winter was discouraging. Willis prepared to continue and obtained ten mules and pack saddles, ropes, and other fixtures for packing. While at the fort they were provided small portions of flour and pork but had to pay for their wood. It was a difficult time for the Willis contingent. They were uneasy in the fort because of the Missourians stationed there. This distrust and dislike dated back to the murder of Joseph Smith and to the mobs in Missouri.

They began the last part of their journey December 4, traveling only ten miles the first day. Richard Brazier, too sick to travel, was left behind with a mule and a dozen others. Thomas Burns and George D. Wilson were among those who remained with Brazier. They were instructed to continue to Turley's ranch when able. Simeon Turley was a settler who lived between Santa Fe and Pueblo.[27] Leaving the sick behind did not set well with the men. George Wilson thought it was a very "bad policy to divide and divert the brethren especially to leave the sick behind among the Spaniards." John Tippets noted that "It is a time of sorrow and mourning with me to see the distress and sorrow of the sick. There hearts are broken. They are wore out. They mourn and weap."[28]

After traveling twenty miles the next day, the main company camped on a stream. The next morning they left one broken-down mule and reached a Spanish town after walking fifteen miles. Alva Calkins requested to remain in town to wait for Brazier and the sick to catch up.

Snow fell and continued until noon the next day. On December 8 they marched twelve miles and rented quarters from a Spaniard where they were able to buy bread, onions, pork, and other supplies, all with their own money. George Coleman was so hungry he overate and was in great distress during the night. Dr. William Rust, one of the company, gave him tincture of lobelia, the only medicine in camp. It provided only partial relief. [29]

Early the next morning Willis left a saddle mule for Coleman to ride and went ahead to Turley's ranch to make arrangements for the group's arrival. The company traveled the last ten miles, reaching the ranch about noon. Turley offered to send his team and a carriage back to bring Coleman, which was a great relief to Captain Willis. That night there was strong discussion about making it over the mountains to Pueblo due to deep snow. Captain Willis told his men he was authorized to draw supplies for the journey only and that he had been spending his own money to obtain supplies for them. He assured the men he was going to follow his instructions to go to Pueblo if he had to go alone. A vote by show of hands revealed all but one man agreed to continue under Captain Willis. The lone hold out later expressed regret at his opposition.

Three days of hard travel in snow from two to four feet deep brought them to the summit. Willis detailed a rear guard of the most able-bodied men to see that no one fell behind on the uphill climb while he continued at the head of the column, breaking the road through deep snow drifts. Only with great exertion and some frost-bitten feet were they able to reach the mountain top. As they looked on the other side and saw less snow and occasional bare ground, the men were relieved and descended in better spirits.

George Ruxton followed the Mormons' trail from Turley's ranch to Pueblo: "There were some twelve or fifteen of them, rawboned . . . with four or five pack-mules carrying their provisions, themselves on foot. They started several hours before me, but I overtook them before they had crossed the mountain, straggling along, some seated on the top of the mule packs, some sitting down every few hundred yards, and all looking tired and miserable."[30] From the Sangre de Cristo Pass, their route continued out of the mountains to the high plains. Near the Greenhorn River, they ate the last of the army rations. Only an accidental meeting with a hunting party of battalion men from Pueblo saved them. That evening they enjoyed a celebration feast of roasted venison.

Willis and his emaciated group reached Pueblo December 20 and found the first two detachments and the Mississippi Saints in what seemed to them very comfortable quarters. They were greeted enthusiastically. "The hearty looks of those who were sick & pale when we parted, assured us of the healthiness of the place. My heart rejoiced that kind providence had at last brought us there" (James Scott).[31] Another member of the Willis detachment wrote, "After much suffering from the hardships from the journey—weak teams, scant supplies of food, illy clad, general sickness among the men, the fall of December snows in the mountain ranges north of Santa Fe, excessive cold, and several deaths; this detachment finally arrived in Pueblo on the 20th of December 1846" (Thomas Bingham).[32]

Arza E. Hinckley had sent all his money back to his family and the Mormon Church. As the Willis detachment crossed the snowy mountain, Arza waded through deep snow in a hickory shirt, blue drill pants, socks, shoes, and a hat. He needed trousers, so when he arrived in Pueblo he traded for two deer skins, tanned them, and made a pair of pants. Each time the pants got wet, they shrank until they were very short and skin tight.

The Willis group went to work immediately building log cabins, one for each mess of six or eight men. Thomas Woolsey and John Tippets left December 23 with four days' provisions for Winter Quarters carrying mail.[33] Their journey lasted fifty-two days, during which they suffered greatly from hunger and cold. The last three days they were without food. They were given a hearty meal by Brigham Young upon arriving in Winter Quarters.

On December 27 Willis sent Gilbert Hunt, of the Higgins group, and a few men back to Turley's for the sick left there. Lieutenant Willis went to Bent's Fort on January 2, 1847, a distance of seventy-five miles, to obtain supplies. He was received kindly by Captain Enos, commander of the post and acting quartermaster, who furnished sixty days' rations for the company and provided transportation to Pueblo with ox teams.

Gilbert Hunt and his party arrived back in Pueblo in mid-January with all the sick—Brazier, Burns, Wilson, Calkins, and eight others—but not George Coleman. Hunt also brought a letter from Turley, who wrote that when he sent his team and carriage back, Coleman could not be located. His body was found later by the side of the road, some distance from where he had been left by Captain Willis. He died sometime in mid-December 1846.

Willis Sick Detachment

William W. Willis, Lieutenant	John Brimhall, Co. C
Lorenzo Babcock, Co. C	Daniel Brown, Co. E
Samuel Badham, Co. D	Thomas R. Burns, Co. E
James Bevan, Co. A	William Burt, Co. C
Thomas Bingham, Co. B	John Bybee, Co. B
Abner Blackburn, Co. C	Alva Calkins, Co. A
Richard Brazier, Co. E	James Camp, Co. B

Richard Carter, Co. B
James Cazier, Co. E
John Cazier, Co. E
Haden W. Church, Co. B
Albert Clark, Co. E
George Coleman, Co. A
George S. Clark, Co. B
Allen Compton, Co. D
Josiah Curtis, Co. A
Edward Dalton, Co. D
Harry Dalton, Co. D
Eli Dodson, Co. A
James Dunn, Co. C
Marcus Eastman, Co. B
David Frederick, Co. A
Elijah Freeman, Co. B
John W. Green, Co. C
Eli B. Hewitt, Co. A
Alfred Higgins, Co. D
Arza E. Hinckley, Co. B
Lucas Hoagland, Co. D
Jesse Johnstun, Co. C

Maxie Maxwell, Co. A
William E. McClellan, Co. E
Erastus D. Mechan, Co. D
Thomas Richardson, Co. E
Benjamin Richmond, Co. C
William W. Rust, Co. C
Joseph Shipley, Co. C
Joseph Skeen, Co. E
William Squires, Co. C
Benjamin Stewart, Co. D
James Stewart, Co. D
Hayward Thomas, Co. D
Nathan Thomas, Co. C
John H. Tippets, Co. D, Courier
William R. Tubbs, Co. D
Madison Welch, Co. C
Francis T. Whitney, Co. B
George Wilson, Co. E
Lysander Woodworth, Co. A
Thomas Woolsey, Co. E, Courier
Isaac N. Wriston, Co. A

One woman, Sophia Tubbs, accompanied the Willis group. There were no children.

All three detachments were situated fairly well in Pueblo by comparison with what they had been through. The weather was cold and wind whipped through the cracks in the log cabins, but it was better than their tents. The snow melted quickly and there was good grazing for the animals. Food was not a problem; supplies obtained from Bent's Fort were supplemented by hunting expeditions that added venison to their menu.

The Willis detachment had traveled the greatest distance, taking three months to complete the journey. The Higgins company completed its journey of 385 miles in about three weeks, while the Brown group reached Pueblo in one month. Life during that winter in Pueblo included dancing as the best entertainment, but the young women did not like the mountaineers' fandangos:

It was certainly a blessing to us that the detachment of Capt Brown came to Pueblo to protect us from the mountaineers and trappers who were in a fort across the river. They were determined that we should mingle with them in their wild living. Some of them had squaws with whom they were living; also some Spanish women were there. We attended a dance in their hall on one occasion. That was enough for us. We refused to go again, or to associate with them. They became very resentful and put up a tall pole in the street between the two rows of houses. They put a red shirt on the top of it to shoot at, and we were very much alarmed at their actions. When the Battalion boys arrived an end was put to all this. We had peace and protection. (Sarah J. Brown)[34]

After Captain Brown's detachment reached Pueblo and the meeting house was built, dances were held in the Mormon settlement with a couple of fiddlers furnishing the music: "There was no nice floors to dance on but we made the gravel fly" (Abner Blackburn).[35] If the mountaineers crossed the Arkansas for the dances, they had to listen to Captain Brown and President A. Porter Dowdle preach before the festivities commenced.[36]

Arnold Stephens wrote a letter to his wife and described life in Pueblo:

I am now dressing dear skins. I and my partner have dressed fifteen and can have all we can do. They are worth about two dollars a piece. . . . Our horses, mules and cattle live here and keep fat without feeding. . . . They raise corn here but have to water their land for a crop by taking the water out of the river in ditches. The corn is of an inferior quality and is the only thing cultivated here.[37]

Excitement prevailed when Mexicans and Indians attacked Taos in a bloody revolt on January 19, 1847. The rebels cruelly murdered Governor Charles Bent in his home and massacred the white population including eight Americans who sought safety at Turley's ranch. All communication between the settlements ceased. Colonel Sterling Price, commander at Santa Fe, promptly assembled the United States forces. With these men and four brass, twelve-pound mountain howitzers, Price successfully fought the Mexican revolutionaries in a series of skirmishes on the road to Taos. The rebels retreated to a church at the edge of Taos, setting it up as a fort. Price attacked the church on February 4, blasting the structure with the howitzers. The roof burst into flames, burning many occupants to death. Ten U.S. soldiers were killed and fifty-two were wounded. The Mexican-Indian coalition lost about one hundred and fifty with an even larger number wounded.

With communication cut off, it was a time of suspense and worry for a few weeks in Pueblo. They prepared to fight or flee. Guards were on duty day and night. Captain Brown sent messengers to Bent's Fort and the settlers living in the Arkansas Valley. His quick action in warning the fort and settlers impressed those at Bent's Fort. One of the officials, Dr. Hempstead, wrote:

Immediately on receiving news of the insurrection, Capt. Brown dispatched an express to this place, reporting to the Quartermaster the readiness of his company for active service should they be required. This promptness speaks well of them as soldiers, whatever may be said of them as citizens.[38]

Finally, on February 25 word was received that Colonel Price had destroyed the rebels and communication between Pueblo and Santa Fe was reopened. In Pueblo, Captain Brown ordered a celebration. Eighteen couples gathered in the meeting house to dance and celebrate by candlelight until midnight.

There were 275 Saints in Pueblo. Several men worked at Bent's Fort during the winter, earning money for the trip west at two dollars per day welding and setting tires for army provision wagons. Others found work in Fort Pueblo when the mountaineers hired several Mormons to dig a canal near the fort. Two weddings took place. Gilbert Hunt, Company A, married Lydia A. Gibson of the Mississippi Saints, and John Chase, Company B, married Almira Higgins, daughter of Captain Higgins.

While most of the sick recovered gradually, there were fifteen deaths in the three sick detachments after leaving the main body of the battalion. Six men died en route, and nine during the winter in Pueblo. Each death brought an outpouring of compassion and religious faith. Full military honors and a musket volley accompanied the services of the men. Five babies were born and two infants died.[39]

There was considerable conflict between the officers and a handful of soldiers. The officers had to lead their detachments to Pueblo with sick men, many women and children, limited rations, and poor transportation and, for the Willis company, cross mountains in the winter. The main complaint from the men seemed to be the harshness of the officers. Stiff punishments, swearing and yelling, and general lack of respect of their charges created resentful feelings toward the officers. They did not feel the officers were living up to the admonition of Brigham Young "to be as fathers to the privates."[40] They felt the officers frequently abused their authority in petty ways. The soldiers were extremely upset when they learned the officers benefited financially at their expense by charging a fee for obtaining their pay for them.

Although the Mississippi Saints had a branch of the Mormon Church organized before the detachments arrived, Captain Brown exerted leadership over the Pueblo settlement and spoke frequently at their religious services. To add fuel to the smouldering antagonism between the officers and the men, several men wrote jingles or poetry, most of which were highly uncomplimentary to the officers. The writings were posted beside doors, scattered around camp, or slipped under the doors of the officers.Captain Brown attempted to maintain strict control over the Pueblo soldiers. They were required to report to roll call every morning and those who failed to do so were suspected of desertion. John Steele recorded, "[Sometimes] we are paraded three times per day and all privileges are taken from us."[41] George Wilson and William Tubbs fled to the mountains so they could write freely in their diaries. When they returned to camp, Wilson complained that the officers threatened death for those writing the poetry.

On December 26, 1846, William Bird wrote a letter to Brigham Young in Council Bluffs stating that "the conduct of Captain Brown toward his troops is outrageous."[42] Captain Brown wrote a letter to Brigham Young dated December 27, 1846:

> I am undergoing to govern the men under my command by the military laws of the United States and the instructions I received . . . at Council Bluffs for I have it imprinted in my hart for I received it as the word of the Lord and by the power of the preasthood, and the grace of God I will do it and carry out the principals for which I was sent.[43]

Apparently conditions did not improve, for the following laws were read to the company at a meeting on January 13:

> That there be no card playing in the company, nor dancing, and any soldier or laundress that should be found speaking against an officer should be put under guard, and if a woman, she should be discharged, and that the houses of the souldiers should be cleared of any of their brethren that might be visiting and no one was to be found out of his quarters after 8 o'clock at night under the penalty of being sent up to the Guard House and tried by a court martial next day.[44]

The men reacted strongly to these strict rules: "That is the way that we have the privileges of Saints. It is martial law in the extreme and he says we are a first-rate set of boys and is that the way to treat good boys to curtail them of every privilege?" (John Steele).[45]

Finally, at a general meeting on February 3, the men were told in no uncertain terms that the jingles and poetry must stop. All soldiers were paraded at nine o'clock and formed in a hollow square. A guard was placed to guard the houses so the women could not pass out. Captain Higgins opened the meeting by speaking about the poetry and naming George Wilson as the writer. The officers did not like the poetry. Captain Brown was upset and called Wilson a "d-md rascal."[46]

John Perkins died on January 19 after a lingering illness and was buried on the 20th at the base of a big cottonwood tree. James Scott died

February 5 after a short period of severe suffering. The description of his funeral affords an idea of the respect and honors the deceased received. Not all deaths were written about in such detail:

> A number of our sisters accompanied the corpse. A company of fine looking soldiers accompanied the corpse with shouldered arms under the command of Lieutenant Willis. When the body was laid in the grave, Brother Chase said a few remarks upon the deceased. . . . "He is gone to the courts above to carry news respecting our Battalion. . . . In the morning of the first resurrection he will come forth for he has fell asleep in Jesus." After that the soldiers fired three vollies of musquetry and then retired, leaving the pall bearers to cover up the grave. (John Steele)[47]

Melcher Oyler, who died February 25, 1847, had been ill almost from the beginning of the westward trek.

Before Captains Brown and Higgins left for Santa Fe on March 18, Brown apologized for any wrong doing on his part. John Steele wrote that he "asked the boys to forgive him if he had done them any harm and promised to do better for the time to come."[48] The apology did not soothe the feelings of the men. Captain Higgins also humbled himself at this same time, encouraging them to have a forgiving spirit. He asked them to pray for him. Steele recorded that "out of 130 men, six or eight said they would."[49]

Eli Dodson died March 21, 1847. Arnold Stephens died the evening of March 26. Stevens was handling a wild mule when he was dragged over several logs and was hurt internally. He lingered five days until a blood vessel burst and suffocated him. He was dressed in his robes and laid in a coffin made of puncheons of cottonwood. These slabs split off like staves. On the Saturday before he died, he called Ebenezer Hanks and Orson Adams to make his will. His mule, saddle, and bridle went to his oldest son and all the rest of his effects were to be given to his wife.[50] On April 10, Mervin S. Blanchard died after a lingering illness.

According to John Brown, "William Casto deserted. Captain Brown was intending to go after him, but was advised to desist. Ebenezer Hanks and John Steele were sent and found him some forty miles [away]. After some persuasion Casto returned with them. He was court martialed and sentenced to hauling wood for camp some days."[51] Captain Brown and Captain Higgins had returned from Santa Fe on April 9. He reported "there was no one there that had power to discharge us or to give us any orders to leave until Colonel Kearny returns from California."[52]

Brown and Higgins went to Santa Fe again on May 1, this time to obtain the soldiers' pay and to seek orders for leaving Pueblo. Several men accompanied them. The soldiers left behind in Pueblo thought the officers took advantage of their position. First, they required the soldiers to give Brown power of attorney to requisition their pay. Next, Captain Brown and Captain Higgins appointed themselves to journey to Santa Fe for the money, giving the men no choice. Finally, they charged the men two and one half percent commission for getting their pay. When Brown and his party returned May 18 with the soldiers' pay, their commission amounted to about $200 on the $8,000 collected. The men did not like the officers profiting on their pay. Brown also returned with orders from the fort commander, Colonel Sterling Price, "to go to California and to start on the 25th of May with two and one half months of provisions."[53]

Several Mississippi families, anxious to be on their way west, left Pueblo and started for Fort Laramie again. They met Brigham Young and the pioneer company at the ferry of the Platte River on June 1.[54] "Six wagons, which are a part of the Mississippi company that wintered at Pueblo, are here. They have been here two weeks, and they report that the remainder of their company were coming on with a detachment of the Mormon battalion, who expected to be paid off and start for this point about the first of June" (Howard Egan).[55]

The date this group left Pueblo is not known, but it arrived at Fort Laramie around the middle of May. It included seventeen persons: Robert and Elizabeth Brown Crow and family, George W. and Matilda Jane Crow Therlkill and family, Archibald Little, James Chesney and Lewis B. Myers, William D. and Margaret Jane Casteel Kartchner, Milton H. Therlkill, and James W. Therlkill.[56]

Brigham Young chose four men to go back to Pueblo to have the remaining Mississippi Saints and the battalion detachments start immediately for Fort Laramie. The men chosen were Amasa Lyman, Thomas Woolsey, John H. Tippets, and Roswell Stephens. Woolsey and Tippets were battalion members who had acted as couriers between Pueblo and Winter Quarters (present Florence, Nebraska). Tippets and Woolsey left the upper Arkansas December 23, 1846, and finally reached the Missouri River fifty-two days later. Stephens had gone to Winter Quarters earlier to carry mail and had not returned to the battalion.

The four men charged by Brigham Young to bring the battalion left Fort Laramie June 3 about 11 A.M. Brigham Young, Heber C. Kimball, Willard Richards, and Orson Pratt accompanied them as far as Laramie Fork. Sitting on a large tree, which had fallen on the bank of the river, they held a council meeting. Afterward, they knelt down, and Brigham Young blessed the men and dedicated them to the Lord.

When Brown and Higgins returned to Pueblo, all efforts were turned to getting ready for the trip west. In six days the three detachments and the remaining Mississippi Saints had their wagons loaded and left Pueblo May 24, 1847, at noon. The soldiers were relieved to depart.

Joseph Skeen recalled his days at Pueblo with remorse and sorrow: "Many things happened while we lay at Perbelow [Pueblo] that it is to mean to mention."[57] George D. Wilson was resentful: "The last few months have been those of the greatest persecution I have ever experienced."[58] Not all of the Pueblo dwellers went west. Thomas Burns, James Glines, Daniel Brown and his wife, Harriet, and perhaps others went to Winter Quarters.

The main party's route was north to Fort Laramie on the Platte River. After a week's travel, John Taylor Brown was born June 2 to James Polly and Eunice Reasor Brown. They reached the Platte River June 3. Continuing along the river, they crossed the South Fork of the Platte on June 5. During the afternoon of June 11, while camped at Lodgepole Creek, they were surprised by the arrival of Amasa M. Lyman, one of the Quorum of Twelve Apostles. He was accompanied by Thomas Woolsey, Roswell Stephens, and John Tippets, all direct from Brigham Young at Fort Laramie. Lyman brought letters from some of their families and the news of the probable destination of the Mormon Church. John Hess expressed his feelings at the meeting by running to Apostle Lyman and kissing him for joy.[59]

Amasa Lyman had been sent by Brigham Young to straighten out the conflicts existing in the Pueblo detachments and to bring them west to join the Young company. Robert Crow, leader of the advance Mississippi unit, had reported the divisive condition within the ranks of the soldiers at Pueblo. Brigham Young had dictated letters for Captain Brown and Elder A. Porter Dowdle, branch president, which Lyman gave to them.

Amasa Lyman spoke to the Pueblo detachments on Sunday, June 13, with a spirit of meekness. He urged the men to follow the principles for which they had enlisted. He pleaded with his brethren to "leave off card playing and profane swearing and return to God."[60] He then told them that they were not as bad as had been reported. In a letter to Brigham Young, Lyman wrote, "I laid the instruction before them which had the effect of quelling the spirit of mutiny and . . . they followed the counsel."[61]

The combined groups resumed their journey west. On June 20, Apostle Lyman addressed them again and once more exhorted them to live as Saints and followers of Jesus Christ and forsake all sins: "Elder Lyman gave us all a good whipping at 2 o'clock and a great deal of good council in relation to the course we should take" (Joel Terrell).[62] Lyman's speech had a noticeable effect on Captain James Brown, who humbled himself by publicly acknowledging some of his faults.

On June 16 they camped one mile from Fort Laramie, 540 miles west of Council Bluffs, which they left eleven months before. At Fort Laramie they learned Brigham Young and the pioneer company were twelve days ahead. They determined to try to catch the pioneer company and left early on the morning of June 17. After crossing the Platte River on June 28 a special party was dispatched with instructions to recover stolen horses. The thirteen scouts caught all but one of the thieves. The missing renegade escaped and headed toward Fort Bridger with the stolen animal. The battalion party was pursuing this thief when they learned the pioneer company was ahead of them. The men rode hard to overtake Young and his band. Battalion men in this group included John Buchannan, William W. Casto, Andrew Shupe, Thomas Bingham, George S. Clark, Allen Compton, Francillo Durphee, Samuel J. Gould, James Oakley, Benjamin Roberts, Joel J. Terrell, and William H. Walker. Thomas H. S. Williams was in charge.

They caught up with Brigham Young and the pioneers at the junction of Big Sandy and Green rivers (Wyoming) on July 4. After the soldiers were ferried across the river and reached the campsite, Wilford Woodruff described the scene: "When we met, it was truly a hearty greeting and shaking of hands."[63] William Walker learned his wife was in the next company, so he left immediately to go back to her company.

The soldiers lined up in military formation to listen to words of greeting from Brigham Young. At the conclusion of his remarks, Young asked for a cheer for the returning battalion members. A great shout of "Hosannah, hosannah, hosannah, give glory to God and the Lamb" rang through the camp. The soldiers then were dismissed and quickly were surrounded by friends eager for news of their adventures during the previous year. After a brief celebration between the two groups, Brigham Young and other church officials met in Willard Richards's wagon to read letters from Amasa Lyman and Captain James Brown, which the soldiers had brought. Heber C. Kimball recorded, "The report of the soldiers is not very favorable and it appears there has been considerable wrong practised by both officers and men."[64]

Four days later Thomas H. S. Williams and Samuel Brannan were sent back to meet Captain Brown and the sick detachments with a message from Brigham Young and to bring them to join the pioneer company. Brannan told Brigham Young he could lead the detachments to California for their discharge and final pay.

The Pueblo detachments and the Mississippi Saints, traveling under Captain James Brown, gradually gained on the vanguard company until they were only a day behind when they reached the ferry on the Platte River. Finding a blacksmith at the ferry, they decided to get the animals shod. While here they saw many emigrants crossing the ferry en route to California and Oregon. From Fort Laramie, Captain Brown led his unit along the Oregon Trail to Fort Bridger in the footsteps of the pioneer party. They followed the Platte River to the Sweetwater River and to Independence Rock, where they camped. It was here Martha Jane Sharp and Harley Mowrey were married July 4, 1847. He was twenty-four years old and she was twenty. She was the young widow of Norman Sharp, who had died on the way to Pueblo. This trail romance had blossomed along the Sweetwater River and was described rather humorously by Abner Blackburn:

> Their was a coupple of young folks in the company spooning . . . ever since we started on the road. The whole company weare tired of it, and they weare persuaded to marry now, and have done with it and not wait until their journeys end. The next evening we had a wedding and a reglar minister to unite them. And after come the supper with the best the plains could furnish. Then came the dance or howe down. The banjo and the violin made us forget the hardships of the plains.[65]

When they reached Devil's Gate, Abner Blackburn was descriptive again:

> Once upon a time the river cut through this mountain and left a chasm several hundred feet deep. It looked as though one could step across on top. If there was any difference in width, the bottom was the widest. Some of our party weare afraid to goe thrugh the gate for fear they might land in the bad place. We went around the gate over a ridge.[66]

The anniversary of their enlistment, July 16, was not forgotten: "At daylight there was a salute of small arms in honor of our enlistment and more especially the finishing of our one year's service to Uncle Sam, and to let every one of Uncle Sam's officers know we were our own men once more. We still kept up our organization, and respected the command as usual, and was rather better than some had been before" (John Steele).[67] Although the men believed their period of service was up, there was no one with authority to discharge them. Then, too, as long as they remained soldiers, they received pay and provisions from the government. They thought they had to go to California to be discharged.

On Sunday, July 18, Captain Brown spoke on discipline, cattle driving and other matters. The Sabbath was not always observed by the soldiers, again candidly reported by Abner Blackburn:

> Some weare in the shade reading . . . some mending clothes, others shoeing cattle, and a number in a tent playing the violin. By an by a runner come around to notify the company that our minister was a going to observe the sabath and preach a sermon. All hands quit work and the fiddle stopt playing. . . . [some] went into a tent to play cards, & few took their guns and went hunting and a few herd the sermon. Such is life on the plains.[68]

The company arrived at Fort Bridger July 19. On July 28 the men had their first view of the Salt Lake Valley. Abner Blackburn and a few friends who climbed a mountain crest were impressed by "the grandest view that ever mortal beheld, the air was clear and perfect for a good view, the great Salt Lake glittering under the suns rays, range after range of mountains in every direction, the great desert to the west, and Utah lake to the south east and the mountains beyond. A more sublime view was seldom seen from a mountain top."[69]

On July 29, 1847, President Brigham Young, Heber C. Kimball, Willard Richards, George Albert Smith, Amasa Lyman, Wilford Woodruff, Ezra T. Benson, and five other authorities rode on horseback from Salt Lake to the mouth of Emigration Canyon, where they met the incoming Pueblo colonists. A violent thunderstorm prevented a grand welcoming in Salt Lake Valley, but a fife and drum corps greeted the arrival of the Pueblo detachments of the Mormon Battalion and the Mississippi Saints. Thomas Bullock described the formation: "Council & officers first, Infantry next with Martial Music, then followed the Cavalry—with baggage wagons bringing up the rear."[70]

Captain Brown led twenty-nine wagons filled with soldiers, their families, and the Mississippi Saints to a campsite about one half mile north of the temple lot.[71] They brought with them wheat raised in Taos, a Mexican town. (When mixed with club-head wheat, this Taos wheat was for many years the staple wheat sown in Utah fields.)

On the morning of July 30, Brigham Young and the Council of Twelve Apostles met with the battalion officers. Young told the veterans of the sick detachment, "Your going into the army has saved the lives of thousands of people." Since their year-long enlistment period in the Mormon Battalion had expired, it was decided to disband the three detachments and that they would not proceed on to California for their severance pay as originally planned. That evening in a general meeting for the Saints, Brigham Young spoke until he was hoarse. He expressed a warm feeling toward the soldiers. He requested that the men build a bowery on the temple lot so they could hold their meetings in the shade.[72]

On July 31, 1847, Brigham Young assumed command of the soldiers and ordered them to gather brush for the bowery. They built a comfortable shelter forty by twenty-eight feet in size. During the week the soldiers worked under church direction, cultivating the soil and making adobes for both living quarters and a fort.

With the arrival of wee Elizabeth Steele on August 9, the first white child was born in Salt Lake Valley. Her parents were John and Catherine Campbell Steele. Her father was a private in Company C of the battalion. She was born at four o'clock in the morning in a tent where the east wall of the Salt Lake Temple now stands.[73]

Concerned over the actions of some ex-soldiers, the council decided to rebaptize all of the men for their health and the remission of sins. A small dam was built on City Creek to divert water into two pools. On Sunday, August 8, the baptisms took place.

The battalion men whose families were still in Winter Quarters left to go to their families. Captain James Brown made one final trip to obtain severance pay due the men who had been on detached duty in Pueblo. He took several ex-battalion members and started for California. Accompanying him were Abner Blackburn, Lysander Woodworth, Jesse S. Brown, John S. Fowler (not a Mormon Battalion soldier), Gilbert Hunt, William Squires, and William Gribble.[74] He carried letters from families and from Mormon Church officials to the discharged veterans in California, whom he met in the Sierra Nevada on September 6.

From Fort Hall the Brown party followed the Oregon Trail down Snake River Canyon to the Raft River where the California Trail turned south. Crossing Goose Creek Mountains, they descended into Thousand Springs Valley. They followed the Humboldt River to Big Meadow at Humboldt Lake (Lovelock, Nevada). Next came the Humboldt Sinks and then the Forty-Mile Desert to the Truckee River. They continued past Johnson's ranch to Sutter's Fort.

Brown and his companions arrived in Monterey only to learn the governor had left for San Francisco. They turned around immediately and overtook him at the old San Juan Mission (San Juan Bautista). The governor informed them the army payrolls were in Monterey. Abner Blackburn and Lysander Woodworth were dispatched back after them. After receiving the payrolls, they returned to the mission exhausted, having covered the same territory four times that day. On the presentation of the claims to Governor Mason for the three months' pay still due, they were allowed. Governor Mason stated, "Paymaster Rich paid to Captain Brown the money due to the [Pueblo] detachment up to that date, according to the rank they bore upon the muster rolls, upon which the Battalion had been mustered out of the service."[75]

This final pay of the Pueblo battalion members taken from California by Brown amounted to about five thousand dollars, mostly in Spanish doubloons.[76] This mustering-out roster, which listed the soldiers by company, provides interesting data about amounts paid to soldiers with different ranks, the ten percent "payout" to James Brown, and the fact that soldiers apparently borrowed from one another and used this mustering-out pay to settle accounts. Examples include the following:

Captain Nelson Higgins: $93, less 10% ($9.30), paid $83.70.
1st Lieutenant Elam Luddington: $78, less $7.80, plus several
payouts so Luddington received only $4.45.

The mustering out rosters of the Pueblo detachments list the men, generally alphabetically, by company. This page shows the amount due the men in Company D, less Brown's 10 percent, and the net payout. Archives, Historical Department, Church of Jesus Christ of Latter-day Saints, Salt Lake City, Utah; used by permission.

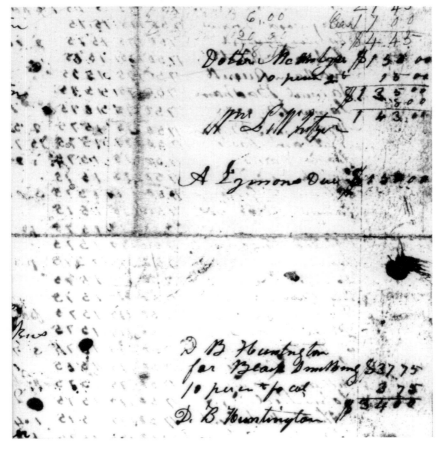

This marginal note from a Pueblo mustering out roster clarifies the whereabouts of
Dr. William McIntire, who does not appear in journal accounts of the later stages of
the battalion's march. He was in Pueblo with the sick detachments. In the company
rosters, McIntire was listed in the margin because he never belonged to a company.
Although Dimick Huntington's name appears with his company for his regular
army pay, this marginal reference shows he received an additional amount of
$37.75 for blacksmith work, less Brown's 10 percent, for a net of $34. Archives,
Historical Department, Church of Jesus Christ of Latter-Saints, Salt Lake City; used
by permission.

2nd Lieutenant Orson Adams: $32.50, less $3.25, paid
$29.25.
Sergeant Thomas Williams: $32.50, less $3.25, paid $29.25.
Corporal Gilbert Hunt: $22.50, less $2.25, paid $20.25.
Private Allen Compton: $17.50, less $1.75, net $15.75.
    Compton apparently owed Thomas Bingham $7 and
    James Hirons $8.75. After paying these debts, Compton
    received nothing.

The rosters also reveal that soldiers were paid extra for certain jobs.
In a marginal note Dimick B. Huntington earned $37.75 for black-
smithing, less Brown's ten percent of $3.75, for a net payment of $34.
Huntington also received his regular private's pay of $17.50, less Brown's
fee. A second marginal note shows Dr. McIntire receiving $150, less
Brown's ten percent, for a net of $135. Someone (name not readable)
owed him $8, so McIntire was paid $143. Since McIntire was on the command staff, he never was on a company roster. The last known reference
to Dr. McIntire on the journey was on September 3, 1846, which was
before all three detachments left. McIntire probably went with the Brown
group. One name—Albert Clark, Company E, Willis detachment—that
was not on previously published lists of the Pueblo detachment was on
these rosters. Several published accounts state that Reuben Allred went to
California rather than Pueblo, but his name is listed on these rosters,
thereby proving that he and his wife went to Pueblo for the winter.

Only three of the men who went to California with Brown returned
with him—his son Jesse, Abner Blackburn, and Lysander Woodworth.
They were joined by Samuel Lewis, who had been discharged from the
battalion earlier in Los Angeles and had been working for Sutter.

We started the 5 of October 1847 on the biggest torn fool erant that
every is known. A whole band of half broke animals to pack and
drive through a rough mountain country and hostile Indians
tribes . . . with our pot gutted horses we packed and unpacked a
dozen times a day and then [had to] herd them again at night. In
this camp there came verry near being a mutiny and nothing but
fair promises and extra pay kept us from it. (Abner Blackburn)[77]

This small returning group had numerous encounters with Indians,
took twice as long to get back as going to California, and encountered
severe weather conditions. A near disaster occurred about fifteen miles
after leaving San Francisco. When Brown and his companions stopped for
the night, the saddle bags containing the Spanish doubloons were missing. Brown sent Abner and one other to retrace their route. Fortunately,
they found the bags about three miles back.

Brown took four bushels of wheat, some corn, and other seeds when he left California. On several occasions they had trouble with their pack animals: "Changed a pack onto another [horse] that had a sound back and by the way he acted we thought he was an old pack horse. [We] did not find out [differently] until the crupper tightened on him a going down a hill and away he went. Tore a hole in the pack and spilt some wheat. We caut him [and] scraped the wheat up clear for it was valuble in this far off land" (Abner Blackburn).[78]

After a few days' travel, a light snow fell in the Sierra mountains and it was very cold. When they reached the site of the Donner tragedy, Abner wrote, "I stood guard in the latter part of the night and thought of all the ghosts and hobgoblins could think of or ever heard of. Beside the sculls, bones, and the dark forest, it was a most dismal place."[79] They ran out of provisions and spent several days crossing the desert without any water. During the last three days of their journey, they existed on soup made from the leather on their saddles and a lean crow.

They arrived in Salt Lake Valley November 16, almost starved and very weak. Hungry as they were, they did not eat the grain they were carrying, realizing it was needed for planting and that many lives would benefit from the harvest of the seeds. Brown's charge of ten percent for the round-trip to California of three months and seven days amounted to a commision of five hundred dollars.[80] "Captain James Brown returned from California . . . making us pay 10% for our money and wanting us to pay 6 cents per lb for all the U.S. oxen that we have eaten since the 16th of July" (John Steele).[81]

At the direction of Mormon Church officials, Brown used $1,950 of battalion money to buy Fort Buenaventura, a trading post, from Miles Goodyear. This settlement was known as Brown's Fort and Brownsville until 1850, when it was named Ogden City and finally shortened to Ogden.[82]

CHAPTER THIRTEEN

Mormon Volunteers

Although members of the battalion had been pressured to enlist for an additional period by the governor of California, army officers, and Mormon officers, they did not reveal their intentions at first to military authorities. Colonel Stevenson wrote to Governor Mason: "Until the day after they were mustered out of the service, there was not the slightest disposition evinced to re-enter, but on the 17th in the afternoon, Capt. Davis and Lieut. Canfield commenced enrolling and on the 20th all were enrolled."[1] Seventy-nine discharged veterans agreed to serve an additional six months. Three young men, who served as officers' aides during the trip west, also enlisted, making a total of eighty-two men in the company. Two wives and two boys completed the group.

John Riser, who had served as a private in Company C, joined the Mormon Volunteers: "I was still embued with military service. I again enlisted with eighty [eighty-two] others into the service of the same."[2]

> While a sufficient number of us have reenlisted to make one Company, I did not like to reenlist, but I had no relatives in the Church to return to. I desired to remain in California til the Church became located, for it is impossible for us to leave here with provisions to last any considerable length of time. And if I Stay here or any number of us, it is better for us to remain together, than to Scatter all over Creation. So we have all enlisted that are going to stop in this lower country. We have been promised by the present Governor of California that we Shall be disbanded next March. By that time we shall know more about the movements of the Church. (Henry G. Boyle)[3]

On July 20, 1847, the company of eighty-two men known as Mormon Volunteers was mustered into the U.S. Army by Lieutenant Andrew J. Smith, First Dragoons. Daniel C. Davis, former captain of Company E,

Mormon Battalion, was appointed captain of the Volunteers: "I suppose Capt. Hunter expected to be captain of the company but Davis was run in by some means or other and Hunter was appointed Indian agent" (William Coray).[4]

Army uniforms were issued and, finally, the volunteers looked like an army unit. It was the first time the men had been in uniform even though they had been in the army over a year. The battalion had sent its clothing allowance to families and the Mormon Church. Their only common article previously was the wide white belt they received in Fort Leavenworth with instructions to keep it clean. In a letter to R. B. Mason, Colonel Stevenson reported: "They uniformed themselves from head to toe in the uniform of my regiment."[5]

Four days later, July 24, the following order was issued to Captain Davis by Colonel Stevenson:

> You will proceed to San Diego with your company and garrison that post. San Diego, San Luis and the surrounding country will be under your command. You will be watchful and vigilant, and especially have a strict eye upon all persons passing in and out of the country and by every mail give me such information as regards the state of the country, as well as deportment of the people towards your command. You are, whenever called upon by the civil authorities, to sustain them in the execution of the laws, and in all things to act with prudence and discretion in the performance of your duties.[6]

The Mormon Volunteers left Los Angeles July 25 and arrived in San Diego August 2. The company was charged mainly with guard duty to protect the citizens from Indian raids and to watch the movement of any rebellious parties until a treaty between the United States and Mexico was signed. Henry G. Boyle reported, "We are comfortably quartered here and have full rations, and nothing to do as far as Soldiers duties are concerned."[7] The residents of San Diego, upon learning a group of Mormons had reenlisted, awaited their arrival anxiously. A few even went out to greet the soldiers the day before they reached San Diego.

Captain Davis found quarters, but the roof leaked, so he asked for permission from Colonel Stevenson to use tile from several of the dilapidated outer buildings of the San Diego mission. Colonel Stevenson wanted the men "as comfortable as possible" and suggested that Lieutenant Clift surpervise the repairs. The soldiers made use of the tile and a table with benches from the mission.

By agreement with the military commander at the time of reenlistment, the men followed in the footsteps of Company B, doing manual and mechanical labor for the citizens when not assigned to military duty. In order to maintain certain sanitary and moral regulations, a daily detail of four men and one non-commissioned officer acted as police. They cleaned the quarters and the yard as well as the parade ground. The volunteers were told to give attention to cleanliness of person and clothing and to have a proper decorum of conduct. Card playing in quarters was not allowed.

Four Mormon officers served in important positions in San Diego: Captain Davis was the post commander. Jesse D. Hunter was appointed by Governor Mason as the Indian agent for the Southern Military District with headquarters in San Luis Rey.[8] After Captain Henry D. Fitch resigned as alcalde of San Diego, Lieutenant Robert Clift, formerly of Company C, became the justice of the peace (alcalde) from June 1847 until March 1848.[9] Lieutenant Ruel Barrus was in charge of a detachment at San Luis Rey, consisting of twenty-five men, a corporal, and a sergeant. This company left San Diego August 10 for San Luis Rey to guard the mission and all other public property and to prevent vandalism.[10] They took twenty days' provisions, one wagon, and a team. They returned the middle of February without experiencing any major incidents.[11]

A problem developed over the death of Charles Soin, a New Yorker living in San Diego. While waiting for a ship to take him to the Hawaiian Islands, he was known to carry a large sum of money. On August 11, Soin disappeared from his boarding house. Later his body was found with marks that indicated he had been murdered. Captain Davis offered a forty-dollar reward to find the killer. Alcalde Robert Clift arrested Richard Freeman, a non-Mormon resident at the same boarding house, but due to lack of evidence he was released. There were no serious problems between the local citizens and the volunteers.

Sergeant Lafayette Frost died September 8, 1847. He was remembered for his bravery when charged by a wild bull and for his character and good deeds. He was buried one half mile southeast of San Diego. Private Henry Packard was promoted to sergeant to fill the vacancy created by the death of Frost.

During his command in San Diego, Captain Davis had a problem with a member of the 7th New York Volunteers, Archibald Waddell. Waddell, a hospital steward under Dr. Alfredo Anseline, had been stealing government medicines and selling them to the soldiers. Davis searched Waddell's personal property and found a government medicine box, various medicines, and a note of obligation from one of the Mormon soldiers for medicine. Captain Davis charged Waddell with embezzling government property. Waddell confessed on October 6, 1847, and was sent on the ship *Barnstable* to be court-martialed in Los Angeles.[12] Private Thomas Morris replaced Waddell as hospital steward.

On November 5, Neal Donald died and was buried near Lafayette Frost. Dr. Alfredo Anseline, army physician for the post, attended both Donald and Frost before they died.[13]

During the time the Mormon Volunteers were stationed in San Diego, there were several rumors of insurrection by the former Mexican leaders, with supposedly three thousand well-armed troops. Just in case an invasion occurred, Captain Davis obtained powder, ball, and a couple more cannon from Colonel Stevenson in Los Angeles. He also warned Lieutenant Barrus in San Luis Rey to be on guard. Jesse Hunter discounted the rumor but said, "if it is the case, we will try and give them the best fight we can."[14] News of the supposed invasion spread throughout San Diego: "The inhabitants here appear much alarmed, and express their fears, that should the reports prove true, you may order us from San Diego, and thus leave them unprotected. I have invariably told them not to fear, that we were amply able with what force we have to defend San Diego from any attack that may be made upon us" (Captain Daniel Davis).[15] William T. Sherman granted Captain Davis full authority if necessary "to arrest any person and upon reasonable grounds of suspicion, that if they are engaged in exciting discontent toward our Government, and if any such there be, you should not wait for overt acts on their part, but should arrest and imprison them and if necessary send them here to Monterey by sea."[16]

Captain Davis did not have to use this authority granted him, but he kept his men on alert as a precaution. The Mormon Volunteers were credited with thwarting any counter-American movement. On March 7, 1848, Henry Boyle wrote:

> Our term of enlistment is nearly out. We have met with nothing of a Serious nature Since we reenlisted. I have been at work in company with four others of my brethren making brick. I have also during the winter been engaged white washing. I have whitewashed nearly all the town, & have been otherwise engaged to the best advantage. We did their blacksmithing, put up a bakery, made and repaired carts and . . . did all we could to benefit ourselves as well as the citizens. We never had any trouble with Californians or Indians.[17]

Their enlistment was up on January 20, 1848, but they were not mustered out for two more months. The Mormon Volunteers were disbanded in San Diego on March 14, 1848, after drawing their pay. They did not receive travel-home allowance as they had been promised, but they were given return rations of beef on-the-hoof. "The citizens became so attached to us that before our term of service expired, they got up a petition to the governor of California to use his influence to keep us in the service. The petition was signed by every citizen in the town. The governor tried hard to keep us for six months longer, but this latter offer was declined"(Henry G. Boyle).[18]

On March 21, 1848, thirty-five men with Henry G. Boyle as their leader started for Salt Lake Valley by the southern route. Susan Davis, wife of Captain Daniel C. Davis, was the only woman. Captain Davis's son, Daniel Jr., traveled with them. The Boyle company arrived at the Williams ranch on March 31 and obtained additional supplies and animals for the trip. They met Porter Rockwell and James Snow, who had traveled the southern route the previous winter. Rockwell and Snow agreed to pilot the Boyle group to Salt Lake Valley.[19] John Riser wrote, "We started on the 12th of April from Rancho El Chino, through the Tejon Pass with one wagon and 135 mules and horses. The majority of us were packers, but this wagon that we took was the first wagon that had ever traveled this route."[20]

They traveled the southern route from San Bernardino, California, via Las Vegas, Nevada, on the Old Spanish Trail until just north of Antelope Spring (near present Cedar City, Utah), where they left the trail and proceeded north to Salt Lake Valley. This was the second time Susan Davis experienced the blazing of a road.[21] The Boyle company arrived in Salt Lake Valley June 5, 1848. Much of their route eventually became Interstate Highway 15.

The "rest" of the Volunteers, possibly the remaining forty-two mentioned, went north to Sutter's Fort, San Francisco, and the gold fields. Ebenezer Brown, his wife Phebe, and her son, Zemira Palmer, traveled with this group to northern California.[22] Only eight names of volunteers who went to the gold fields are known at this writing: Ebenezer Brown, Isaac Harrison, John C. Naegle, Lot Smith, John L. Wheeler, Andrew Workman, Oliver Workman, and Jerome Zabriskie.

Since no lists are available to detail this division of who went with Boyle and who went to the gold fields, it is not possible to plot further the movement of the eighty-two Mormon Volunteers at this time.

Mormon Volunteers

Officers:

Daniel C. Davis, Captain
Cyrus C. Canfield, 1st
    Lieutenant
Ruel Barrus, 2nd Lieutenant
Robert Clift, 3rd Lieutenant
Edmund L. Brown, 1st
    Sergeant
Samuel Myers, 2nd Sergeant
Benjamin F. Mayfield, 3rd
    Sergeant

Lafayette Frost, 3rd Sergeant
    (Died in San Diego)
Henry Packard, 4th Sergeant
Thorit Peck, 1st Corporal
Isaac Harrison, 2nd Corporal
Hiram B. Mount, 3rd Corporal
Edwin Walker, 4th Corporal
Richard D. Sprague, Musician
Henry W. Jackson, Musician

Privates:

Addison Bailey
Jefferson Bailey
Gordon S. Beckstead
Henry Bowing*
Henry G. Boyle
Benjamin Brass
Henry Brizzee
Ebenezer Brown
William W. Brown
John S. Bryant
Edwin Calkins
Thomas W. Callahan
Isaac P. Carter
Riley G. Clark
John R. Clawson
James Clift
Jeptha S. Condit
John Q. A. Covil
Neal Donald (Died in San
    Diego)
Willard Y. Dayton
Thomas P. Dutcher
Jacob S. Earl
Justice C. Earl
William Evans
Ezra Fatoute
Hiram W. Fellows
Philander Fletcher
Ebenezer Harmon
Lorenzo F. Harmon
Oliver Harmon
James S. Hart
William Hickenlooper
James Kibby

William Lance
James W. Lemmon
Benjamin Maggard
Harlem McBride
Thomas Morris
James Mowrey*
John T. Mowrey
John C. Naegle
Christian Noler
James P. Park
Edwin M. Peck
Isaac Peck
Peter F. Richards
John J. Riser
John Ritter
Levi Runyan
George S. Sexton
Aurora Shumway
Lot Smith
Willard G. Smith
George E. Steele
Isaiah C. Steele
Andrew J. Steers
Miles J. Thompson
John S. Watts
Benjamin West
Henry Wheeler
John L. Wheeler
James V. Williams
Jacob Winters
Andrew J. Workman
Oliver G. Workman
Nathan Young*
Jerome Zabriskie

*The eighty-two enlistees in the Mormon Volunteers included these three former officer aides from the Mormon Battalion. Because of this service as volunteers, they were eligible for pensions. They were never in the Mormon Battalion, but their names on the pension rolls has caused them to be listed incorrectly on other lists of battalion members.

The women with the volunteers were Susan Davis, wife of Captain Daniel Davis, and Phebe Palmer Brown, wife of Sergeant Ebenezer Brown. Each couple had a son with them: six-year-old Daniel Davis Jr. and seventeen-year-old Zemira Palmer.

Melissa Burton Coray Kimball.

In 1851 Sarah Allen exchanged her gold flakes for cash and goods. She wrote, "I gathered my little means together and hired me a wagon made, purchased another cow and a yoke of cattle," but she reserved "enough of the gold to make me a wedding ring." She arrived in Salt Lake Valley September 14, 1852, and later married Joel Ricks. She wore the ring for the rest of her life.

Sarah Fiske Allen Ricks. Courtesy of International Society, Daughters of Utah Pioneers, Salt Lake City, Utah.

Epilogue

Sometimes there are exceedingly brief periods which determine a long future.
—Bernard DeVoto, *Year of Decision, 1846*

The Mormon Battalion was involved in numerous significant events in western history between 1846 and 1849. They blazed the wagon route that became the southern route to California; they demonstrated the importance of the San Pedro and Santa Cruz rivers as transportation corridors, which led to the Gadsden Purchase; they took part in the conquest of California to claim it as part of the United States. The battalion aided the 1847 move to Utah by the Mormons. Fifteen veterans escorted General Stephen Kearny to Fort Leavenworth when he took John C. Frémont to be court-martialed. They participated in the discovery of gold and opened the highway over Carson Pass in the Sierra Nevada. Now called the Mormon-Carson Pass Emigrant Trail, this road became the main entrance to California for approximately 200,000 gold-seeking immigrants during 1849–56. Six ex-soldiers carried two thousand copies of *The California Star* east that told the world gold had been discovered. Finally, they drove the first wagons over the Old Spanish Trail and the Salt Lake Cutoff of the California Trail.

As impressive as these accomplishments are, it is the day-to-day stories of these men and their epic march that remain indelibly stamped on our minds. Traveling together, experiencing everything in common, bonded the men together in a way that lasted for the rest of their lives. David Pettegrew stated at a reunion in Salt Lake City, "the connection and acquaintance we found when in the service can never be blotted out."[1] Melissa Coray, in speaking about the kindness and assistance she received as her husband's health deteriorated, said, "They are good friends we shall ever remember."[2]

They traveled in small groups or messes of six men to a tent; messmates seemed to have a particularly strong bonding. Frequently, after camping for the night, the weary, starving men carried canteens of water back to their comrades who had fallen along the trail, too weak and too ill to continue. Helping their fallen comrades, the men arrived back in camp in early morning hours, just in time to begin the next day's march. Recipients of this kind treatment recorded in their journals they may have perished had not their friends returned for them.

One of their greatest challenges was burying a comrade in a desolate, lonely spot. If the burial was to be early in the morning, the body was kept in the tent of the deceased's messmates during the night. Even though the grave was in a remote, lonely spot, and the bodies were wrapped only in blankets or tree bark, the burials were conducted with dignity, respect, and caring. A friend was gone, bringing thoughts such as those of John Tippets: "At present it is our daily prayer that there will be no more deaths in our midst for truly it is grievous to see our breatherin left by the side of the road."[3]

Members of families in the battalion were very loyal and caring in looking after one another. Sixteen-year-old Orin Hatch became so ill he could not keep up with his company and was left by the side of the trail. Meltiar Hatch, who celebrated his twenty-first birthday by joining the battalion, had looked after his younger brother since their mother's death. Each night Meltiar and a messmate returned to find Orin. Walking, one on each side, they literally carried him into the camp, where they attended to his needs the best they could. This scene was repeated night after night until his condition improved.

A general festival of the battalion was held in the Social Hall in Salt Lake City February 6–7, 1855.[4] All ex-soldiers in the area met for this first reunion. There were many speeches both by Mormon Church authorities and by the ex-soldiers, which expressed the warm feelings they had for each other. Any differences they may have had during the journey seemed to disappear with the passing years. Brigham Young predicted, "The Mormon Battalion will be held in honorable remembrance to the latest generation. . . . I will prophesy that the children of those who have been in the army in defense of their country will grow up and bless their fathers for what they did at that time." William Hyde, who had been on foreign missions since his discharge, remarked:

> I am truly happy . . . to meet with you in this capacity. . . . I have not language to express my feelings on this occasion. . . . I have been separated from my brethren in Zion for a long time, thousands of miles of sea and land have lain between us, and I have never forgotten you. . . . I have been looking for a day of this kind ever since we left the service, but it has seemed as though we never should have a chance of meeting all together again. Sometimes a few have met, but now a large majority have the privilege of meeting . . . and

rejoicing all together. I cannot express the joy of my heart on this ever-to-be-remembered day; it is a glorious day to me.

During the same reunion, Captain James Brown stated, "This is one of the happiest days I have had since I enlisted in the Mormon Battalion . . . I have not language to express the feelings of my mind in meeting with the battalion on this occasion."

In 1887 John J. Riser wrote an eight-page summary of his life. With a retrospective view of his military service, he wrote, "I often wonder why no writer or speechmaker either in the army or out of it ever dares to list the services of that Battalion to our country in the Mexican War, where they have been found so ready on all occasions to keep before the country the services of all others engaged in that war."[5]

The soldiers were aware that their actions, good or bad, reflected on the Mormon Church. To their credit, starting with their first command-ing officer, Lieutenant Colonel James Allen, all reports were favorable. Colonel Allen was overheard at Fort Leavenworth to say he "had not been under the necessity of giving the word of command the second time. The men, though unacquainted with military tactics, were willing to obey orders."[6]

Colonel J. D. Stevenson wrote to Brigham Young that serving "with the men of the battalion since their arrival had dispelled the prejudices and that having had occasion to visit all the prominent places from Santa Barbara to San Diego, he had found a strong feeling of respect entertained for the Mormon people, both by the native and foreign population."[7]

Governor Richard B. Mason wrote in his reports to Washington, D.C.:

Of services of the Mormon Battalion, of their patience, subordina-tion and good conduct, you have already heard and I take great pleasure in adding that as a body of men they have religiously respected the rights and feelings of these conquered people, and not a syllable of complaint has reached my ears of a single insult or outrage done by a Mormon volunteer. So high an opinion did I entertain for the Battalion, and of their special fitness for duties now performed by the garrisons in this country that I made strenuous efforts to engage their services for another year.[8]

Colonel Doniphan attended a social function in St. Louis after his return from the West at which he told Senator Thomas A. Benton: "I can take one thousand Mormon boys, and do more efficient service against Mexico than you can with the whole American army."[9]

When Johnston's Army passed through Salt Lake City on June 26, 1858, in the aftermath of the so-called Utah War, which had temporarily pitted the federal government against the Mormons, Colonel Cooke was one of Johnston's officers. In deference to the men who had served under him in the Mormon Battalion, Cooke took off his hat and rode through the deserted city with his head uncovered.[10]

Hubert H. Bancroft, California's prolific historian, wrote of the battalion:

> While the honor of making the discovery of gold may not be claimed for them, nor the honor of making the conquest of California, that which is infinitely better than either of these achievements . . . may be claimed for them—the honor of writing into the annals of California, and of the world's history, this example of fidelity to duty . . . which is not over matched in any of the records written by men. Thus . . . at the call of duty, or what they deemed to be duty, these devotees of their religion unhesitatingly laid down their wealth-winning implements, turned their back on what all the world was just then making ready with hot haste and mustered strength to grasp at and struggle for, and marched through new toils and dangers to meet their exiled brethren in the desert.[11]

Being in the Mormon Battalion changed the men and their families forever. As soldiers, they were exposed to situations they may never have experienced otherwise. They returned different men from when they left. While their cultural and world views were expanded, they were like rough diamonds that needed polishing. After living in the outdoors for so long, adjustments had to be made when they reached their families. A number of the men had health problems relating to battalion service for the rest of their lives.

The family of Zadock Judd arrived in Salt Lake Valley in 1848 a few weeks before he did. He described his first night home. His stepmother, Jane Stoddard Judd, made him "a bed on the floor with several heavy quilts folded underneath, but I have been so used to sleeping on the hard-board [ground] that I could not go to sleep. . . . In order to rest, I had to take the top quilt off and roll myself up in it on the floor with no other quilts underneath. Then sleep soon overcame me."[12]

The arrival was a happy one for those whose families were in Salt Lake Valley to greet them. Henry Bigler was "received with open arms, both by friends and dear relatives bidding us welcome, welcome, thrice welcome!"[13] Anticipation soon turned to disappointment when others reached Salt Lake Valley and learned their families had not yet arrived:

> The first man I saw was T. Bingham my old Mess Mate . . . from him I learned my Family were not here [Salt Lake Valley] which was one of the Greatest trials of my Life; to think that I had left them with the Expectation to meet them here & had suffered almost every thing

but Death & traveled some 1500 miles since the 21st of July with Joyful hope of Meeting them here and thought of the Happiness of their society again to be disappointed; to hear they were 1100 miles still from me & no possible Chance of getting to them in 8 or 10 months to come is almost to much for me to bear & without any means to Get Provisions or Clothing for the Season that is approaching. If I could cross the Mts I would not rest till I saw them but the Mts are now covered with Snow and my animals would die & I should perish among the Mts. and never see them here. Therefore I must wail till Spring before I can go to them; I ask God the Eternal Father to bless them & presirve them in health until I meet them once more.(Robert Bliss) [14]

Newman Bulkley arrived in Salt Lake Valley in the fall of 1847, too destitute to continue:

My provisions were gone. I had no money and there was nothing to buy even if I had been able to buy it. My clothes were gone. I was tired, in fact, exhausted, 1,000 miles from my family with winter at hand. I hauled wood for D. B. Huntington to pay for my board and two buckskins. I hauled wood to pay for having them made into pants. I then went to work for Brother Stratton and while there his wife made me two shirts and two pair of drawers out of an old tent. [15]

Bulkley, typical of many so destitute they could not continue on, left Salt Lake Valley in August 1848 and finally reached his wife, child, and father and mother, still ragged and destitute. Although he started planning immediately to take them west, he and his family did not reach the valley until October 9, 1852.

Of those who had to journey back to Council Bluffs, most found their families. Others did not. Both Horace Alexander and Levi McCullough reached Winter Quarters to find their wives and one child of each of them had died. Who can forget the scene when McCullough's young son looked at the three men standing before him and asked: "Which one of these ragged men is my father?" [16]

The women who traveled with the battalion—the twenty-nine who spent the winter in Pueblo and the four who walked all the way to California—had unusual experiences never to be forgotten. John Hess wrote about his wife's mode of travel:

The government provided two to six mule teams to each company. I was solicited to drive one of them and, for the comfort and convenience of my wife, I consented to do so and many times I was thankful that I had done so as these teams had to haul the camp equipage which consisted of tents, tent poles, camp kettles, etc., which filled up the wagons to the bows and the women would have to crawl in as best they could and lie in that position until we would stop to camp. As I had the management of the loading I could make the situation a little more comfortable for my wife. For this and other reasons I will not mention, I was glad I was a teamster.[17]

When Melissa Coray was interviewed by a reporter in 1901 about walking to California with the battalion, she replied: "I didn't mind it. I walked because I wanted to. My husband had to walk and I went along by his side." Melissa Coray made a second trip to California during her later years. In Monterey she walked quietly in the cemetery looking for the grave of her infant son she and her husband had buried there in 1847. She hunted over the hillside for the tiny mound, but time and the elements had changed the terrain and she could not locate baby William's grave. The Corays reached Utah in October 1848. A baby daughter was born in February 1849 and a month later, March 1849, her beloved husband died of tuberculosis. A short time later she wrote a letter to Howard Coray to tell him of his brother's death: " I do not feel to complain yet I think my trials are great for one so young."[18] Melissa was twenty years old. Two years later she became the second wife of polygamist William Kimball, which resulted in the U.S. government's rejection of her application for the pension of her first husband, William Coray.[19]

Pensions the men received, although small by today's standards, provided many veterans with necessities in their later years. In some cases, the pensions even furnished a few luxuries. Lorenzo Babcock was twenty-three years old when he enlisted as a private in Company C. He traveled to Pueblo with the Willis sick detachment. When he was sixty years old in 1883, he applied for his pension. His first check was $450, which covered many years. He continued to receive a small pension, paid semi-annually until he died in 1903 at the age of eighty.[20]

It was heart-wrenching for the mothers, as in any war, to see their sons leave. Drusilla Hendricks at first forbade her son William to join the battalion. Later, as she remembered the morning of the final call for men, she wrote:

> William raised his eyes and looked me in the face. I knew then that he would go. . . . I could not swallow one bite of breakfast, but I waited on the rest thinking I might never have my family all together again. I had no photograph of him but I took one in my mind and said to myself, "If I never see you again until the morning of the resurrection I shall know you are my child."[21]

Years after his stint in the battalion, James Ferguson delivered a lecture in England and told about Wealthy Richards, the mother of his

Department of the Interior.
PENSION OFFICE.

Washington, D.C. March 19, 1884

Sir:

In response to your letter addressed to Hon. John T. Caine, and by him referred to this office relative to the claim of Melissa Coray, I have the honor to state that the evidence shows that soldier died in 1849 and no claim was filed until July 25 1879.

The claimant having contracted a Polygamous marriage prior to filing her claim, the case was found to be inadmissible, and was rejected in accordance with the provisions of the Act of August 7 1882.

Very respectfully,

_____
Acting Commissioner

The rejection of Melissa's request for the pension of her deceased husband William Coray. Her request was not granted because she was the second of polygamist William Kimball's five wives.

comrade, Joseph W. Richards, who died in Pueblo. In remembering the time of enlistment in Council Bluffs, he said:

> There was one scene that was particularly touching. An aged mother, to whom the call of the government and the wish of the President was made known, came forward. She had five sons—one was murdered and now lay buried deep and unavenged in the tragic well in Missouri. Two were in a foreign land preaching the faith for which their brother's blood was shed; one was still too young . . . and needed care and comfort. The other was a young man, the sentinel and protector of her tottering steps. Even in her aged heart, withered and broken as it was, the love of country burned deep and strong. She yielded up her son and never saw him more.[22]

For the women, waiting in Winter Quarters or Council Bluffs for husbands to return, trying to keep body and soul together and to provide for their children, changed their lives too. After surviving through long, lonely months, they looked forward to their husbands' return. Sarah Fiske Allen was one of these waiting women. While Ezra Allen was in the battalion, she experienced many challenges and worked hard to supply necessities for herself and her two children. Her journal reveals her feelings:

> In the spring of 1848, I began to look forward to the return of my husband. The Lord had blessed my efforts to provide for my family. And the Brethren and Sisters had been kind to me. But a long journey lay before me and I looked forward to the time when his strong arms would lift these burdens of care from my shoulders. I gathered grapes from the lowland near the river and made wine and prepared such dainties as I could that would please him. At length the news came that a company of brethren was expected to cross the river in a few days. I felt anxious to go to the ferry to meet him, but circumstances would not permit, so I remained at home waiting and watching, listening to the sound of every footstep that approached my door. After several days word was brought to me that some of the brethren had arrived home and that my husband and two other of the brethren had been killed by Indians in the California Mountains . . . I learned that a purse containing $120.00 in gold dust had been found belonging to my husband and it was being brought to me.
>
> Thus, when my hopes and expectations [were] blasted in a moment, what could I do but trust in God. I had no relative in the Church, two small children and a journey of 1000 miles before me. For some time I felt I would sink under my burden of grief and anguish of heart. Then I aroused myself and began to meditate on

what course to pursue, how to provide for my family and prepare for the journey. I therefore determined to make every effort in my power to accomplish this desireable undertaking and leave the event in the hands of God. In a few days, the purse . . . which had belonged to my husband was brought to me. There were marks of blood upon it and it seemed to me as the price of his life.[23]

These pioneer journalists wrote about hunger and unbearable thirst for days at a time, about threadbare clothing and shoes that didn't exist. They told of animals so weak they couldn't pull a full load. Yet, with all their hardships, they never questioned serving in the battalion. To the very end, they considered their year in the army as a mission to help their church. Complaints were few; they simply wrote direct, factual statements of their condition as they saw it at the time, such as Newman Bulkley's remark, "I've walked 3,000 miles—half of it on bare feet."[24]

The stories of the Mormon Battalion are powerful, reaching across the years to connect us with those soldiers who made that incredible journey 150 years ago. They experienced important historical moments in the early days of California's golden era. They blazed the first wagon tracks in four different areas over nearly two thousand miles. Their gold provided financial aid at a crucial time. The seeds, cuttings, equipment, horses, cattle, and other "in kind" payment for their labors were most helpful to the struggling Salt Lake settlement. They were seasoned, experienced frontiersmen, who became leaders in colonizing outlying areas in the western states as assigned by Brigham Young. Knowledge of irrigation, observed as they passed through the Indian country, was beneficial in communities where they settled. Their contributions to dozens of colonies is another story waiting to be told.

They transmitted knowledge and values and feelings. The structure and tempo of their daily lives touch those who read their story. In their writings they gave themselves identities that carry from one generation to the next. In retrospect, one must ask if those priceless journals, written on small pages by the light of campfires, are not their most important legacy. One cannot read the diaries without being impressed with the sustaining power of faith as they recorded not only their experiences, but a belief that God protected them and that promises made to them by their leaders would be fulfilled.

They dug wells as they walked the trails, leaving the wells for those who followed. In their writings, they leave a well of inspirational stories to be told and retold. Along the way, collectively, they preserved several chapters of American history that otherwise would have been lost. Through their journals, their footprints still echo along the trails.

MOVEMENT WITHIN THE MORMON BATTALION

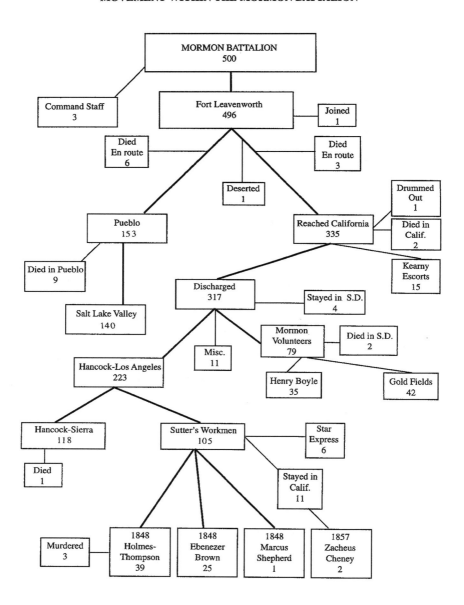

Numbers indicate men involved in each category.

Analysis of Movement within the Mormon Battalion

Reconstructed Alphabetical Roster (appendix B)		500
Less Glines, Shelton, Dykes (on command roster), and John Allen (joined later)		−4
Official Rosters of Allen, July 31, 1846, and Smith, August 31, 1846 (both confirmed by Coray)		496

* * * * *

		500
Died enroute to California—Boley, Phelps, Hampton	3	
Higgins Family Detachment, excluding Tippets & Woolsey (chap. 12)	11	
Brown Sick Detachment, excluding Dr. McIntire (chap. 12)	91	
Willis Sick Detachment, including Tippets & Woolsey (chap. 12)	57	
Gully, resigned, 10/46	1	
Stephens, courier, 10/46	1	
Gilbert, deserted	1	−165
Total Arrived in California (appendix C)		335
Died in California—Dunham, Smith	2	
Kearny Escorts (chap. 7)	15	
John Allen, drummed out	1	−18
Discharged in Los Angeles		317
Independents—Alexander, Bulkley, Colton, Curtis, Day (chap. 8)	5	
Stayed in San Diego—Hunter, Hunter, Brown, Allen (chap. 8)	4	
Mormon Volunteers (chap. 13)	79	
Bates group, Williams ranch (chap. 8)	6	−94
Hancock-Los Angeles Company (appendix D)		223
Sutter's Workmen (appendix F)		−105
Hancock-Sierra Company (appendix E)		118

Compiling the Reconstructed Roster

The firm figure of 496 men listed twice on official company rosters made me wonder why there was such variance (500–540) in published lists of the battalion. Many names on the enlistment roll had lines drawn through them. These crossed-out names did not appear subsequently on the muster-out roll or the pension roll.

There are several reasons why individuals may have signed up on the enlistment roll but were not accepted into the battalion and thus had a line drawn through their names: First, age—they were either too young or too old. Second, size—two boys were rejected because they were too short. They later stood on stumps behind someone to appear taller and were accepted. Another stood on his toes to pass. Third, illness—Calvin Reed and Samuel Boley had the same illness. Dr. William McIntire told Reed he could not go because he was too ill. Perhaps he told Boley the same thing and Boley didn't listen. In any event, Boley died after only three days on the trail. Reed didn't go and lived until 1895. At the July 17 enlistment another man, in Company B, was rejected and no reason was given.

At Fort Leavenworth the roster was used to issue guns and accoutrements, clothing allowances, and other military supplies. The rosters were reviewed frequently during the year of enlistment—on the trip, in San Diego and Los Angeles, and, finally, at discharge. It is inconceivable that, with all these reviews of the official roster, a name could be left off.

These are the men whose names were crossed out on the enlistment roll (muster-in roll) and who did not appear on the subsequent muster-out or pension rolls. These names are not included in the reconstructed roster herein, although some of them are aliases for men who do appear there under other names.

Billings, Orson	Fife, Peter M.	Murdock, Price
Bowen, James	Findley, John	Packard, James W.
Brown, George	Forgandson, Samuel	Parke, James B.
Bryan, J.	Garner, Riley	Peck, Thomas
Bybee, Henry G.	Harrison, Israel	Rawlins, John
Call, Thomas.	Hayward, Thomas	Reed, Calvin
Clawson, George	Higbee, Henry G.	Richards, L.
Coleman, William	Holman, John G.	Richardson, J.
Cowin, Elbridge J.	Holman, N. C.	Rollins, John (Roylance)
Curtis, Samuel T.	Houston, John	Scott, James R.
Dart, James L.	Hovey, Silas G.	Snyder, William W.
Davis, Walter L.	Howarth, Charles T.	Taylor, Norman
Dayton, William J.	Howell, William	Thompson, Henry
Dickmott, John	Hulse, Lewis	Ure, Martin
Earl, Jesse	Joyce, Thomas C.	Ure, William
Eldred, James	Miller, Henry G. (Boyle)	Young, John R.
Ewell, Martin F.	Miller, James (Myler)	

Other factors have led to previous inaccuracies in determining an accurate roster for the battalion. There were at least twelve young men who served as aides to the officers but were not enlisted in the battalion. Three later enlisted in the Mormon Volunteers, creating further confusion when their names appeared only on pension rolls. The twelve were the following:

1.   Henry A. Bowing: Enlisted in Mormon Volunteers in San Diego, but was not in Mormon Battalion.

2.   Neuman Brown: Teamster; father: James P. Brown; went to Pueblo.
3.   Robert Brown: Teamster; father: James P. Brown; went to Pueblo.
4.   Charles E. Colton: Aide to Adjutant P. C. Merrill; ran away and caught up with battalion to be with father.
5.   George E. Elliot: Nothing known.
6.   Nathan Hart: Father: James S. Hart.
7.   Nelson D. Higgins: Father: Nelson Higgins; went to Pueblo.
8.   James Mowrey: Aide to Lieutenants George W. Rosecrans, Samuel Thompson, and Robert Clift; enlisted in Mormon Volunteers; was not in Mormon Battalion.
9.   William Byram Pace: Aide to father: Lieutenant James Pace; cousin to number 10.
10.   Wilson Daniel Pace: Aide to Lieutenant Andrew Lytle; fifteen years old, cousin to number 9.
11.   Zemira Palmer: Son of Phebe Brown; aide to Colonel Allen, then Doctor Sanderson from Fort Worth to Santa Fe, then Lieutenant Lorenzo Clark until discharge.
12.   Nathan Young: Nephew of Brigham Young; aide to Captain Jesse Hunter to San Diego; enlisted in Mormon Volunteers, was not in Mormon Battalion. Immediately after discharge from the Volunteers, he went by boat to Australia and did not go to Utah until many years later.

Several men have appeared on lists under different names, a few of which were aliases. Others were misspellings:

John Roylance appears as John Rollins: Family tradition relates that John had a strong British accent and spoke rapidly. When he said his name, it sounded like Rollins.
Henry Green Boyle appears as Henry G. Miller.
Isaac N. Wriston appears as Isaac N. Clifford, and John P. Wriston appears as John P. Clifford: These two brothers used their stepfather's name, Wriston. Brigham Young later told them to use their father's name, Clifford.
Riley Garner Clark appears as Riley Garner.
John Conrad Naegle appears as John C. Naille.

Others have appeared twice—under both first and last names, such as Hayward Thomas, Thomas Hayward, and Foster Curtis, Curtis Foster—thereby doubling the count.

Two men, John Bosco and Elisha Smith, were hired teamsters and were not in the battalion. Both died en route to California. Many journals record their deaths and published rosters include their names. Since these men did not belong to the battalion, their names were removed from the roster reconstructed here.

John Allen, a disruptive man who joined the battalion at Fort Leavenworth, was not included on the first Allen and Coray rosters because he enlisted after the first record was made July 31, 1846. A soldier, Thomas Gilbert, deserted August 23, which was before the second roster (Smith and Coray) count, August 31. His desertion countered Allen's increase, keeping the total at 496 in the second count. For the thirteen days between Allen's enlistment and Gilbert's leaving, there were 497 men enrolled on the company rosters.

By eliminating the names in these groups, the reconstructed roster of the Mormon Battalion in appendix B totals 500. The practice of not listing the command staff in the company rosters was illustrated when Philemon Merrill told his friends he would like to resign his command position and go back on the company roster (see February 2, 1847, chap. 4). Deleting the names of the three men assigned to the command staff from the company rosters brings the reconstructed total to 497. Subtracting either the name of John Allen or of Thomas Gilbert makes a total of 496, the same as Allen, Smith, and Coray recorded (see July 31, chap. 1 and August 31, chap. 2). After years of careful posting and several months spent in recreating the roster, and with totals that duplicate Allen, Smith, and Coray, I am confident in the accuracy of the reconstructed roster, appendix B.

Appendix B

Alphabetical Reconstructed Roster

Mormon Battalion

Name (spouse) / Battalion Company / Later Group or Fate

Abbott, Joshua (Ruth Markham) / D / Brown

Adair, G. Wesley / C / Sutter's Workmen; Holmes-Thompson

Adams, Orson B. (Susan Smith) / C / Brown

Alexander, Horace M. / B / Independents

Allen, Albern / A / Hancock

Allen, Elijah / B / Stayed in San Diego

Allen, Ezra H. / C / Sutter; Murdered, Tragedy Spring

Allen, Franklin / B / Brown

Allen, George A. / B / Hancock

Allen, John / E / Drummed out in Los Angeles

Allen, Rufus C. / A / Sutter

Allred, James R. / A / Sutter; Holmes-Thompson

Allred, James T. (Elizabeth Manwaring) / A / Brown

Allred, Reddick N. / A / Hancock

Allred, Reuben W. (Ezadie Ford) / A / Brown

Averett, Elisha / A / Hancock

Averett, Jeduthan / D / Brown

Babcock, Lorenzo / C / Willis

Badham, Samuel / D / Willis

Bailey, Addison / C / Mormon Volunteers

Bailey, James / A / Sutter

Bailey, Jefferson / C / Volunteers

Barger, William H. / D / Sutter

Barney, Walter, Sr. / C / Williams; Sutter

Barrus, Ruel / B / Volunteers

Bates, Joseph W. / E / Williams; Ebenezer Brown

Beckstead, Gordon S. / A / Volunteers

Beckstead, Orin M. / A / Hancock

Beckstead, William E. / C / Brown

Beddome, William / E / Hancock

Beers, William / E / Sutter; Ebenezer Brown

Bevan, James / A / Willis

Bickmore, Gilbert / A / Hancock

Bigler, Henry W. / B / Sutter; Holmes-Thompson

Bingham, Erastus, Jr. / B / Brown

Bingham, Thomas Sr. / B / Willis

Binley, John W. / E / Kearny

Bird, William / B / Brown

Blanchard, Mervin S. / A / Brown; Died in Pueblo

Bliss, Robert S. / B / Hancock

Blackburn, Abner / C / Willis
Boley, Samuel / B / Died en
route
Borrowman, John / B / Sutter;
Ebenezer Brown
Boyd, George W. / B / Sutter;
Ebenezer Brown
Boyd, William W. / D / Sutter;
California until 1851
Boyle, Henry G. (a.k.a. Miller,
Henry G.) / C / Volunteers
Brackenbury, Benjamin B. / B /
Sutter; Ebenezer Brown
Brass, Benjamin / A / Volunteers
Brazier, Richard / E / Willis
Brimhall, John / C / Willis
Brizzee, Henry W. / E /
Volunteers
Bronson, Clinton D. / A /
Hancock
Browett, Daniel / E / Sutter;
Murdered, Tragedy Spring
Brown, Alexander / C / Brown
Brown, Daniel (Harriet St. John;
Brown sick) / E / Willis
Brown, Ebenezer (Phebe Palmer)
/ A / Volunteers; Ebenezer
Brown
Brown, Edmond L. (Agnes; Brown
sick) / E / Volunteers
Brown, Francis / B / Stayed in
San Diego
Brown, James (Mary McCree) / C
/ Brown
Brown, James P. (Eunice Reasor)
/ D / Higgins
Brown, James S. / D / Sutter;
Holmes-Thompson
Brown, Jesse S. / C / Brown
Brown, John / A / Hancock
Brown, William W. / A /
Volunteers
Brownell, Russell G. / C /
Hancock
Bryant, John S. / A / Volunteers
Buchannan, John / D / Brown
Bulkley, Newman / E /
Independents
Bunker, Edward / E / Hancock
Burns, Thomas R. / E / Willis
Burt, William / C / Willis

Bush, Richard / B / Sutter;
Holmes-Thompson
Bush, William / C / Hancock
Butterfield, Jacob K. / A / Sutter
Button, Montgomery (Mary
Bittels) / D / Higgins
Bybee, John M. / B / Willis
Caldwell, Matthew / E / Kearny
Calkins, Alva C. / A / Willis
Calkins, Edwin R. / A /
Volunteers
Calkins, James W. / A / Brown
Calkins, Sylvanus / A / Hancock
Callahan, Thomas W. / B /
Volunteers
Calvert, John H. / C / Brown
Camp, James G. / B / Willis
Campbell, Jonathan, Jr. / E /
Hancock
Campbell, Samuel / E / Sutter
Canfield, Cyrus C. / D /
Volunteers
Carpenter, Isaac / C / Brown
Carpenter, William H. / C /
Brown
Carter, Isaac P. / B / Volunteers
Carter, Richard / B / Willis; Died
en route to Pueblo
Casper, William W. / A / Hancock
Casto, James / D / Hancock
Casto, William W. / D / Brown
Catlin, George W. / C / Hancock
Cazier, James / E / Willis
Cazier, John / E / Willis
Chapin, Samuel G. / E / Sutter
Chase, Abner / D / Brown; Died
en route to Pueblo
Chase, Hiram B. / A / Hancock
Chase, John D. / B / Brown
Cheney, Zacheus / B / Cheney
company, to Utah in 1857
Church, Haden W. / B / Willis
Clark, Albert / E / Willis
Clark, George S. / B / Willis
Clark, Joseph / E / Sutter;
Ebenezer Brown
Clark, Joseph L. / A / Hancock
Clark, Lorenzo / A / Hancock
Clark, Riley G. / A / Volunteers;
Boyle
Clark, Samuel G. / E / Kearny

Clawson, John R. / D / Volunteers

Clift, James / C / Volunteers

Clift, Robert / C / Volunteers

Cole, James B. / D / Hancock

Coleman, George / A / Willis; Died en route to Pueblo

Collins, Robert H. / D / Hancock

Colton, Philander / B / Independents

Compton, Allen / D / Willis

Condit, Jeptha S. / C / Volunteers

Coons, William A. / D / Sutter; California until after 1854

Coray, William (Melissa Burton) / B / Sutter; Holmes-Thompson.

Covil, John Q. / C / Volunteers

Cox, Amos / D / Kearny

Cox, Henderson / A / Sutter; Murdered, Tragedy Spring

Cox, John / E / Sutter; Holmes-Thompson

Cummings, George W. / E / Brown

Curtis, Dorr P. / B / Independents

Curtis, Foster / D / Sutter

Curtis, Josiah / A / Willis

Dalton, Edward / C / Willis

Dalton, Harry / C / Willis

Dalton, Henry S. / B / Sutter; Stayed in California

Davis, Daniel C. (Susan Moses) / E / Volunteers

Davis, Eleazer / D / Hancock

Davis, James / D / Brown

Davis, Sterling / D / Hancock

Davis, Walter L. / E / Hancock

Day, Abraham / E / Independents

Dayton, Willard T. / B / Volunteers

Decker, Zachariah B. / A / Sutter

Dennett, Daniel Q. / E / Sutter; Holmes-Thompson

Dobson, Joseph / A / Sutter; Holmes-Thompson

Dodge, Augustus E. / C / Hancock

Dodson, Eli / A / Willis; Died in Pueblo

Donald, Neal / C / Volunteers; Died in San Diego

Douglas, James / D / Sutter; Holmes-Thompson

Douglas, Ralph / D / Brown

Dunham, Albert / B / Died in San Diego

Dunn, James / C / Willis

Dunn, Thomas J. / B / Sutter

Durphee, Francillo / C / Brown

Dutcher, Thomas P. / B / Volunteers

Dyke, Simeon / E / Hancock

Dykes, George P. / D / Hancock

Earl, James S. / E / Volunteers

Earl, James C. / A / Brown

Earl, Justice C. / E / Volunteers

Eastman, Marcus N. / B / Willis

Egbert, Robert C. / A / Hancock

Elmer, Elijah / C / Sutter; Holmes-Thompson

Evans, Israel / B / Sutter; Holmes-Thompson

Evans, William / E / Hancock

Ewell, John M. / E / Hancock

Ewell, William F. / A / Hancock

Fairbanks, Henry / A / Hancock

Fatoute, Ezra / D / Volunteers

Fauney, Fredrick / E / Hancock

Fellows, Hiram W. / C / Volunteers

Ferguson, James / A / Sutter; Ebenezer Brown

Fife, John / C / Hancock

Fifield, Levi J. / C / Sutter; Ebenezer Brown

Finlay, Thomas B. / D / Hancock

Fletcher, Philander / D / Volunteers

Follett, William A. / B / Sutter

Follett, William T. / E / Sutter

Forbush, Lorin E. / C / Hancock

Forsgreen, John E. / D / Hancock

Frazier, Thomas L. / D / Hancock

Frederick, David I. / A / Willis

Freeman, Elijah N. / B / Willis; Died en route to Pueblo

Frost, Lafayette N. / A / Volunteers; Died in San Diego

Garner, David / A / Brown

Garner, Philip / B / Brown

Garner, William A. / B / Sutter;
Holmes-Thompson
Gibson, Thomas / C / Sutter
Gifford, William W. / D / Brown
Gilbert, John R. / D / Hancock
Gilbert, Thomas / D / Deserted
August 23, 1846
Glazier, Luther W. / E / Brown
Glines, James H. / A / Brown
Goodwin, Andrew / A / Hancock
Gordon, Gilman / A / Kearny
Gould, John C. / C / Brown
Gould, Samuel J. / C / Brown
Green, Ephraim / B /
Sutter/Holmes-Thompson
Green, John W. / C / Willis; Died
en route to Pueblo
Gribble, William / D / Brown
Gully, Samuel / E / Resigned
October 19, 1846
Hampton, James / A / Died en
route to California
Hancock, Charles B. / C /
Hancock
Hancock, George W. / C /
Hancock
Hancock, Levi W. / E / Hancock
Hanks, Ebenezer (Jane Wells
Cooper) / E / Brown
Hanks, Ephraim K. / B /
Hancock
Harmon, Ebenezer / C /
Volunteers
Harmon, Lorenzo F. / C /
Volunteers
Harmon, Oliver N. / E /
Volunteers
Harris, Robert, Jr. / E / Hancock
Harris, Silas / B / Sutter; *Star
Express*
Harrison, Isaac / E / Volunteers;
Cheney in 1857
Hart, James S. / E / Volunteers
Haskell, George N. / B /
Hancock
Hatch, Meltiar / C / Sutter;
Holmes-Thompson
Hatch, Orin / C / Sutter; Holmes-
Thompson
Hawk, Nathan / B / Sutter; *Star
Express*

Hawk, William / B / Sutter; *Star
Express*
Hawkins, Benjamin T. / A /
Sutter
Haws, Alpheus / D / Hancock
Hendricks, William D. / D /
Hancock
Hendrickson, James / C / Higgins
Henrie, Daniel / D / California
until 1849
Hess, John W. (Emeline Bigler) /
E / Brown
Hewitt, Eli B. / A / Willis
Hickenlooper, William E. / A /
Volunteers
Hickmott, John / E / Hancock
Higgins, Alfred / D / Willis
Higgins, Nelson (Sarah
Blackman) / D / Higgins
Hinckley, Arza E. / B / Willis
Hirons, James P. (Mary Ann) / D
/ Brown
Hoagland, Lucas / D / Willis
Hoffeins, Jacob / B / Sutter
Holdaway, Shadrack / C /
Williams; Sutter
Holden, Elijah E. / A / Brown
Holmes, Jonathan H. / D /
Sutter; Holmes-Thompson
Holt, William / C / Sutter;
Holmes-Thompson
Hopkins, Charles A. / E / Brown
Hoskins, Henry / E / Brown
Howell, Thomas C. / E /
Hancock
Hoyt, Henry P. / A / Hancock;
Died in Sierra Nevada
Hoyt, Timothy S. / A / Sutter;
Ebenezer Brown
Hudson, Wilford H. / A / Sutter;
Holmes-Thompson
Hulet, Schuyler / A / Brown
Hulet, Sylvester / D / Kearny
Hunsaker, Abraham / D /
Hancock
Hunt, Gilbert / A / Higgins
Hunt, Jefferson (Celia Mounts,
Higgins; Matilda Nease,
Brown) / A / Hancock
Hunt, Marshall / A / Hancock
Hunter, Edward / B / Sutter

Hunter, Jesse D. (Lydia Edmonds, Died in San Diego) / B / Stayed in California

Hunter, William / B / Stayed in California

Huntington, Dimick B. (Fanny Maria Allen) / D / Higgins

Huntsman, Isaiah / B / Hancock

Hyde, William / B / Hancock

Ivie, Richard A. / A / Hancock

Ivie, Thomas C. / C / Kearny

Jackson, Charles A. / A / Brown

Jackson, Henry W. / D / Volunteers

Jacobs, Henry B. / E / Brown

Jacobs, Sanford / D / Sutter; *Star* Express

Jameson, Charles / E / Hancock

Johnson, Henry M. / A / Hancock

Johnson, Jarvis / C / Brown

Johnstun, Jesse W. / C / Willis

Johnstun, William J. / C / Sutter; Holmes-Thompson

Jones, David H. / B / Sutter

Jones, Nathaniel V. / D / Kearny

Judd, Hyram / E / Hancock

Judd, Zadock / E / Sutter; Holmes-Thompson

Karren, Thomas, III / E / Brown

Kelley, George / E / Sutter; Holmes-Thompson

Kelley, Milton (Malinda Allison) / E / Higgins; Died in Pueblo

Kelley, Nicholas (Sarah) / A / Higgins

Kelley, William / A / Sutter

Kenney, Loren E. / D / Brown

Keysor, Guy M. / B / Sutter; California until 1850

Kibby, James / A / Volunteers

King, John M. / B / Hancock

Kirk, Thomas / B / Hancock

Knapp, Albert / E / Williams; Ebenezer Brown

Lake, Barnabas / A / Brown

Lamb, Lisbon / D / Brown

Lance, William / E / Volunteers

Landers, Ebenezer / C / Kearny

Lane, Lewis / D / Hancock

Larson, Thurston / C / Brown

Laughlin, David S. / D / Brown

Lawson, John / B / Hancock

Layton, Christopher / C / Williams; Sutter; England; Salt Lake, 1852

Lemmon, James W. / A / Volunteers; Boyle

Lewis, Samuel / C / Sutter; Went with James Brown, Dec. 1847

Luddington, Elam (Mary Eliza Clark) / B / Brown.

Lytle, Andrew / E / Hancock

Maggard, Benjamin / C / Volunteers

Martin, Edward / C / Hancock

Martin, Jesse B. / B / Sutter; Holmes-Thompson

Maxwell, Maxie / A / Willis

Maxwell, William B. / D / Sutter

Mayfield, Benjamin F. / A / Volunteers

Mead, Orlando F. / C / Sutter; Ebenezer Brown

Mecham, Erastus D. / D / Willis

Merrill, Ferdinand / D / Hancock

Merrill, Philemon C. / B / Hancock

Mesick, Peter I. / D / Brown

Miles, Samuel, Jr. / B / Sutter

Miller, Daniel M. / E / Brown

Miller, Miles / E / Sutter; Holmes-Thompson

Moore, Calvin W. / C / Williams/Ebenezer Brown

Morris, Thomas / B / Volunteers

Moss, David / A / Sutter; Holmes-Thompson

Mount, Hiram B. / B / Volunteers

Mowrey, Harley W. / C / Higgins

Mowrey, John T. / C / Volunteers

Muir, William S. / A / Sutter; Holmes-Thompson

Murdock, John R. / B / Sutter

Murdock, Orrice C. / B / Sutter

Myers, Samuel / B / Volunteers

Myler, James / C / Hancock

McArthur, Henry M. / D / Hancock

McBride, Harlem / E / Volunteers

McCarty, Nelson / B / Hancock

McClelland, William C. / E /
Willis
McCord, Alexander / A /
Hancock
McCullough, Levi H. / C /
Hancock
Naegle, John C. / A / Volunteers;
Stayed in California
Noler, Christian / B / Volunteers
Nowlin, Jabez T. / C / Brown
Oakley, James E. / D / Brown
Olmstead, Hiram / C / Hancock
Oman, George W. / A / Hancock
Owen, James C. / D / Sutter
Owen, Robert / B / Hancock
Oyler, Melcher / A / Brown; Died
in Pueblo
Pace, James, / E / Hancock
Packard, Henry / A / Volunteers
Park, James P. (1) / B / Volunteers
Park, James P. (2) / B / Sutter;
Ebenezer Brown
Park, William A. / E / Brown
Pearson, Ephraim, Jr. / B / Sutter
Peck, Edwin M. / D / Volunteers;
Boyle
Peck, Isaac / C / Volunteers;
Boyle
Peck, Thorit / C / Volunteers
Perkins, David M. / C / Brown
Perkins, John / C / Brown; Died
in Pueblo
Perrin, Charles / A / Hancock
Pettegrew, David / E / Hancock
Pettegrew, James P. / D /
Hancock
Phelps, Alva / E / Died en route
to California
Pickup, George / C / Sutter;
Holmes-Thompson
Pierson, Ebenezer / A / Sutter
Pierson, Harmon D. / B / Brown
Pierson, Judson A. / C / Brown
Pixton, Robert / E / Sutter;
Holmes-Thompson
Porter, Sanford / E / Hancock
Prows, William C. / B / Sutter;
Ebenezer Brown
Pugmire, Jonathan, Jr. / E /
Brown
Pulsipher, David / C / Hancock

Rainey, David P. / B / Hancock
Rawson, Daniel B. / D / Sutter;
Star Express
Raymond, Alonzo P. / D /
Hancock
Reynolds, William F. / C / Kearny
Richards, Joseph W. / A / Brown;
Died in Pueblo
Richards, Peter F. / B /
Volunteers
Richardson, Thomas L. / E /
Willis
Richie, Benjamin W. / C /
Hancock
Richmond, Benjamin B. / C /
Willis
Richmond, William / D /
Hancock
Riser, John J. / C / Volunteers;
Boyle
Ritter, John / A / Volunteers
Roberts, Benjamin M. / D /
Brown
Roberts, Levi / E / Hancock
Robinson, William J. / D /
Hancock
Rogers, Samuel H. / B / Sutter;
Holmes-Thompson
Rosecrans, George W. / C /
Hancock
Rowe, Caratat C. / A / Brown
Rowe, William / D / Brown
Roylance, John / D / Sutter
Runyan, Levi / D / Volunteers
Rust, William W. / C / Willis
Sanders, Richard T. / E /
Hancock
Sanderson, Henry W. / D /
Brown
Sargent, Abel M. / D / Brown
Savage, Levi / D / Hancock
Scott, James A. / E / Brown; Died
in Pueblo
Scott, Leonard M. / E / Hancock
Sessions, John (Mary Emeline) /
A / Brown
Sessions, Richard / A / Hancock
Sessions, William B. / A /
Hancock
Sexton, George S. / A /
Volunteers

Sharp, Albert / D / Brown

Sharp, Norman (Martha Jane Sargent) / D / Higgins; Died en route to Pueblo

Shelton, Sebert C. (Elizabeth Trains) / D / Higgins

Shepherd, Marcus L. / A / Sutter; Shepherd

Shipley, Joseph / C / Willis

Shumway, Aurora / C / Volunteers

Shupe, Andrew J. / C / Brown.

Shupe, James W. (Sarah Coates Prunty) / C / Brown

Simmons, William A. / B / Sutter

Skeen, Joseph / E / Willis

Slater, Richard / E / Sutter; *Star* Express

Sly, James C. / B / Sutter; Holmes-Thompson

Smith, Albert / B / Hancock

Smith, Azariah / B / Sutter; Holmes-Thompson

Smith, David / E / Died in San Luis Rey

Smith, John G. / D / Brown

Smith, Lot / E / Volunteers

Smith, Milton / C / Brown; Died en route to Pueblo

Smith, Richard D. / C / Brown

Smith, Willard G. / D / Volunteers; Boyle

Spencer, William W. / D / Kearny

Spidle, John / E / Hancock

Sprague, Richard D. / C / Volunteers

Squires, William / C / Willis

St. John, Steven / E / Hancock

Standage, Henry / E / Hancock

Steele, George E. / A / Volunteers

Steele, Isaiah C. / A / Volunteers

Steele, John (Catherine Campbell) / D / Brown

Steers, Andrew J. / B / Volunteers

Stephens, Alexander / D / Holmes-Thompson

Stephens, Arnold / D / Brown; Died in Pueblo

Stephens, Roswell / E / With Lee to Council Bluffs; Pioneer company

Stevens, Lyman / B / Brown

Stewart, Benjamin F. / D / Willis

Stewart, James / D / Willis

Stewart, Robert B. / D / Hancock

Stillman, Clark / D / Brown

Stillman, Dexter / B / Brown

Stoddard, John R. / B / Sutter; Ebenezer Brown

Strong, William / E / Sutter; Holmes-Thompson

Study, David / B / Hancock

Swarthout, Hamilton / A / Hancock

Swarthout, Nathan / D / Hancock

Taggart, George W. / B / Hancock

Tanner, Albert M. / E / Hancock

Tanner, Myron / D / Brown

Taylor, Joseph A. / A / Kearny

Terrell, Joel J. / C / Brown

Thomas, Elijah / C / Sutter; Ebenezer Brown

Thomas, Hayward / D / Willis

Thomas, Nathan T. / C / Willis

Thompson, James L. / C / Hancock

Thompson, John C. / A / Hancock

Thompson, Miles J. / D / Volunteers

Thompson, Samuel / C / Sutter; Holmes-Thompson

Tindell, Solomon / C / Brown

Tippets, John H. / D / Willis; Council Bluffs; Pioneer company

Treat, Thomas W. / D / Sutter

Truman, Jacob M. / C / Sutter; Holmes-Thompson

Tubbs, William (Sophia) / D / Willis

Tuttle, Elanson / C / Kearny

Tuttle, Luther T. / D / Hancock

Twitchell, Anciel / D / Hancock

Tyler, Daniel / C / Hancock

Vradenburg, Adna / A / Hancock

Wade, Edward E. / C / Sutter

Wade, Moses / C / Hancock

Walker, Edwin / D / Volunteers

Walker, William H. / B / Brown

Watts, John S. / B / Volunteers

Weaver, Franklin / A / Sutter; Ebenezer Brown

Weaver, Miles / A / Sutter; Ebenezer Brown

Webb, Charles Y. / A / Kearny

Weir, Thomas / A / Sutter; Holmes-Thompson

Welch, Madison J. / C / Willis

West, Benjamin / E / Volunteers

Wheeler, Henry / C / Volunteers

Wheeler, John L. / B / Volunteers; Stayed in California

Wheeler, Merrill W. / A / Hancock

White, John S. / C / Sutter; Holmes-Thompson

White, Joseph / A / Hancock

White, Samuel S. / A / Sutter

Whiting, Almon / D / Brown

Whiting, Edmond W. / D / Brown

Whitney, Francis T. / D / Willis

Whitworth, Robert W. / E / Hancock

Wilcox, Edward / B / Sutter

Wilcox, Henry / B / Hancock

Wilcox, Matthew / C / Hancock

Wilkin, David (Isabella McNair) / C / Brown

Willes, Ira J. / B / Sutter; Holmes-Thompson

Willes, W. Sidney / B / Sutter; Holmes-Thompson

Willey, Jeremiah / A / Kearny

Williams, James V. / E / Volunteers

Williams, Thomas S. (Albina Merrill) / D / Brown

Willis, William W. / A / Willis

Wilson, Alfred G. / A / Sutter; Stayed in California

Wilson, George D. / E / Willis

Winn, Dennis W. / A / Hancock

Winters, Jacob / B / Volunteers

Wood, William / C / Sutter; Ebenezer Brown

Woodward, Francis S. / D / Sutter

Woodworth, Lysander / A / Willis

Woolsey, Thomas / E / Willis; Council Bluff; Pioneer company

Workman, Andrew J. / B / Volunteers; California until 1855

Workman, Oliver G. / B / Volunteers; Holmes-Thompson

Wright, Charles / B / Brown

Wright, Phineas R. / A / Sutter; Ebenezer Brown

Wriston, Isaac N. (a.k.a. Clifford, Isaac N.) / A / Willis

Wriston, John P. (a.k.a. Clifford, John P.) / A / Brown

Zabriskie, Jerome / B / Volunteers; Stayed in California

Appendix C

Men Who Reached California

Adair, G. Wesley
Alexander, Horace M.
Allen, Albern
Allen, Elijah
Allen, Ezra Hela
Allen, George A.
Allen, John
Allen, Rufus C.
Allred, James R.
Allred, Reddick N.
Averett, Elisha
Bailey, Addison
Bailey, James
Bailey, Jefferson
Barger, William
Barney, Walter, Sr.
Barrus, Ruel
Bates, Joseph W.
Beckstead, Gordon S.
Beckstead, Orin M.
Beddome, William
Beers, William
Bickmore, Gilbert
Bigler, Henry W.
Binley, John W.
Bliss, Robert S.
Borrowman, John
Boyd, George W.
Boyd, William W.
Boyle, Henry G.
Brackenbury, Benjamin B.
Brass, Benjamin
Brizzee, Henry W.

Bronson, Clinton D.
Browett, Daniel
Brown, Ebenezer
Brown, Edmond L.
Brown, Francis
Brown, James S.
Brown, John
Brown, William W.
Brownell, Russell G.
Bryant, John S.
Bulkley, Newman
Bunker, Edward
Bush, Richard
Bush, William
Butterfield, Jacob K.
Caldwell, Matthew
Calkins, Edwin R.
Calkins, Sylvanus
Callahan, Thomas W.
Campbell, Jonathan, Jr.
Campbell, Samuel
Canfield, Cyrus C.
Carter, Isaac P.
Casper, William W.
Casto, James
Catlin, George W.
Chapin, Samuel G.
Chase, Hiram B.
Cheney, Zacheus
Clark, Joseph
Clark, Joseph L.
Clark, Lorenzo
Clark, Riley G.
Clark, Samuel G.

Clawson, John R.
Clift, James
Clift, Robert
Cole, James B.
Collins, Robert H.
Colton, Philander
Condit, Jeptha S.
Coons, William A.
Coray, William
Covil, John Q.
Cox, Amos
Cox, Henderson
Cox, John
Curtis, Dorr P.
Curtis, Foster
Dalton, Henry S.
Davis, Daniel C.
Davis, Eleazer
Davis, Sterling
Davis, Walter L.
Day, Abraham
Dayton, Willard T.
Decker, Zachariah B.
Dennett, Daniel Q.
Dobson, Joseph
Dodge, Augustus E.
Donald, Neal
Douglas, James
Dunham, Albert
Dunn, Thomas J.
Dutcher, Thomas P.
Dyke, Simon
Dykes, George P.
Earl, James S.

Earl, Justice C.
Egbert, Robert C.
Elmer, Elijah
Evans, Israel
Evans, William
Ewell, John M.
Ewell, William F.
Fairbanks, Henry
Fatoute, Ezra
Fauney, Fredrick
Fellows, Hiram W.
Ferguson, James
Fife, John
Fifield, Levi J.
Finlay, Thomas B.
Fletcher, Philander
Follett, William A.
Follett, William T.
Forbush, Lorin E.
Forsgreen, John E.
Frazier, Thomas L.
Frost, Lafayette N.
Garner, William A.
Gibson, Thomas
Gilbert, John R.
Goodwin, Andrew
Gordon, Gilman
Green, Ephraim
Hancock, Charles B.
Hancock, George W.
Hancock, Levi W.
Hanks, Ephraim K.
Harmon, Ebenezer
Harmon, Lorenzo F.
Harmon, Oliver N.
Harris, Robert, Jr.
Harris, Silas
Harrison, Isaac
Hart, James S.
Haskell, George N.
Hatch, Meltiar
Hatch, Orin
Hawk, Nathan
Hawk, William
Hawkins, Benjamin
Haws, Alpheus
Hendricks, William D.
Henrie, Daniel
Hickenlooper, William E.
Hickmott, John
Hoffeins, Jacob

Holdaway, Shadrack
Holmes, Jonathan H.
Holt, William
Howell, Thomas C.
Hoyt, Henry P.
Hoyt, Timothy S.
Hudson, Wilford H.
Hulet, Sylvester
Hunsaker, Abraham
Hunt, Jefferson
Hunt, Marshall
Hunter, Edward
Hunter, Jessie D.
Hunter, William
Huntsman, Isaiah
Hyde, William
Ivie, Richard A.
Ivie, Thomas C.
Jackson, Henry W.
Jacobs, Sanford
Jameson, Charles
Johnson, Henry M.
Johnstun, William J.
Jones, David H.
Jones, Nathaniel V.
Judd, Hyrum
Judd, Zadock
Kelley, George
Kelley, William
Keysor, Guy M.
Kibby, James
King, John M.
Kirk, Thomas
Knapp, Albert
Lance, William
Landers, Ebenezer
Lane, Lewis
Lawson, John
Layton, Christopher
Lemmon, James W.
Lewis, Samuel
Lytle, Andrew
Maggard, Benjamin
Martin, Edward
Martin, Jesse B.
Maxwell, William B.
Mayfield, Benjamin F.
Mead, Orlando F.
Merrill, Ferdinand
Merrill, Philemon C.
Miles, Samuel, Jr.

Miller, Miles
Moore, Calvin W.
Morris, Thomas
Moss, David
Mount, Hiram B.
Mowrey, John T.
Muir, William S.
Murdock, John R.
Murdock, Orrice C.
Myers, Samuel
Myler, James
McArthur, Henry M.
McBride, Harlem
McCarty, Nelson
McCord, Alexander
McCullough, Levi H.
Naegle, John C.
Noler, Christian
Olmstead, Hiram
Oman, George W.
Owen, James C.
Owen, Robert
Pace, James
Packard, Henry
Park, James P., I
Park, James P., II
Pearson, Ephraim, Jr.
Peck, Edwin M.
Peck, Isaac
Peck, Thorit
Perrin, Charles
Pettegrew, David
Pettegrew, James P.
Pickup, George
Pierson, Ebenezer
Pixton, Robert
Porter, Sanford
Prows, William C.
Pulsipher, David
Rainey, David P.
Rawson, Daniel B.
Raymond, Alonzo P.
Reynolds, William F.
Richards, Peter F.
Richie, Benjamin W.
Richmond, William
Riser, John J.
Ritter, John
Roberts, Levi
Robinson, William J.
Rogers, Samuel H.

Rosecrans, George W.
Roylance, John
Runyan, Levi
Sanders, Richard T.
Savage, Levi
Scott, Leonard M.
Sessions, Richard
Sessions, William B.
Sexton, George S.
Shepherd, Marcus L.
Shumway, Aurora
Simmons, William A.
Slater, Richard
Sly, James C.
Smith, Albert
Smith, Azariah
Smith, David
Smith, Lot
Smith, Willard G.
Spencer, William W.
Spidle, John
Sprague, Richard D.
St. John, Stephen
Standage, Henry
Steele, George E.
Steele, Isaiah C.
Steers, Andrew J.

Stephens, Alexander
Stewart, Robert B.
Stoddard, John R.
Strong, William
Study, David
Swarthout, Hamilton
Swarthout, Nathan
Taggart, George W.
Tanner, Albert M.
Taylor, Joseph A.
Thomas, Elijah
Thompson, James L.
Thompson, John C.
Thompson, Miles J.
Thompson, Samuel
Treat, Thomas W.
Truman, Jacob M.
Tuttle, Elanson
Tuttle, Luther T.
Twitchell, Anciel
Tyler, Daniel
Vradenburg, Adna
Wade, Edward D.
Wade, Moses
Walker, Edwin
Watts, John S.
Weaver, Franklin

Weaver, Miles
Webb, Charles Y.
Weir, Thomas
West, Benjamin
Wheeler, Henry
Wheeler, John L.
Wheeler, Merrill W.
White, John S.
White, Joseph
White, Samuel S.
Whitworth, Robert W.
Wilcox, Edward
Wilcox, Henry
Wilcox, Matthew
Willes, Ira J.
Willes, W. Sidney
Willey, Jeremiah
Williams, James V.
Wilson, Alfred G.
Winn, Dennis W.
Winters, Jacob
Wood, William
Woodward, Francis S.
Workman, Andrew J.
Workman, Oliver G.
Wright, Phineas R.
Zabriskie, Jerome

Total Men to Reach California: 335

APPENDIX D

Hancock-Los Angeles Company

Following the pattern established previously for travel, this group of 223 men and one woman was divided into companies of two hundreds, four fifties, and twenty tens. Andrew Lytle and James Pace were captains of hundreds, while William Hyde, Daniel Tyler, Reddick Allred, and Jefferson Hunt commanded the fifties. It is impossible to identify these groups of fifty.

Jefferson Hunt took his company of fifty-one and went to San Francisco on the established coastal route, El Camino Real. After a short stay in San Francisco, he went to Sutter's Fort. The other three fifties went up California's central valleys to Sutter's Fort, where they met Jefferson Hunt and continued on together. This entire group leaving Los Angeles is referred to as the Hancock-Los Angeles company. It included one woman, Melissa Coray.

Adair, G. Wesley	Boyd, George W.	Chase, Hiram B.
Allen, Albern	Boyd, William W.	Cheney, Zacheus
Allen, Ezra H.	Brackenbury, Benjamin	Clark, Joseph
Allen, George A.	B.	Clark, Joseph L.
Allen, Rufus C.	Bronson, Clinton D.	Clark, Lorenzo
Allred, James R.	Browett, Daniel	Cole, James B.
Allred, Reddick N.	Brown, James S.	Collins, Robert H.
Averett, Elisha	Brown, John	Coons, William A.*
Bailey, James	Brownell, Russell G.	Coray, William and
Barger, William H.	Bunker, Edward	wife, Melissa Burton
Beckstead, Orin M.	Bush, Richard	Coray*
Beddome, William	Bush, William N.	Cox, Henderson
Beers, William	Butterfield, Jacob K.	Cox, John*
Bickmore, Gilbert	Calkins, Sylvanus	Curtis, Foster
Bigler, Henry W.	Campbell, Jonathan, Jr.	Dalton, Henry S.
Bliss, Robert S.	Campbell, Samuel	Davis, Eleazer
Borrowman, John (By	Casper, William W.	Davis, Sterling
boat to San	Casto, James	Davis, Walter L.
Francisco, rejoined	Catlin, George W.	Decker, Zachariah B.
at Sutter's Fort)	Chapin, Samuel G.	Dennett, Daniel Q.

*Went with Hunt fifty to Monterey and San Francisco.

294

Dobson, Joseph
Dodge, Augustus E.*
Douglas, James
Dunn, Thomas J.*
Dyke, Simon
Dykes, George P.
Egbert, Robert C.
Elmer, Elijah*
Evans, Israel
Ewell, John M.
Ewell, William F.
Fairbanks, Henry
Fauney, Fredrick
Ferguson, James*
Fife, John
Fifield, Levi J.
Finlay, Thomas B.
Follett, William A.
Follett, William T.
Forbush, Lorin E.
Forsgreen, John E.
Frazier, Thomas L.
Garner, William A.
Gibson, Thomas
Gilbert, John R.
Goodwin, Andrew
Green, Ephraim
Hancock, Charles B.
Hancock, George W.
Hancock, Levi W.
Hanks, Ephraim K.
Harris, Robert, Jr.
Harris, Silas
Haskell, George N.
Hatch, Meltair*
Hatch, Orin*
Hawk, Nathan
Hawk, William
Hawkins, Benjamin
Haws, Alpheus
Hendricks, William D.
Henrie, Daniel
Hickmott, John
Hoffeins, Jacob
Holmes, Jonathan H.
Holt, William
Howell, Thomas C.
Hoyt, Henry P.
Hoyt, Timothy S.
Hudson, Wilford H.
Hunsaker, Abraham H.

Hunt, Jefferson
Hunt, Marshall
Hunter, Edward
Huntsman, Isaiah
Hyde, William
Ivie, Richard A.
Jacobs, Sanford
Jameson, Charles
Johnson, Henry M.
Johnstun, William J.
Jones, David H.
Judd, Hyrum
Judd, Zadock*
Kelley, George
Kelley, William
Keysor, Guy M.
King, John M.
Kirk, Thomas
Lane, Lewis
Lawson, John
Lewis, Samuel
Lytle, Andrew
Martin, Edward
Martin, Jesse B
Maxwell, William B.
Mead, Orlando F.
Merrill, Ferdinand
Merrill, Philemon C.*
Miles, Samuel, Jr.
Miller, Miles
Moss, David
Muir, William S.
Murdock, John R.
Murdock, Orrice C.
Myler, James
McArthur, Henry
McCarty, Nelson
McCord, Alexander
McCullough, Levi H.
Olmstead, Hiram
Oman, George W.
Owen, James C.
Owen, Robert
Pace, James
Park, James, II (By boat
   to San Francisco,
   rejoined at Sutter's
   Fort)
Pearson, Ephraim, Jr.
Perrin, Charles
Pettegrew, David

Pettegrew, James P.
Pickup, George
Pierson, Ebenezer
Pixton, Robert
Porter, Sanford
Prows, William C.
Pulsipher, David
Rainey, David P.
Rawson, Daniel B.
Raymond, Alonzo P.
Richie, Benjamin W.
Richmond, William
Roberts, Levi
Robinson, William J.
Rogers, Samuel H.
Rosecrans, George W.
Roylance, John
Sanders, Richard T.
Savage, Levi
Scott, Leonard M.
Sessions, Richard
Sessions, William B.
Shepherd, Marcus L.
Simmons, William A.
Slater, Richard
Sly, James C.
Smith, Albert
Smith, Azariah
Spidle, John
St. John, Stephen
Standage, Henry
Stephens, Alexander
Stewart, Robert B.*
Stoddard, John R.
Strong, William
Study, David
Swarthout, Hamilton
Swarthout, Nathan
Taggart, George W.
Tanner, Albert M.
Thomas, Elijah
Thompson, James L.
Thompson, John C.
Thompson, Samuel*
Treat, Thomas W.*
Truman, Jacob M.
Tuttle, Luther T.
Twitchell, Anciel
Tyler, Daniel
Vradenburg, Adna
Wade, Edward D.

Wade, Moses
Weaver, Franklin
Weaver, Miles
Weir, Thomas
Wheeler, Merrill W.
White, John S.*
White, Joseph

White, Samuel S.
Whitworth, Robert W.
Wilcox, Edward
Wilcox, Henry
Wilcox, Matthew
Willes, Ira J.

Willes, W. Sidney
Wilson, Alfred G.
Winn, Dennis W.
Wood, William
Woodward, Francis S.
Wright, Phineas R.

Total Hancock-Los Angeles Company: 223

Appendix E

Hancock-Sierra Company

The Hancock-Sierra company went directly to Salt Lake Valley in 1847. They were the "half" who continued on after meeting James Brown.

Allen, Albern
Allen, George A.
Allen, Rufus C.
Allred, Reddick N.*
Averett, Elisha*
Beckstead, Orin M.
Beddome, William
Bickmore, Gilbert
Bliss, Robert S.*
Bronson, Clinton D.
Brown, John
Brownell, Russell G.
Bunker, Edward*
Bush, William
Calkins, Sylvanus
Campbell, Jonathan, Jr.
Casper, William W.
Casto, James
Catlin, George W.
Chase, Hiram B.
Clark, Joseph L.
Clark, Lorenzo
Cole, James B.
Davis, Eleazer
Davis, Sterling
Davis, Walter L.
Dodge, Augustus E.
Dyke, Simon

Dykes, George P.
Egbert, Robert C.
Ewell, John M.
Ewell, William F.
Fairbanks, Henry
Fauney, Fredrick
Fife, John
Finlay, Thomas B.
Forbush, Lorin E.
Forsgreen, John E.
Gilbert, John R.
Goodwin, Andrew
Hancock, Charles B.
Hancock, George W.
Hancock, Levi W.*
Hanks, Ephraim K.
Harris, Robert, Jr.*
Haskell, George N.*
Haws, Alpheus
Hendericks, William D.
Hickmott, John
Howell, Thomas C.
Hoyt, Henry (Died in
    Sierra Nevada)
Hunsaker, Abraham*
Hunt, Jefferson
Hunt, Marshall
Huntsman, Isaiah

Hyde, William*
Ivie, Richard A.
Jameson, Charles*
Johnson, Henry M.
Judd, Hyrum
King, John M.
Kirk, Thomas
Lane, Lewis
Lawson, John
Lytle, Andrew*
McArthur, Henry M.
McCarty, Nelson
McCord, Alexander
McCullough, Levi H.*
Martin, Edward
Merrill, Ferdinand
Merrill, Philemon C.
Murdock, John R.
Myler, James*
Olmstead, Hiram
Oman, George W.*
Owen, Robert
Pace, James*
Perrin, Charles
Pettegrew, David*
Pettegrew, James P.
Porter, Sanford
Pulsipher, David

---

*These are those names known of the thirty-two men who, after two days of rest in the Salt Lake Valley, continued on to Council Bluffs.

Rainey, David P.*
Raymond, Alonzo P.*
Richie, Benjamin W.
Richmond, William
Roberts, Levi*
Robinson, William J.
Rosecrans, George W.
St. John, Stephen
Sanders, Richard T.
Savage, Levi
Scott, Leonard M.
Sessions, Richard

Sessions, William B.
Smith, Albert
Spidle, John
Standage, Henry
Stewart, Robert B.
Study, David
Swarthout, Hamilton
Swarthout, Nathan
Taggart, George W.*
Tanner, Albert M.
Thompson, James L.
Thompson, John C.

Tuttle, Luther T.*
Twitchell, Anciel
Tyler, Daniel*
Vradenburg, Adna
Wade, Moses
Wheeler, Merrill W.
White, Joseph*
Whitworth, Robert W.
Wilcox, Henry
Wilcox, Matthew
Winn, Dennis W.

Total Hancock-Sierra Company: 118

Sutter's Workmen

When the Hancock-Los Angeles company left Sutter's Fort, a handful of men stayed behind to work for Sutter. When the company met James Brown in the Sierra Nevada, several diarists recorded that half continued and half returned, while others stated about a hundred went on and a hundred returned. Sutter's workmen are the men who returned. The names of Sutter's 105 workers were verified from Sutter's records and individual journals. By subtracting these known Sutter names from the Hancock-Los Angeles company, it is reasonable to assume that most of the remaining names belong in the Hancock-Sierra company. With Lytle and Pace having about fifty men traveling with each of them as they finally left California (chapter 8), and with Jefferson Hunt out in front with nine, these lists are close to complete.

Adair, G. Wesley
Allen, Ezra H.
Allred, James R.
Bailey, James
Barger, William H.
Beers, William
Bigler, Henry W.
Borrowman, John
Boyd, George W.
Boyd, William W.
Brackenbury, Benjamin B.
Browett, Daniel
Brown, James S.
Bush, Richard
Butterfield, Jacob E.
Campbell, Samuel
Chapin, Samuel G.
Cheney, Zacheus
Clark, Joseph
Collins, Robert H.
Coons, William A.
Coray, William and wife

Cox, Henderson
Cox, John
Curtis, Foster
Dalton, Henry S.
Decker, Zachariah B.
Dennett, Daniel Q.
Dobson, Joseph
Douglas, James
Dunn, Thomas J.
Elmer, Elijah
Evans, Israel
Ferguson, James
Fifield, Levi J.
Follett, William A.
Follett, William T.
Frazier, Thomas L.
Garner, William A.
Gibson, Thomas
Green, Ephraim
Harris, Silas
Hatch, Meltiar
Hatch, Orin
Hawk, Nathan

Hawk, William
Hawkins, Benjamin
Henrie, Daniel
Hoffeins, Jacob
Holmes, Jonathan H.
Holt, William
Hoyt, Timothy S.
Hudson, Wilford H.
Hunter, Edward
Jacobs, Sanford
Johnstun, William J.
Jones, David H.
Judd, Zadock
Kelley, George
Kelley, William
Keysor, Guy M.
Lewis, Samuel
Martin, Jesse B.
Maxwell, William B.
Mead, Orlando F.
Miles, Samuel, Jr.
Miller, Miles
Moss, David

Muir, William S.
Murdock, Orrice C.
Owen, James C.
Park, James, II
Pearson, Ephraim, Jr.
Pickup, George
Pierson, Ebenezer
Pixton, Robert
Prows, William C.
Rawson, Daniel B.
Rogers, Samuel H.
Roylance, John
Shepherd, Marcus L.

Simmons, William A.
Slater, Richard
Sly, James C.
Smith, Azariah
Stephens, Alexander
Stoddard, John R.
Strong, William
Thomas, Elijah
Thompson, Samuel
Treat, Thomas W.
Truman, Jacob M.
Wade, Edward D.

Weaver, Franklin
Weaver, Miles
Weir, Thomas
White, John S.
White, Samuel
Wilcox, Edward
Willes, Ira J.
Willes, W. Sidney
Wilson, Alfred G.
Wood, William
Woodward, Francis S.
Wright, Phineas R.

Total Sutter's Workmen: 105

Most of these men left in organized companies in the summer of 1848. Those identified with a company are named in chapter 11. How and when the rest left California is not known, but by 1857 few ex-soldiers were in California.

Remained in California

William W. Boyd, left 1851
William Coons, left after 1854
Zacheus Cheney, left 1857
Henry Dalton
Isaac Harrison, left 1857
Daniel Henrie, left 1849

Guy H. Keysor, left 1850
John L. Wheeler
Alfred Wilson
Alfred J. Workman, left 1855
Jerome Zabriskie, left 1849

APPENDIX G

Purchase of Sutter's Russian Cannon

The ex-soldiers of the battalion decided to buy two small, decorated brass parade cannon from Captain John Sutter to take to the leaders of the Mormon Church. The cannon had been left behind in Moscow as the defeated Napoleon fled during the winter of 1812–13. Later the cannon were brought to Fort Ross in northern California, the Russian fur trade outpost. Sutter purchased the cannon from the Russians, along with other supplies, when the Russians closed Fort Ross.

The two brass cannon, a four pounder and a six pounder, were put on runners and carried in a wagon by the Holmes-Thompson company to Great Salt Lake Valley. Daniel Browett acted as agent for the company in collecting the money and paying Sutter for the cannon. There is confusion as to how much Sutter received. Perhaps Browett had not collected all the money from his comrades and advanced some of his own gold to complete the sale (see chapter 11, September 21 and 23). Several diarists mentioned payment was in gold flakes. It is not known where the cannon are today.

J. D. Perkey*	25.00	Jonathan H. Holmes	10.00
Sanford Jacobs	5.60	William H. Johnstun	10.00
Samuel Brannan*	25.00	Jacob M. Truman	15.40
C. C. Smith*	12.50	John White	10.00
James C. Sly	10.00	Henderson Cox	6.00
Ezra H. Allen	10.00	Ephraim Pearson	5.00
Daniel Browett	10.00	Ephraim Green	10.00
Philo M. Behunin*	15.00	William Kelley	20.00
W. S. S. Willes	20.00	Robert Pixton	20.00
Wilford Hudson	20.00	John Cox	20.00
James S. Brown	10.00	William Strong	6.00
Alexander Stephens	10.00	Richard Bush	20.00
Samuel H. Rogers	10.00	George Pickup	10.00
Daniel Q. Dennett	10.00	John Eagar*	5.00
Israel Evans	10.00	Jesse B. Martin	10.00
Henry W. Bigler	5.00	Ebenezer Pierson	7.00
David Moss	10.00	George Kelley	5.00
Joseph Dobson	20.00	Azariah Smith	5.00
Francis S. Woodard	10.00	Thomas Weir	10.00
Samuel White	1.50	James Douglas	5.00

Wesley Adair	10.00	William Coray	5.00
James R. Allred	10.00	Miles Miller	5.00
Ira J. Willes	15.00	William Barger**	7.00
Total subscription	$512.00		

---

*These men were not members of the Mormon Battalion.

**Barger's name is in the file at Sutter's Fort. It is not on the list in Journal History, May 1848, page 3, HDC.

APPENDIX H

Military Documents

The first of these two military documents resulted in the formation of the Mormon Battalion and is taken from the Stephen W. Kearny Diary and Letter Book 1846–47, Missouri Historical Society, St. Louis. The second marked the completion of the battalion's march to the Pacific Ocean.

Colonel Stephen Kearny's Order to Captain James Allen

Head Quarters, Army of the West
Fort Leavenworth, June 19, 1846
Sir:

It is understood that there is a large body of Mormons who are desirous of emigrating to California, for the purpose of settling in that country, and I have, therefore, to direct that you will proceed to their camps and endeavor to raise from among them four or five companies of volunteers to join me in my expedition to that country, each company to consist of any number between 73 and 109; the officers of each company will be a captain, first lieutenant and second lieutenant, who will be elected by the privates and subject to your approval, and the captains then appoint the non- commissioned officers, also subject to your approval. The companies, upon being thus organized, will be mustered by you into the service of the United States, and from that day will commence to receive the pay, rations and other allowances given to the other infantry volunteers, each according to his rank. You will, upon mustering into the service the fourth company, be considered as having the rank, pay and emoluments of a lieutenant-colonel of infantry and are authorized to appoint an adjutant, sergeant-major and quartermaster-sergeant for the battalion.

The companies, after being organized, will be marched to this post where they will be armed and prepared for the field, after which they will, under your command, follow on my trail in the direction of Santa Fe, and where you will receive further orders from me.

You will, upon organizing the companies, require provisions, wagons, horses, mules, etc. You must purchase everything that is necessary and give the necessary drafts upon the quartermaster and commissary departments at this post, which drafts will be paid upon presentation.

You will have the Mormons distinctly to understand that I wish to have them as volunteers for twelve months, that they will be marched to California, receiving pay and allowances during the above time, and at its expiration they will be discharged, and allowed to retain, as their private property, the guns and accoutrements furnished to them at this post. Each company will be allowed four women as laundresses, who will travel with the company, receiving rations and other allowances given to the laundresses of our army.

With the foregoing conditions, which are hereby pledged to the Mormons, and which will be faithfully kept by me and other officers in behalf of the government of the United States, I cannot doubt but that you will, in a few days, be able to raise five hundred young and efficient men for this expedition.

	Very respectfully, your obedient servant,
To Captain James Allen	(Signed) S.F. Kearny
First, Regular Dragoons,	Colonel of First Dragoons Fort Leavenworth

On January 30, 1847, Lieutenant Colonel Cooke wrote the following statement in San Diego (from Cooke, *The Conquest of New Mexico and California in 1846–1848*). It was not read to the battalion until February 4 in San Luis Rey.

The Lieutenant Colonel commanding congratulates the Battalion on their safe arrival on the shore of the Pacific Ocean and the conclusion of their march of over 2000 miles. History may be searched in vain for an equal march of infantry. Half of it has been through a wilderness where nothing but savages and wild beasts are found. There, with almost hopeless labor we have dug wells, which the future traveler will enjoy. Without a guide who had traversed them, we have ventured into trackless tablelands where water was not found for several marches. With crowbar and pick and ax in hand, we have worked our way over the mountains, which seemed to defy aught save the wild goat, and hewed a passage through a chasm of living rock more narrow than our wagons. To bring these first wagons to the Pacific we have preserved the strength of our mules by herding them over large tracts which you have laboriously guarded without loss. Thus, marching half naked, and half fed, and living upon wild animals, we have discovered and made a road of great value to our country.

Arrived at the first settlement of California after a single day's rest, you cheerfully turned off from the route to this point of promised repose, to enter upon a campaign, and meet, as we supposed, the approach of an enemy; and this, too, without salt to season your sole subsistence of fresh meat. Lieut. A. J. Smith and George Stoneman, of the First Dragoons, have shared and given valuable aid in all these labors.

Thus, volunteers, you have exhibited some high and essential qualities of veterans. But much remains undone. Soon you will turn your attention to the drill, to system and order, to forms, also, which are all necessary to the soldier.

By order of Lt. Col. P. St. George Cooke
P. C. Merrill, Adjutant

Appendix I

Music and Poetry

Faced with incredible hardships and extreme conditions, the soldiers bolstered their spirits by debating, reciting poetry, singing songs, and dancing around the campfires at night. An unidentified soldier had tucked a fiddle in a captain's wagon as they left Council Bluffs. When the companies were all together, this fiddle was passed around during an evening. Different men played their favorite tunes, providing a wide variety in selection and style.

Songs frequently mentioned in the journals of the soldiers include "Jefferson's Liberty," "Over the River to Charley," "The Girl I Left Behind," "White Cockade," and "California March" (played often). Patriotic songs included "Star Spangled Banner," "Hail Columbia," and "Yankee Doodle." One song, "Jim Along Joe," was played by the fifers each morning as the men, who were ill, marched to the wagon of Dr. George Sanderson, the army physician.

At night fifes and mouth organs (and occasionally the fiddle if the companies were together) were brought out. They sang about going to the Pacific Ocean, favorite hymns or new songs made up along the way. Levi Hancock was prolific throughout the journey in writing both poems and songs, which he scattered throughout his journals. Azariah Smith, who was usually optimistic, wrote poems that told of his longing for family and home. As the Holmes-Thompson company neared Salt Lake Valley, several journalists recorded that Daniel Dennett composed and sang a song celebrating the end of the journey.

A few songs and poems are included to illustrate the soldiers' thoughts and feelings.

"The Desert Route"
Levi W. Hancock

While here beneath a sultry sky,
Our famished mules and cattle die;
Scarce aught but skin and bones remain
To feed poor soldiers on the plain.

Chorus: How hard, to starve and wear us out,
Upon this sandy, desert route.

We sometimes now for lack of bread,
Are less than quarter rations fed,
And soon expect, for all of meat,
Naught less than broke-down mules, to eat.
Now, half-starved oxen, over-drilled,
Too weak to draw, for beef are killed;
And gnawing hunger prompting men
To eat small entrails and the skin.

Our hardships reach their rough extremes,
When valiant men are roped with teams,
Hour after hour, and day by day,
To wear our strength and lives away.

The teams can hardly drag their loads
Along the hilly, sandy roads,
While trav'ling near the Rio Grande,
O'er hills and dales of heated sand.

We see some twenty men, or more,
With empty stomachs, and foot-sore,
Bound to one wagon, plodding on
Thro' sand, beneath a burning sun.

(When the officers weren't near, the men sang these two verses about Doctor
Sanderson in hushed tones:)

A Doctor, which the Government
Has furnished, proves a punishment!
At his rude call of "Jim Along Joe,"
The sick and halt to him must go.

Both night and morn, this call is heard;
Our indignation then is stirred,
And we sincerely wish in hell,
His arsenic and calomel. . . .

"Mormon Battalion Song"
Thomas Morris
(Written after arriving in Salt Lake Valley)

All hail the brave Battalion!
The noble, valiant band,
That went and served our country
With willing heart and hand.
Altho' we're called disloyal
By many a tongue and pen,
Our nation boasts no soldiers
So true as "Mormon" men.

O'er many a barren desert
Our weary feet have trod
To find, where, unmolested,
The Saints can worship God.
We've built up many cities—
We're building temples, too;
Which prove to all beholders
What "Mormon" hands can do.

We settled here in Utah,
Upon a sterile soil,
And by our faith and patience
And hard, unfliching toil,
And thro' the daily blessings
Our Father, God, bestows,
The once forbidding desert
Now blossoms as the rose.

What tho' the wicked hate us,
And 'gainst our rights contend;
And, through their vile aggressions,
Our brotherhood would rend!
The keys of truth and knowledge,
And power to us belong;
And we'll extend our borders
And make our bulwarks strong.

Our sons are growing mighty,
And they are spreading forth,
To multiply our numbers
And beautify the earth.
All hail, the brave Battalion!
The noble, valiant band,
That went and served our country
With willing heart and hand.

(Source: Tyler, *Concise History*, 375.)

Azariah Smith didn't get fancy with the name of his efforts. He simply titled it:

"Song"
(Composed when quartered in San Diego)

In forty-six we bade adieu
To loving friends and kindred too:
For one year's service, one and all
Enlisted at our country's call,
    In these hard times.

We onward marched until we gained
Fort Leavenworth, where we obtained

Our outfit—each a musket drew—
Canteen, knapsack, and money, too,
    In these hard times.

Our Colonel died—Smith took his place,
And marched us on at rapid pace;
O'er hills and plains, we had to go,
Through herds of deer and buffalo,
    In these hard times.

O'er mountains and through valleys too—
We town and villages went through;
Through forests dense, with mazes twined
Our tedious step we had to wind,
    In these hard times.

At length we came to Santa Fe,
As much fatigued as men could be;
With only ten days there to stay,
When orders came to march away,
    In these hard times.

Three days and twenty we march'd down
Rio Del Norte, past many a town;
Then changed our course—resolved to go
Across the mountains, high or low,
    In these hard times.

We found the mountains very high,
Our patience and our strength to try;
For, on half rations, day by day,
O'er mountain heights we made our way,
    In these hard times.

Some pushed the wagons up the hill,
Some drove the teams, some pack'd the mules,
Some stood on guard by night and day,
Lest haplessly our teams should stray,
    In these hard times.

We traveled twenty days or more,
Adown the Gila River's shore—
Crossed o'er the Colorado then,
And marched upon a sandy plain,
    In these hard times.

We thirsted much from day to day,
And mules were dying by the way,
When lo! to view, a glad scene burst,
Where all could quench our burning thirst,
    In these hard times.

We traveled on without delay,
And quartered at San Luis Rey;
We halted there some thirty days,
And now are quartered in this place,
    In these hard times.

A "Mormon" soldier band we are:
May our great Father's watchful care
In safety kindly guide our feet,
Till we, again, our friends shall meet,
    And have good times.

O yes, we trust to meet our friends
Where truth its light to all extends—
Where love prevails in every breast,
Throughout the province of the blest.
    And have good times.

Melissa Coray told her daughter and grandchildren she and Lydia Hunter sang church hymns and other favorites, such as "Lucy Long," as they walked along or rode in the Hunter wagon. A bond of friendship, forged under trial, existed among the men. Sylvester Hulet expressed it in this verse, extracted from his history:

"Friendship"

How sweet is friendship's cheering voice,
When far from kindred parted;
It makes the lonely breast rejoice,
Or cheers the gloomy-hearted.
Although in distant lands we roam,
Disconsolate and weary,
From old companions and from home,
In regions lone and dreary.

Then Friendship's sweet angelic sound
Can cheer those scenes of sorrow,
And joys more pure in them are found
Than wealth can buy or borrow.
If from celestial realms of Bliss
This principle we sever,
No happiness could there exist,
No heaven there . . . no never.

Robert Bliss, Company B, described July 4, 1847, in San Diego in his journal: "The day was spent with firing of cannons and small arms with suitable toasts. The inhabitants participated with us most cordially and on the whole it ended with no accident, but with the best of feelings with both soldiers and people. We have now received orders to march forthwith to the City of Angels to be there the 16th to receive our discharge." Bliss followed his journal entry with this poem. No title was given:

> A few days more and we shall go
> To see our wives and children too
> And friends so dear we've left below.
> To save the Church from overthrow.
> Our absence from them has been long
> But, oh, the time will soon be gone
> When we shall meet once more on earth
> And praise the God who gave us birth.

Azariah Smith noted that Sunday, May 23, 1847, was a "beautiful" day and "everything goes on very well, but still this is not a home to me." He wrote two poems in his journal that day. This is one:

> On the Pacific Ocean some thousand miles from home,
> Across the rocky mountains I had a cause to roam,
> Enlisting for a soldier and leave my native land,
> And with my friends and kindred I took the parting hand.
>
> Far from my dear Mother and Sisters I am,
> But by the grace of God I will see them again.
> And live in Zion's city most glorious to behold,
> Whose walls are made of jasper and streets of purest gold.
>
> With thanks and adoration to God forever more,
> And sing a song of Zion, the great I am adore,
> When the lamb and the Lion together shall lie down,
> Then Christ will be the standard and nations flock around.

(Source: Smith, *Gold Discovery Journal,* 84.)

"The Bull Fight on the San Pedro"
Levi W. Hancock

> Under command of Colonel Cooke,
> When passing down San Pedro's brook,
> Where cane-grass, growing rank and high,
> Was waving as the breeze pass'd by;
>
> There, as we gain'd ascending ground,
> Out from the grass, with fearful bound,
> a wild ferocious bull appear'd,
> And challeng'd fight, with horns uprear'd.
>
> "Stop, stop!" said one, "just see that brute!"
> "Hold!" was responded, "let me shoot."
> He flashed, but failed to fire the gun—Both stood
> their ground and would not run.
>
> The man exclaimed, "I want some meat,
> I think that bull will do to eat,"

And saying thus, again he shot
And fell'd the creature on the spot:

It soon arose to run away,
And then the guns began to play;
All hands at work—amid the roar,
The bull was dropp'd to rise no more.

But lo! it did not end the fight—
A furious herd rushed into sight,
And then the bulls and men around,
Seemed all resolved to stand their ground.

In nature's pasture, all unfenc'd,
A dreadful battle was commenc'd;
We knew we must ourselves defend,
And each, to others, aid extend.

The bulls with madden's fury raged—
The men a skillful warfare waged;
Tho' some, from danger, had to flee
And hide or clamber up a tree.

A bull at one man made a pass,
Who hid himself amid the grass,
And breathless lay until the brute
Pass'd him and took another shoot.

The bulls rushed on like unicorns,
And gored the mules with piercing horns,
As if the battleground to gain,
When men and mules should all be slain.

With brutal strength and iron will,
Poised on his horns with master skill,
A bull, one mule o'er mule did throw,
Then made the latter's entrails flow.

One bull was shot and when he fell,
A butcher ran his blood to spill,
The bull threw up his horns and caught
The butcher's cap upon the spot.

"Give up my cap!" exclaimed the man,
And chased the bull as on he ran;
The butcher beat, and with his knife
Cut the bull's throat and closed his life.

O, Cox, from one bull's horns was thrown
Ten feet in the air. When he came down,
A gaping flesh wound met his eye—
The vicious beast had gored his thigh.

The Colonel and his staff were there,
Mounted, and witnessing the war:
A bull, one hundred yards away,
Eyed Colonel Cooke as easy prey.

But Corp'ral Frost stood bravely by,
And watch's the bull with steady eye;
The brute approach'd near and more near,
But Frost betray'd no sign of fear.

The Colonel ordered him to run—
Unmov'd he stood with loaded gun;
The bull came up with daring tread,
When near his feet, Frost shot him dead.

Whatever cause, we did not know,
But something prompted them to go;
When all at once in frantic fright,
The bulls ran bellowing out of sight.

And when the fearful fight was o'er,
And sound of muskets heard no more,
At length a score of bulls were found,
And the mules dead upon the ground.

"Death of the Wolves"
Levi W. Hancock
(Written in memory of Elisha Smith's death and burial)

The Battalion encamped
    By the side of a grove,
Where the pure waters flowed
    From the mountains above.
Our brave hunters came in
    From the chase of wild bulls—
All around 'rose the din
    Of the howling of wolves.

When the guards were all placed
    On their outposts around,
The low hills and broad wastes
    Were alive with the sound,
Though the cold wind blew high
    Down the huge mountain shelves,
All was rife with the cry
    Of the ravenous wolves.

Thus we watched the last breath
    Of the teamster, who lay

In the cold grasp of death,
　　As his life wore away.
In deep anguish he moaned
　　As if mocking his pain,
When the dying man groaned
　　The wolves howled a refrain.

For it seem'd the wolves knew
　　There was death in our camp,
As their tones louder grew,
　　And more hurried their tramp,
While the dead lay within,
　　With our grief to the full,
O, how horrid a din
　　Was the howl of the wolves!

Then we dug a deep grave,
　　And we buried him there—
All alone by the grove—
　　Not a stone to tell where!
But we piled brush and wood
　　And burnt it over his grave,
For a cheat, to delude
　　Both the savage and the wolf.

'Twas a sad, doleful night!
　　We by sunrise, next day,
When the drums and the fifes
　　Had performed *reveille*—
When the teams were brought nigh,
　　And our baggage arranged,
One and all, bid *Good bye*,
　　To the grave and to the wolves.

James Scott was en route to Pueblo in the Brown sick detachment on October 31, 1846, when he wrote these few lines in his diary in typical Nineteenth Century prose:

Pass by, days of subjection to Gentile tyrants and let the oppressed Mormon soldier, who under unparallelled circumstances, voluntarily, for the sake & to obtain a resting place for his brethren, made a sacrifice of feelings of both body and Mind & yielded the inducements of worldly interests (at least for the present) to a sense of duty, feelings of love & to obtain far in the west a home for the Saints. Eight months more & we meet those for whom we suffered . . . & in connection with them raise our houses, cultivate our soil, live once more upon the good things of life, build our God a house & enjoy the sweets of Liberty undisturbed by mobs.

Scott, described as a "promising young man," died "of winter fever and liver complaint" after a brief illness in Pueblo on February 5, 1847. He did not get to enjoy the "sweets of liberty" he wrote about.

On the evening of September 22, 1848, a few days before reaching the Salt Lake Valley, members of the Holmes-Thompson company celebrated the near-end of their journey with a large common campfire. After supper the camp enjoyed singing songs, recalling events of the trail, and telling jokes on each other. Daniel Dennett composed a special song and sang it for his comrades that night. Although several journals mention Dennett's musical contribution, the song itself remained lost. Recently the Dennett family sent the author thirty-eight pages of his prose. No verses in the loose pages were identified as the song he sang. In the following verses Dennett tells of his trip to Salt Lake Valley with the Holmes-Thompson company. Several verses have been eliminated due to length, but this may be part of the song he sang:

A lengthy chain is formed to draw
In this year forty seven
It answers every link the law
We mean the law of heaven.

(At discharge, military authority ceased, and Levi Hancock became leader.)

It has drawn from the army all the strength
That ever yet was in it.
And now their foes can go their length
They never back can win it.

They send runners to our place
To try to win it back,
They have a fair and flattering face
But our confidence they lack.

(Refers to efforts to reenlist the battalion.)

Levi is the middle link
And Elisha the forward hook
So Levi keeps the chain from breaking
And Elisha ahead to look.

(Levi Hancock was leader as the company left Los Angeles. Elisha Averett and ten scouts were assigned to find the route.)

David he now forms the ring
He is a man of a good heart
And he would suffer almost anything
Before the chain should part.

(David Pettegrew)

Every tenth in strength now blends
And every fiftyeth higher
And on the hundreds much depends
But they've all been proved by fire.

(Organization when traveling: 100s, 50s, and 10s)

Levi now is in command,
He's a skillful navigator,
He can make any mountain or point of land
There are none among us greater.

(Levi Hancock)

The chain drawing over the mountains height
The two ends went over first
And before it could straighten out right
It by the center burst.

The hook and ring and middle link
And the largest links we had
Made up their minds quicker than you can think,
And left us sorry and sad.

(Refers to the meeting with
James Brown in the Sierra)

This chain of which we made such boast
Has made a dreadful break
One half has gone towards the coast
The other towards the lake.

(Half went to Salt Lake
Valley and half returned to
Sutter's Fort.)

The broken links are now in use
In dirt and wood & leather
From Sutter's Fort to Santa Cruz,
Exposed to the weather.

(Those who went back
were working for Sutter
and on many projects.)

Jonathan is now on hand
He is also David's brother.
He belongs to the mechanic band
And David was another.

(Jonathan Holmes was
leader after Browett was
murdered. Brother is a
common salutation among
Mormons.)

He is a man for love and peace
And anger does not cherish.
He likes to see good will increase
And all its opposites perish.

A Samuel we now can praise,
And he can for us plan.
For us weak ones he often prays,
And does all the good he can.

(Samuel Thompson,
captain of the fifty in the
Holmes-Thompson
company)

Addison now is in from [the] sea
And has joined us in our effort.
He likes to see all people free
And freedom in the fish port.

(Addison Pratt returned
from Hawaii and joined
the group. He was ill and
was assigned to fish until
he recovered.)

But if he takes a hook & line,
As others do around,
Out of one hundred he takes 99
A boss in him they have found.

Our mechanics now have left the shop
The forge is growing cold,
But we don't believe that they will stop
For trifles such as gold.

(The men working for
Sutter quit and began
looking for gold.)

The gold it has a power surprising,
It turns men out of their course
Instead of helping them when rising
It draws them down by force.

Our mechanics are now at work again
We can hear the anvil ring

(They began gathering and
getting ready for the trip to
Salt Lake Valley.)

Of the links they are forming a chain
And the iron to them we bring.

We've a train of wagons seventeen   (Description of Browett-
And animals four hundred   Holmes company)
And [forty-five] Mormons keen
Who have well the gold mine plundered.

This road is new and unexplored   (They took the first wagons
But we are the boys who can see it   over Carson Pass, building
Though lions through this way have roared   a new road.)
When they see the chain they flee it.

The chain has moved many stone   (They had to chisel rocks
The canyon much have raised.   to get wagons through.)
This chain can do so much alone
By strangers it is praised.

When this chain gets its full motion   (The Mormon Church will
Its links it will increase   grow.)
On every continent, isle and ocean
Will be here and there a piece.

We think ourselves quite lucky,   (They traveled over Carson
We missed monster Truckee   Pass to avoid crossing the
Its crossings are unlucky   Truckee River many
They [number twenty-seven].   times.)

They more for California have done
Than all the American Nation
Thirty mills have built, ready to run
They are now in operation.

Fremont's men they cannot shine,
For Hancock's men are better,
The former are governed by brandy and wine,
But wisdom governs the latter.

Old [Lilburn] Boggs thought when he came here   (Boggs was an old Mormon
To live in peace and plenty,   enemy from Missouri then
But now he is filled with dread & fear.   living in the Sacramento
For [Mormons] here, he has found twenty.   area.)

We are in the city of the blest,
We think to take a permanent rest.
From our foes both east & west
For now we are at home.

We congratulate all both great & small,
And would like every separate name to call,
But the curtain of night would on us fall
Before we accomplished this.

Notes

Introduction

1. Daniel Tyler, *A Concise History of the Mormon Battalion in the Mexican War, 1846–1848* (1881; 4th ed., Glorieta, N.Mex.: Rio Grande Press, 1988), 112.
2. Tyler, *Concise History,* 357.
3. Hosea Stout, *On the Mormon Frontier: The Diary of Hosea Stout,* ed. Juanita Brooks (Salt Lake City: University of Utah Press, 1964), 1:164.
4. Henry W. Bigler, Journal, July 15, 1846, Huntington Library, San Marino, Calif.
5. James Polk, *The Diary of James K. Polk during His Presidency, 1845 to 1848,* ed. Milo Milton Quaife (Chicago: A. C. McClurg, 1910), 1:205–6.
6. Leroy Hafen, W. Eugene Hollon, and Carl Coke Rister, *Western America: The Exploration, Settlement, and Development of the Region beyond the Mississippi* (Englewood Cliffs, N.J.: Prentice-Hall, 1970), 220.
7. William B. Ide brought his wife and eight children to California in 1845. Ide purchased part of a Mexican land grant, Rancho de la Barranca Colorada, on Highway 99, north of Red Bluff. His adobe home is a state historical monument, maintained by the Department of Beaches and Parks, State of California. Before coming west, Ide was the presiding elder of a branch of the Mormon Church in Sangamon County, Illinois. He was a delegate to the convention that nominated Joseph Smith, the Mormon prophet, as a candidate for the presidency of the United States. Ide was propelled to fame when he and other northern California settlers thought the Mexican authorities intended to drive out all Americans. These early settlers banded together to secure their land rights. They captured the pueblo Sonoma, north of San Francisco, and took the Mexican officials prisoners. They fashioned a flag, with a star and bear in its field, and raised it in the plaza June 14, 1846. The crudely fashioned flag gave their cause its name—Bear Flag Revolt. For the next twenty-five days Ide was president of the Republic of California before Lieutenant John C. Frémont, U.S. Army, arrived and flew the Stars and Stripes. The California-Oregon Trail crossed the Sacramento River near his adobe and he established a ferry in 1850. He was elected judge of Colusa County and held other civic positions before dying in 1852 at age 56. As far as can be determined the Ides were the first Mormons to arrive in California, two years before Brigham Young reached Salt Lake Valley in 1847.

8. On September 17, 1847, Santa Anna surrendered in Mexico City to Zachary Taylor. The Treaty of Guadalupe Hidalgo, which ended the war, was signed February 2, 1848. John F. Yurtinus, *A Ram in the Thicket: The Mormon Battalion in the Mexican War* (Ph.D. diss., Brigham Young University, 1975), 2:606.
9. Esther Brown Judd and Elva N. Judd, eds., "Reminiscences of Zadock Knapp Judd, Senior," n.d., 17.
10. Tyler, *Concise History*, 118.
11. Eugene Edward Campbell, *A History of the Church of Jesus Christ of Latter-day Saints in California, 1846–1946* (Ph.D. diss., University of Southern California, 1952), 70.
12. Tyler, *Concise History*, 354.
13. Journal History (hereafter JH), July 18, 1846, Archives, Historical Department, Church of Jesus Christ of Latter-day Saints, Salt Lake City.
14. William Coray, Journal, Nov. 11–16, 1846.
15. Tyler, *Concise History*, 146.
16. William Wood, Autobiography.
17. Although several wrote about this incident, the soldier's name was not recorded.
18. Philip St. George Cooke, *Conquest of New Mexico and California in 1846–1848* (1878; reprint, Glorieta, N.Mex.: Rio Grande Press, 1964), 91.
19. Henry Standage, Journal, November 17, 1846.
20. Brigham Young Papers, April 5, 1848, Archives, Historical Department, Church of Jesus Christ of Latter-day Saints, Salt Lake City (hereafter HDC).

CHAPTER ONE
The Enlistment

1. Mount Pisgah, located near present-day Talmadge, became a supply center, an assembly point, and a resting place for the exiles for several years. William Huntington was chosen to preside in Mount Pisgah while Brigham Young and other Mormon Church officials traveled between settlements to assist and to encourage the scattered church members. Wilford Woodruff, an apostle, was passing through Mount Pisgah when Allen arrived. Joseph Fielding Smith, *Essentials in Church History* (Salt Lake City: Deseret News Press, 1944), 271.
2. Frank A. Golder, *The March of the Mormon Battalion from Council Bluffs to California Taken from the Journal of Henry Standage* (New York: Century, 1928).
3. S. W. Kearny to J. Allen, June 19, 1846, Miscellaneous Papers, Mexican War, National Archives, Washington, D.C.
4. William Hyde, Private Journal of William Hyde, June 28, 1846, Brigham Young University, Provo.
5. Kate B. Carter, ed., *The Mormon Battalion, 1846–1848* (Salt Lake City: Daughters of Utah Pioneers, 1956), 134.
6. Norma B. Ricketts, *Melissa's Journey with the Mormon Battalion* (Salt Lake City: Daughters of Utah Pioneers, 1994), 12, 121.
7. George W. Taggart, Diaries, 1846–47, July 5, 1846.
8. Daniel B. Rawson, Family History, n.d., 9.
9. Henry G. Boyle, Autobiography and Diary, 1:13.

10. Heber C. Kimball motioned at the meeting in Council Bluffs that a battalion of five hundred men be raised in conformity with the requisition of the government. This motion was seconded by Elder Willard Richards and carried unanimously. Brigham Young, Letter to Saints in Mt. Pisgah, July 7, 1846, JH.

11. Brigham Young, Letter to Samuel Bent, Mt. Pisgah, July 7, 1846, JH.

12. When John Riser wrote his brief history in 1887, he stated he was not a member of the Mormon Church. However, as a young man he worked on the Nauvoo temple, received his endowments, was ordained a seventy, and went on a mission through Ohio with his brother, George. He did not accept the doctrine of polygamy, and several financial problems with members during his farming days around Fremont perhaps contributed to his 1887 statement.

    There may have been six non-members of the Mormon Church in the battalion. When Eli Dodson died in Pueblo, one diarist recorded he was not a member of the church. On August 18, Levi Hancock wrote he baptized Leonard Scott into the church. At least three others whose names were not given were "baptized for the first time." First-time baptisms are performed for those converting to the Mormon Church. Rebaptisms were also performed at the time of enlistment to renew covenants of the faith or for washing away sins. John J. Riser, History, March 18, 1887, Bancroft Library, Berkeley, Calif., 2.

13. B. H. Roberts, *The Mormon Battalion: Its History and Achievements* (Salt Lake City: Deseret Press, 1919), 19.

14. James Allen to Brigadier General Roger Jones, Fort Leavenworth, August 2, 1846, Miscellaneous Papers, Mexican War, National Archives, Washington, D.C.

15. Peter A. Sarpy was the government's licensed merchant. This trading post, eight miles south of Council Bluffs, located on the Missouri River, consisted of about twenty houses built of hewn logs that had been whitewashed on the outside. The soldiers were issued blankets at Sarpy's before they left. Most of the soldiers' supplies were obtained at Fort Leavenworth. Erwin C. Gudde, ed., *Bigler's Chronicle of the West: The Conquest of California, Discovery of Gold, and Mormon Settlement as Reflected in Henry William Bigler's Diaries* (Berkeley: University of California Press, 1962), 19.

16. Carter, ed., *Mormon Battalion*, 68.

17. This was a significant statement because it was the first time the officers learned the ultimate destination of the main body of the Mormon Church. Willard Richards, Journal, JH, July 19, 1846.

18. Thomas L. Kane, "The Mormons, A Discourse Delivered before the Historical Society of Pennsylvania," March 26, 1850.

19. Carter, ed., *Mormon Battalion*, 75.

20. Zacheus Cheney, Journal, July 20, 1846.

21. David Pettegrew, Journal, 1840–1860, Brigham Young University, Provo, 69.

22. John Steele, Diary of John Steele, July 17, 1846, Brigham Young University, Provo.

23. Abner Blackburn, Autobiography, Nevada State Historical Society, Reno, 5.

24. Henry W. Sanderson, Diary of Henry Weeks Sanderson, Brigham Young University, Provo, 37.

25. Levi Hancock, Journal, July 26, 1846.
26. William Coray, Journal, July 31, 1846. James Allen, Return for July 1846, Mormon Battalion, Mexican War Service Records, 1845–1848, National Archives, Washington, D.C. (hereafter MWSR).
27. Order No. 3, Head Quarters, Mormon Battalion, Council Bluffs, Iowa, July 16, 1846, quoted in Tyler, *A Concise History*, 127.
28. Ricketts, *Melissa's Journey*, 118.
29. John W. Hess, Autobiography, Brigham Young University, Provo.

CHAPTER TWO
Fort Leavenworth: Knapsacks and Muskets

1. Fort Leavenworth, near present Kansas City, is the oldest U.S. Army post west of the Mississippi River still in existence. It was founded on the Missouri River in 1827 by Colonel Henry Leavenworth, Third Infantry, to protect the Santa Fe Trail. Abner Blackburn, *Frontiersman: Abner Blackburn's Narrative,* ed. Will Bagley (Salt Lake City: University of Utah Press, 1992), 43.
2. The author located a typed copy of William Coray's journal in the summer of 1994. Because he wrote in greater detail than most of his contemporaries and because his journal has not previously been quoted extensively, it is used frequently in this work. The date of each quotation from Coray is the same as that for the events described in the text where the quotation appears, and therefore, the journal is not cited in notes hereafter.
3. Each company had a baggage wagon and the men placed their personal equipment in these wagons. On occasions as a matter of discipline, they were required to carry everything. As the journey progressed and as the animals grew weaker, the men were ordered to carry their outfits. Toward the end of the journey the baggage wagons were left behind.
4. Tyler, *Concise History*, 137.
5. The late arrivals evidently had been assigned to a company in Council Bluffs, since they went into different companies (not all into Company E, the last to be formed) and since the total number of men in each company did not change with these additions. A second roster count made August 31, 1846, a month after the first, was identical to the first record—496 men on company rosters—the number also recorded by William Coray. James Allen, Return for July 1846, and A. J. Smith, Return for August 1846, Mormon Battalion, MWSR.
6. The doctrine of plural marriage was not announced publicly until August 28, 1852, at a special conference in Salt Lake City. It had been practiced privately by selected Mormon leaders as it was taught to them in Nauvoo by Joseph Smith before his death. The fact Hunt took two wives on this journey is interesting because it was before the doctrine was announced publicly.
7. David Pettegrew, Journal, 1846–1860, August 9, 1846, Brigham Young University, Provo.
8. Thomas Dunn, Private Journal, August 9, 1846, Utah State Historical Society, Salt Lake City.
9. John Tippets, Journal, August 9, 1846, Merrill Library Special Collections, Utah State University, Logan.

10. Tyler, *Concise History*, 138.
11. The battalion began traveling on the Santa Fe Trail, an old established corridor for trade, from Missouri west. They followed the trail until they took the Cimarron Cutoff into Santa Fe.
12. John Steele, Diary, August 19, 1846.
13. Pettegrew, Journal, 70.
14. Levi Hancock was the only general authority of the Mormon Church in the battalion. He was one of seven members of the First Council of the Seventy. The actions of a few of the Mormon troops prompted Hancock to grasp for religious leadership in the battalion. From the time the men chose him as their spiritual leader, he urged them to stop drinking and swearing and to live good lives. This eventually produced an authority conflict between the church and the military—all Mormons— that split the battalion at times into rival factions. Whenever Brigham Young sent dispatches to the battalion, Young always addressed them to Jefferson Hunt as the senior officer. Eugene E. Campbell, "Authority Conflicts in the Mormon Battalion," *BYU Studies* 8 (Winter 1968): 127–42.
15. Hyde, Private Journal, August 20, 1846.
16. James Pace, 1847 Trail Diary, HDC.
17. Golder, ed., *Journal of Henry Standage*, 149. According to the teachings of the Book of Mormon, the Nephites were an early American people who were destroyed after a series of wars.
18. Elmer J. Carr, ed., *In Honorable Remembrance: The San Diego Master List of the Mormon Battalion* (San Diego: Mormon Battalion Visitors Center, 1972–78), 29. Mormon Battalion Files, HDC.
19. Pace, Trail Diary.
20. Hyde, Private Journal, August 26, 1846.
21. Thirty-eight-year-old James Allen was the first officer to die since the establishment of Fort Leavenworth in 1827. He was well liked by the Mormon soldiers. He was attached to the soldiers in his command and said after arriving in Fort Leavenworth that he had never commanded a finer or more orderly company. "Indeed, everyone here (ladies too) speak highly of this battalion." *St. Louis Morning Missouri Republican*, August 31, 1846.

   Lieutenants Samuel Gully and James Pace were at Fort Leavenworth with a detail of ten men to transport the staff wagons to the battalion and remained with Colonel Allen during his last night. Major Clifton Wharton, commander of the post, suggested James Pace return to Council Bluffs to inform Mormon leaders of Allen's death. Gully had quartermaster duties, so he did not go with Pace. Pace left immediately for Council Bluffs and Gully returned to the battalion.
22. Hyde, Private Journal, August 29, 1846.
23. In a letter dated October 17, 1846, written from Santa Fe, Jefferson Hunt wrote to Brigham Young and the Council of the Twelve Apostles, explaining why the command was transferred to Lt. Andrew J. Smith:

    Our commander [Smith], I have no doubt, would have acted well with us, had it not been for a bad influence which the doctor and pilot used with him. We had an opportunity of seeing two or three times the benefit derived from having him our commander. We had no provisions to last us more than half way to Santa Fe and should consequently have had to go on one fourth or one half rations, but he made a requisition on Col. Price and made him give us about 12 days rations. This Price would not have done for us under any consideration had we been alone. It is true we have had a forced and wearisome march; there was for the better part of the time, however, occasion for this, as we would soon be out of provisions and were now past the time Gen. Kearny had expected us at Santa Fe. We have, however, with much anxiety got thus far, and shall continue our journey under Lt. Col. Cooke. There are other matters which cannot all be included in this letter. I shall, therefore, write you another. In the mean time, I am your obedient servant, Jefferson Hunt.

Pauline Udall Smith, *Captain Jefferson Hunt of the Mormon Battalion* (Salt Lake City: Nicholas G. Morgan Sr. Foundation, 1958), 76.

24. Samuel Hollister Rogers, Journal, August 31, 1846.
25. Pettegrew, Journal, August 3, 1846.
26. Hyde, Private Journal, September 3, 1846.
27. Judd and Judd, "Reminiscences," 14.
28. Tyler, *Concise History*, 147.
29. Pawnee Rock was a well-known landmark for western travelers, many of whom wrote their names on the rock. Several Indian attacks had occurred in the vicinity. Extra guards were mounted while the battalion passed Pawnee Rock. It is located near Larned, Kansas.
30. Robert Bliss, "The Journal of Robert S. Bliss with the Mormon Battalion," *Utah Historical Quarterly* 4 (July–October 1931), 72.
31. Hancock, Journal, 6.
32. Tyler, *Concise History*, 147.
33. Francis Parkman became a well-known American historian. He was on an expedition on the Great Plains to recover his health when he saw the Mormon Battalion encampment at the Arkansas Crossing. His description revealed his attitude toward the Mormons and brought to life the activity of their camp. Francis Parkman, *The Oregon Trail: Sketches of Prairie and Rocky-Mountain Life* (New York: Modern Library), 348–49.
34. Henry Bigler, Diary of Henry W. Bigler, September 1, 1846, in Brigham Young, History of Brigham Young, HDC.
35. Samuel Gully to Brigham Young, September 17, 1846, Brigham Young Papers, HDC.
36. Henry Weeks Sanderson, Diary of Henry Weeks Sanderson, Brigham Young University, Provo, 38.
37. Blackburn, *Frontiersman*, 41.
38. James Scott, Diary, September 26, 1846.
39. Rabbit Ears or Rabbit Ear Mountain is located about two hundred miles from Santa Fe, near Seneca, New Mexico.
40. Steele, Diary, September 29, 1846. The Nephites are the principal people in the Book of Mormon.
41. John D. Lee, "Diary of the Mormon Battalion Mission: John D. Lee," ed. Juanita Brooks, *New Mexico Historical Review* 42 (July–October 1967): 191.
42. Two months before, in Las Vegas, Kearny had proclaimed New Mexico to be part of the United States. Smith, *Gold Discovery Journal*, 31n52.

43. Santa Fe, capital of New Mexico, was located at the junction of the Chihuahua Trail from Mexico, the Spanish Trail from California, and the Santa Fe Trail from Missouri. When the battalion passed through, Santa Fe was over two hundred years old and was the center of the Spanish civilization in the Southwest, with about three thousand residents.

Colonel Alexander W. Doniphan was an old friend of the Mormons. He commanded a regiment of the First Missouri Mounted Volunteers, who had marched from Fort Leavenworth with the Army of the West to conquer New Mexico. His regiment took part in the capture of Santa Fe on August 18, a few weeks before the battalion arrived.

44. George Rutledge Gibson, *Journal of a Soldier under Kearny and Doniphan 1846–47,* ed. Ralph F. Bisher (Glendale, Calif.: Arthur H. Clark, 1935), 3:250–251.

CHAPTER THREE
Santa Fe: Colonel Cooke Assumes Command

1. In 1837 when Missouri governor Lilburn W. Boggs demanded that the Mormons be exterminated or driven from the state of Missouri, Doniphan replied the order was illegal. As a militia commander Doniphan induced the Mormons to surrender their arms and leaders at the Battle of Crooked River. Once this was accomplished a superior officer ordered Doniphan to take Joseph Smith and other Mormon prisoners to the public square in Far West and shoot them. Doniphan's reply made him a steadfast friend of the Latter-day Saints: "It is cold-blooded murder. I will not obey your order. . . . if you execute these men, I will hold you responsible before an earthly tribunal, so help me God." He became a prominent Missouri lawyer, who tried to keep Missouri neutral during the Civil War. Gregory P. Maynard, "Alexander William Doniphan, the Forgotten Man from Missouri" (master's thesis, Brigham Young University, 1968). Smith, *Essentials in Church History,* 171, 241.

2. Colonel Philip St. George Cooke assumed command of the Mormon Battalion October 13, 1846. Born near Leesburg, Virginia, June 13, 1809, Cooke's roots ran deep in the aristocratic South's heritage. While Philip was a youngster, his father died and the family fortune vanished. As a result he applied to the new U.S. Military Academy at West Point, New York. Cooke graduated when he was eighteen years old and was commissioned as a brevet 2nd lieutenant of infantry. He reported for duty at Jefferson Barracks near St. Louis, Missouri. Prior to the battalion, Cooke served primarily on the Great Plains frontier. In 1829 he left Jefferson Barracks for Fort Leavenworth to serve Major Bennet Riley's expedition on the Santa Fe Trail. In the early 1830s, Cooke engaged in the Black Hawk War. Cooke secured an appointment as a 1st lieutenant in the elite First Dragoons. In 1843 Colonel Stephen W. Kearny chose him to escort the annual traders caravan along the Santa Fe Trail. Two years later he led a company of the First Dragoons over the Oregon Trail to the Souh Pass. By the outbreak of the Mexican War, Cooke was an experienced commander, highly respected by Kearny. He was the commander of Company K, First Dragoons, in Fort Crawford, Wiconsin, to keep a watchful eye on the Sioux. In order to implement a plan to

conquer Mexico, President James K. Polk ordered Kearny to capture New Mexico and California.

3. Cooke's Wagon Road connecting the Rio Grande with the Gila River was one of the battalion's foremost contributions to southwestern history. This 474-mile section from just south of Socorro followed the Rio Grande River to the Pima Villages on the Gila River north of Tucson. This section of road was pioneered for the most part by the Mormon Battalion under Cooke's direction. Although there were other, older trails in the region, none was adequate for the purpose of running a direct line between the two river valleys that could convey any large number of wagons. General Stephen W. Kearny's trail to the north was practical for mules, but not serviceable for wagons. A previously established Spanish trail linking El Paso with Janos, Fronteras, Santa Cruz, and Tucson not only ran too far south but entered the fortified garrison towns of Mexico's northern frontier.

When Cooke traveled to Santa Fe with Kearny before taking command of the battalion, he wrote about families traveling in carts with solid wooden wheels, drawn by oxen. Some of these carts had mattresses in them for the comfort of passengers, with blanket awnings. He also described families arriving at Santa Fe in primitive wagons, rough boxes on solid wooden wheels. This historic Gila River route was first opened in 1774 by Padre Francisco Garcés, Franciscan missionary and founder of Tucson. Juan Bautista de Anza, commander of the presidio at Tubac, also used this route. Cooke's command took the first modern-day wagons over these existing trails for about 250 miles.

The Mormon Battalion forged Cooke's Wagon Road generally north of Mexico's northern frontier towns, yet it lay south of the Apache strongholds. Although it crossed two trying deserts (the forty-mile desert to Lake Playas and the seventy-mile desert from the Santa Cruz River to the Gila River), well-equipped wagon trains could travel Cooke's Wagon Road successfully. It became a vital link in east-west communications, joining the major Mexican roads uniting Mexico City with Santa Fe and Tucson. The Gila River's southern tributaries were important for transportation and commerce. In 1853 the U.S. Senate ratified the Gadsden Purchase from Mexico for ten million dollars, which completed the modern geographical configuration of the United States. Cooke, *Conquest*, 65, 281. Azariah Smith, *Gold Discovery Journal of Azariah Smith*, ed. David Bigler (1990; reprint, Logan, Utah: Utah State University Press, 1996), 40, 59. George Ruhlen, "Kearny's Route from the Rio Grande to the Gila River," *New Mexico Historical Review* 2 (July 1957): 213–20.

4. Cooke, *Conquest*, 91, 92–93.
5. Orders No. 10. Headquarters Mormon Battalion, Santa Fe, October 15, 1846, Mormon Battalion Files, HDC.
6. Hess, Autobiography, 4.
7. Ibid.
8. Smith, *Gold Discovery Journal*, 41.
9. Tippets, Journal, October 15, 1846.
10. Leo J. Muir, *A Century of Mormon Activities in California* (Salt Lake City: Deseret News Press, n.d.), 17.
11. Roswell Stephens did not return to the battalion. He, Gully, Egan, and Lee arrived at Winter Quarters November 21. In the spring of 1847 he

was selected to go with the pioneer company and Brigham Young. Three weeks after arriving in Salt Lake Valley in July 1847, he returned to Winter Quarters with Brigham Young. He was appointed to help care for the families of men in the battalion. Two other battalion members were in this first pioneer company to enter Salt Lake Valley—Thomas Woolsey and John Tippets. Daughters of Utah Pioneers, *The First Company to Enter Salt Lake Valley* (Salt Lake City, 1993), 32.

12. Cooke, *Conquest*, 92–93.

13. Pauline Weaver was a French half-breed who had trapped the Gila River from its headwaters in New Mexico to its mouth at the Colorado River. Yurtinus, *A Ram in the Thicket*, 1:199. Dr. Stephen Foster, a native of Maine, was graduated from Yale College. He had practiced medicine in several states, including Missouri. He enlisted in Santa Fe in the Army of the West when the Mexican War broke out as an interpreter and translator. His pay was $475 per month and rations. He was twenty-six years old. Cooke recognized his talents and gave him several difficult assignments. He later became the first American mayor of Los Angeles.

Convinced that Cooke could not take wagons to San Diego, Kearny later sent Antoine Leroux to the Mormon Battalion with instructions to follow a more southerly route. Leroux served in the Ashley-Henry expedition to the headwaters of the Missouri River in 1822. He hunted in the San Juan Basin and the San Luis Valley. Leroux also spent several years trapping the Gila and Colorado Rivers. When the Mexican War started, he was a naturalized Mexican citizen but immediately joined the United States when General Kearny proclaimed New Mexico conquered. Unlike many of the mountain men, Leroux was both literate and wealthy. He was Kearny's guide during the march down the Rio Grande in late September. Smith, *Gold Discovery Journal*, 40–41.

14. Cooke, *Conquest*, 95.

15. Pettegrew, Journal, 75.

16. Albuquerque, founded in 1706, was named after New Mexico's twenty-eighth governor, the Duque de Albuquerque. The battalion crossed the river and followed the Chihuahua Trail. They met Captain John H. Burgwin, First Dragoons, and two mounted companies General Kearny had ordered to stay in New Mexico. Burgwin was wounded fatally in the uprising at Taos three months later when Colonel Price put down the revolt. Smith, *Gold Discovery Journal*, 44, n13.

17. Jean Baptiste Charbonneau was born February 11, 1804, to Touissant Charbonneau, a Frenchman, and his Indian wife, Sacajawea. He served as a guide and she as an interpreter for the Lewis and Clark Expedition, 1804–1806. Clark took a liking to the young boy and persuaded the Charbonneaus to let him educate him. When Baptiste was about six, his parents took him to Clark in St. Louis, where he was enrolled in a church academy and grew up as Clark's adopted son. At eight years he went to Germany, where he learned German, French, and Spanish and traveled in France, England, Germany, and North Africa. He returned to America in 1829 and became a mountain man for the American Fur Company for the next seventeen years. For the U.S. government he helped explore southern Colorado, New Mexico, northwest Texas, and Oklahoma, and guided parties along the Santa Fe Trail. When the Mexican War began, he was assigned as guide to Colonel Philip St.

George Cooke, commander of the battalion from Santa Fe to California. He died in 1866 en route to Montana, his birthplace.

18. Cooke, *Conquest,* 98.
19. During his travels with the battalion, Zemira Palmer acquired a taste for the burned bread his mother saved for him. He later stated he preferred burned bread to a piece of pie or cake.
20. Henry G. Boyle, Autobiography and Diary, Brigham Young University, Provo, 1:18.
21. Nelson Higgins had been ordered by Lieutenant Andrew J. Smith to take his detachment to Pueblo. Once the Higgins company reached Pueblo, Higgins was to return to the battalion. Failing to return was cause for court-martial.
22. Pettegrew, Journal, 76.
23. Hyde, Journal, November 4, 1846.
24. Guy M. Keysor, Journal, November 6, 1846.
25. Cooke, *Conquest,* 104.
26. Tippetts, Journal, November 9, 1846.
27. Hyde, Journal, November 10, 1846.
28. Sophia's husband, William Tubbs, a private in Company D, also was in Lieutenant Willis's sick detachment that wintered in Pueblo. There has been some confusion as to who was the fifth wife allowed to continue. This confusion may have been caused by a newspaper interview with Melissa Coray, not long before she died, when she incorrectly included the wife of Eleazer Davis. It is believed she meant to refer to Ebenezer Brown's wife. The similarity of the two first names—Eleazer and Ebenezer—may have confused Melissa seventy-five years later when she was interviewed. Or perhaps the reporter misunderstood what Melissa said. There is no record that Eleazer Davis's wife started with the battalion. Carr, ed., *In Honorable Remembrance,* 78.
29. Cooke, *Conquest,* 108.
30. Standage, Journal, 21.
31. Yurtinus, *A Ram in the Thicket,* 1:245. Margaret F. Maxwell, "The March of the Mormon Battalion, 1846" (unpublished MS, n.d.).
32. The location of Foster's Hole was unknown until it was found recently by Carmen and Omer Smith on the SS Ranch, owned by Michael Hall, in Sierra County, New Mexico. It was named after battalion guide Stephen Foster, who found it. Cooke wrote, "The water is about one hundred feet lower than the camp in a rocky chasm difficult of descent for animals; the chief supply is a natural rock-bound well thirty feet in diameter and twenty-four feet deep. It contains about fifty-five thousands gallons." Cooke directed the watering of the animals from a ledge above for two hours. The passageway to the water was so narrow the animals had to enter single file. Carmen Smith and Omer Smith, "The Lost Well of the Mormon Battalion Rediscovered," *Utah Historical Quarterly* 57, no. 3 (Summer 1989): 177–86.
33. Boyle, Autobiography, 1:30.
34. Samuel Rogers, Journal, November 17, 1846.
35. Cooke, *Conquest,* 127.
36. There may have been several black servants who served Lieutenant A. J. Smith and Dr. George Sanderson. Daniel Tyler wrote of "servants" on

one occasion. That is the only known reference to black servants other than this escapade between Nathan Young and the servant of Lieutenant Smith. Tyler was ill and had been to see Dr. Sanderson. He described the mixture of bayberry bark and camomile flowers given to each patient in the rusty spoon. Tyler said there was supposed to be a drop of brandy, furnished by the government, added to each spoonful. Since the Mormons received no brandy in their spoons, they "understood [it] was drank by the Doctor and Smith and their immediate associates, including their negro servants, who sometimes got rather tipsy." Tyler, *Concise History*, 150.

37. Rogers, Journal, November 23, 1846.
38. Boyle, Autobiography, 1:21.
39. Henry W. Bigler, Journal, November 31, 1846, Huntington Library, San Marino, Calif.
40. Rogers, Journal, December 1, 1846.
41. Ibid., December 2, 1846.
42. Boyle, Autobiography, 1:23.
43. Hyde, Journal, December 4, 1846.
44. Carl V. Larson, ed., *A Data Base of the Mormon Battalion* (Providence, Utah: Watkins and Sons, 1987), 26.
45. Tyler, *Concise History*, 218.
46. Gudde, ed., *Bigler's Chronicle*, 82.
47. Cooke, *Conquest*, 143–44.
48. Gudde, ed., *Bigler's Chronicle*, 33.
49. Cooke, *Conquest*, 148.
50. Ibid., 225.
51. Boyle, Autobiography, 1:26.
52. The Spaniards established a presidio at Tucson in 1776. As the result of a serious Indian uprising in 1802, the successful Mexican revolt (1821) against Spain, and another Indian uprising in 1821, almost all of the Arizona settlements and missions were abandoned. Cooke, *Conquest*, 147–51.
53. Layton family tradition states Private Christopher Layton, Company C, raised the old American flag that had flown over Nauvoo and under which the volunteers had been sworn into the Mormon Battalion in Council Bluffs. In Council Bluffs the flag was identified as the one from Nauvoo. After the battalion had left San Luis Rey, a torn, faded flag was found in one of the mission rooms. Since it is not known what happened to the Nauvoo flag after Council Bluffs, this may be the same flag.
54. Cooke, *Conquest*, 152.
55. Pettegrew, Journal, 82.
56. Boyle, Autobiography, 1:27.
57. This historic route was first opened in 1774 by Padre Francisco Garcés, Franciscan missionary and founder of Tucson, and Juan Bautista de Anza, who was the commander of the presidio at Tubac. In 1775 Colonel Anza led an espedition on this trail to the San Gabriel Mission near Los Angeles. He continued north to the San Francisco Bay, where he founded the presidio and Mission Delores in 1776 that became San Francisco.

CHAPTER FOUR
Pima and Maricopa Indian Villages

1. Later, when Captain William H. Emory, Corps of Topographical Engineers on General Kearny's staff, made a map with instruments that measured latitude and longitude, he determined Cooke's rude map covered 474 miles. Cooke's map was so accurate Emory called it "Colonel Cooke's wagon route" and incorporated it in the map he was preparing in Washington. Cooke, *Conquest*, 138.
2. Ibid., 162.
3. Pettegrew, Journal, 83.
4. Thirty soldiers later settled in Arizona: G. Wesley Adair, Reuben W. Allred, Henry G. Boyle, Henry W. Brizzee, James S. Brown, Edward Bunker, George P. Dykes, William A. Follett, Schuyler Hulet, John Hunt, Marshall Hunt, William Johnstun, Hyrum Judd, Zadock Judd, Christopher Layton, Samuel Lewis, William B. Maxwell, William C. McClelland, Philemon C. Merrill, James Pace, Wilson D. Pace, Sanford Porter, William S. Prows, David Pulsipher, Samuel H. Rogers, Henry Standage, George E. Steele, John Steele, Lot Smith, and Samuel Thompson. All contributed greatly to the colonization of Arizona. Maxwell, "The March of the Mormon Battalion, 1846," 17. Juanita Brooks, "The Mormon Battalion," *Arizona Highways* (May 1943): 42.
5. Carter, ed., *Mormon Battalion*, 102.
6. Cooke, *Conquest*, 163.
7. These petroglyphs cover less than an acre and are located fourteen miles west of Gila Bend, Arizona, in the Painted Rocks Historic Park.
8. William Money had gone to Sonora in 1837, where he married a Mexican wife. His Protestant religious views were not well received in the San Antonio de Oquitoa mission. The Moneys were on their way from California to Sonora, where her father lived. Money's information was the first time the battalion knew Samuel Brannan and 238 Mormons had sailed from New York in the ship *Brooklyn* around Cape Horn to San Francisco.
9. Cooke, *Conquest*, 205.
10. Pettegrew, Journal, 83.
11. Ibid., 85.
12. Carrizo Creek flows intermittently on the Southern Emigrant Trail. Cooke, *Conquest*, 67.
13. Boyle, Autobiography, 1:31.
14. Tyler, *Conquest*, 245.
15. Standage, Journal, January 18, 1847.
16. Warner's Ranch served a similar role to western immigrants on the Gila Trail as Sutter's Fort did for travelers on the California Trail. Both Warner and Sutter welcomed weary travelers and fed them. Cooke estimated Warner's Ranch to be 1,125 miles from Santa Fe. Jonathan T. Warner, born in Connecticut in 1807, joined the Smith-Jackson-Sublette trading expedition to Santa Fe and California in 1831. After Smith was killed by Comanches, Warner went to California and became a Mexican citizen. He changed his name to Juan Jose Warner and received a Mexican land grant of 49,000 acres. He married Anita Gaile and lived there for eleven years. He became a successful merchant in Los Angeles. He was familiar with the war situation and told

Cooke that Kearny had captured Los Angeles. He also told the battalion that Kearny was in a power struggle with John C. Frémont over who was to be governor of California. The Mormons arrived in California just in time for a confrontation between American military leaders over who was in charge of the newly occupied province. Joseph H. Hill, *The History of Warner's Ranch and Its Environs* (Los Angeles: privately printed, 1927).

17. Boyle, Autobiography, January 27, 1847.
18. Cooke, Journal, January 27, 1847.
19. Bliss, Journal, 86.
20. Nathaniel V. Jones, Journal, January 30, 1847, HDC.
21. Ibid., February 1, 1847.
22. Bliss, Journal, 86.
23. See official proclamation, Appendix K. Cooke, Order No. 1, January 30, 1847. Read to battalion in San Luis Rey February 4, 1847. Mormon Battalion Files, HDC.
24. Tyler, *Concise History*, 264.
25. Riser, History, 7.
26. Standage, Journal, February 6, 1847.
27. John Borrowman, Journal, 1846–1860, February 7, 1847.
28. Ibid., February 13, 1847.
29. Ibid., February 16, 1847.
30. Jones, Journal, February 18, 1847.
31. Borrowman, Journal, February 19, 1847.
32. Ibid., February 21, 1847.
33. Ibid., February 22, 1847.
34. Ibid., February 26, 1847. Borrowman erred when he wrote he was sentenced to *three* days of guard duty. The court-martial stated *six* days.

CHAPTER FIVE
San Diego: Company B Makes Friends

1. Bernard DeVoto, *The Year of Decision 1846* (Boston: Houghton Mifflin, 1942), 367–98.
2. General Stephen W. Kearny to Roger Jones, Los Angeles, January 17, 1847, Stephen W. Kearny Diary and Letter Book 1846–47, Missouri Historical Society, St. Louis.
3. Yurtinus, *A Ram in the Thicket*, 2:498.
4. Cooke, *Conquest*, 283.
5. Yurtinus, *A Ram in the Thicket*, 2:498.
6. Father Junípero Serra established the mission in San Diego in 1768 six miles up the San Diego River. It was the first in the chain of Spanish missions in California. Eventually there were 1,500 Christian Indians and a school, vineyards, gardens, and grazing lands. When the Mormons arrived, the mission, abandoned for many years, was dilapidated and full of debris and fleas. Company B camped near town at the foot of Presidio Hill. The settlement included a Mexican plaza, surrounded by a church, several stores, a few dozen adobe houses, and a population of several hundred Spanish natives and Americans. Theodore W. Fuller, *San Diego Originals* (Pleasant Hill, Calif.: Profiles Publications, 1987). Smith, *Gold Discovery Journal*, 74.

7. John S. Griffin, "A Doctor Comes to California: The Diary of John S. Griffin, Assistant Surgeon with Kearny's Dragoons. 1846–47," ed. George Walcott Ames Jr. *California Historical Society Quarterly* 22 (January 1943): 54.

8. The fort on Presidio Hill near San Diego had been occupied by several troops before the Mormon Battalion arrived. A Mexican fort was built over the ruins of the old presidio. When Captain Samuel F. Dupont, U.S. warsloop *Cyane,* put his men ashore to claim the fort during July 1846, he renamed it Fort Dupont. The California insurgents took over the fort and occupied it until November, when Commodore Stockton sent one hundred marines from his ship, the *Congress,* to recapture the fort. It was renamed Fort Stockton at that time, three months before the arrival of the battalion. Smith, *Gold Discovery Journal,* 80.

The Spanish established presidios, or garrisoned forts, in the 1700s at San Diego first, followed by Santa Barbara, Monterey, and San Francisco. The forts were weak defense against Indians and usually housed about eighty horsemen, some auxiliaries and small detachments of artillery. They consisted of a square enclosed with adobe walls with a chapel and a store. The Franciscan missions usually located near these garrisons. The Spanish government was overthrown by the Mexican revolution of 1822 and the missions began to decline in wealth and power by 1824. A decree for the expulsion of priests was enforced and by 1836 the fathers were stripped of their possessions and the missions sank into decline. Cooke, *Conquest,* 198.

9. Dunn, Private Journal, May 12, 1847.

10. Sheltering San Diego from the deep swells of the Pacific was a peninsula, five miles in length, named Point Loma, which enclosed San Diego bay on the west. Fort Rosecrans, located on the eastern slope of Point Loma, was established as a National Cemetery in 1852. Prior to this, it served as the burial place for soldiers and scouts who fell in the battle of San Pascal in 1846. Lydia Hunter was buried near these men. In 1905 a boiler exploded on the ship *Bennington,* killing more than half its crew of 179. For a short time following the disaster, the burial site was known as the Bennington Cemetery. Fort Rosecrans National Cemetery is under the jurisdiction of the Veterans Administration. Herbert Lockwood, "The Mormon Coal Mine," *The Western Explorer* (Cabrillo Historical Association, Point Loma, Calif.) 2, no. 3 (April 1964): 14.

11. A small group of Mormons lived at Haun's Mill, twelve miles east of Far West, Missouri. On the afternoon of October 29, 1838, the settlement was engaged in normal activites—men in the fields and shops, women attending to homes and children. Without warning, Captain William O. Jennings of the Missouri State Militia and a force of men attacked the settlers. When the attack was over, seventeen men were dead, many more were wounded, including women and children. Before they left, they robbed the houses, wagons, and tents, and stripped the bodies of the slain.

12. General Alexander Doniphan won a battle with the Spaniards and Indians December 25, 1846, at El Brazito, and a second one at the Pass of the Sacramento, fifteen miles from Chihuahua on February 28, 1847. Smith, *Gold Discovery Journal,* 54.

13. Bliss, Journal, June 1, 1847.

14. On September 17, 1847, Santa Anna surrendered at Mexico City to General Zachary Taylor. The Treaty of Guadalupe Hidalgo, which officially ended the war, was signed February 2, 1848. Yurtinus, *A Ram in the Thicket*, 2:606.

15. Cooke was relieved of duty as commander of the battalion at his own request. He returned to Fort Leavenworth with General Kearny and his escorts when they took John C. Frémont east for his court-martial. Colonel Jonathan D. Stevenson, New York politician, replaced Cooke on April 28 but did not go to San Diego until June 13. He and his regiment, the First New York Volunteers, arrived by boat from San Francisco.

16. Since the men were already members of other quorums, they formed the mass quorum in Los Angeles as a temporary organization to conduct church business. A seventy is one of the general officers of the Mormon Church, assigned to assist the First Presidency and the Quorum of Twelve Apostles.

17. Twenty-nine battalion veterans reenlisted at the request of Colonel Stevenson of the New York Volunteers. Others might have done so but felt he insulted them when he said:

    > Your patriotism and obedience to your officers have done much towards removing the prejudice of the government and the community at large, and I am satisfied that another year's service would place you on a level with other communities.

    Smith, *Essentials in Church History*, 431.

18. Carter, ed., *Mormon Battalion*, 92.

19. One of the most interesting jobs performed by Mormon soldiers in San Diego was working the coal mine on Point Loma in 1847. Although not too successful for the battalion men, the mine was quite an operation at its peak. The storage platform, which measured 511 feet by 462 feet, had a capacity of 50,000 tons of coal. The coaling tower, located on the fueling pier, had a capacity of 75 tons per hour. After naval vessels were converted from coal-burning to fuel-oil burning, the issuance of coal to naval vessels was discontinued. The last 12,000 tons of coal remaining at the depot were sold in November 1936. The adit was filled in 1962, but some traces of the mine can be found north of the Sewage Treatment Plant on Point Loma. Lockwood, "Mormon Coal Mine," 14–15.

CHAPTER SIX
Los Angeles: Building Fort Moore

1. Zadock Judd, Autobiography, 15.
2. Pettegrew, Journal, 93.
3. Dwight L. Clarke, *Stephen Watts Kearny, Soldier of the West* (Norman: University of Oklahoma Press, 1961), 303.
4. Cooke, *Conquest*, 295.
5. Stephen Clark Foster, *Los Angeles from '47 to '49* (Berkeley: H. H. Bancroft, University of California, 1877), 21.
6. The statement that Sylvester Hulet resigned from the army is confusing. One record indicates he wanted to return to his family and resigned. A short time later, Hulet was one of fifteen battalion soldiers chosen to go as escorts with General Kearny to take John C. Frémont to Fort

Leavenworth for court martial. Perhaps Hulet intended to resign but found he could stay in the army and serve as an escort while on his way back to his family. As an escort, Hulet still had his rank, obeyed orders, and participated actively with his battalion comrades in performing military duties. On July 19, 1847, Kearny's contingent met a group of Utah-bound emigrants. Hulet had family members with the emigrants and, since it was three days past his enlistment period, he asked for permission to go west with his relatives. His request was granted.

7. Rebecca M. Jones, "Life Sketch of Nathaniel V. Jones," *Utah Historical Quarterly* 4, no.1 (January 1931): 15.

8. See chapter 5, note 16.

9. Allen joined the battalion in Fort Leavenworth. His companions later thought he was not sincerely converted to Mormonism and was baptized only as a means to get to California. From the beginning he was undisciplined and a problem.

10. Yurtinus, *A Ram in the Thicket*, 2:500–4. Hafen, Hollon, and Rister, *Western America*, 220.

11. When Kearny began building the Army of the West at Fort Leavenworth, men from Missouri volunteered for duty on horseback. A mounted infantry battalion was added to Kearny's forces. Known as the First Missouri Mounted Volunteers, they served under Colonel Alexander W. Doniphan. Doniphan left Fort Leavenworth in June 1846, assigned to conquer New Mexico. The Second Regiment of Missouri Mounted Volunteers served under Colonel Sterling Price at Santa Fe and mounted an expedition in 1848 into northern Mexico during the closing days of the war. Price was openly antagonistic toward the Mormons on several occasions. The Mormons did not trust the Missouri volunteers because of their role in driving them from Missouri in 1838–39. On several occasions the Mormon soldiers prepared for a surprise attack. Polk, *The Diary of James K. Polk*, 1:443.

12. Standage, Journal, April 28, 1847.

13. Cooke, *Conquest*, 6.

14. Standage, Journal, May 2, 1847.

15. Tyler, *Concise History*, 282.

16. Boyle, Journal, June 1, 1847.

17. The early Californians enjoyed frequent festivals and religious holidays, many of which are no longer observed in the Catholic Church. Local Catholic authorities say the names of many of these early holidays have been lost.

18. J. H. Bonnycastle to Jefferson Hunt, Los Angeles, June 3, 1847, Mormon Battalion Files, HDC.

19. Standage, Journal, June 7, 1847.

20. Isaac Williams owned Rancho Santa Anna del Chino, forty miles east of Los Angeles. He offered to sell it to Jefferson Hunt in 1847 for five hundred dollars down, with payments for the balance. This was the land the Mormons later decided to purchase when Amasa Lyman, Charles C. Rich, and Jefferson Hunt were sent to establish a colony of five hundred Mormons in the area to aid travelers en route to the sea port. Williams withdrew his offer upon their arrival in California, leaving the Mormons with no place to settle. They subsequently purchased Rancho San Bernardino from the Lugo family. Blackburn, *Frontiersman*, 199.

Ephraim Green, *A Road from El Dorado: The 1848 Trail Journal of Ephraim Green*, ed. Will Bagley (Salt Lake City: Prairie Dog Press, 1991), 45.

21. George R. Stewart, *Ordeal by Hunger* (1936; reprint, New York: Houghton Mifflin, 1960).
22. Standage, Journal, June 18, 1847.
23. Ibid., June 19, 1847.
24. Ibid., June 24, 1847.
25. Pettegrew, Journal, 81.
26. Joseph Fielding Smith, *Essentials in Church History* (Salt Lake City: Deseret News Press, 1944), 431.

CHAPTER SEVEN
General Kearny's Escort to Fort Leavenworth

1. *The Church News*, September 23, 1989. Larry C. Porter, "From California to Council Bluffs," *Ensign*, August 1989, 42–46.
2. In his memoirs he wrote: "This gave me the best kind of opportunity for seeing the country, which was very sparsely populated indeed, except by a few families at the various missions. We had no wheeled vehicles, but packed our food and clothing on mules driven ahead, and we slept on the ground in the open air, the rainy season having passed." William Tecumseh Sherman, *Memoirs of General William T. Sherman* (New York: D. Appleton, 1875), 1:28.
3. Henry S. Turner, "Journal of Brig. Genl. S. W. Kearny's Return from California in the Summer of 1847," Kearny Papers, Missouri Historical Society, St. Louis, Mo.
4. Joshua S. Vincent, Diary, May 31, 1847, San Diego Historical Society, San Diego, Calif.
5. This was New Hope, the settlement Brannan planned for the Mormon Church when it reached California. He had assigned twenty men from the *Brooklyn* to build houses and plant crops.
6. C. C. Smith had come into California early in 1846. He later became a partner with Brannan in a store at Sutter's Fort called C. C. Smith and Company. Brannan was the "and Company." Smith was recognized by members of Brigham Young's company at Green River (Wyoming) as a former resident of Nauvoo. During the fall of 1848, Brannan bought Smith out for $50,000 and renamed the store "S. Brannan & Co." Brannan also opened stores up at Coloma and Mormon Island, which gave Brannan a monopoly on the gold rush trade. Samuel Brannan, "A Biographical Sketch Based on a Dictation," Bancroft Library, University of California, Berkeley, 6.
7. Edwin Bryant was a member of an 1846 migration across the Hastings Cutoff. He authored an excellent trail account of his trip. Edwin Bryant, *What I Saw in California, 1846–47* (New York: D. Appleton, 1849), 330–31.
8. Matthew Caldwell, Journal, June 22, 1847.
9. Robert Hoshide and Will Bagley, eds. "Sooter's Fort to Salt Lake Valley," *Crossroads Newsletter* 4, no.4 (Winter 1993): 6.
10. Sylvester Hulet, Biographical Sketch, n.d., University of Utah, Salt Lake City, 5.
11. Dan Talbot, *A Historical Guide to the Mormon Battalion and Butterfield Trail* (Tucson, Ariz.: Westernlore Press, 1992), 19.

12. Jones, Journal, August 4, 1847.
13. Ibid., August 7, 1847.
14. Ibid., August 22, 1847.
15. Porter, "From California to Council Bluffs," 45.
16. Ibid.

CHAPTER EIGHT
After Discharge

1. Standage, Journal, July 19, 1847.
2. Ricketts, *Melissa's Journey,* 79.
3. Bigler, Journal, August 7, 1847, 118.
4. Samuel Brannan was in charge of bringing 238 Mormons around Cape Horn, South America, in the ship *Brooklyn,* landing in Yerba Buena (San Francisco) July 31, 1846. Brannan sent twenty men and their families to the north bank of the Stanislaus River, at its junction with the San Joaquin River near present-day Stockton. The men built a log house and fenced and planted eighty acres. The venture was abandoned by October 1847 after Brannan returned from Green River (Wyoming) with Brigham Young's assurance the pioneers would not settle in California. Blackburn, *Frontiersman,* 104.
5. The letters they received in Los Angeles and San Diego, written before the pioneers left Iowa, had been en route for some time, and contained personal news.
6. Thomas Rhoades and his large family came to California in October 1846 in the Harlan-Young party and settled between Dry Creek and the Cosumnes River. He and his sons were very successful in the gold mines. After his wife died, he took their four youngest children to Utah in 1849. Records in the Gold Account of Brigham Young indicate Thomas deposited $10,826 upon his arrival. In return for his generosity he was given a choice lot near the Salt Lake Temple. Thomas became a polygamist, the first treasurer of Salt Lake County, and a representative in the first Utah Legislature. Two of Thomas' sons, John and Daniel, were in the first Donner Party rescue team. John made several more trips until the rescue was completed. Will Bagley and Robert Hoshide, eds., "The Last Crossing of the River: The 1847 William and James Pace Trail Diaries," *Crossroads Newsletter* 4, no. 2 (Spring 1993), 9. Norma B. Ricketts, *Historic Cosumnes and the Slough House Pioneer Cemetery* (Salt Lake City: Daughters of Utah Pioneers, 1978), 56.
7. Hoshide and Bagley, eds. "Sooter's Fort to Salt Lake Valley," 4.
8. Johnson's Ranch is located three miles east of present Wheatland. In June 1847 Johnson married Mary Murphy, a member of the ill-fated Donner party. Mary was very young and Johnson's Ranch was the first stop after getting out of the snow. After losing six members of her family in the snow, marrying Johnson might have seemed a solution to such a young woman. A few months later Mary left him and had the marriage annulled. She settled in Marysville, which was named for her. Her mother, Lavina Murphy, was a poor, fifty-year-old widow, originally from Tennessee. After she joined the Mormons, she moved to Missouri and then Nauvoo. When the church began its western exodus, she agreed to cook and wash for the Donner party as a means of getting her large

family west without help from the Mormon Church. The Murphy family included John Landrum, 15; Mary M., 13; Lemuel B., 12; William G., 11; and Simon P., 10. Two married daughters and their husbands were included: William M. Foster, ca. 28, and Sarah Murphy Foster, 23, and their son, George, about 4; William M. Pike, ca. 25, and Harriet Murphy Pike, ca. 21, and their two children, Naomi, 3, and Catherine, 1. All of her daughters survived. Both sons-in-law perished as did her grandchildren except for Naomi Pike, whom John Rhoades carried inside his coat next to his body on the way to Sutter's Fort to keep her from perishing. Lavina and her son, John L., also died, leaving seven survivors of a family of thirteen. Stewart, *Ordeal by Hunger*, 292. Jack Steed, *The Donner Party Rescue Site, Johnson's Ranch on Bear River* (Fresno, Calif.: Pioneer Publishing, 1988).

9. Bigler, Journal, August 29, 1847, H-18, 118.
10. William Coray became ill during the rainy days of January 1847 as the battalion approached San Diego. Coray died of consumption (tuberculosis) March 7, 1849, just four months after reaching Salt Lake Valley. Ricketts, *Melissa's Journey*, 100.
11. Hancock, Journal, September 2, 1847. Hoshide and Bagley, eds., "Sooter's Fort to Salt Lake Valley," 5.
12. Bagley and Hoshide, eds., "The William and James Pace Diaries," 9.
13. Details of Captain Brown's trip to California are in chapter 8, "Detached Service."
14. Andrew Jenson, "The Mormon Battalion," *The Historical Record* 8 (January 1888): 930.
15. Three weeks after Brigham Young and the Mormon pioneers arrived in the valley, two groups returned east to guide the waiting families westward. The arrival of the sick detachments of the battalion and the members from Mississippi increased the population of Salt Lake Valley to about 450 persons. Brigham Young returned in 1848 with more than two thousand people and four thousand animals. Stanley B. Kimball, *Historic Resource Study: Mormon Pioneer National Historic Trail* (Washington, D.C.: U.S. Department of Interior, National Park Service, 1991), 137. Hal Knight and Stanley B. Kimball, *111 Days to Zion* (Salt Lake City: Deseret Press, 1978), 206.
16. Albert Smith, Journal, September 7, 1847, California Room, California State Library, Sacramento.
17. Bagley and Hoshide, eds., "The William and James Pace Diaries," 9.
18. Pettegrew, Journal, September 17, 1847.
19. Carter, ed., *Mormon Battalion*, 92.
20. Jefferson Hunt had an added incentive to reach Salt Lake Valley when he learned from Captain James Brown that the sick detachments were there. His two wives and nine children traveled with the Pueblo group that arrived July 29, 1847, five days after Brigham Young and his company.
21. Stewart, *Ordeal by Hunger*, 141–49.
22. The early trappers called the Humboldt River Mary's River. The crossing west of its sink became known as the Forty-Mile Desert, located between the Truckee River near present Wadsworth and the place where the river is consumed by the desert. It was a torturous stretch with no water or grass except a sulfurous hot spring (Boiling Springs) about halfway. Smith, *Gold Discovery Journal*, 132.

23. Bliss, Journal, September 20, 1847.
24. Hastings Cutoff left the California Trail about 230 miles up the river from the Humboldt Sink, near present-day Elko, Nevada. Crossing the southern end of the Ruby Mountains, the cutoff turned northward, passed Pilot Peak and Donner Spring, and crossed the Great Salt Lake Desert, going southeast and around the south end of the Great Salt Lake. Lansford W. Hastings traveled over the Oregon Trail in 1842. In 1843 he went south from Oregon to California. Hastings learned about the cutoff from John C. Frémont's topographic surveying party, who had explored the south shore of the Great Salt Lake. In April 1846, Hastings, James Clyman, and James M. Hudspeth followed Frémont's tracks east across the Great Salt Lake Desert. They were hunting a shorter route to Fort Bridger. The ill-fated Donner party and others, including Thomas Rhoades with the Harlan-Young party, followed the cutoff west later in 1846.
25. The divide referred to appears to be the rim of the Great Basin between Thousand Springs Valley, north of Wells, Nevada, and the Humboldt River. Smith, *Gold Discovery Journal*, 142.
26. The junction of the California Trail and the Oregon Trail was south of Fort Hall, where the Raft and Snake Rivers meet.
27. Bagley and Hoshide, "The William and James Pace Diaries," 9.
28. Jenson, "The Mormon Battalion," 932.
29. Abraham Hunsaker, Journal, 60.
30. Ibid.
31. Tyler, *Concise History*, 385.
32. Carter, ed., *Mormon Battalion*, 105.

CHAPTER NINE
Monterey, San Francisco, and the Brooklyn

1. Coray, Journal, 57.
2. Judd, Autobiography, 47.
3. Paul D. Bailey, *Sam Brannan and the California Mormons* (Los Angeles: Westernlore Press, 1953), 97.
4. Knight and Kimball, *111 Days*, 133.
5. Mormons pay ten percent of their increase as tithes to the church.
6. Coray, Journal, 57.
7. Ibid.
8. Borrowman, Journal, October 24, 1847.
9. Francis A. Hammond, Autobiography.
10. The first baptism was a sailor named Beckwourth from the ship *Congress* by James Garner, Company B, in San Diego April 10, 1847.
11. Marriages between battalion men and *Brooklyn* women included the following: Zacheus Cheney married Mary Ann Fisher, who died January 1, 1851, in San Francisco. He married Amanda Evans January 10, 1853. They left California August 28, 1857, arriving in Salt Lake Valley November 3, 1857. William Coons and young Emerette Goodwin eloped to Washington Township, Santa Clara County, and were married November 4, 1852. Two children were born in Sacramento, the last in 1854. Franklin Weaver and Christina R. Reed were married March 12, 1848, by Addison Pratt. James Ferguson married Lucy Nutting March

12, 1848. Perhaps Addison Pratt also married the Fergusons since the wedding date is the same as the Weavers. William Squires courted a "widow" who lost her husband during the *Brooklyn* voyage. Since there were two widows whose husbands were buried at sea, both of whom went to Utah, it is believed the courtship was unsuccessful. Squires died in Sacramento of cholera in 1850. Isaac Harrison, who reenlisted in the Mormon Volunteers, married Catherine Smith sometime after 1855, the year of her husband Robert's death. Henry Dalton married Elizabeth Kittleman in March 1848 in San Francisco. They went to the gold fields in May and stayed until June 1849, when they went to Utah. Thomas W. Howell married Elizabeth Poole in 1856 in Utah. Henry Brizzee married Eliza Smith and they settled in Arizona.

12. Norma B. Ricketts, "The California Star Express," *Golden Notes* (Sacramento County Historical Society) 28, no.1 (Spring 1982): 5.

13. John A. Sutter, Sutter's Fort Record, 1848, April 7, 1848, Archives, California State Library, Sacramento.

14. Ricketts, "California Star Express," 9.

15. Ibid., 10.

16. J. S. Holliday, *The World Rushed In* (New York: Simon and Schuster, 1981), 45.

17. President Polk learned of the gold discovery from an official communiqué from Colonel Mason, governor of California, to the army adjutant general in Washington. Accompanying the written report was a tea caddy containing more than 230 ounces of gold. The report was carried to Washington by Lieutenant Loeser, who traveled eastward via the Isthmus of Panama and arrived in the capital December 7, 1848. A duplicate copy of Mason's report was sent overland and arrived in Washington November 22, 1848. It was on this duplicate copy that President Polk based his proclamation, delivered in an annual message to Congress on December 5, 1848. Two days later the arrival of the tea caddy full of gold confirmed that the president's report was correct. James D. Richardson, ed., *A Compilation of the Messages and Papers of the Presidents* (Washington, D.C.: Bureau of National Literature, 1911), 4:2486.

 An earlier report reached Washington about the discovery of gold. This was sent by Navy Commodore Thomas Catesby Jones to the secretary of state and secretary of the navy. Jones's report was carried by Lieutenant Edward Beale, who made an arduous crossing of Mexico from San Blas to Veracruz and arrived in Washington September 16, 1848. Beale also carried a small quantity of gold, some of which was put on public display in the U.S. Patent Office. A story about Beale's news was published in the Washington *Union* September 17, 1848.

18. Coray, Journal, 58.

19. William Glover, *The Mormons in California* (Los Angeles: Glen Dawson, 1954).

20. Zacheus Cheney and James Bailey commenced a kiln in April 1848. Cheney went to the gold fields, but Bailey had burned 50,000 bricks by June. Mervin Blanchard set up a blacksmith shop. James Harley, *Brooklyn*, and John Mowrey were boat builders and built several docks. Two in the east bay are named for them. William Evans opened a tailor shop on the corner of what is now Market Street and Van Ness Avenue.

They dug wells, repaired boats in the harbor, and generally used their skills all over the Bay Area. Other firsts included first jury trial, first colonists under the American flag, first school, first newspaper boy, first express wagon. The *Brooklyn* pioneers were the first Anglo-Americans to arrive by water. They established a ferry that served Fremont and San Francisco, and founded the Brooklyn township, which later was incorporated into the city of Oakland. The Mormon Temple in Oakland is in the original Brooklyn Township. They farmed at Mission San José, in southern Alameda County, and in other Bay Area locations. Angela Lovett was the first school teacher in San Francisco. Samuel Brannan owned considerable property in San Francisco and Sacramento and was California's first millionaire.

21. *Deseret News,* Salt Lake City, September 14, 1903.

CHAPTER TEN
Sutter's Workmen

1. Will Bagley, "Across the Snowy Mountain," (unpublished MS), 21, n72.
2. Robert Pixton, Family History, 7.
3. John A. Sutter, *New Helvetia Diary: A Record of Events Kept by John A. Sutter and His Clerks at New Helvetia, California* (San Francisco: Grabhorn Press, 1939), August 25, 1847.
4. Tyler, *Concise History,* 332.
5. Alan Beilharz, "Early Exploration," *Golden Flakes* (Gold Discovery Park Association, Coloma, Calif.) 6, no. 5 (Summer 1995).
6. Smith, *Gold Discovery Journal,* December 18, 1847.
7. Sutter, *New Helvetia Diary,* January 6, 1848.
8. Bigler, Journal, January 24, 1848.
9. Smith, *Gold Discovery Journal,* January 30, 1848.
10. Green, *Road from El Dorado,* 7.
11. Confusion exists about who found gold at Mormon Island first. Levi Fifield's name is sometimes identified as being with Sidney Willes and Wilford Hudson when they found the island. Fifield and Henry Bigler returned from Coloma to Fort Sutter on the road as recorded in Bigler's journal. Willes and Hudson walked along the river, and Fifield was not with them. After Sidney Willes and Hudson later showed the island to a few comrades, including Ephraim Green and Ira Willes, the names of Green and Ira Willes were included as discovering the site along with the first two men. It is correct to say that Green and Ira Willes were among the first to pan for gold on Mormon Island, but they did not make the initial sighting. At one time there were about two hundred Mormons on Mormon Island, including battalion members, men from the ship *Brooklyn,* as well as Thomas Rhoades and his sons. When Folsom Dam was built, Mormon Island was inundated. A marker, placed by the Daughters of Utah Pioneers, overlooks the site of Mormon Island.
12. Thomas Rhoades and his sons worked for a week, tossing their gold into a common pot. At the end of the week, each man received his share of $17,000.
13. Green, *Road from El Dorado,* ii.
14. Borrowman, Journal, May 18, 1848.

15. Ibid., May 19, 1848.
16. Shepherd and Hawkins discovered the rich placer at Negro Bar, across the south fork of the American River from Mormon Island.
17. Interview with Nathan Hawk, *Sacramento Bee,* January 4, 1906.
18. Azariah Smith, Journal, May 11–23, 1848, California Room, California State Library, Sacramento.
19. Campbell, "History of the Church," 133.
20. Ibid., 134.
21. Sutter, *New Helvetia Diary.*
22. Holliday, *The World Rushed In,* 37.
23. Rogers, Journal, 89.
24. Green, *Road from El Dorado,* 8.
25. Campbell, "History of the Church," 130.
26. Sutter, *New Helvetia Diary,* May 28, 1848.
27. Ibid.
28. These two brass cannon were decorated parade cannon, which Napoleon left behind when he fled Russia during the winter of 1912–13. When the state of California restored Fort Ross, an extensive search over several years was made to find them. The last battalion account places them in Salt Lake City in 1848. A general statement at a reunion in 1855 mentions bringing the cannon to Mormon Church authorities without giving any names involved. However, the cannon are not among the seven owned presently by the church.

    One may have been used, along with furniture, to fill a well. The second may have been a doorstop at a store in Utah for many years. In the 1970s, this store cannon was sold at a gun show in Reno, Nevada. An elderly gentleman said the cannon had been a doorstop in his family's store. He got about ten feet inside the gun show when the cannon was sold. During the next three months the cannon changed owners four times and skipped across the country to Michigan and then to Europe. Each time the cannon changed hands during this three-month period the price doubled. Because of the quick sales and the rapid increase in the selling price, this may well have been one of Napoleon's cannon.

    The cannon at the Temple Visitors Center in St. George, Utah, is not one of the cannon the battlion bought although many believe it is one of the Russian cannon simply because it came from California. The St. George cannon has historical significance since it was used due to its weight and durability as a pile driver in the marsh-like foundation of the St. George Temple.

    Norman Wilson, retired archeologist for the state of California, confirmed that the St. George cannon is not Napoleon's brass cannon, but is an iron naval cannon. He stated a brass cannon would not be strong enough nor heavy enough to be used as a pile driver. Sutter also referred to them as the "brass pieces."
29. Green, *Road from El Dorado,* 8.
30. Jonathan H. Holmes, Journal, July 19, 1848.
31. For many years this group was nameless; sometimes it was known as the Tragedy company, referring to the three men murdered at Tragedy Spring. In 1975, J. F. Yurtinus in his doctoral dissertation, referred to it as the Holmes company, following the pattern of the emigrant companies calling their companies after their leaders. It also has been referred

to as the Samuel Thompson company after Samuel Thompson, captain
of the four tens. Recently, it became the Browett-Holmes company,
named after its first leader, Daniel Browett, who was murdered, and
Jonathan Holmes, who succeeded Browett as president of the company
and saw the journey to completion. When men of this company applied
for land after arriving in Salt Lake Valley, they were listed as being with
Jonathan Holmes. This fact verifies that Yurtinus was correct in following the established policy of naming companies after their leaders.
However, in order to eliminate further confusion, historian Will Bagley
came up with a solution. By calling it the Holmes-Thompson company,
its identity is not lost in past or future research.

CHAPTER ELEVEN
Journey's End

1. Elijah Elmer, "Elijah Elmer Diary," ed. Will Bagley, *Crossroads Newsletter*
   4, no. 3 (Summer 1993): 5.
2. Green, *Road from El Dorado*, 17, 20.
3. Rogers, Journal, July 18, 1848. Ricketts, *Melissa's Journey,* 88.
4. Preston Nibley, *Faith Promoting Stories* (Salt Lake City: Deseret Book,
   1943), 93.
5. Holmes, Journal, July 19, 1848.
6. Norma B. Ricketts, *Tragedy Spring and the Pouch of Gold* (Sacramento:
   Ricketts Publishing, 1983), 22–25.
7. James Diamond traveled to Oregon in 1847, then sailed by ship to San
   Francisco. He was not a member of the Mormon Church when he traveled with the Holmes-Thompson company to Salt Lake Valley. Shortly
   after arriving in Utah he joined the church and settled in Manti in
   1849. He later moved to Springville, Utah, where he died in 1908.
8. Judd, Autobiography, 17.
9. Green, *Road from El Dorado*, 27.
10. Hazen Kimball served as a captain of ten in the company of one hun-
    dred led by Jedediah M. Grant, which arrived in Salt Lake October 2,
    1847. He became disaffected with the Mormon Church and took his
    family to California.
11. James Clyman, 56, was a noted frontiersman who had come to
    California as early as 1823. The Clyman company was the first group of
    emigrants going west to use the newly opened road over Carson Pass.
    Evelyn Van Noy, ed., "Autobiography of James Clyman" (typescript, n.p.,
    n.d.).
12. This group of 25 wagons may be the Pierre Barlow Cornwall train,
    which also followed the new Carson Pass route. Green, *Road from El
    Dorado*, 28. Smith, *Gold Discovery Journal,* 136, 140.
13. Green, *Road from El Dorado*, 31.
14. W. W. Riter, son of Levi Riter, wrote of his father's unsuccessful trip to
    California:
    > The goods my father shipped by the ship *Brooklyn* were of con-
    > siderable value in New York and of much great value in
    > California, so he decided to go and take possession of his
    > goods. . . . Other parties who had sent goods . . . made him their
    > agent to dispose of their goods . . . as he thought best. When he

arrived in San Francisco, he found Brannan had appropriated not only his property but that of others, for which he was agent. High prices prevailing enabled brannan to realize a very large sum of money from these illegally gooten goods . . . Brannan was drinking very heavily and could never be found in a condition to do business. There was no law in the country, which was passing from Mexican rule to American rule and it was a forlorn hope to get anything from him. My father went into Brannan's home and found he had taken largely from father's goods to furnish his house. Father took from the house what he could identify. . . . When he returned to Salt Lake he brought them with him.

Riter was successful in the gold fields. He returned to Utah in the spring of 1849 with a party of *Brooklyn* Saints and several members of the Mormon Battalion. Green, *Road from El Dorado*, 20.

15. Samuel Hensley's group of ten were the first to pack west over the Salt Lake Cutoff in August 1848. On Nevada's Humboldt River they encountered the discharged battalion members and told them of the new route. The battalion veterans took their wagons over the trail, converting it into a wagon road. Richard L. Rieck, "The Trails of the Gold Rush," *Overland Journal* 12, no.1 (1994): 31. Hoshide and Bagley, eds., "Sooter's Fort," 3.

16. Rogers, Journal, September 18, 1848.

17. The statement that a payment was due the widow of Daniel Browett for work he did "before he was murdered" is confusing. No reference has been found as to why money was due Browett. Rogers, Journal, September 21, 1848.

18. Addison Pratt, Journal, November 17, 1846, HDC.

19. Smith, *Gold Discovery Journal*, 146.

20. Green, *Road from El Dorado*, 15.

21. Rogers, July 18, 1848.

22. Lydia Hunter, the fourth woman, died shortly after arriving in San Diego. Susan Davis went the southern route along the Spanish Trail, through Las Vegas, and into Salt Lake Valley in 1848. Melissa Coray was with the Holmes-Thompson company.

23. Green, *Road to El Dorado*, 45.

24. Borrowman, Journal, August 26, 1848.

25. Carter, ed., *Mormon Battalion*, 75. Daughters of Utah Pioneers, "The Mormons in California," *Heart Throbs of the West* (Salt Lake City, 1946), 7:405.

26. For names and story of the Mormon Volunteers, see chapter 13.

27. History of Brigham Young, 1849, HDC, 144.

28. John S. Woodbury, Journal, August 27–28, 1857, Lorin K. Hansen Library, Fremont, Calif.

CHAPTER TWELVE
Detached Service

1. Included in the John Brown group of fourteen families were James and Mary Ann Smithson Harmon and (1) James Bartley Harmon, (2) Mary Eliza Harmon, left in Mississippi, (3) Sarah

Elizabeth Harmon, (4) Paralene America Harmon, (5) Josephine Smithson Harmon, (6) John Taylor Harmon, born in Pueblo April 6, 1847

William and Elizabeth Bankhead Mathews and (1) Mahalia Mathews, (2) Thomas Marion Mathews, (3) Jane Elizabeth Mathews, (4). John Lynn Mathews, (5) Ezekiel C. Mathews, (6) Marie Celeste Mathews, (7) Elvira Mathews, (8) Narcissa Mathews, (9) Benjamin Mathews, (10) Emma Louise Mathews, (11) Martha Roxanna Mathews, (12) Sina Adeline Mathews

Benjamin and Temperance Weeks Mathews and Mary Elizabeth Mathews plus two children

Allen Freeman and Letitia Holladay Smithson and (1) John Bartley Smithson, (2) Sarah Catherine Smithson, (3) James Davis Smithson, (4) Mary Emma Smithson

William Cox Smithson

George W. and Lorena Roberds Sparks

Absalom Porter and Sarah Ann Holladay Dowdle

George W. and Mary Ann Sparks Gibson and (1) Mary Denisia, married merchant in Santa Fe and did not continue west; (2) Lydia A. Gibson, married Gilbert Hunt, Pueblo; (3) Robert B. Gibson; (4) Frances Abigail Gibson; (5) William G. Gibson; (6) Laura Altha Gibson; (7) Moses Gibson; (8) Manomas Gibson; (9) Joseph Gibson

James A. Smithson (returned to Mississippi with Brown)

Six families not known

Lee, "Diary of the Mormon Battalion Mission," 188. Colorado Springs Colorado North Stake, *The Stone Rolls Forth: A History of the Church of Jesus Christ of Latter-day Saints in Southeastern Colorado, 1846–1986* (Bountiful, Utah: Horizon Publishers, 1988), 62, 68.

2.   Included in this group at Independence were thirteen adults with ten men, three women, and a number of children:

Robert and Elizabeth Brown Crow and (1) Harriet Crow, (2) Benjamin B. Crow,(3) Walter Hamilton Crow, (4) John McHenry Crow, (5) William Parks Crow, (6) Matilda Jane Crow, (7) Iravinda Exene Crow, (8) Iraminda Almarene Crow (Iravinda and Iraminda were twins), (9) Elizabeth Jane Crow

George W. and Marilla Jane Crow Therlkill and (1) Milton H. Therlkill, 3 years old, 1st death in Salt Lake Valley; (2) daughter born August 15, 1847, 2nd death in Salt Lake Valley

William D. and Margaret Jane Casteel Kartchner and Sara Emma, born August 17, 1846, in Pueblo, first child born to United States citizens in Colorado

And men without families: Archibald Little, James A. Chesney, Lewis B. Myers, Milton Howard Therlkill, James William Therlkill, and two others whose names are unknown

Knight and Kimball, *111 Days,* 133.

3.   John Brown, Journal, *Our Pioneer Heritage* (Salt Lake City: Daughters of Utah Pioneers, 1969), 2:428.

4.   Ibid., 427.

5.   Ibid.

6.   Ibid.

7. Ibid., 428.
8. Colorado Springs North Stake, *The Stone Rolls Forth*, 68.
9. Parkman, *The Oregon Trail*, 282.
10. Brown, Journal, September 1, 1846, p. 2430.
11. John S. Brown, "Pioneer Journeys: From Nauvoo, Illinois, to Pueblo, Colorado, in 1846, and over the Plains in 1847," *Improvement Era* (July 1910): 23.
12. Hancock, Journal, 1846–1847, September 13, 1846.
13. Carter, ed., *Mormon Battalion*, 117.
14. Ibid., 71.
15. Joel J. Terrell, Record, October 25, 1846.
16. Hess, Autobiography, 4.
17. Steele, Diary, November 7, 1846.
18. Tyler, *A Concise History*, 171,
19. George F. Ruxton, *Life in the Far West* (Edinburgh: W. Blackwood, 1849), 204.
20. Joseph W. Richards was a brother of future Mormon apostle Franklin D. Richards. LeRoy R. Hafen and Frank M. Young, "The Mormon Settlement at Pueblo, Colorado, during the Mexican War," *The Colorado Magazine* 9, no. 4 (July 1932): 136. According to *The Contributor* (Salt Lake City, 1880), 7:296–7:

> Franklin D. Richards, went to Pueblo in 1880 to find the grave of his brother, Joseph W. Richards. He brought a plan of the settlement and cemetery drawn by Caratat Rowe. With Lewis Conley, an old resident of Pueblo, Richards searched for the burial place. Richards wrote later: "We spared nothing which could assist us in the effort to find the burial places of our dead, but without avail. Every trace was obliterated. The earthly tabernacles of our friends had been deposited within the sound of the never-ceasing Arkansas [River]. Thrice during the long interval of time, which had elapsed since the melancholy event, the turbulent river had inundated the surrounding country, each time changing its channel and has carried away upon its raging bosom the habitations of death and life. No hillock of any kind now marks the last resting place of the Battalion boys who died in Pueblo. . . . The only result of this extra effort was to fully satisfy us that we had done everything in the matter which could be accomplished."

21. Hancock, Journal, November 10, 1846.
22. Tippets, Journal, November 16, 1846.
23. Carter, ed., *Mormon Battalion*, 53.
24. Tippets, Journal, November 26, 1846.
25. Blackburn, Autobiography, 7.
26. Ibid., 8.
27. Simeon Turley had a mill and distillery at Arroyo Hondo, twelve miles north of Taos. He was killed in the January 1847 rebellion at Taos. Blackburn, *Frontiersman*, 47, n.65.
28. Tippets, Journal, December 6, 1846.
29. Carter, ed., *Mormon Battalion*, 112.
29. William Walker Rust had graduated from medical school. He was assigned to Company C as assistant surgeon. He was kicked by a mule,

resulting in a serious injury and was assigned to the Willis detachment. Carter, ed., *Mormon Battalion,* 112.

30. George F. Ruxton, *Adventures in Mexico and the Rocky Mountains* (1847; reprint, Glorieta, N.Mex.: Rio Grande Press, 1973), 204.
31. Scott, Journal, December 21, 1846.
32. Thomas Bingham Jr., Biography of Thomas Sr. and Thomas Jr., 1824–1906, 4.
33. JH, December 23, 1846, and February 15, 1847. Woolsey and Tippetts arrived at Winter Quarters on February 15, 1847.
34. Sarah J. Brown Lowry, Statement, December 27, 1846, HDC.
35. Blackburn, Autobiography, 9.
36. Ruxton, *Adventures,* 162.
37. Letters, Mormon Battalion Files, HDC.
38. *St. Louis Daily New Era,* March 19, 1847.
39. Six children were born and two infants died in the Mormon Battalion group during the winter in Pueblo: (1) Betsy Prescinda Huntington, born October 21, 1846; died November 4, 1846; parents: Dimick B. and Fanny Maria Huntington. (2) Sarah Ellen Sharp, born November 28, 1846; parents: Norman and Martha Jane Sargent Sharp. (3) Phoebe Williams, born January 15, 1847; parents: Thomas Stephen and Albina Merrill Williams. (4) Malinda Catherine Kelley, born February 7, 1847; parents: Milton and Malinda Allison Kelley. (5) Elizabeth Margaret Shupe, born March 2, 1847; parents: James W. and Sarah Prunty Shupe. (6) Wealtha M. Higgins, born May 2, 1847; parents: Nelson and Sarah Blackburn Higgins. On January 1, 1847, Parley Hunt, eighteen-month-old twin son of Jefferson and Celia Mounts Hunt, died.

There were two known births in Pueblo in the Mississippi group: (1) Sara Emma Kartchner, born August 17, 1846, the first child born in Colorado of American citizens; parents: William D. and Margaret Casteel Kartchner. (2) John Taylor Harmon, born April 6, 1847; parents: James and Mary Ann Smithson Harmon.
40. Richards, Journal, July 18, 1846.
41. Steele, Diary, December 24–27, 1846.
42. John D. Lee, *Journals of John D. Lee 1846–47 and 1859,* ed. Charles Kelly (Salt Lake City: Western Printing, 1938), 117.
43. James Brown to Brigham Young, Pueblo, December 27, 1846, Brigham Young Papers, HDC.
44. Steele, Diary, January 13, 1847.
45. Ibid., January 14, 1847.
46. George Wilson, Journal, February 6, 1847.
47. Steele, Diary, February 5, 1847.
48. Ibid., March 18, 1847.
49. Ibid.
50. Steele, Diary, March 20, 1847.
51. Daughters of Utah Pioneers, *Our Pioneer Heritage,* 2:442.
52. Steele, Diary, April 9, 1847.
53. Ibid., May 18, 1847.
54. Knight and Kimball, *111 Days,* 206.
55. Howard Egan, *Pioneering the West, 1846–1878: Major Howard Egan's Diary,* ed. W. E. Egan (private printing, 1917), 67. William Clayton, Journal, 207.

56. Hafen and Young, "The Mormon Settlement," 134.
57. Joseph Skeen, Reminiscences and Diary, HDC.
58. Wilson, Journal, April 6, 1847.
59. Daughters of Utah Pioneers, *Our Pioneer Heritage*, 2:443.
60. Steele, Diary, June 13, 1847.
61. Amasa Lyman to Brigham Young, June 16, 1847, Amasa Lyman, *History of Amasa Mason Lyman Family* (Delta, Utah: Melvin A. Lyman, 1957), 1:170.
62. Terrell, Record, June 20, 1847.
63. Knight and Kimball, *111 Days,* 209.
64. Heber C. Kimball, Diary, July 4, 1847, HDC.
65. Blackburn, Autobiography, 9.
66. Ibid., 9.
67. Steele, Diary, July 16, 1847.
68. Blackburn, Autobiography, 9.
69. Ibid., 10.
70. Thomas Bullock, Journal, July 29, 1847, HDC.
71. There were 157 persons in the pioneer company that arrived July 24: 152 men, 3 women, and 2 children. The arrival of the 140 battalion soldiers and families (29 women, 46 children) and 42 men and women, plus an unknown number of children of Mississippi Saints increased the valley's population to about 450 persons. Brigham Young was concerned for the Mormons still scattered in Iowa and took two groups back east within a month after arriving in the valley. On August 16, 71 men left Salt Lake Valley and on August 26, 108 men departed for the East, including Young and Heber C. Kimball. This left approximately 113 men, 50 women, and less than 100 children in the valley. Since only 3 women and 2 children came in the pioneer company, these figures illustrate the important role of the battalion detachments and the Mississippi Saints during those first months in the Salt Lake Valley. They were left to plant crops and build homes and a fort, all with very little food of their own. Their numbers were increased by late September and early October when 1,500 persons with 556 wagons reached the valley. This group was known as the big company. Brigham Young and other leaders returned with 2,000 Mormons in 1848.

    Joseph Fielding Smith (*Essentials in Church History,* 455) commented on the three groups of women in the valley at this time:

    > It is quite generally understood that there were three women who entered the Salt Lake Valley with the pioneers . . . July, 1847. The fact has been overlooked by many that there were other noble women besides these three who . . . braved the dangers and hardships of the journey to the west. Among the Mississippi Saints . . . were: Elizabeth Crow, Harriet Crow, Elizabeth J. Crow, Iravinda E. Crow, Irmaninda A. Crow, and Marilla Jane Therlkill.

    There were probably eighteen women among the Mississippi Saints, whose names are not all known. They and the twenty-nine battalion women have been largely unrecognized as pioneers of 1847. Knight and Kimball, "Epilogue," *111 Days;* Smith, *Essentials in Church History,* 455.
72. Bagley and Hoshide, "William and James Pace Diaries," 4.
73. Steele, Diary, 2.

74. The names listed here are confirmed by historian Will Bagley. All but John S. Fowler were battalion members. Fowler's wife and children were in California, having sailed there on the ship *Brooklyn*. Quite a number from the Pueblo detachments showed up in California about this same time: Ebenezer Hanks, Thomas Williams, Edward Dalton, Montgomery Button, Samuel G. Clark, Benjamin F. Stewart, Daniel Miller, Sebert Shelton, James Oakley, M. James Welch, and Richard D. Smith. How and when these men reached California is not known.

75. Roberts, *Mormon Battalion*, 61.

76. Smith, *Gold Discovery Journal*, 145.

77. Blackburn, *Frontiersman*, 112.

78. Ibid., 118.

79. Ibid., 103.

80. Shortly after arriving in Great Salt Lake City, Blackburn and Lysander Woodworth brought Captain Brown before a Mormon Church court for breach of contract, indicating Brown did not pay them for their services during the return to Utah. On November 27 the High Council, the ruling body of the Mormon colony, met to consider the matter. Blackburn and Lysander Woodworth preferred a charge against Captain James Brown for not supplying them with beef according to contract. Willard Snow spoke for the plaintiff and Abraham O. Smoot for the defendants. The decision was unanimous that Captain Brown should furnish four hundred pounds of beef to each man and, if that was not enough, he should furnish sufficient to last them until the next spring. Ibid., 119.

81. Steele, Diary.

82. Smith, *Gold Discovery Journal*, 145.

CHAPTER THIRTEEN
Mormon Volunteers

1. J. D. Stevenson to R. B. Mason, Los Angeles, July 25, 1847, Letters, 10 Military Department, National Archives, Washington, D.C.

2. John Riser returned to California in 1850 with his wife and one daughter. The family stayed briefly in Sacramento, the gold fields, and Auburn, before moving to Alameda in June 1851. He became a "moderately successful" farmer. In 1885 he sold his farm and moved to Centerville for the rest of his life. Riser had become a disaffected Mormon, claiming in his hand-written autobiography that he had never joined the church. Riser, History, 2.

3. Boyle, Autobiography and Diary, 1:39.

4. Coray, Journal, 57.

5. Talbot, *Historical Guide*, 74.

6. This was the first order issued to the newly formed Mormon Volunteers.

7. Boyle, Autobiography and Diary, 1:40.

8. Hunter joined two outstanding Indian agents, also appointed by General Kearny: John A. Sutter for the Central Valley and Mariano Vallejo for the Sonora District. Colonel Stevenson recommended Hunter for the position because he was well known and was "universally esteemed by all." One of his duties was to inventory the farms, horses, cattle, and property belonging to San Luis Rey mission and to guard it

from destruction. Although the mission had been abandoned, Hunter
was to provide rooms and sustenance from the mission farms should
the Catholic fathers return. R. B. Mason to J. D. Hunter, Santa Barbara,
August 5, 1847, Letters, 10 Military Department, National Archives,
Washington, D.C.

9. Clift also served as the acting assistant quartermaster and commissary
officer in San Diego. Colonel Stevenson thought highly of Robert Clift,
calling him the most competent officer in the Mormon Volunteers. J. D.
Stevenson to R. B. Mason, Los Angeles, November 2, 1847, Letters, 10
Military Department, National Archives, Washington, D.C.

10. The soldiers did their best to protect the abandoned mission and its
contents, which had been badly vandalized before their arrival.

11. Ruel Barrus to D. C. Davis, San Luis Rey, January 16, 1848, Mormon
Battalion Files, HDC.

12. J. D. Stevenson to D. C. Davis, Los Angeles, October 10, 1847; D. C.
Davis to J. D. Stevenson, San Diego, October 17, 1847, Mormon
Battalion Files, HDC.

13. The government retained Dr. Anseline for $87.33⅓ per month, for no
other "competent physician could be obtained at a lower rate." W. T.
Sherman to J. D. Stevenson, Los Angeles, October 29, 1847, Mormon
Battalion Files, HDC.

14. J. D. Hunter to D. C. Davis, San Luis Rey, September 19, 1847, Mormon
Battalion Files, HDC.

15. D. C. Davis to J. D. Stevenson, San Diego, September 10, 1847,
Mormon Battalion Files, HDC.

16. W. T. Sherman to D. C. Davis, Monterey, December 29, 1847, Mormon
Battalion Files, HDC.

17. Boyle, Autobiography and Diary,1:40.

18. Ibid., 41.

19. Ibid., 42.

20. Riser, History, 3.

21. The Mormon Battalion is credited with blazing four wagon roads, cover-
ing nearly two thousand miles. The first was the last 700 miles to San
Diego, of which Cooke's Wagon Road consisted of 474 miles and the
other 226 miles followed existing trails. See maps 4 and 5. All four
women with the battalion witnessed the building of the San Diego road.
Melissa Coray witnessed two others—over Carson Pass and the Salt Lake
Cutoff. Susan Davis witnessed one other—the southern route to Salt
Lake Valley through San Bernardino and Las Vegas following the Old
Spanish Trail.

22. The Browns left California in the fall of 1848 when he captained a company of ex-battalion soldiers and families from the ship *Brooklyn* to Salt
Lake Valley.

Epilogue

1. Tyler, *Concise History,* 348.

2. May A. Sorensen, "With a Pebble in Her Mouth" (unpublished MS,
n.d.).

3. Tippets, Journal, November 22, 2856.

4. Carter, ed., *Mormon Battalion,* 132.

5. Riser, History, 6.
6. Tyler, *Concise History,* 137.
7. Ibid., 343
8. Smith, *Essentials in Church History,* 431.
9. Tyler, *Concise History,* 353.
10. Ibid., 370.
11. H. H. Bancroft, *History of California* (San Francisco: History Company, 1884–1890), 6:49.
12. Judd and Judd, eds., "Reminiscences," 17.
13. Green, *Road from El Dorado,* 48.
14. Bliss, Journal, October 24, 1847.
15. Carter, ed., *Mormon Battalion,* 132.
16. Ibid., 105.
17. Hess, Autobiography.
18. Letter from Melissa Coray to Howard Coray, April 2, 1849.
19. Ricketts, *Melissa's Journey,* 118.
20. Carter, ed., *Mormon Battalion,* 101.
21. Kenneth W. Godfrey, Audrey M. Godfrey, and Jill Mulvey, *Women's Voices: An Untold History of the Latter-day Saints, 1830–1902* (Salt Lake City: Deseret Book, 1984), 11.
22. Carr, *Honorable Remembrance,* 95.
23. Sarah taught school until 1851 when she exchanged the gold dust for cash and goods with plans to start west. She did not record the hardships of the journey to Utah, but simply stated, "We arrived in Salt Lake City in good health September 14, 1852." Nibley, *Faith Promoting Stories,* 48. Ricketts, *Tragedy Spring,* 29–31.
24. Carter, ed., *Mormon Battalion,* 132.

Bibliography

The principal sources for this work have been government documents and journals, diaries, autobiographies, letters, and memoirs written by members of the Mormon Battalion or their contemporaries. The author has collected copies of these, during many years of research, from descendants of battalion members and other sources. As indicated below, many of these are now part of the Ricketts Collection in the author's possession. Where originals documents or copies are available in public repositories, that location is referenced, so far as it is known. Documents other than the government sources are unpublished typescripts except those listed as manuscripts (MS), as microfilm, or with publication data.

Primary Sources

Journals, Letters, and Memoirs

Bagley, Will, and Robert Hoshide, eds. "The Last Crossing of the River: The 1847 William and James Pace Trail Diaries." *Crossroads Quarterly Newsletter* 4, no. 2 (Spring 1993).

Bigler, Henry W. Diary of Henry W. Bigler. Brigham Young University, Provo, Utah.

———. Journal. Huntington Library, San Marino, Calif.

Bingham, Thomas, Jr. Biography of Thomas Sr. and Thomas Jr. Copy in Ricketts Collection.

Blackburn, Abner. Autobiography. Nevada State Historical Society, Reno.

———. *Frontiersman: Abner Blackburn's Narrative.* Ed. Will Bagley. Salt Lake City: University of Utah Press, 1992.

Bliss, Robert S. "The Journal of Robert S. Bliss with the Mormon Battalion," *Utah Historical Quarterly* 4 (July–October 1931).

Borrowman, John. Journal, 1846–1860. Vol. 3. Joel E. Ricks Collection of Transcriptions, Utah State University, Logan.

Boyle, Henry G. Autobiography and Diary. 2 vols. Brigham Young University, Provo, Utah.

Brannan, Samuel. "A Biographical Sketch Based on a Dictation." Bancroft Library, University of California, Berkeley.

Brigham Young Papers. Archives, Historical Department, Church of Jesus Christ of Latter-day Saints, Salt Lake City.

Brown, John. Journal. *Our Pioneer Heritage.* Vol. 2. Salt Lake City: Daughters of Utah Pioneers, 1969.

Brown, John S. "Pioneer Journeys: From Nauvoo, Illinois, to Pueblo, Colorado, in 1846 and over the Plains in 1847." *Improvement Era,* July 1910.

Bryant, Edwin. *What I Saw in California, 1846–47*. New York: D. Appleton, 1849.

Bullock, Thomas. Journal. Archives, Historical Department, Church of Jesus Christ of Latter-day Saints, Salt Lake City.

Caldwell, Matthew. Journal. Copy in Ricketts Collection.

Cheney, Zacheus. Journal. Archives, Historical Department, Church of Jesus Christ of Latter-day Saints, Salt Lake City.

Clayton, William. Journal. Archives, Historical Department, Church of Jesus Christ of Latter-day Saints, Salt Lake City.

Colton, Philander. Biography. Copy in Ricketts Collection.

Cooke, Philip St. George. *The Conquest of New Mexico and California in 1846–1848*. 1878. Reprint, Glorieta, N.Mex.: Rio Grande Press, 1964.

Coray, William. Journal. Copy in Ricketts Collection.

Dennett, Daniel Q. History. Copy in Ricketts Collection.

Dunn, Thomas. Private Journal. Utah State Historical Society, Salt Lake City.

Egan, Howard. *Pioneering the West, 1846–1878: Major Howard Egan's Diary*. Ed. W. E. Egan. Private printing, 1917.

Elmer, Elijah. "Elijah Elmer Diary." Ed. Will Bagley. *Crossroads Newsletter* 4, no. 3 (Summer 1993).

Elmer, Elijah. Journal. San Diego Historical Society, San Diego, Calif.

Garner, William. Family History. Copy in Ricketts Collection.

Gibson, George Rutledge. *Journal of a Soldier under Kearny and Doniphan 1846–47*. Ed. Ralph F. Bisher. Glendale, Calif.: Arthur H. Clark, 1935.

Golder, Frank A., ed. *The March of the Mormon Battalion from Council Bluffs to California Taken from the Journal of Henry Standage*. New York: Century, 1928.

Green, Ephraim. Journal. Archives, Historical Department, Church of Jesus Christ of Latter-day Saints, Salt Lake City.

———. *A Road from El Dorado: The 1848 Trail Journal of Ephraim Green*. Ed. Will Bagley. Salt Lake City: Prairie Dog Press, 1991.

Griffin, John S. "A Doctor Comes to California: The Diary of John S. Griffin, Assistant Surgeon with Kearny's Dragoons, 1846–47." Ed. George Walcott Ames Jr. *California Historical Society Quarterly* 22 (January 1943).

Gudde, Erwin G., ed. *Bigler's Chronicle of the West: The Conquest of California, Discovery of Gold, and Mormon Settlement as Reflected in Henry Bigler's Diaries*. Berkeley: University of California Press, 1962.

Hafen, LeRoy R., and Ann W. Hafen, eds. *The Utah Expedition, 1857–1858: A Documentary Account of the United States Military Movement under Colonel Albert Sidney Johnston, and the Resistance by Brigham Young and the Mormon Nauvoo Legion*. Glendale, Calif.: Arthur H. Clark, 1958.

Hammond, Francis A. Autobiography. Copy in Ricketts Collection.

Hancock, Charles. Family History. Copy in Ricketts Collection.

Hancock, Levi. Journal, 1846–47. Levi Hancock Journals. Microfilm. Archives, Historical Department, Church of Jesus Christ of Latter-day Saints, Salt Lake City.

Hanks, Ephraim. "Scouting on the Western Frontier." Mormon Battalion Visitors Center, San Diego, Calif.

Hawk, Nathan. Family History. Copy in Ricketts Collection.

———. Interview. *Sacramento Bee*. January 4, 1906.

Henrie, Daniel. History of Daniel and Amanda Brandley Henrie. University of Utah, Salt Lake City.

Hess, John W.. Autobiography. Brigham Young University, Provo, Utah.

Holmes, Jonathan H. *Jonathan Harrison Holmes: Trail Journal of 1848*. Ed. Will
     Bagley. Salt Lake City: Prairie Dog Press, 1991.
————. Journal. Copy in Ricketts Collection.
Hulet, Sylvester. Biographical Sketch. University of Utah, Salt Lake City.
Hunsaker, Abraham. Journal. Copy in Ricketts Collection.
Hunt, Jefferson. Journal. Copy in Ricketts Collection.
Hyde, William. Private Journal of William Hyde. Brigham Young University,
     Provo, Utah.
Jones, Nathaniel V. Journal. Archives, Historical Department, Church of Jesus
     Christ of Latter-day Saints, Salt Lake City.
————. "Journal." *The Utah Historical Quarterly* 4, no. 1 (January 1931).
Journal History. Archives, Historical Department, Church of Jesus Christ of
     Latter-day Saints, Salt Lake City.
Judd, Esther Brown, and Elva N. Judd, eds. "Reminiscences of Zadock Knapp
     Judd, Senior." Copy in Ricketts Collection.
Judd, Zadock. Autobiography. Copy in Ricketts Collection.
Kane, Thomas L. "The Mormons: A Discourse Delivered before the Historical
     Society of Pennsylvania." March 26, 1850.
Kearny, Stephen W. Kearny Diary and Letter Book 1846–47. Kearny Papers,
     Missouri Historical Society, St. Louis.
Keysor, Guy M. Journal. Copy in Ricketts Collection.
Kimball, Heber C. Diary. Microfilm. Archives, Historical Department, Church of
     Jesus Christ of Latter-day Saints, Salt Lake City.
Lee, John D. "Diary of the Mormon Battalion Mission: John D. Lee." Ed. Juanita
     Brooks. *New Mexico Historical Review* 42 (July–October 1967).
————. *Journals of John D. Lee 1846–47 and 1859*. Ed. Charles Kelly. Salt Lake
     City: Western Printing, 1938.
Lowry, Sarah J. Brown. Statement. Archives, Historical Department, Church of
     Jesus Christ of Latter-day Saints, Salt Lake City.
Lyman, Amasa. *History of Amasa Mason Lyman Family*. Delta, Utah: Melvin A.
     Lyman, 1957.
Merrill, Philemon. Family History. Copy in Ricketts Collection.
Mormon Battalion Files. Archives, Historical Department, Church of Jesus Christ
     of Latter-day Saints, Salt Lake City.
Pace, James. 1847 Trail Diary. Archives, Historical Department, Church of Jesus
     Christ of Latter-day Saints, Salt Lake City.
Pace, William Byram. 1847 Trail Diary. Archives, Historical Department, Church
     of Jesus Christ of Latter-day Saints, Salt Lake City.
Parkman, Francis. *The Oregon Trail: Sketches of Prairie and Rocky-Mountain Life*. New
     York: Modern Library.
Pettegrew, David. Autobiography. Utah State Historical Society, Salt Lake City.
————. Journal, 1846–1860. Brigham Young University, Provo, Utah.
Pixton, Robert. Family History. Copy in Ricketts Collection.
Polk, James K. *The Diary of James K. Polk during His Presidency, 1845 to 1848*. Ed.
     Milo Milton Quaife. 4 vols. Chicago: A. C. McClurg, 1910.
Pratt, Addison. Journal. Archives, Historical Department, Church of Jesus Christ
     of Latter-day Saints, Salt Lake City.
Pratt, Parley P. *Autobiography of Parley Parker Pratt*. Salt Lake City: Deseret Book,
     1980.
Prows (Prouse), William C. Family History. Copy in Ricketts Collection.
Rawson, Daniel B. Family History. Copy in Ricketts Collection.

Richards, Willard. Journal. Archives, Historical Department, Church of Jesus
    Christ of Latter-day Saints, Salt Lake City.
Riser, John J. Autobiography. 1887. Bancroft Library, Berkeley, Calif.
Rogers, Samuel H. Journal. Copy in Ricketts Collection.
Ruxton, George F. *Adventures in Mexico and the Rocky Mountains.* 1847. Reprint,
    Glorieta, N.Mex.: Rio Grande Press, 1973.
———. *Life in the Far West.* Edinburgh: W. Blackwood, 1849.
Sanderson, Henry W. Diary of Henry Weeks Sanderson. Brigham Young
    University, Provo, Utah.
Scott, James. Diary. Copy in Ricketts Collection.
Sherman, William Tecumseh. *Memoirs of General William T. Sherman.* New York: D.
    Appleton, 1875.
Skeen, Joseph. Reminiscences and Diary. Archives, Historical Department,
    Church of Jesus Christ of Latter-day Saints, Salt Lake City.
Sly, James C. Family History. Copy in Ricketts Collection.
Smith, Albert. Journal. California Room, California State Library, Sacramento.
Smith, Azariah. *The Gold Discovery Journal of Azariah Smith.* Ed. David Bigler. 1990.
    Reprint, Logan, Utah: Utah State University Press, 1996.
———. Journal. California Room, California State Library, Sacramento.
Standage, Henry. Journal. Standage Family. Copy in Ricketts Collection.
Steele, John. Diary of John Steele. Brigham Young University, Provo, Utah.
Stout, Hosea. *On the Mormon Frontier: The Diary of Hosea Stout, 1844–1861.* Ed.
    Juanita Brooks. 2 vols. Salt Lake City: University of Utah Press and Utah
    State Historical Society, 1965.
Sutter, John A. *New Helvetia Diary: A Record of Events Kept by John A. Sutter and His
    Clerks at New Helvetia, California.* San Francisco: Grabhorn Press, 1939.
———. *Sutter's Fort Record. 1848.* Archives, California State Library, Sacramento.
Taggart, George W. Diaries, 1846–47. Archives, Historical Department, Church
    of Jesus Christ of Latter-day Saints, Salt Lake City.
Terrell, Joel J. Record. Copy in Ricketts Collection.
Tippets, John H. Journal. Merrill Library Special Collections, Utah State
    University, Logan.
Turner, Henry S. "Journal of Brig. Genl. S. W. Kearny's Return from California
    in the Summer of 1847." Kearny Papers, Missouri Historical Society, St.
    Louis.
Tyler, Daniel. *A Concise History of the Mormon Battalion in the Mexican War,
    1846–1848.* 1881. 4th ed., Glorieta, N.Mex.: Rio Grande Press, 1988.
Van Noy, Evelyn. Autobiography of James Clyman. Unpublished. Copy in
    Ricketts Collection.
Vincent, Joshua S. Diary. San Diego Historical Society, San Diego, Calif.
White, Joseph. Family History. Copy in Ricketts Collection.
White, John S. Family History. Copy in Ricketts Collection.
Wilson, George. Journal. Copy in Ricketts Collection.
Wood, William. Autobiography. Copy in Ricketts Collection.
Woodbury, John S. Journal. Lorin Hansen Library, Fremont, Calif.
Workman, Oliver. Family History. Copy in Ricketts Collection.
Young, Brigham. History of Brigham Young. Archives, Historical Department,
    Church of Jesus Christ of Latter-day Saints, Salt Lake City.

Government Documents

Cooke, Philip St. George. *Report of Lieut. Col. P. St. George Cooke of His March from Santa Fe, New Mexico, to San Diego, Upper California.* 38th Congress, 1st session, 1848. H. Exec. Doc. 41.

Letters, 10 Military Department, National Archives, Washington, D.C.

Mexican War Service Records 1845–1848. Microfilm 351–1, 351–2, 351–3. National Archives, Washington, D.C.

———. Microfilm 471,465; 471,517; and 471,518. LDS Family History Center, Salt Lake City.

Miscellaneous Papers, Mexican War. National Archives, Washington, D.C.

Richardson, James D., ed. *A Compilation of the Messages and Papers of the Presidents.* Washington, D.C.: Bureau of National Literature, 1911.

Roster and Record of Iowa Soldiers in the Mexican War. Adjutant-General's Office, State of Iowa, Des Moines, Iowa. 6:837–75.

U.S. Government Pension Records. Microfilm T81196, parts 1–21. National Archives, Washington, D.C.

———. Microfilm 480, 129–480, 149. LDS Family History Center, Salt Lake City.

Secondary Sources

Arrington, Leonard. "Mississippi Mormons." *The Ensign,* June 1977.

———. "Sakajawea's Mormon Connection." *This People,* Fall 1991.

Bagley, Will. "Across the Snowy Mountain." Unpublished.

———. "Primary Sources on the Opening of the Salt Lake Cutoff." *Crossroads Quarterly Newsletter* 5, no. 2 (Spring 1992).

Bailey, Paul D. *Sam Brannan and the California Mormons.* Los Angeles: Westernlore Press, 1953.

Bancroft, Hubert Howe. *History of California.* 5 vols. San Francisco: History Company, 1886.

Beilharz, Alan. "Early Exploration." *Golden Flakes* (Gold Discovery Park Association, Coloma, Calif.) 6, no. 5 (Summer 1995).

Bitton, Davis. *Guide to Mormon Diaries and Autobiographies.* Provo, Utah: Brigham Young University Press, 1930.

Broadbent, Dee A., ed. "Return of the Mormon Battalion from the Gold Fields." Unpublished. Copy in Ricketts Collection.

Brooks, Juanita. "The Mormon Battalion." *Arizona Highways,* May 1943.

Campbell, Eugene Edward. "The Apostasy of Samuel Brannan." *Utah Historical Quarterly* 27 (April 1959).

———. "Authority Conflicts in the Mormon Battalion." *BYU Studies* 8 (Winter 1968).

———. *A History of the Church of Jesus Christ of Latter-day Saints in California, 1846–1946.* Ph.D. diss., University of Southern California, Los Angeles, 1952.

Cannon, George Q. "Twenty Years Ago." *Juvenile Instructor* 4 (1869).

Carr, Elmer J., ed. *Honorable Remembrance: The San Diego Master List of the Mormon Battalion.* San Diego, Calif.: Mormon Battalion Visitors Center, 1978.

Carter, Kate B., ed. *The Mormon Battalion.* Salt Lake City, 1986.

Church News, September 23, 1989.

Clarke, Dwight L. *Stephen Watts Kearny: Soldier of the West.* Norman: University of Oklahoma Press, 1961.

Clegg, Dennis A. *Levi Ward Hancock; Pioneer, Soldier, Political and Religious Leader of Early Utah.* Master's thesis, Brigham Young University, Provo, Utah, 1966.

Colorado Springs Colorado North Stake. *The Stone Rolls Forth: A History of the Church of Jesus Christ of Latter-day Saints in Southeastern Colorado, 1846–1986.* Bountiful, Utah: Horizon Publishers, 1988.

Daughters of Utah Pioneers. *An Enduring Legacy.* 12 vols. Salt Lake City, 1978–1990.

———. *Chronicles of Courage.* 7 vols. Salt Lake City, 1990–1996.

———. *The First Company to Enter Salt Lake Valley.* Salt Lake City, 1993.

———. *Heart Throbs of the West.* Ed. Kate B. Carter. 10 vols. Salt Lake City, 1942–1951.

———. *Our Pioneer Heritage.* Ed. Kate B. Carter. 20 vols. Salt Lake City, 1958–1977.

———. *Treasures of Pioneer History.* Ed. Kate B. Carter. 6 vols. Salt Lake City, 1952–1957.

Davies, J. Kenneth. *Mormon Gold: The Story of California's Mormon Argonauts.* Salt Lake City: Olympus Publishing.

DeVoto, Bernard. *The Year of Decision 1846.* Boston: Houghton Mifflin, 1942.

Egan, Ferol. "Incident at Tragedy Spring." *The American West* (January 1971).

Esshom, Frank, comp. *Pioneers and Prominent Men of Utah.* Salt Lake City: Utah Pioneers Book Publishing, 1913.

Faulk, Odie B. *Destiny Road: The Gila Trail and the Opening of the Southwest.* New York: Oxford University, 1973.

Foster, Stephen Clark. *Los Angeles from '47 to '49.* Berkeley: H. H. Bancroft, University of California, 1877.

Fuller, Theodore W. *San Diego Originals.* Pleasant Hill, Calif.: Profiles Publications, 1987.

Furniss, Norman F. *The Mormon Conflict.* New Haven, Conn.: Yale University Press, 1960.

Gentry, Leland H. "The Mormon Way Stations: Garden Grove and Mt. Pisgah." *BYU Studies* 21, no. 4 (Fall 1981).

Glover, William. *The Mormons in California.* Los Angeles: Glen Dawson, 1954.

Godfrey, Kenneth W., Audrey M. Godfrey, and Jill Mulvey. *Women's Voices: An Untold History of the Latter-day Saints, 1830–1902.* 1904. 3rd printing, Salt Lake City: Deseret Book, 1984.

Gudde, Erwin G. *California Place Names: The Origin and Etymology of Current Geographical Names.* Berkeley: University of California Press, 1969.

Hafen, Leroy, W. Eugene Hollon, and Carl Coke Rister. *Western America: The Exploration, Settlement, and Development of the Region beyond the Mississippi.* Englewood Cliffs, N.J.: Prentice-Hall, 1970.

Hafen, LeRoy R., and Frank M. Young. "The Mormon Settlement at Pueblo, Colorado, during the Mexican War." *The Colorado Magazine* 9, no. 4 (July 1932).

Harris, Benjamin Butler. *The Gila Trail: The Texas Argonauts and the California Gold Rush.* Ed. Richard H. Dillon. Norman: University of Oklahoma Press, 1960.

Harris, E. W. *The Overland Emigrant Trail to California.* Reno: Nevada Emigrant Trail Marking Committee, Inc. Nevada Historical Society, 1980.

Hill, Joseph H. *The History of Warner's Ranch and Its Environs.* Los Angeles: privately printed, 1927.

Holliday, J. S. *The World Rushed In.* New York: Simon and Schuster, 1981.

Hoshide, Robert, and Will Bagley. "Sooter's Fort to Salt Lake Valley." *Crossroads Newsletter* 4, no. 4 (Winter 1993).

Jenson, Andrew. *Latter-day Saints Biographical Encyclopedia.* 4 vols. Salt Lake City: Andrew Jenson History Company, 1901–1936.

———. "The Mormon Battalion." *The Historical Record* 8 (January 1888).

Jones, Rebecca M. "Life Sketch of Nathaniel V. Jones." *Utah Historical Quarterly* 4, no. 1 (January 1973).

Kemble, Edward C. *A Kemble Reader.* Berkeley: California Historical Society, Howell-North Press, 1963.

———. "Yerba Buena—1846." *Sacramento Daily Union,* August 26, 1871; October 14, 1871.

Kimball, Stanley B. *Heber C. Kimball: Mormon Patriarch and Pioneer.* Chicago: University of Illinois Press, 1981.

———. *Historic Resource Study: Mormon Pioneer National Historic Trail.* Washington, D.C.: U.S. Department of Interior, National Park Service, 1991.

———. *Historic Sites and Markers: The Mormon and Other Great Western Trails.* Chicago: University of Illinois Press, 1988.

Knight, Hal, and Stanley B. Kimball. *111 Days to Zion.* Salt Lake City: Deseret News, 1978.

Kohler, Charmaine Lay. *Southern Grace: A Story of the Mississippi Saints.* Boise, Idaho: Beagle Creek Press, 1995.

Larson, Carl V. *A Data Base of the Mormon Battalion.* Providence, Utah: Watkins and Sons Printing, 1987.

Lockwood, Herbert. "The Mormon Coal Mine." *The Western Explorer* (Cabrillo Historical Association, Cabrillo National Monument, Point Loma, Calif.) 2, no. 3 (April 1964).

Maxwell, Margaret F. "The March of the Mormon Battalion, 1846." Unpublished MS, n.d. Copy in Ricketts Collection.

Maynard, Gregory P. *Alexander William Doniphan, the Forgotten Man from Missouri.* Master's thesis, Brigham Young University, 1968.

McClintock, James H. *Mormon Settlements in Arizona.* Tucson: University of Arizona Press, 1985.

"Mississippi Saints Headed West in 1846." *Church News,* July 13, 1996.

Muir, Leo J. *A Century of Mormon Activities in California.* Salt Lake City: Deseret News Press, n.d.

Nibley, Preston. *Faith Promoting Stories.* Salt Lake City: Deseret Book, 1943.

Parrish, William E. "The Mississippi Saints." *The Historian: A Journal of History.* Toledo: University of Toledo, 1989.

Porter, Larry C. "From California to Council Bluffs." *Ensign,* August 1989.

Ricketts, Norma B. "The California Star Express." *Golden Notes* (Sacramento County Historical Society) 28, no. 1 (Spring 1982).

———. *Historic Cosumnes and the Slough House Pioneer Cemetery.* Salt Lake City: Daughters of Utah Pioneers, 1978.

———. *Melissa's Journey with the Mormon Battalion.* Salt Lake City: Daughters of Utah Pioneers, 1994.

———. *Mormons and the Discovery of Gold.* Placerville, Calif.: Pioneer Press, 1966.

———. *Tragedy Spring and the Pouch of Gold.* Sacramento: Ricketts Publishing, 1983.

Rieck, Richard L. "The Trails of the Gold Rush." *Overland Journal* 12, no. 1 (1994).

Roberts, B. H. *The Mormon Battalion: Its History and Achievements.* Salt Lake City: Deseret News, 1919.

Ruhlen, George. "Kearny's Route from the Rio Grande to the Gila River." *New Mexico Historical Review* 2 (July 1957).

Seegmiller, Janet Burton. *The Life Story of Robert Burton Taylor.* Salt Lake City: Robert Taylor Burton Family Organization, 1988.

Smith, Carmen, and Omer Smith. "The Lost Well of the Mormon Battalion Rediscovered." *Utah Historical Quarterly,* Summer 1989.

Smith, Joseph Fielding. *Essentials in Church History.* Salt Lake City: Deseret News Press, 1944.

Smith, Pauline Udall. *Captain Jefferson Hunt of the Mormon Battalion.* Salt Lake City: Nicholas G. Morgan Sr. Foundation, 1958.

Sorensen, May A. "With a Pebble in Her Mouth." Unpublished MS, n.d. Copy in Ricketts Collection.

Steed, Jack. *The Donner Party Rescue Site, Johnson's Ranch on Bear River.* Fresno, Calif.: Pioneer Publishing, 1988.

Stewart, George R. *Ordeal by Hunger.* 1936. Reprint, New York: Houghton Mifflin, 1960.

Talbot, Dan. *A Historical Guide to the Mormon Battalion and the Butterfield Trail.* Tucson, Ariz.: Westernlore Press, 1992.

Watson, Jeanne H. "The Carson Emigrant Road." *Overland Journal* (Oregon-California Trails Association), Summer 1986.

Whitney, Orson F. *Life of Heber C. Kimball.* 3rd ed. Salt Lake City: Bookcraft, 1967.

Yurtinus, John F. *A Ram in the Thicket: The Mormon Battalion in the Mexican War.* 2 vols. Ph.D. diss., Brigham Young University, Provo, Utah, 1975.

Index

Brown, Ebenezer, Sgt., 21, 30–31, 70–71, 147, 223, 265–66
Brown, Edmund L., Sgt., 27, 31, 239, 265
Brown, Eunice Reasor, 31, 233, 251
Brown, Francis, Pvt., 23, 134, 137, 169
Brown, Harriet St. John, 29, 31, 239, 251
Brown, James, Capt., 24, 29, 31, 37, 238–39, 246–54, 259, 271, 328, 346; to California for mustering-out pay, 175–76, 193, 255, 258–59; differences with Brannan, 175–76; differences with Rosecrans, 43–44; settlement on Ogden River, 220; sick detachment to Pueblo, 67–69, 238–39
Brown, James Polly, Pvt., 26, 31, 233, 251
Brown, James S., Pvt., 26, 195, 204, 218, 221–22, 255
Brown, Jesse Sowell, Pvt., 24, 238, 258
Brown, John (Mississippi), 53, 229–31, 341
Brown, John, Pvt., 21
Brown, John Taylor, 251
Brown, Martha Stephens, 31
Brown, Mary Ann, 31, 233
Brown, Mary McCree Black, 29, 31, 239
Brown, Neuman, 31, 33, 233
Brown, Phebe Draper Palmer, 30–31, 70, 75, 136, 147, 223, 265, 267
Brown, Robert, 31, 33, 233
Brown, Sarah, 31, 233, 246
Brown, William W., Pvt., 21, 266
Brown detachment. See detachments
Brownell, Russell G., Pvt./Cpl., 24, 68
Bryant, Edwin, 164, 333
Bryant, John S., Pvt., 21, 266
Buchannan, John, Cpl., 25, 238, 252
buffalo, 51–52; dung as fuel,, 53, 59
Bulkley, Newman, Pvt., 27, 169, 273
Bullen, (*Brooklyn*), Newell (husband), Clarissa Atkinson (wife), and

Andrew, Herschel, and John Joseph (children), 224
bull fights, 155, 159
bulls stampede, 94–95
Bunker, Edward, Pvt., 27, 180, 193, 328
Burgwin, John, Capt., 74, 79, 242, 325
burials, 30, 48, 76, 93, 116, 134, 137, 139, 164, 174–75, 186, 208–9, 211, 234–36, 240–41, 248–49, 263, 270
Burns, Thomas R., Pvt./Cpl., 27, 242, 244, 251
Burr (*Brooklyn*), Charles Clark (husband), Sarah Sloat (wife), and John Atlantic and Nathan Jr. (children), 224
Burr (*Brooklyn*), Nathan (husband), Chloe Clarke (wife), and Amasa and Charles Clark Jr. (children), 224
Burt, William, Pvt., 24, 244
Burton, Rebecca, 29
Bush, Richard, Pvt., 23, 222
Bush, William H., Pvt., 24, 138
Butterfield, Jacob K., Pvt., 15, 21, 61
Button, James, 31, 160, 233
Button, Jutson, 31, 233
Button, Louisa, 31, 233
Button, Mary Bittels, 31, 233
Button, Montgomery, Pvt., 26, 223, 233, 346
Button, Samuel, 31, 233
Bybee, John McCann, Pvt., 23, 244

C
cactus, described, 83–84, 96
Cahuenga Capitulation, 161
Cajon Pass, 148–49
Caldwell, Matthew, Pvt., 27, 162, 167–68
California, 30, 40, 107, 255; colonists, 185–86; conflict over command, 132; conquest, 131, 269; migrants to, 214–15, 217; remaining there

Gribble, William, Pvt., 26, 238, 255
Griffin, John S., Dr., 133, 136, 330
grizzly bears, 87, 195
guides: hired and assigned, 71, 74, 85,
    87, 105; performance of, 82, 88
Gully, Samuel L., Lt., 19, 27, 37, 43,
    45–48, 55, 60, 69–70, 321, 324

H
Hall, Willard P., 162
Hammond, Francis, 187, 195, 207,
    213
Hampton, James, Pvt., 22, 76, 240
Hancock, Charles B., Pvt., 14, 24, 108
Hancock, Clarissa, 176
Hancock, George W., Pvt., 24, 108,
    157
Hancock, Levi W., Musician, 27, 40,
    42–44, 48, 52, 54–55, 57, 60–61,
    69, 75–76, 79, 146, 149, 158–59,
    176, 180, 240, 319; as leader of
    discharged men, 171, 174, 178;
    poem, 120; son born, 176; as spiri-
    tual leader, 43, 82, 84, 116, 122,
    124–27, 139, 147, 155, 157,
    172–73, 321
Hancock company, 171, 177, 185,
    193; Allred fifty, 171, 177; Allred-
    Tyler-Hyde fifties, 171–74; Averett
    ten (scouts), 171–72, 174, 178;
    Curtis ten, 171; Hunt fifty, 171,
    177–79, 185; Hyde fifty, 171, 177;
    Lytle hundred, 173–75, 177–79;
    Pace hundred, 171, 173–75,
    177–79; Savage ten, 171; Tuttle
    ten, 171; Tyler fifty, 171, 177
Hancock-Sierra company, 177–78,
    180, 202
Hanks, Ebenezer, Sgt., 27, 32,
    238–39, 249, 346
Hanks, Ephraim K., Pvt., 23, 82, 137
Hanks, Jane Wells Cooper, 32, 239
Harley, James (Brooklyn), 337
Harmon, Ebenezer, Pvt., 24, 127, 266
Harmon, James (Mississippi), 229,
    341, 344
Harmon, Lorenzo F., Pvt., 25, 266

Harmon, Oliver N., Pvt., 28, 266
Harris, Robert, Jr., Pvt., 28, 180, 193
Harris, Silas, Pvt., 23, 189
Harrison, Catherine Smith, and chil-
    dren (Brooklyn), 226–27, 337
Harrison, Isaac, Pvt., 28, 226–27, 265,
    337
Harrison, James (Mississippi), 229
Hart, James S., Pvt., 28, 266
Haskell, George N., Pvt., 23
Hastings Cutoff, 179, 217, 225, 333,
    336
Hatch, Meltiar, Pvt., 25, 187, 222, 270
Hatch, Orin, Pvt., 25, 187, 222, 270
Haun's Mill massacre, 136, 330
Hawk, Nathan, Pvt., 23, 188–90, 200
Hawk, William, Pvt., 23, 189–90
Hawkins, Benjamin, Pvt., 22, 339
Haws, Alpheus, Sgt., 25, 172
Hempstead, Dr., 246–47
Hendricks, William D., Pvt., 26, 274
Hendrickson, James, Pvt., 25, 233
Henrie, Daniel, Pvt., 26, 82, 195, 226
Hensley, Samuel, Capt., 217–19, 341
Hess, Emeline Bigler, 30, 32, 68, 70,
    239
Hess, John W., Pvt., 28–30, 32, 68, 70,
    236, 238–39, 273
Hewitt, Eli B., Pvt., 22, 245
Hickenlooper, William E., Pvt., 22,
    266
Hickmott, John, Pvt., 28
Higgins, Alfred, Pvt., 26, 32, 233, 245
Higgins, Almira, 32, 233, 247
Higgins, Carlos, 32, 233
Higgins, Driscilla, 32, 233
Higgins, Heber, 32, 233
Higgins, Nelson, Capt., 25, 32, 44, 48,
    54–55, 76–77, 233–35, 248–50,
    255, 326
Higgins, Nelson D., 32–33
Higgins, Sarah Blackman, 32, 233
Higgins detachment. See detachments
Hinckley, Arza E., Pvt., 23, 244–45
Hirons, James P., Pvt., 26, 32, 238–39,
    258
Hirons, Mary Ann Jameson, 32, 239

| 111° 46' W. Long.

Coyoteros

sill River

Pima Village

Rio Gila

water pools

no water

small water hole in the Rocks.

Gold District.

a Soma.
(a new mining town)

Gold District.

Sandy Desert.
with irregular mountains.

Lost

water

Tucson

Pima Vill.

no water

Indian Village

San Pedro

very mountains
or broken

- of part of the march

from San

From a point on Grande River, (their w

& followed t

Believed by Mr Leroux to be an open pr

Cañon
San Pedro
Bull Run.

Deserted Ranche.

Numerous herds of wild Cattle from
San Bernadino to the point where the
San Pedro river is left.

water

Coyotero trail for
plundered Cattle & mules

Santa Cruz mountain.

From

△ Camps

Explanations etc. Distances between marked in figures;
Water at all camps, unless the
contrary is stated

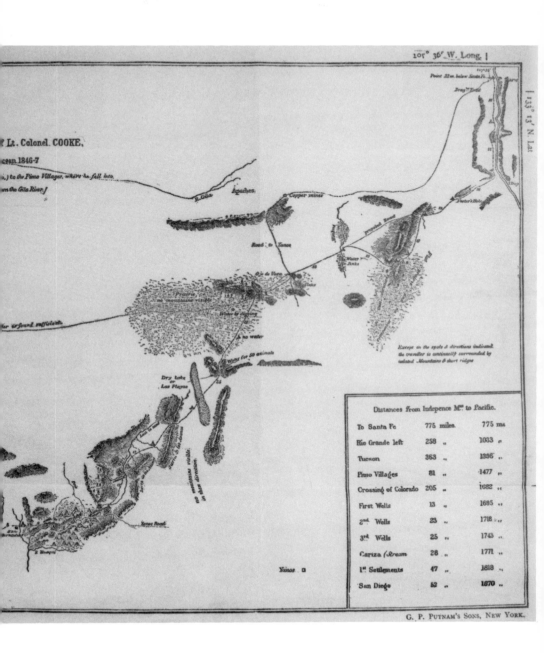

105° 36′ W. Long.

33° 13′ N. Lat.

of Lt. Colonel. COOKE,

cean 1846-7

) to the Pimo Villages, where he fell into,

from the Gila River.

R. Gila   Apaches.

Copper mines

Point 52 m. below Santa Fe.

Dragoon Wells

Presidio Road

Foster's Hole

Road to Janos

Water Sinks

Ojo de Vaca   Lake

Prairie
no mountains visible

Except on the spots & directions indicated,
the traveller is continually surrounded by
isolated Mountains & short ridges

Water & grazing

No water

Water for 30 animals

Dry Lake
or
Las Playas

Gila

no mountains visible
in these directions

Janos Road

Sonoyta

S. Bisnaga

Yanos. □

G. P. PUTNAM'S SONS, NEW YORK.

Distances from Indepence M⁰⁰ to Pacific.		
To Santa Fe	775 miles	775 ma
Rio Grande left	258 "	1033 "
Tucson	363 "	1395 "
Pimo Villages	81 "	1477 "
Crossing of Colorado	205 "	1682 "
First Wells	13 "	1695 "
2ᵈ Wells	23 "	1718 "
3ᵈ Wells	25 "	1743 "
Cariza (Stream	28 "	1771 "
1ˢᵗ Settlements	47 "	1818 "
San Diego	52 "	1870 "